James Craik

The Divine Life and the New Birth

Vol. 1

James Craik

The Divine Life and the New Birth
Vol. 1

ISBN/EAN: 9783337780227

Printed in Europe, USA, Canada, Australia, Japan

Cover: Foto ©Lupo / pixelio.de

More available books at **www.hansebooks.com**

THE DIVINE LIFE AND NEW BIRTH

WITH A SUPPLEMENT ON

THE INCARNATION.

BY THE

REV. JAMES CRAIK, D. D.,

RECTOR OF CHRIST CHURCH, LOUISVILLE; AUTHOR OF "SEARCH OF TRUTH,"
"OLD AND NEW," ETC.

THIRD EDITION.

LOUISVILLE.

JOHN P. MORTON AND COMPANY.

NEW YORK: E. P. DUTTON AND COMPANY

LONDON: TRÜBNER & CO.

1876.

TO THE

Congregation of Christ Church, Louisville,

IN MEMORY OF THE TWENTY-ONE YEARS

IN WHICH WE HAVE BEEN

FELLOW-WORKERS

IN THE

KINGDOM OF GOD,

AS MINISTER AND PEOPLE,

THIS BOOK

IS AFFECTIONATELY DEDICATED,

AUGUST 1ST, 1865.

PREFATORY NOTE.

Two pamphlet editions of a material portion of this work, under the same title, were published in 1850. The same portion was afterwards incorporated into the volume entitled "Search of Truth." The original work, and some other of the more practical parts of the volume just named, form the basis of the present publication. To these materials large additions have been made upon kindred branches of Christian knowledge, with the hope that the whole will prove to be a Manual adapted to the needs of our time.

For the reception of my first efforts by the Church at large, and by many of her most gifted sons, I have been profoundly grateful. Much of the opposition which these publications encountered proceeded from local disturbances which have long since passed away, and the rest, I think, from misapprehensions growing out of the excited temper of the times.

Contention and party spirit may hardly ever be expected to cease from the Church, yet the perils of the present day have produced a very general conviction that Christians must come closer together to strive successfully for the faith once delivered. It is hoped, therefore, that all will welcome the feeblest effort to add to the unity and strength of the Christian host, and to furnish a guide to inquiring souls.

CONTENTS.

(iii)

CHAPTER IV.

CHAPTER V.

CHAPTER VI.

CHAPTER VII.

CHAPTER VIII.

CHAPTER IX.

CHAPTER X.

CHAPTER XI.

CHAPTER XII.

CHAPTER XIII.

CHAPTER XIV.

CHAPTER XV.

CHAPTER XVI.

CHAPTER XVII.

CHAPTER XVIII.

CHAPTER XIX.

SUPPLEMENT.

CHAPTER I.

CHAPTER II.

INTRODUCTION.

In *The Christian Remembrancer* (London, January, 1863), there is a very noticeable article in relation to the famous "Essays and Reviews." The writer affirms, and, I think, proves, that Modern Skepticism is a natural reaction from the narrowness of the popular theology. He further undertakes to show that "the genuine theology of Christ and His Church" is not liable to the assaults of this skepticism; and he therefore counsels, as its most effectual refutation, a reform of the popular theology, so as to make it the real teaching of Christ and the Church. A position very similar to this was taken by Dr. M'Cosh and other eminent men, at the meeting of the Evangelical Alliance, in Edinburgh, in July, 1864.

It is gratifying to find that this truth is beginning to be so generally perceived by the leaders of religious opinion in the mother country. A profound conviction of the same truth induced the writer of the following work—first in 1850, and then in 1855—to throw in his little mite towards the correction of that popular theology as it is professed in our own country. In those publications an attempt was made to prove that the Bible and the Church teach a religion far more catholic, and better adapted to human need and intelligence, than much of the prevalent theology of our time.

In speaking thus freely of systems which have so extensively prevailed, let us not forget that the most injurious dogmas of some of them were the result of a violent reaction of the Christian mind from that deadly form of ecclesiastical pharisaism which destroyed all the individuality of the human soul, and degraded religion into a superstitious round of propitiatory observances. Thus our nature is ever oscillating between two vicious extremes, and is with the utmost difficulty stayed in the just equilibrium of pure and simple truth.

It was not from books or reviews that my knowledge of the truth, announced from these various quarters, was principally derived. A familiar intercourse with many of the educated and uneducated men of America had made me acquainted with their thoughts and feelings, their doubts and perplexities; and, although downright infidelity was comparatively rare, yet there was among the educated classes a reasonable and intelligent repugnance to the popular religion, as something outside of their nature and inconsistent with their deepest convictions. This made them insensible to all the appeals of the Gospel, because those appeals were based upon a system which they could not reconcile with the facts of observation and consciousness. To this class my little book was addressed, and I have the happiness of knowing that, within the limited sphere of its circulation, it gave effectual relief to many inquiring minds.

It is painful to be compelled to say that the specific remedy proposed by the *Remembrancer* for the evil it has pointed out seems to be partial, one-sided, and insufficient. For one false system it has substituted another just as narrow, and just as much in conflict with human experience and human consciousness. In place of one set of dogmas, restricting the grace of God and the operations of His Spirit to the elect, or to the converted, it proposes the Romish theory, which restrains these and other benefits of the incarnation and sacrifice of Christ to the baptized members of His Church. The writer says: "It is to the Sacraments that man must look, both for the beginning and the continuance of Divine Grace. In Baptism Grace is first infused."

The maintenance of such opprobria of technical theology as this and the opposite prevailing theories, each contradicted alike by human consciousness and by universal experience, the swaying back and forth of such large parties between indefensible opinions, unhappily confounded with Christianity, are among the chief causes which have alienated multitudes from Christianity itself, and raised up in the Church a school of such latitudinarian construction as almost to take away the foundations of the Christian religion.

To claim for the baptized, or for a class deemed elect, or for the professedly converted, an exclusive interest in the work and mediation of Christ; to declare that in these alone the Spirit of Christ resides to guide and instruct them, while men just as good, and in some instances a great deal better, exhibiting far more genuine evidences of the work of the Spirit in their temper and conduct, are represented as having as yet received no benefit from the incarnation and death of Christ, and as utterly destitute of the Spirit of life, is to expose Christianity to contempt and denial. "By their fruits ye shall know them" is at least one Christian rule which the world universally applies. To take a community whose members are living and acting together apparently on the same principles and in the very same way, and separate them by an arbitrary line so broad and deep, that all on one side are declared to be the special favorites of heaven, guided and illuminated by the Spirit of God dwelling in them, while all on the other side are represented as abandoned to the polluting force of

natural corruption and to the absolute dominion of the devil,
is so manifestly false, so utterly irreconcilable with the facts of
the case, as to provoke opposition and to challenge rejection.

Instead of these narrow and insufficient theories, the
Scriptures and the Church teach that the Grace of God is
co-extensive with the sinfulness of man—that the quickening power of the Second Man, who is the Lord from heaven,
is equal to and parallel with the destroying and death-entail-
ing influence of the first man—that the healing virtue of the
Second Representative of the human race is commensurate
with the taint and corruption derived from the first.   Therefore, all who die without actual sin are undoubtedly saved,
because they are Christ's.   Therefore, He said, "Suffer little
children to come unto me"—not to make them His, but
because they were His already—"*for of such is the kingdom
of Heaven.*"

As Christ tasted death for every man, so He sends His
ministers to preach the Gospel, not to insensible reprobates,
not to the mere carnal mind, which can not discern spiritual
things, but to the partakers of His own nature—to men
made alive in Him, quickened by the Holy Ghost, and *thus*
imbued with spiritual power to apprehend, believe, obey, and
love the truth.   Therefore, every man who commits sin resists and strives against the Spirit given unto him, *else he
could be in no condemnation for his sin.*   The Spirit of Christ,
given to all, places all alike in a state of trial and probation
for heaven or for hell; and the rule of judgment will be the
use which each man has made of his opportunities to be and
to do good, under the guidance of that Spirit of Life and
Light.   In this rule is involved the Divinely enunciated
principle, that to whom much is given, of him, and of him
alone, will much be required.

Between this teaching and the human consciousness there

is no repugnance, but a perfect and delightful harmony; and this teaching of the Bible and the Church would seem to be the most effective way of bringing men to Christ; for when they know that all the good they feel and enjoy is the witness of the Spirit of Christ within them, who would thus draw them to HIMSELF, to make them partakers of His eternal blessedness, and that a refusal to come to Him will deprive them forever of that Spirit, and leave them to the baseness and darkness and misery of unrelieved corruption, every right and generous feeling, every sense of beauty and goodness, every aspiration after nobleness and true greatness, will draw them to Him who is the Fountain of Life, the Regenerator of humanity, JESUS CHRIST THE SAVIOR OF THE WORLD.

The state of opinion among all cultivated peoples requires that these important truths should now be brought prominently forward, as the best solvent of most of the religious questions of the age. To connect, logically and fairly, the broad catholic truths which are at the foundation of religion, with that great fact in the history and method of redemption, the KINGDOM OF GOD, "the Church which is His body, the fullness of Him that filleth all in all," is the special object of the following work. Unless this connection be established, some minds will rest in the mere technicalities of Churchmanship, ignoring those truths, and thus exposing religion to the contempt of the most enlightened portion of the community; while another class of minds will run off into that reckless rejection of all that is distinctive in Christianity, which characterizes the German and English rationalistic schools. The recognition of that Divinely ordained connection leaves unimpaired those great catholic verities which belong to mankind, while it shows the imperative obligation of union with the Church, on the part of all those to whom the whole Gospel is sufficiently proposed.

Now, in this period of unsettled opinion, when the human mind is breaking loose from the moorings of the past, is the time for the Church of God to show herself the conserver and advocate, not only of a certain class of positive truths, but of human freedom as well. "Where the Spirit of the Lord is, there is liberty." (2 Cor., iii, 17.) Let the world see that in the Church alone is true liberty, that her teachings are the noblest and only genuine catholicity.

The objection to some of the conclusions of this work, that we must not attempt to be wise above what is written, is sufficiently answered by a proposition just as true, that we are bound to seek for wisdom enough to understand what is written. And when human systems of theology so interpret certain positive and general expressions of Scripture as to make them assert contradictory propositions, and to be at variance with the very principles upon which all Scriptural teaching is founded, then it is obvious that these systems have perverted and misunderstood what is written: and it is of essential consequence to bring the Christian mind back to the comprehension of that which God's blessed Word does really and truly teach. This duty is the more imperative when it becomes apparent in the progress of society that this unwarranted change of the meaning of God's Word is a cause of offense and a formidable obstacle to the candid reception of the Gospel.

THE DIVINE LIFE AND THE NEW BIRTH.

CHAPTER I.

REDEMPTION.

THE central fact of all Revelation is the Redemption of mankind in Christ Jesus. The fact of the redemption of

§1. MAN FALLEN AND REDEEMED. man presupposes two other facts as its reason and foundation. First, the upright creation of man; and, secondly, his fall from that condition. These are not mere doctrines, but facts. God created man in His own image, and a part of that image was the power to know Him as God, and to trust in Him as Good. This power is Faith, the very highest exercise of human reason and affection. Human reason perceives and decides upon the evidences of truth. The purest exertion of human affection is to love and trust in that God—that Infinite Good—whom the truth reveals. So false is the notion that faith and reason are antagonistic; true faith is the highest reach, the noblest exercise of reason. That such a faculty as Faith belongs to man, either in a sound or in a diseased state, is certain; for he attempts to exercise it. And every abortive attempt is just as much a proof of the original existence of the faculty, as a successful exertion of the same faculty would be.

The second fact assumed and presupposed by the great fact of Redemption is, the fall of man—the depravement, the vitia-

2

tion of his whole nature, of all his powers, faculties, and affections. Of this fact every man has the witness in himself, in the consciousness of his own imperfection, frailty and sinfulness. It is a fact strongly written upon every page of human history. The credulity with which men have ever adopted the vilest religious impostures is an especial attestation of this fact. For one of the most melancholy parts of this superinduced pravity of human nature is the conversion of faith into credulity. Credulity is the vitiated, the corrupted state of faith. Faith, as we have seen, is the exercise of human reason apprehending truth upon sufficient evidence, and of human affections moving towards the good thus apprehended. Credulity is the effort of infirm reason, accrediting falsehood upon insufficient evidence; and of corrupt affections seizing hold upon the falsehood thus received.

Now, as when you prove that a man has a broken limb, or a diseased organ, you as certainly prove the existence of the limb or of the organ; so the universal prevalence of that credulity which, in every age, has admitted and relied upon the grossest impostures, proves both the great facts which we have stated, viz: the original gift to man of that noble faculty by which he was enabled to apprehend and love the truth; and the corruption of that faculty which induces him rather to receive and to trust in a falsehood.

The Redemption of man, by some Divine intervention, from this ruin is, again, a fact, the proof of which is patent and inscribed upon the whole history and condition of the race. For, if truth is at all received among men, and has ever triumphed over error; if real goodness is loved, and genuine Godliness is practiced, these are facts which prove the more general fact of this Divine restoration of humanity. For, a bitter fountain can not send forth sweet waters; a diseased organ can not-perform a healthy function; imbecile credulity can not convert itself into enlightened faith.

The corruption of human nature is abundantly proved by many phenomena of our being. But it is strikingly and mournfully manifested in the history of revealed religion.

The common dealing of man with religion has ever been to corrupt and debase it. This could only be true upon the supposition that the human heart and mind are essentially corrupt.

It is a popular fallacy that the lowest forms and conceptions of religion are to be found in the infancy of society and of the race. The evidence of history proves, on the contrary, that the nearer you approach, in *time* and *place*, to the origin of the human race, the purer is the religion of the people. An unintended testimony to this fact was given lately by an antichristian writer in the *Westminster Review*, who was obliged to confess that the religion and morality of the book of Job were nobler, purer, and more refined than the most beautiful speculations of modern philosophy.*

---

* "In the writer of the Book of Job there is an awful moral earnestness, before which we bend as in the presence of a superior being." "If we ask ourselves how much during this time has been actually added to the sum of our knowledge in these matters, what—in all the thousands upon thousands of sermons, and theologies, and philosophies, with which Europe has been deluged—has been gained for mankind beyond what we have found in this very book of Job, for instance; how far all this has advanced us in the 'progress of humanity,' it were hard, or rather it is easy to answer. How far we have fallen below, let Paley and the rest bear witness; but what moral question can be asked which admits now of a nobler solution than was offered two, perhaps three thousand years ago."—*Westminster Review*, for October, 1853. p. 233. American edition.

The same writer frequently speaks, with hearty scorn and contempt, of the dogma of "the corruption of humanity," as "a lie." But in another part of the same article he furnishes this strong testimony to the truth he had thus boldly denounced : "But it seems from our present experience of what—in some, at least, of its modern forms—Christianity has been capable of becoming, that there is no doctrine in itself so pure but what the poorer nature which is in us can disarm and distort it, and adapt it to its own littleness."

The article, like many of the writings of its class, has many noble thoughts. The great error, out of which all the capital for infidelity is made by this writer, is the quiet assumption that Calvinism is orthodox Christianity.

This popular fallacy about the natural and progressive improvement of religion, is founded upon a comparison of the state f religion among the barbarous tribes of men, living far beyond the bounds of civilization, and the state of religion among those same tribes after they had become civilized and cultivated nations. But the comparison proves nothing at all, unless it could be shown that the civilization and religious improvement of these nations proceeded from themselves, without external help or prompting. But this fact, so indispensable to the validity of the popular conclusion, has never been shown, even in a single instance. The unvarying testimony of history upon this subject is, that every improvement of the religion of a people has been brought to that people from an external source. The Bible alone tells us whence came that light which has thus been gradually diffused among the nations, civilizing, refining, and elevating them. In every instance it was a distinct revelation from God—that revelation being made fuller and more complete under each dispensation of His Grace, according as it seemed meet to His unsearchable wisdom.

In creating man, God conferred upon him all the gifts that were necessary to his well-being. He gave him, therefore, the true religion—the knowledge of God and of the subsisting relations between God and man. He bestowed this great benefit, as every other, to be used or abused, to be improved and cultivated, or to be deteriorated and lost, as men might determine for themselves, in the exercise of the fearful responsibility thus thrown upon them. The history of the whole human race proclaims the melancholy fact that men, manifesting in this, as in other ways, the malign influence of their own apostasy, have universally corrupted the religion which God revealed. The effect of this corruption has been to make religion, indeed, more popular, more congenial to the natural heart; but at the same time to take away, more or less, according to the extent of the vitiation, the purifying, life-giving, and elevating power of religion. And the true religion has only been preserved, pure and unadulterate, in the world, by the continual interposition of the Almighty, co-operating with ordinary human powers by supernatural agencies. For this purpose—to counteract the tendency of men to corrupt the true religion—God has given, in successive ages, prophets, apostles, written revelations, holy sacraments, and a divine society called the Church.

When men wandered away in tribes and families from the early seats of civilization and knowledge, they rapidly sunk into barbarism; and the religion which they took with them, already corrupted, became more stupid and senseless as they declined in intellectual and moral power. The plan of Divine Providence for the reclamation of these innumerable wanderers has been to send them, by various human agencies, the truth which He had already revealed.

Again, the upright creation of man is shown by the correspondence between human nature and the law of God. · The fall of man is as plainly manifested by the opposition between his nature and that same holy law.

Every man who examines thoroughly the moral law, sees that it is the law of his nature—the constitution of the Almighty written upon his soul, and demanding his obedience. He finds that this law, if perfectly obeyed, would produce the highest development, and the greatest happiness of which his nature is capable. This correspondence between a perfect law and the soul of man, proves that the soul was originally created as perfect as the law which is thus a part of its essential constitution.

But every man finds that this same law, although evidently ordained to be a law of life, is to him a law of condemnation.

because he has broken the law. Instead of securing, by obedience, the happiness it promised, and which it manifestly tends to produce, he has incurred its penalty by disobedience. He is compelled, therefore, to concur with St. Paul in the declaration, "The commandment which was ordained to life, I found to be unto death. Wherefore, the law is holy and the commandment holy, and just, and good." (Rom. vii, 10, 12.) But the creature for whom it was ordained has left his first estate—fallen from the uprightness which corresponded with the law, and finds himself now under the curse of that same holy, just, and good commandment.

This is the plain teaching of nature, without the aid of revelation. The Word of God simply affirms the same thing: "And God said, Let us make man in our image, after our likeness." "So God created man in His own image, in the image of God created He him." (Gen. i, 26, 27.) Here was man perfect in himself, and with a perfect law adapted to his nature. Life and happiness were the conditions of obedience to this law; death and misery its penalties for disobedience. An external test and witness of man's continual allegiance to the law of life was at the same time appointed. "In the day that thou eatest thereof thou shalt surely die." (Gen. ii, 17.) After the disobedience and the expulsion from Paradise, "God saw that the wickedness of man was great in the earth, and that every imagination of the thoughts of his heart was only evil continually." "And God looked upon the earth, and behold it was corrupt; for all flesh had corrupted his way upon the earth." (Gen. vi, 5, 12.)

St. Paul tells us "There is none righteous, no, not one." "By the offense of one, judgment came upon all men to condemnation." "By the deeds of the law there shall no flesh be justified in His sight; for by the law is the knowledge of sin." (Rom. iii, 10, 20, and v, 18.) The Scriptural teaching upon this subject is therefore but the reiteration of the universal consciousness and observation of men.

Christian religion assures us that a new element of life has been given to the race of mankind through the man Christ Jesus. An ancient and a modern heresy maintains that the corruption of human nature never was such as to prevent men from recovering themselves from the power of sin, and obeying perfectly the law of God. Without confronting this dogma with the clear testimony of Scripture, let it be tried by the single test of observation. Let one community, in all the long catalogue of nations, be shown where this result has been accomplished. Let this result be shown, even in a single man, beyond the range of the Christian revelation. Christianity allows that the grace of God has appeared unto all men, and that some gleams of revealed truth have been retained among all nations. By these facts she accounts for the good that is found in the most desperate conditions of humanity.

If the hypothesis of the self-restorative powers of human nature be true, we ought to see the full evolution and the complete success of these powers, in a fair proportion of cases, in every country. So far from making this exhibit, without which the hypothesis must be dismissed as utterly destitute of foundation, the actual phenomena are all in the opposite direction. No nation or tribe of men has ever been known to improve its religious system, or to make one single step in advance towards that object, without the assistance, direct or indirect, of Judaism or of Christianity—that is, of Divine revelation. On the contrary, whenever communities have been removed from the influence of this external aid, the only progress has been downward—their only change increasing degeneracy.

This fact is the complete and utter refutation of the Pelagian heresy, which claims for man a self-renovating power. But it displays in still bolder relief the strange absurdity of the position of some modern illuminati, which maintains that Christianity itself is the unassisted product of the human mind; and that, at the present stage of human progress, a new evolution, of a higher religion than Christianity, from the same teeming fountain, is required. But after eighteen centuries of Christian progress, where shall we look for a man superior to the man Christ Jesus, to be the author of this new religion, and the model of a higher style of humanity? Shall we take any one of the German trans-cendentalists? Or one of their English or American copyists? The proposition is painfully incongruous, and shows the blind credulity of dreaming unbelief.

Jesus Christ is the only perfect man that has yet appeared upon the earth since the fall. He alone displayed in His whole life the entire correspondence between human nature and the Divine law. He alone was without sin. He is the author of redemption. God in Christ is the restorer of man, and the perfect model for our imitation and example. From Him is derived that new life, that quickening power, by which His followers are enabled to grow in likeness to Him. The same Spirit by which He was conceived in the womb of the Virgin and assumed man's nature, is given unto us to change that nature in us into the image of Himself, into the like-ness of his perfect manhood.

§2. The First and the Second Adam. It is impossible to understand the relation of man to the Gospel of salvation, unless we clearly recognize the antagonism, the conflict of opposing forces, in his present condition, resulting from these two great facts—the Fall and the Redemption.

The creative act which brought into being the first man and his consort, involved likewise the successive existence of the countless myriads of men who, in each generation, have lived, and acted, and suffered. The one fiat of creation goes on, extending and perpetuating its power, making the first man to live continuously in his posterity, and to fill the earth with the multitude of those who are identical with him in nature. This is a great mystery.

This head and beginning of the human race, falling from original righteousness, was himself corrupt; and all his descendants are like him, in this, as in every other part of their nature. For his being is their being, his nature is their nature. What he was they are. By natural procreation they have no other life or being than his. The inclination of this fallen and degenerate nature is to evil. Its tendency is downward. It spoils and defiles every thing it touches. The taint of sin pervades the whole mass of human feelings, interests, and pursuits. The noblest gifts of God, the purest, the holiest, the loveliest things of earth, it perverts, abuses, and pollutes. Cut off from God, the Fountain of Good, it goes, by the fatal momentum of its own evil disposition, further and further from Him. It continues to sink lower and lower in the scale of moral excellence, until, if no other power interposed, it would reach that lowest depth of degeneracy, which can say, "Evil, be thou my good." When this consummation of man's evil tendencies is reached, all possibilities of happiness and joy are at an end. The tortured slave of relentless passions will then passively submit to their control, and writhe in pitiable impotence beneath their power.

It is not permitted to man fully to realize this description of his natural state and of its result in this world. But every man is conscious of enough in his own nature and disposition to enable him to verify the first part of it, as at least a partial description of himself. And a few persons

3

are allowed to live, who, by long continued habits of iniquity, and of loathsome viciousness, have almost reached that horrid consummation of the evil tendencies of their nature.

Thanks be to God for His unspeakable gift, that natural tendency to evil is but a partial account of man, in his present state, redeemed by the blood of Christ from the dominion of sin, from the power of the Devil. There is a force within him which opposes this natural tendency to evil, and which, if unobstructed and obediently submitted to, will conduct every man in the pathway of righteousness, to God, to heaven, and to happiness. This other force, this Divine power, this holier, Godward tendency, is derived, to the *whole race* of man, from the Second Adam—THE MAN—who is the Lord from heaven. This also is a great mystery! Not more mysterious, but more glorious than the other mystery of creative energy. "Since by man came death, by man came also the resurrection of the dead. For as in Adam all die, even so in Christ shall all be made alive." "The first man Adam was made a living soul; the last Adam was made a quickening spirit." "The first man is of the earth, earthy; the Second Man is the Lord from heaven." "As we have borne the image of the earthy, we shall also bear the image of the heavenly." (1st Cor. xv, 21, 22, 45, 47, 49 verses.)

The first Adam was the Son of God by creation, and was made in the likeness of his Creator, and pronounced to be very good. By simple depravation he corrupted himself, sinking down from the Eternal Source of goodness and purity. As the progenitor of the human race had thus become the source of uncleanness and corruption to his posterity, God provides for the race of mankind a new beginning, a fountain of strength and holiness and purity. Christ is this second and nobler Adam—the new head and representative of the human race, from whom and through whom all men derive the inclination and the power to do good.

§3. The Second Adam is God and Man. Who is this Second Man, this better and purer fountain of humanity, the Regenerator and Restorer of a fallen race? Is He a second creation, a new and faultless being, formed by the Almighty and sent into this world to teach men how they should live, and what they should do? Then is he a stranger to *our humanity*, and has no claim to the title which He assumed— The Son of Man. And all the precepts of practical morality he delivered had been taught before. The Bible every-where negatives the hypothesis of a new creation, but tells of a Being all powerful, and doing His own will, who, because the creatures he would redeem were "partakers of flesh and blood, He also himself likewise took part of the same; that through death He might destroy him that had the power of death, that is, the Devil." (Heb. ii, 14—16.)

The exalted Being who thus, by an act of his own will, took upon Him our humanity, is represented in the Scripture under the twofold relation of a Divine and a human nature. His true humanity is strongly insisted upon, and frequently declared. His Divine nature is not less emphatically mentioned. The titles by which His Divinity is set forth, although very strong, are much less decisive upon this point than the attributes ascribed to Him. His eternity, His self-existence, His creative power, His omnipresence, His universal sovereignty, His uncontrolled and omnipotent will, His right to the worship of all creatures, His occasional assumption of equality with the Supreme Deity, drive us to one of three conclusions: either, 1. That Christianity is a revelation of a system of idolatry—the elevation of a creature to the place of the Creator in human estimation and regard; or, 2. That it is a revelation of a system of Polytheism—the acknowledgment and worship of several Gods; or, 3. That it is a revelation of the old Christian Creed of One God in three persons—Father, Son, and Holy Ghost; and that the second Person of this adorable Godhead, "for us men, and for our salvation, came down from heaven, and was incarnate by the Holy Ghost of the Virgin Mary, and was made man;" became the second Head and Fountain of life, and strength, and purity, and power, to the race He essayed to redeem, to save and to ennoble.

§4. THE TRUE DEITY OF CHRIST AN ESSENTIAL PART OF THE DOCTRINE OF RE- DEMPTION. That the exigency of Divine and human relations brought about by the sinfulness of man was an adequate occasion for the wondrous condescension of God, manifested in the redemption of the world by the gift and sacrifice of His Son Jesus Christ, is shown by the fact that Infinite Wisdom so wrought our redemption; and certainly no conceivable exhibition of the atrociousness of sin and of the goodness of God could equal this.

Goodness is the eternal and immutable condition of happiness to moral beings. Sin, by an eternal necessity, involves the forfeiture of that happiness. This truth, wrought into the constitution of every moral being, can only be fully known and apprehended by those who have felt the dread penalty of transgression. The meaning and purpose of redemption is to bring man back to goodness, to God-likeness. To drive a reluctant sinner into heaven is a contradiction in terms. It is an incongruous mingling of antagonistic and mutually destroying propositions. Heaven is the place and the state of the good, of those who, being like God, love Him, and enjoy a portion of His happiness.

To accomplish this redemption two conditions are required: 1st. Man must see and understand the necessity of goodness, the odiousness, heinousness, and destructive power of sin.

2d. Man must be enabled to fulfill the first and great commandment of the law—"Thou shalt love the Lord thy God with all thy heart, and mind, and strength." Now it is incompatible with man's intended restoration to holiness and happiness, to make him understand the first of these truths, by bringing upon him the penalty of sin, the curse of the law, the very destruction from which he is to be rescued. The Infinite God taking our nature, suffering in that nature for sin, and paying down in His own person a full satisfaction to the violated law, impresses in the strongest possible manner upon the soul of man, and proclaims to all created intelligences, these great truths—the absolute necessity of goodness; the hatefulness and the destructive power of sin.

This same exhibition of love accomplishes most effectually that other correlative condition of redemption, by furnishing to men the occasion and the power to fulfill the first and great commandment—"Thou shalt love the Lord thy God with all thy heart, and mind, and strength." Obedience to this law is the essential condition of happiness to all free and intelligent beings. But how shall a creature estranged from God begin to fulfill it? How shall a being, the slave of sense, so apprehend the purely spiritual and eternal I AM, as to be capable of passing by all the objects of affection and delight with which God has surrounded his creatures, and fixing upon this impalpable and unapproachable Majesty the holiest and best affections of a heart that is but overwhelmed with amazement and awe at the contemplation of His greatness? The question is answered, and can only be answered in the mystery of the Incarnation, in the mystery of the Cross. There the Infinite stoops to our necessities, descends to our apprehensions, veils in human flesh the majesty of the Godhead, becomes man as we are, sympathizes with every affection and feeling, with every pain, and sorrow, and joy of humanity. The question was answered by the blessed Savior Himself when, speaking of His death, He said: "And I, if I be lifted up from the earth, will draw all men unto Me." (St. John xii, 32.) It is God in Christ who draws to Himself the hearts of men.

The Infinite God surely challenges the supreme affection of all men, because as man He can be known, and as man has manifested a love to them past conception. He challenges our love, for " He first loved us, and gave Himself for us, the Just for the unjust." He assumed our place as sinners, and suffered the punishment due to our offenses. The heroic girl who, with devoted affection, threw herself before the body of the man she loved, and received the ball of his adversary into her own bosom, undoubtedly deserved a return of affection only limited by the capacity of the heart of this man to love. Who can dispute her claim to his *supreme affection* but that glorious Savior who gave to her, from His infinite fullness, the sensibility and the power to merit this love, and who has proved His own affection in a manner yet more attractive and illustrious? IMMANUEL—God with us— the Eternal Son, suffering as man the woes of humanity, and thus relieving us from the bitter pains of eternal death which we had incurred, makes possible our obedience to the first and great commandment.

Let, now, this Lamb of God that taketh away the sin of the world, be any created substitute, be other than God, and where would be the efficacy of this transaction to enable man to fulfill that great commandment? Our supreme affection would be given to the creature who had so loved us, and so redeemed us. But our GOD, lifted up for our offenses, and drawing all men to him through the power of love, realizes in human experience the fulfillment of that command. Thus are men to be drawn to God. Thus they are to be made like unto Him by constant intercourse and communion with the

Being whom they love. And thus are they to acquire that nature—that Godliness—of which perfect happiness is the essential state and condition.

§5. Consonance of this Adorable Mystery with the Far-Reaching Influence of Redemption. Why should we falter at this conception of the method of human redemption, except as the human mind, in its present weakness, falters at the unveiled contemplation of every fact of nature? We deal easily with superficial and transient appearances; but when we come to the permanent, the essential, the reality of being, the understanding fails and is incapable. Yet the same reason which conducts the mind to this point assures us of the certain existence of the permanent, the essential, the substantial, which yet that mind can not conceive.

Moral good and evil are facts which would seem—*ex necessitate*—to traverse the whole range of spiritual being. Moral good and evil—what are they but the preservation, or the violation, of the order of the entire spiritual universe! Can moral evil exist at all, in the slightest degree, at any point, without affecting the whole sphere of the intellectual creation? If we can not answer this question absolutely in the affirmative, much less can we venture even a conjectural answer in the negative. All our conceptions of spiritual being would lead to an affirmative answer.

Well, we have in this world a part of that spiritual creation in which moral evil exists as a fact—a portentous fact—to which the woes, the crimes, and the groans of humanity have testified with terrific emphasis for six thousand years. Again, we have the proof, as strong as of any other moral truth, that the Creator of the material and of the spiritual universe has appeared, on the part of humanity, as a Participant in this conflict. In His own essential nature, far beyond our conceiving, He became man, that He might be the all-sufficient Helper of man in the effort to overcome moral evil—the poison of spiritual being, the destroyer of spiritual life.

The contest is in its nature moral, and therefore precludes all possibility of a decision by mere force, by any sort of necessity, by resistless law, or by resistless influence. The almightiness, the mere power of God, finds here no place for action. It is essentially the struggle of a free, spiritual intelligence against corruption, bondage, death—the struggle to throw off the poison that has permeated the whole nature, and is benumbing and destroying every power—the struggle to burst asunder the chains by which the soul has already been bound—the struggle to rise up from subjection to the power of an endless death to the conscious enjoyment of a new and glorious life.

But if corruption, bondage, and death are already present—the actual condition of the soul—as all human consciousness, all history, and the revealed Word of God, concur in testifying, whence the power of resistance, whence even the desire to be free, and the living energy that can achieve freedom and conquer death? The answer to these questions is the glorious mystery of the Gospel. It is the mystery of the incarnation, by which God became man, and as man entered upon this all-concerning conflict; and in virtue of this union, and for the accomplishment of its sublime purpose, gave to all humanity the Holy Spirit as a fresh endowment of freedom, health, and life, from the primal fount of life and being. Thus the contest for freedom and health and life— the battle against moral evil—is perpetually renewed in every human being, with assurance of a triumphant issue to all those who receive and use this grace of God aright.

Here a common objection comes, almost in the same language, from flippant ignorance and from vain-glorious wisdom.

"What is the use of all this complicated machinery of salvation? If God willed the salvation of man, why did He not save him at once? If He desired the destruction of evil, why did not He, whose will is omnipotence, destroy it?"

If we could do no more than point to this revelation as a proved communication from Heaven, that would be answer enough. That God appointed this complicated system is sufficient to satisfy any ingenuous soul that this is the true and the right way. But the futility of the objection may be shown even by a more conclusive answer. The objection itself utterly ignores all the terms of the problem to be solved. It puts at defiance the very meaning of the words it uses. Apart from all teaching of the Word of God, the objection is naught, is worse than idle, because it contradicts the very nature of the thing about which it professes to speak. Moral evil could not be destroyed by a simple act of Omnipotence without destroying moral good as well, and so destroying the whole sphere of moral being, and reducing the Universe to one blank, dreary system of material necessity.

The actual Universe is composed of two very dissimilar parts—MATTER, of which the essential condition is NECESSITY, and SPIRIT, of which the essential condition is FREEDOM. To choose, to love, and to do right freely, is moral good, the happiness and glory of all spiritual intelligences. The power, therefore, to commit sin, to break the law of righteousness, to introduce moral evil into the Universe, is an essential condition of spiritual existence.

Sin—moral evil—is here, in human nature, triumphing over it, and rioting in it. This is simply a fact. Can we wonder that the whole Universe of spiritual intelligences, more than commensurate, it may be, with the material world, beholds with awe-inspired interest, this portentous fact?

Certainly the Eternal Father has looked upon it with in-

conceivable interest—an interest which He has manifested by
more than six thousand years of effective intervention on
behalf of diseased humanity.   From the nature of the case,
as we have seen, this intervention could not be by an exertion
of Omnipotence.   In human nature was the evil, and in
human nature must be found the remedy.   To expel and
conquer moral evil, the very nature, tainted and subdued,
must be brought to choose, love, and do right freely.   We
do not, dare not say, that God was shut up to the one mode
of effecting this result, which the Bible tells us He actually
adopted.   But we may surely affirm that this mode is sublime
and glorious beyond all human imagining, and should be
greeted with no other feeling than that of meek, adoring
gratitude.

If the universe of spiritual intelligences contemplated with
awe and consternation the ruin of a portion of their own nature
by sin, what wondrous emotions of reverence and love must
have thrilled through the whole realm of being when they be-
held the transcendent plan by which sin was to be conquered,
and truth and righteousness maintained.   By the incarnation of
the Son of God, and by the gift of the Holy Ghost, a new
Divine Life was imparted to humanity, to enable it for the
struggle, and to assure to it the victory in the conflict
against sin and death.   For many thousand years a prepar-
atory dispensation preceded the full revelation of this adorable
mystery.   But in all that time its benefits were partially enjoyed by the subjects of this wondrous contest.

Can we wonder that during all these ages the innumerable
hosts of angels who dwell in the presence of God earnestly
desired to look into this mystery?   But when the Son of God
actually entered upon His mission of love and mercy, and on
behalf of all spiritual being became man, "abhorred not the
Virgin's womb," and submitted to all the incidents, weak-

nesses, and miseries of the humanity He was to save and purify, what must have been the emotions of those adoring, conscious intelligences. Well might the Universe resound with the sublime anthem, "Glory to God in the highest, on earth peace, good will to man."

This strange condescension of the Almighty is hard to believe, it is said. And so it is. But it does not therefore follow that we ought not to believe it. The whole sphere of human belief is composed of inconceivable mysteries, which, when we try to understand them, escape from our mental grasp. "Come, now, and let us reason together, saith the Lord." (Is. i, 18.) Let us compare this Divine mystery with all other conceptions of Deity, and of the relations of that Deity to the Universe.

The impotent efforts of ancient and modern philosophy to comprehend the Infinite have clearly demonstrated that it is not only impossible to conceive God as The Infinite Spirit, but that the attempt to do so leads to the conception of Him as an assemblage of contradictions, or as nothing. God can only be apprehended by the human mind in relation, which is a negation of the Infinite. And when, to attain the conception of the Infinite, we try to abstract from the Deity all relation, the issue is, as in several of the German schools, the "Absolute Nothing."

Better than this have been most of the Polytheistic forms of religion that have prevailed in the world. All of these have been human corruptions and perversions of the promised incarnation of Deity, and of those sensible manifestations of the Son of God which anticipated that incarnation. The facility with which the universal soul of man has seized upon this conception, and worked it up into innumerable forms of beauty or hideousness, proves that the conception is within the grasp of human powers.

The third and most fatal of all the attempted conceptions of Deity either makes Him to be the soul of the world, so that He is alike in every thing, or identifies Him outright with the material universe.   And this last is the actual issue of the ancient Asiatic philosophy, and of all the recent anti-christian philosophy of Europe and America.

Compare with these beliefs the humble but profound Christian philosophy embodied in the creed of the Christian Church, and so touchingly expressed by the God-man himself, when an Apostle said to Him, "Lord, show us the Father and it sufficeth us.   Jesus said unto him, Have I been so long time with you, and yet hast thou not known Me, Philip?   He that hath seen Me hath seen the Father; and how sayest thou, then, Show us the Father?"   (St. John xiv, 8, 9.)

Which now is noblest and most credible, God as NOTHING, the result of one philosophy?   God as a mob of Divinities, according to another issue of human wisdom?   God as every-thing, rock, and reptile, and all brute matter, the highest reach of the latest infidel speculation?   Or, God a Spirit and a Person, becoming man, assuming, for a grand and beneficent purpose—a purpose that includes within its far-reaching scope the whole Universe of spiritual being—this ruined humanity of ours, that by such Divine indwelling man might successfully contend against and triumph over MORAL EVIL, and achieve for eternity freedom, holiness, happiness?

Which of these beliefs best commends itself to a noble and ingenuous nature?   And when we add to this vast difference between the quality of these several beliefs, that the former are but the vagaries of a wanton and wearied imagination, and that the last is accredited to us by an undoubted revela-tion from God, who will refuse to come with adoring humility and say, "Lord, I believe; help Thou my unbelief!"

And if this be true, if the tremendous contest with moral evil, on behalf of the Spirit world, is waged by the Almighty in our human nature, then all other phenomena of being easily arrange themselves around this wondrous fact and in close subordination to it.

With admirable significance was the earth formed and fitted, by ages of preparation, to be the theater of this mighty conflict. With increasing meaning, and in nearer sympathy, were all living creatures on this earth made, by the Divine pre-arrangement, *to symbolize in their life and death the incidents of this fearful contest.* Thus it was literally true that "by sin death entered into the world" long before that sin had actually been committed. And thus is the full meaning of that other wonderful declaration of St. Paul amply vindicated, "For we know that *the whole creation* groaneth and travaileth in pain together until now: Because the creature itself also shall be delivered from the bondage of corruption into the glorious liberty of the children of God." (Rom. viii, 21, 22.)

With prophetic vision of that glorious consummation, as we may believe, did Isaiah sing, "The wolf also shall dwell with the lamb, and the leopard shall lie down with the kid, and the calf and the young lion and the fatling together; and a little child shall lead them. And the sucking child shall play on the hole of the asp, and the weaned child shall put his hand on the cockatrice's den. They shall not hurt nor destroy in all my holy mountain; for the earth shall be full of the knowledge of the Lord, as the waters cover the sea."

> " O, long-expected year ! begin ;
> Dawn on this world of woe and sin."

Who will so frustrate the grace of God, and the capacities of his own redeemed nature, as to lie down in passive submission to the bondage of sin and death, and refuse to enter

upon that transcendent conflict with moral evil with which
the Universe of being is in awful sympathy! Who will be
so recreant to himself and to the infinite mercy of God as
to choose evil rather than good, and with mean perverseness
refuse, with the Lord of glory as his leader, to contend for
life, freedom, immortality, happiness and Heaven!

CHAPTER II.

THE KINGDOM OF GOD.

THE Scriptures teach us that Christ came into the world at a prearranged period—in the fullness of time—when all §1. HISTORICAL things were ready. One preparation for His RETROSPECT. coming was the subjection of the most important portions of the world to a common government, so that the greatest facility might be afforded for the establishment of that kingdom which, though not of this world, was to be set up in it, as the refuge and the home of diseased humanity.

Another, and it may be a higher preparation for that coming of the Son of God, was that, in the previous ages, all the powers and resources of the human mind, and of human society, for the promotion of the well-being of man, had been tried to the utmost, under every variety of circumstance and modification, and had resulted only in disastrous and humiliating failure.

The Patriarchal religion, and the earliest types of civilization, had settled down, in Eastern Asia, into the benumbing, crushing, and soul-withering systems of mingled superstition, atheism and pantheism, which we find there at the present day.

Again and again, in Central Asia, in Western Asia, on the Mediterranean shores of Europe and of Africa, to the furthest western coasts. as the tide of emigration rolled on to the Atlantic, was the experiment of a newer, fresher, and more vigorous civilization tried, with every advantage and under the most varied conditions. All that human faculties could do in their highest development was accomplished then. Again and again the result was failure and blank despair. The better and higher class of minds, who could not submit to the degradation of atheistic unbelief, found a retreat from that lowest depth of human corruption in the rugged recesses of fatalistic stoicism. But the masses, and the large majority of educated men, unreservedly adopted the atheistic and Epicurean alternative, that man can not know the truth, that he can learn nothing of his origin, his nature, or his destiny, and that the highest wisdom is to gratify his appetites, with no other restraint than prudence and a regard for health may supply.

It was when human nature had reached, by its own futile efforts, this lowest deep, and when it must have inevitably perished in its own corruption, that the GOD-MAN appeared, to be the Savior of this fallen humanity, to bear witness to the truth, to bring life and immortality to light.

God, indeed, had never left Himself without a witness in the world, besides that testimony which is borne to Him by the works of nature. The primitive revelation had descended, in gradually decreasing influence, to all races and nations. Instead of improving this revelation, and attaining, from the vantage ground which it gave them, to a better and purer religion, as modern speculation would require, men simply depraved, vitiated, and obscured the knowledge first imparted, until, as we have seen, nearly all was lost.

Even beyond all this, God was pleased, in that long trial of humanity, to help the infirmities and to instruct the ignorance of men. Early in the apostasy, He selected a family and nation to be special witnesses to the truth. To

this nation—then the kingdom of God—the truth was presented by a continuous revelation, submitted to constant
proof and verification. And these witnesses for God were
placed, by the special care of the Almighty, at the base of
the Mediterranean sea, and just between the two earliest
centers of civilization and empire. This testimony, like all
the rest, was disregarded, and the fact of man's incapacity
even to retain, *much less to discover and advance, the true religion, was fully proved.*

And now the revelation of the truth was to be made full
and perfect. Now the whole mind of God, in the creation
and RESTORATION of man, was to be disclosed. Now the
adorable mystery, so long hidden in shadow, type and figure,
of a higher life in humanity, proceeding from the Divine
Manhood of the incarnate Deity, was to be fully manifested.
And now, therefore, to make that revelation effectual, for its
purpose of mercy and grace, to give it influence and power
over mankind, the kingdom of God was to be formally
established among all nations.

At the very crisis of this Divine legation, the objective
truth, which saves and ennobles, was brought, in the person
of our Savior Christ, into immediate contact and conflict with
the best results of mere human wisdom, represented by Pontius Pilate, the Roman Governor of Judea. The Revealer
of the truth stands at the tribunal of the lordly representative of human power and wisdom. To this man the blessed
Jesus makes the sublime annunciation which every ingenuous soul should have hailed as the dayspring from on high:
"For this cause came I into the world, that I should bear
witness unto the truth. Every one that is of the truth heareth my voice."

The answer of Pilate is a contemptuous epitome of the
philosophy of his times. "What is truth?" was not a ques-

4

tion reverently addressed to the incarnate Truth, but the impatient exclamation of a man familiar with the results of human learning and speculation, knowing that truth had been long and earnestly sought and never found, and who had settled down in the despairing conviction that Truth was nothing but a high-sounding word with which to cheat and betray fools and visionaries.

The subsequent conduct of Pilate was in perfect keeping with this rejection of all that gives sanctity to human life and character. He had no ill will towards the extraordinary person who had been brought before him. On the contrary, he repeatedly affirmed his innocence, was evidently impressed by the majestic meekness of his bearing, and was very anxious to discharge him unharmed. But, because to have acted thus in his judicial office, upon his own clear convictions of truth and righteousness, might have caused him some trouble, some perplexity, some complication with his government; and, *knowing these things to be realities,* (whereas truth and righteousness were to him but vain illusions,) he deliberately and wantonly prostitutes the highest of all earthly offices, and condemns to death the man whom, in the very sentence, he proclaimed innocent and just. And this was the actual condition of the whole world at that period, as we learn from other and independent authorities. With such principles at its heart, human society could not have subsisted much longer. And in reading the history of the early ages of Christianity, we must recollect that it was upon such a festering mass of corruption that the leaven of Christian truth was compelled to work.

We now stand upon the vantage ground of eighteen centuries of Christian culture. The kingdom which Christ established was early planted among all the civilized and in some of the barbarous nations of the earth; and the truth which

Jesus came to reveal, and of which that kingdom is the appointed witness, has been permeating and renovating diseased humanity ever since.

Two causes have been at work to renew in our time an image of the period in which the Savior lived. For several generations an infidel philosophy has prevailed, which, consciously shutting out the light of truth that God revealed, has been burrowing in the darkness of the human soul for truth. The result has been a reproduction, in curious succession, of the very systems and fancies which had been found and tried, and exploded in the days of Pontius Pilate, the later philosophies leaving no residuum but a skeptical atheism like his.

A sadder cause has tended to the same conclusion. First, the corruptions of Christianity itself, and then the melancholy divisions among Christians which sprung out of the effort to remove those corruptions, have obscured the light of truth, and given rise to painful perplexities and uncertainties in the minds of multitudes, whether, amid such diversity of jarring dogmas, there is any truth which the mind of man can sufficiently discern and firmly hold.

The thoughts of earnest Christians all over the world are directed to this painful subject. And, surely, the dangers and difficulties of the times are sufficient to turn all hearts and minds to try if haply a remedy may be found. False religion and irreligion, sometimes separate, often combined, arraying all their powers against the truth, should summon all who hold alike the great fundamental saving articles of that truth, to join together in one compact body of believing champions for the defense of the common faith against its proud and insulting foes.

In a question of preserving the integrity of the truth against the powers of darkness, it will not do to begin by an attempt to compromise any portion of that truth, and thus to band together in mere negations those who hold positively the most conflicting dogmas.

Neither will it at all meet the exigency to rest in that merely spiritual unity which results from the consciousness of having certain principles and feelings in common. This is a very blessed unity, indeed, for which we daily pray in the liturgy. But the demand of the present crisis of the struggle of Christianity against the kingdom of darkness, is for that visible, external unity, that organization, which gives strength for defense and for aggression.

§2. ESTABLISH-
MENT OF THE
KINGDOM. Human wisdom could hardly suggest a solution of so hard a problem; but Divine Wisdom had anticipated the puzzling complication produced by human weakness and error, and had provided the amplest solution.

We have seen that at the coming of Christ the disorganization of society, of religion, of philosophy, and of the human mind, was extreme, so that ruthless atheism and moral dissoluteness were rioting over the prostrate nations, and defacing utterly the image of God in man.

At the very crisis of this disorganization, the manifested truth undertook to gather the redeemed into one all-pervading UNITY, which should equally respect the sacredness of truth and the freedom of the human soul, dogmatically prescribe the terms of salvation, and yet allow full scope for the action of all reasonable diversities of mind, character, and circumstances.

For this purpose Christ established a kingdom, with a full and perfect organization, for the effective propagation and perpetuation of the truth, and to secure the salutary power of that truth upon man and upon society. Nothing in the Gospels is presented more prominently than the establishment and pervading influence of this kingdom. All other truth is studiously and constantly taught as the principles, the laws, or the administration of the kingdom of God. Christ alone is King, but a succession of earthly officers was carefully provided, and His last official act was the promulgation of its great CHARTER, "All power is given unto ME in heaven and in earth. Go ye, therefore, and disciple all nations, baptizing them in the name of the Father, and of the Son, and of the Holy Ghost; teaching them to observe all things whatsoever I have commanded you; and lo, I am with you alway, even unto the end of the world." (St. Matt. xxviii, 18, 20.)

In this comprehensive charter we see, *as simple facts*, the kingdom itself, its chief officers, its aggressive constitution, its faith, its sacramental pledges, its perpetuity, its Divine power by the perpetual presence of Christ.

While the visibility and effective external organization of this kingdom of God are carefully provided for, its supernatural, mystical, and spiritual nature is not less clearly declared. It is sometimes called the "spouse of Christ." More emphatically still, " HIS BODY, THE FULLNESS OF HIM THAT FILLETH ALL IN ALL." (Ephes. i, 23.)

The baptismal formula contained in this great Charter, requiring an intelligent faith, was expanded, by those to whom the commission was first given, into those brief explanations of its terms and meaning which, as now collected and preserved, we call, respectively, the Apostles' and the Nicene CREED. These *determine, and take out of the region of question and debate, all essential truth*, yet leave a magnificent domain for the excursion of the human mind in perfect freedom of adventurous speculation. And so, for many ages, the whole Church understood the meaning of the charter, and therefore, with the largest diversity of thought and opinion, continued ONE.

The only practical remedy for the unhappy divisions of Christendom now, is to return to the ancient and divinely-established basis of unity—the recognition of the KINGDOM OF GOD, as originally organized by the Divine care, and with its few and simple terms of communion. The primitive organization, and the terms of communion, are witnessed by the Scriptures, and by the whole subsequent history of Christendom. For in that subsequent history every change, every departure from the primitive order, becomes a witness to that first Divinely-ordained prescription.

When God would make known the way of salvation, He was not so unmindful of His own previous work in ordaining the nature of man as to send forth revealed truth as an abstraction, a mere spoken word, or written treatise. In that way of communication the truth could have exerted no influence whatever upon man and upon society. When God wrote the Ten Commandments upon two tables of stone, He did not leave them upon Mount Sinai, to be found and appropriated by the wanderers of the Arabian desert. He did not even give them to Moses, as a private person, to be subject to the chances of individual life and family transmission; but He placed them in the official custody of a "Kingdom of Priests," whose whole corporate being was founded upon the duty and purpose of safely keeping and transmitting from generation to generation these and other witnesses and memorials of the truth—*this kingdom being itself, in its corporate character, the chief and concurring witness to the same truth.*

And so in the Christian dispensation. The revelation is not merely a discourse or a written treatise. It is the solemn establishment of a kingdom, thoroughly organized, to which the revelation is committed in varied forms—of oral discourse afterward reduced to writing, of letters, sacraments, and creeds. And, again, *the kingdom*, in its Christian form, becomes, as before, and by the necessity of the case, the most prominent and important witness of all.

So fundamental is the kingdom of God in the purpose and method of salvation, that all the practical precepts of the Bible, and the most graphic and concerning illustrations of Divine truth, are given as incidents and peculiar features of this one all-comprehending fact. It is the kingdom of heaven that is declared to be the leaven of the world and of society. The truths of the Gospel are called "the mysteries of the kingdom." The very principles of the Divine administration are announced, as the laws of this kingdom. Nearly all the parables of our blessed Lord are founded upon the assumption of the kingdom as the fundamental fact in Christianity, consequent upon the incarnation, sacrifice, and mediation of Christ our Redeemer. And that adorable Redeemer occupied the wondrous interval between the resurrection and His ascension into heaven in "speaking of the things pertaining to the KINGDOM OF GOD."

§3. CONSTITUTION OF THE KINGDOM. A kingdom without a regular and orderly gradation of offices, in due and fitting relation to each other, would be a mere Babel of confusion, a perpetual source of discord, strife, and lawlessness. "God is not the author of confusion, but of peace," "that there should be no schism in the body." Accordingly we learn that there is a glorious hierarchy in heaven. Much more necessary, and much more distinctly revealed, is the progression and subordination of offices in the earthly kingdom of Christ.

There is no conflict, no sort of opposition, as some strangely imagine, between the Church of God and the saving truth of which she is the appointed witness and keeper. The original constitution of the Church combined into harmonious concord all the best and most legitimate elements of human government. Men, dissatisfied with this Divine concord of what they supposed to be discordant elements, and unwilling to exercise the intelligence and the moral restraint necessary to the right working of such a system, have ever sought to improve and simplify the product of Divine wisdom by changing His beautiful and complex harmony into a simple, crushing autocracy on the one hand, or into an equally simple and despotic supremacy of the shifting popular will on the other.

The witness of the Bible and of history alike rebukes this human tampering with Divinely established order, and presents to us, in clear outline, the original constitution of Christ's earthly kingdom.

The first official act of our blessed Lord in the organization of His kingdom is thus related by St. Luke: "And it came to pass in those days that he went out into a mountain to pray, and continued all night in prayer to God. And when it was day he called unto him his disciples: and of them he chose twelve, whom also he named Apostles." "And he sent them to preach the Kingdom of God." (vi, 12, 13; ix, 2.) "After these things the Lord appointed other seventy also, and sent them two and two before his face into every city and place, whither he himself would come." And these also were commissioned to preach "the kingdom of God," with this solemn sanction: "He that heareth you heareth me; and he that despiseth you despiseth me; and he that despiseth me despiseth him that sent me." (x, 1–16.)

During the remainder of our Lord's sojourn upon earth, while the kingdom was restricted to the narrow limits of the Holy Land, this was its organization: 1. Christ, the visible head. 2. The Apostles. 3. The Seventy. 4. The whole body of disciples.

After the resurrection, when the kingdom was to be extended over the whole earth, and Christ, the only King, was to be no longer visible, it was meet that a visible head should be provided, who might be seen and acknowledged, and who might superintend the administration of the kingdom *in every part of it.* This is not stated as an abstract proposition to which the facts of the Divine Record must be ingeniously conformed; but it is simply the apparent *rationale* of the *unquestionable facts of the case.* To the whole college of the Apostles Jesus studiously gave the visible headship which He Himself had hitherto exercised. "As my Father hath sent me, even so send I you. And when he had said this he breathed on them, and saith unto them, Receive ye the Holy Ghost. Whosesoever sins ye remit, they are remitted unto them; and whosesoever sins ye retain, they are retained." (St. John xx, 21–23.) "Then the eleven disciples went away into Galilee, into a mountain where Jesus had appointed them. And Jesus came and spake unto them, saying, All power is given unto me in heaven and in earth. Go ye therefore and disciple all nations, baptizing them in the name of the Father, and of the Son, and of the Holy Ghost; teaching them to observe all things whatsoever I have commanded you: and lo, I am with you alway, even unto the end of the world." (St. Matt. xxviii, 16–20.)

The first thing the Apostles do, in pursuance of this plenary commission, is to add to their own number. And the subsequent narrative shows that this addition goes on indefinitely, as the exigencies of the ever-enlarging kingdom demanded. The next recorded act in this connection is the formal ordination of Deacons. The orderly organization of the kingdom was then as follows: 1. The Apostles. 2. The Order represented by the original Seventy, presently called Elders and sometimes Bishops—Overseers—and indefinitely multiplied wherever the Church was planted. 3. The Deacons. 4. The body of believers.

5

With this organization the canon of Scripture closes. And if the simple authority of Scripture is to determine the primitive constitution of the Church, there is the decision.

Every page of ecclesiastical history, after the close of the canon, presents to us this identical constitution of the Church, *prevailing and unquestioned every-where.* Only one change is at first observable. The successors to the Apostolic office, out of reverence to the first Apostles, gradually dropped that title, and assumed one which had been sometimes given to the second order of the Ministry, the title Bishop.

To make our conception of the essential constitution of the Church more distinct, one other element of confusion should be removed.

We find in Scripture, and in subsequent ecclesiastical history, mention of other offices in the Church besides the three grades of the Ministry just enumerated: such as Evangelists, Prophets, the gift of tongues, etc., in the first age; and Archdeacons, Archbishops, Patriarchs, and many others, in later times. Two criteria discriminate clearly between these two classes of offices: 1. The second class are, manifestly, variable expediencies, adapted to temporary circumstances; either coming soon to an end, or beginning long after the Divine organization of the Church was completed. The first class are constant, and have continued unchanged from the time when the Apostles were assembled at Jerusalem to this day. 2. A still more decisive mark separates the two classes of offices. Each of the Divine offices is filled, and can only be filled, by a Divinely prescribed ORDINATION, *by those to whom Christ committed the administration of His Church.* Every Bishop, every Presbyter, every Deacon, in the Church of God, has received his office by the solemn "Laying on of hands," for that purpose and with that intention, of an Apostle, or of a Successor of an Apostle. Whereas, to the other offices mentioned in Scripture, no such ordination is mentioned. And from the Apostles' days to this day, no other office in the Church of God has ever been conferred by ordination. No Subdeacon, Archdeacon, Dean, Archbishop, Patriarch, or Pope, has ever been made such by Ordination, but is simply appointed to the office by human authority, as a merely human expediency.

The pregnant inference from this fact is strengthened by another most suggestive fact. There is one other ordination, or "laying on of hands," known to the Church of God, and but one other. It was uniformly practised by the Apostles, and has been uninterruptedly continued ever since. It does not admit to a special ministerial office in the Church, but to the common *fellowship* or general Priesthood of the Church, as the complement of Baptism. It is usually called Confirmation.

Thus there are four ordinations, by Apostolic hands, known to the Church of God, of Divine institution, and perpetual obligation: First, that which confers the general Priesthood that belongs to every member of the Body of Christ; second, that which confers the lowest *ministerial* office in that Priesthood; third, that which admits to a higher Order in the same Ministry; fourth, that which confers the highest of all, the Episcopal office. Each of these grades in the orderly arrangement of Christ's kingdom is a Divine gift, witnessed by a Divine ordinance. All other offices in the Church are human, temporary, and transient; and in the darkest days of corruption no one ever dared to put upon them the sanction of Divine appointment by an attempted Ordination.

The purpose of this work does not permit me to furnish any more detailed proofs of the nature and constitution of the kingdom of God. This has been effectually done in many popular books.*

§4. THE KING-
DOM OF GOD A
WITNESS TO THE
TRUTH.

Such, in brief outline, is the constitution of that Divine Kingdom which God has set up in this world to be His WITNESS, the refuge and home of His redeemed children. This is the fundamental fact in revealed religion, upon which all other revealed truth depends for its authentication, and from which it proceeds as its starting point. No wonder, when this fact was ignored, or counted as nothing, that men began first to doubt and then to deny all other revealed truth.

The Church executes her office as God's WITNESS in the earth. 1st. By keeping and bearing testimony to the Holy Scriptures as God's Word written. To the Church of God under the Mosaic dispensation we owe the Canon of the Old Testament. The Church alone, as a perpetual body corporate, could have preserved these books from age to age; and her authentication alone can compose the separate portions of the Canon into the ONE Book of the Almighty. Even as a mere human corporation having perpetuity, the Church could authenticate and give unity to the Bible *as her own continuous record.* But without this corporate existence of the Church as ONE, there was no human possibility of the collection and transmission of the *Bible as one book*, and there could be no authentication of it. Such is the necessity of the Church, even when we eliminate from her constitution and from her continuous record the Divine element. The Church and the Bible even thus become concurrent witnesses to the truth and to each other.

But when the Kingdom of God and the Holy Record of

---

*Among these are Chapman's Sermons, Kip's Double Witness, Wilson's Church Identified, and the Churchman's Reasons for his Faith and Practice, by Dr. N. S. Richardson.

that kingdom are taken together, as they have actually come down to us, the Divine element can not reasonably be eliminated from either. For the existence of the Church itself from long before the beginning of any other authentic history, down through all the revolutions of the world to our own day, is itself the most stupendous of miracles. The Church, thus Divinely preserved, keeps and transmits, from age to age, a record, telling of her Divine origin, and of numerous Divine attestations, by miracle and prophecy, in successive ages. To each one of these Divine attestations all the myriads composing the Church at the time of their occurrence are the witnesses, and, by virtue of the corporate character of the Church, their testimony is transmitted in the record to all succeeding ages.

The testimony of the Church to the New Testament is just the same as to the Old. Only, from the general extension of the Christian Church, that testimony is even more conclusive. The Christian Church was long before any book of the New Testament, and is, of necessity, the only witness to each and all of them. The testimony is stronger than that of the ancient Church, because that ancient Church consisted of but one people, speaking one language, and there was a possibility therefore of tampering with the record, if we put out of view the Divine care. But there was no such possibility in regard to the testimony of the Christian Church. For the various books composing the New Testament were collected, held, and witnessed by innumerable Christian bodies, in all parts of the world, speaking different languages, and having no connection but their oneness in the body of Christ.

2. The Church is the Witness of God in yet another way. God has ever sealed His mercy and truth by visible sacraments. The constant administration of these by the Church continually proclaimed that mercy and truth, while the insti-

tution of those sacraments was made a part of the written record. Thus the Divine care provided for the satisfaction of the reasonable nature of man three distinct, concurring, mutually dependent, and mutually sustaining witnesses to His truth—the Church by her simple corporate existence, the written Word which she preserved, and the sacraments which she continuously administered.

§5. FATAL EF-   Now see the effect of separating the things
FECTS OF DISRE-   that God had joined together. Romanism
GARDING THIS   began by making the Church, or, rather, a
TESTIMONY.   part of it, superior to the Word and Sacraments, and independent of them, as if she were the sole witness to the truth. The miserable corruptions consequent upon that daring subversion of God's appointed order, led to the extreme reaction which put almost out of view, and entirely out of just estimation, both Church and Sacraments, and left the Bible to be the sole witness of God in the world. These two opposite modes of departure from the Divine prescription have produced for each a terrible retribution.

Unity was God's ordinance; Separation is man's fatal device. God gave His Church, His written Word, and His holy Sacraments, as distinct yet concurring and joint witnesses to the same truth. Rome first divided the Church in the West from the Church in the East. Then she divided this Western fraction, as subsisting in any passing age, from the Catholic Church of all the ages. For the maimed and distorted body, produced by this twofold division, she then arrogated the privilege of being the exclusive witness for God. By the testimony of such a witness she assumed to give Divine sanction to all the mediæval corruptions of religion, and secured the power of adding to those corruptions just as fast as the degeneracy of morals and manners might require. Had it not been for the check given to this process by the Reformation, it may safely be affirmed that by this time the light of Christian truth would have been almost extinguished. Even as it is, the educated classes in Romish countries are, for the most part, skeptical or atheistic; while to the ignorant masses religion is little better than an unreasoning superstition.

What, again, is the result of that mode of separating the things which God had joined together, which ignores the Church and the Sacraments as witnesses to the truth, and sets up the Bible as the only and all-sufficient witness?

Even thus alone, the Bible was reverenced for awhile. But, deprived of the concurring testimony which the Church and the Sacraments give to the great, fundamental truth spread over all the pages of the Bible, men began to find in it, *according to the variations of their own minds*, so many apparently conflicting truths, and thereupon to divide off into so many rival and discordant sects, that the world was confounded by these contrary utterances. The Divine criterion of truth— its unity—was lost. The heathen said, "Agree upon your religion before you come to persuade us to adopt it." Multitudes in Christian lands found an excuse for doubt, indecision, and a practical rejection of the Gospel, in this Babel of confused and jarring testimony.

The evil of this form of separation did not stop here. The Bible, dissevered from the Divine connections which gave to it its UNITY, its authentication, and its sanction as the Word of God, was taken up by learned men as a thing by itself, without a history, and just discovered. The book, thus isolated, was dissected into parts, and torn into fragments, and so subjected to the critical processes of these self-sufficient judges. First one and then another book was disposed of as spurious, then the inspiration of the whole, or any part of it, was denied, and all its miracles rejected. All that they have left us is the ferocious atheism of one sect of philosophers, or the wretched inanities of the sentimental Frenchman who has essayed to turn the life of Jesus into a Pastoral.

God's blessed prescription, God's appointed union of the Church, the Scriptures, and the Sacraments, as diverse but consentient and mutually sustaining witnesses to the same eternal truth, testifying without variation or shadow of change in all the ages, is the cure, and the only cure, for these fatal diseases.

The very latest issue of virulent enmity to Christianity, the Westminster Review for October, 1864, uses as the chief weapon of attack the separation of the Scriptures from the Church. "Divide and conquer" is the motto of infidelity, not only as to Christian people, but as applicable, even more effectively, to the appointed witnesses and muniments of the truth. It attacks each as if it were alone, and loudly boasts an easy victory. Thus it sums up the present aspect of the conflict: "These contests must lead ultimately to a discussion of the basis of the orthodox creed. Hitherto, though contrary to reason, it has been supported by a supposition of the infallibility of the Church, or of the infallibility of Scripture. When each of these is given up it must come to the ground." (p. 228.)

It is painful to remember that the occasion for this advantage was first given by Christian teachers, profanely separating what God had joined together. Christian religion is not founded upon any one unconnected dogma, the infallibility of the Church, or the infallibility of the Scripture, considered each as an isolated fact. It rests upon a concurrence of Divine Witnesses, the Church, the Scriptures, and the Sacraments, provided by the Divine care, authenticating each other and testifying jointly to the same essential truth. The Almighty thus meets and satisfies the highest requirements of human reason, the utmost demands of the nature He has made. This threefold cord can not be broken. Infidelity has never even attempted to answer the argument of Leslie, derived from the strength of this merciful provision.* It is only when Christians have untwisted the cord and laid its parts asunder, and rely upon the strength of a single portion, that infidelity seizes the advantage thus given to it, and makes those continuous assaults which have resulted so disastrously to the cause of revealed religion. Surely it is time to cease this tame surrender of the Christian strength; this mistaken confederacy with evil; this wretched composition with the adversary of God and man.

Another of the favorite devices of the enemy, eagerly adopted from the weak concessions of Christian people, is to represent the Kingdom of God depicted in the Gospel as merely a moral idea, a fancy, or an affection, instead of a real, visible kingdom, set up in the world with power, perpetuity, and Divine authority.

The recognition of the Kingdom of God with its established connections, puts an end to the whole craft and professed science of modern unbelief. The loss of the true conception of that kingdom for some ages past has tended more than all other causes, it seems to me, to nurture that unbelief. We have already seen some illustrations of the truth of this position. There is another which we will briefly consider.

The foremost dogma of this antichristian science is that a miracle is impossible, or so antecedently incredible that no amount of testimony can prove its occurrence. The conclusion from this dogma is that the miracles recorded in the Christian Scriptures discredit those Scriptures, and resolve their contents into myth and fable.

*Short and Easy Method with a Deist.

And why is a miracle thus summarily pronounced impossible by the diminutive spirit of unbelieving sciolism? Is not all nature a perpetual miracle? The universe and its minutest atoms, are they not all stupendous miracles of Almighty power and wisdom, far away beyond our power of comprehension? Has human science yet fathomed the mystery of being, of life, in its most insignificant form? The antichristian advocate replies, These phenomena of nature, with all their incomprehensible wonders, are credible because they proceed in orderly course and are the subject of constant experience, and can be formulated into a scientific arrangement. The position then amounts to this: "Any number of ordinary miracles is credible, and such miracles are the constituents of all science. No extraordinary miracle is credible, and when any such is alleged it must be contemptuously dismissed as a fable and a superstition." This, and no more, is the mystery and meaning of that vaunted science of historical criticism which professes to have discredited the Scriptures and overturned Christianity.

The common sense of mankind must scout this dogma as little better than the idiocy of philosophic pretension. Let us analyze the dogma, and see if the verdict of the common mind is not logically and scientifically correct.

Why is an alleged extraordinary miracle incredible? But two possible reasons can be given for this dogma. Either, first, there is no God—no PERSONAL WILL and MIND—to whom such a miracle can be referred; or, secondly, no human testimony can authenticate such a miracle. The first reason is bald and naked atheism. The second is the oft-refuted sophism of David Hume, in the last century. The whole of this vain boasting, then, goes back to the philosophy which is as old at least as the time when a wise man announced, "The fool hath said in his heart, 'There is no God;'" or to the ingenious riddle of a self-confessed sophist of the eighteenth century.

Indeed, this latter alternative, adopted from Hume by the latest unbelief, resolves itself into the former. For the notion of a God who can not communicate His will to His reasonable creatures, except by the established and ordinary course of natural phenomena—can make known to men no truth but such as is contained in those phenomena—is really equivalent to the denial of any God, out of and above nature, which is simple atheism.

All the force and ingenuity of Hume's riddle proceeds from ignoring the kingdom of God, as a supernatural society, coeval, not indeed with nature, but with human society. This kingdom has subsisted, *as a fact*, from the fall of man, and has come down through all the ages, in continued coincidence with the progress and development of human nature. The communication of the will of God, as a Moral Governor, over and above the course of physical phenomena, has been the normal state, the established rule of this kingdom from the beginning. Such a communication, however attested, in the regular development of the kingdom of God, is not properly extraordinary, is not an isolated, unconnected wonder, which we may ascribe to delusion or deceit, but is part of an orderly, regular, and established sequence.

The phenomena of conscience in every man attest a moral Governor, and a spiritual sphere of being subject to the moral law, just as certainly as physical phenomena attest a physical law, and a creative power. A VISIBLE KINGDOM has been the outward witness of God, as the Moral Governor of this spiritual sphere of being, through all the ages; and its official record is older than all the sciences, and than any other human history.

A communication from God, beyond and above nature,

and manifesting a control of all physical phenomena, is the rule and ordinary procedure of this kingdom, *at every great conjuncture of its history.* The official record has attested these communications, and the manner of them, at the respective times in which they were made. And the Divine care has provided, in the very constitution of the kingdom, that all the members of it, living at the time of these communications, should be, in various ways, concurrent witnesses to the facts stated in the record.

This elaborate provision at once authenticates the truth beyond reasonable question, and separates it by a broad gulf from all the impostures or delusions with which the Devil has attempted to simulate the voice of God. A true miracle might never have been questioned but for this cunning device of the Adversary, by which he accomplishes a double purpose, to build up his own kingdom of darkness, and to discredit the Divine communications. And this vile deceit is really the foundation of the pretended modern science which repudiates miracles as incredible. Because miracles have been alleged in behalf of every form of false religion, and as an habitual mode of practicing upon superstitious weakness, therefore it is concluded that every alleged miracle must be referred either to fraud or delusion.

The reasonable conclusion, on the contrary, from these premises, would seem to be that there must be a foundation in truth and reality for a phenomenon so universal. Every counterfeit presupposes the genuine thing which it tries to represent. Imposture would never have pretended, or superstition imagined, a false miracle, except upon the condition that true miracles had actually been performed on behalf of God's truth, or were reasonably to be looked for. Take away this condition and you leave one of the most prominent phenomena in the history of man without a cause, without a possible foundation. Admit this condition and you destroy that fragile erection of historical criticism which rejects all miracles as incredible.

Turn now to the official record of the Kingdom of God, and you find both the parts of this unquestionable phenomenon of human history. True miracles are recorded, wrought by Divine power in attestation of the truth, and "lying wonders" are mentioned with equal distinctness, wrought either by satanic agency or by human fraud, deriving all their force and influence from the true miracles which they counterfeit, or from the reasonable conviction of the human soul that God would so attest His truth to man. Both facts are presented fully and in their proper relations in the Bible. The New Testament continues the plain testimony of the Old in this regard, and further announces that this method of deception will continue all through the Christian dispensation. The blessed Savior says: "There shall arise false Christs and false prophets, and shall show great signs and wonders." (St. Matt. xxiv, 24.) And St. Paul declares: "The mystery of iniquity doth already work," anticipating the approach of him "whose coming is after the working of Satan, with all power, and signs, and lying wonders." (2 Thess. ii, 7–9.)

Look at the miracles recorded in Scripture which attest the power and presence of God, and see how broad the distinction between them and all human or satanic counterfeits. God's miracles are wrought in orderly course, as a part of the development of His kingdom. They belong emphatically to each changing period in the history of that kingdom, when new disclosures of the mysteries of Grace required additional attestations from on high. And the nature of these miracles is in beautiful accordance with the revealed character of God as the Father of His people and the Curer of all disorders.

The counterfeits, on the contrary, occur without method, and with no other apparent purpose than to practice upon credulity and fear, to keep the people in quiet submission to their temporal or spiritual rulers. And, again, in their character most of these counterfeits are either ferocious manifestations of enmity to mankind, designed to inspire terror, or they are trifling, meaningless, silly mummeries, a very mockery of man as well as an insult to the Deity. This whole description applies as truly to Popish as to Heathen miracles. Winking or weeping Madonnas, flying chapels, and liquefying blood, are no better, no more like to God's working in the glorious economy of His kingdom than the wildest and silliest legends of heathendom, or than the table turnings and monkey tricks of modern necromancy.

Allowing, therefore, to the argument of Hume and his imitators all that it claims, a miracle, in the orderly development of the kingdom of heaven, when the occasion for it occurs, is just as much to be expected as any physical phenomena, and can be as certainly authenticated by sufficient testimony.

A miracle, however authenticated, simply by itself, isolated from all these Divine connections, is no witness for God. It may be the product of human or satanic fraud, or the creature of mere delusion. But when it appeals to us as an integral part of God's established order, in that kingdom which He set up in the world and has continually maintained from the beginning; when it is one of a regular series of Divine workings in that kingdom, and for the promotion of its ordained purpose; when thus supported by a consistent order of antecedents and consequents, it is just as capable of complete authentication as any physical fact or event of human history. It then becomes the unmistakable witness of God, accrediting the messenger He sends or the truth He would make known. We see, therefore, how fatal in every aspect has been the error of that modern popular phase of Christianity which ignores the Church of God as an integral and essential part of revealed religion.

The Incarnation, God becoming man, "for us and for our salvation," is the great miracle and the central fact of this revealed religion. To this all history points. Around it all human interests and events revolve. The religious rites of all time and of all nations derive from this fact their meaning and significance. They are either the ordinances of God to show forth this fact and its appointed consequents, or imitations, travesties, and corruptions of those ordinances, and of the truths which they signify.

It may reasonably be asked, "As the Christian world is now divided, however wrongfully, into discordant sects, how are we to know that kingdom of God which Christ reorganized in its latest form, and to which He gave such power and authority?"

The preceding discussion helps to answer this very pertinent inquiry. The Christian body which can show its historical continuity with the Apostolic Church; which has never put asunder the things that God had joined together, retaining inviolate and unbroken His whole institution, the same organization, the same ministry; which teaches, and requires to be believed for salvation, the ONE FAITH—no more, no less—taught and required by that Church; and which continues to administer the same Sacraments instituted and administered then, is not only beyond peradventure an integral part, but is plainly a sound and healthy part of that Divine kingdom. For the detailed solution of this question I must refer again to the admirable works formerly mentioned.

Another essential purpose of God's earthly kingdom,

besides being a witness to the truth, is to be the refuge and the home of His redeemed children. It is her duty to teach them what to believe and what to do in order to be saved; to take them into her bosom and seal them for heaven by Christ's own Sacraments; to nurture them by instruction in God's holy Word and in His holy worship, and so to train them in His holy fear and love that they shall be meet for an entrance into His EVERLASTING KINGDOM.

We proceed to the consideration of this great and all-con-cerning purpose of the Church.

CHAPTER III.

TERMS OF ADMISSION TO THE WAY OF SALVATION.

WHEN we go to the Word of God for the answer to the question, "What must we do to be saved?" we find some very brief, precise, and emphatic answers. In the great commission which our Savior gave to His Apostles just before his ascension, he said: "He that believeth and is baptized shall be saved." (St. Mark xvi, 16.) The same august authority had before declared, "Except a man be born again he can not see the kingdom of God." "Except a man be born of water and of the Spirit, he can not enter into the kingdom of God." "God so loved the world, that he gave His only begotten Son, that whosoever believeth in Him should not perish, but have everlasting life." (St. John iii, 3, 5, 16.) In the first sermon preached by the assembled Apostles after the ascension of our Lord, this very question was answered by the injunction, "Repent, and be baptized every one of you in the name of Jesus Christ for the remission of sins." (Acts ii, 38.) In the next recorded discourse the Apostles state the way of salvation in these terms: "Repent ye, therefore, and be converted, that your sins may be blotted out." (Acts iii, 19.)

It is unnecessary to accumulate here the numerous passages of Scripture in which salvation is ascribed to faith alone, or to repentance alone. The prominence thus given to these two graces as representative of the whole plan of

6

salvation, is due to their fundamental, continuing, and pervading agency in the economy of salvation. Christian religion is the revelation of a system of Divinely instituted *means of grace*, whereby a guilty sinner is to receive the pardon of his sins, and supernatural power to change his corrupt nature into the likeness of the Son of God. In this entire scheme of redemption, man is treated according to his nature, as an intelligent and free agent. He therefore must be informed of the way of his salvation, acquiesce in it, and actively co-operate with his Maker and Redeemer in its accomplishment. To this end he must believe the facts and doctrines communicated by the revelation, and must trust in the will and power of Christ his Savior to effect the purpose of the revelation—the salvation of his soul. This belief and trust in Christ, when sincere and active, is the saving faith of the Gospel. Faith, therefore, is fundamental and indispensable. It lies at the foundation of Christianity, and is the first beginning, and the continuing impulse, of every part and step of the way of salvation. In one important particular, too, faith is truly and emphatically *alone* in the work of salvation. For faith alone can bring the sinner to Christ, the Author of salvation. Faith alone can bring the child of corruption to the fountain of cleanliness, and purity, and health—the heir of death to the Source and Giver of Life. Faith has, therefore, been rightly termed the hand put forth to take the cup of salvation.

Repentance, too, is an indispensable and continuing condition in the whole work of salvation. For this is an agency which the Holy Spirit uses and sanctifies for the production of the very object and meaning of salvation, the change of a foul and sinful into a pure and holy being. Repentance, thus endued with healthful energy by the power of the Holy Ghost, brings us to loathe and abhor our own corruption and our wickedness, and to seek earnestly and diligently for cleansing grace, and for pardoning grace, from the Infinite Fountain of all grace, God in Christ, reconciling the world unto himself.

I have before said that many passages of Scripture might be cited in which faith alone is mentioned as the means of salvation. Others again speak only of repentance as the condition. But in the first class is repentance set aside? And in the second is faith excluded? Not at all. The Gospel, although composed of so many fragmentary portions, is a connected whole, and every verse is constructed with a distinct reference to the analogy or "proportion of faith."

Every part of the Bible recognizes the Bible and Christianity as a whole. When repentance is declared to be the condition of salvation, faith is presupposed; and when faith is so distinguished, it is because the faith spoken of includes repentance. The word faith is used in several senses in the Bible. In its lowest meaning it is mere intellectual belief of a truth. In its highest sense, as saving faith, it always includes repentance, conversion, trust in Christ as a Savior, and the actual going to Christ for salvation.

Repentance is also used in a higher and lower sense. In the latter, in its own simple meaning, repentance is the looking back upon a thing that has been done, and is therefore past recall, with sorrow, pain, and grief. In the Gospel use of the term there is added to this a full determination to forsake and avoid the evil thing that has produced this sorrow, pain, and grief. The actual accomplishment of the resolve included in repentance—the actual forsaking of evil and turning to good—is Conversion. When Repentance is spoken of as the sole condition of salvation, it becomes, like faith when similarly used, a complex term, standing for all the things necessarily connected with it in the Gospel plan of salvation.

The frequent and conspicuous employment of these two words in the Gospel, and their connection with two other expressions—"Baptism" and "The Kingdom of God"—make certain these three great features of the way of salvation: 1. That a conviction of sin, and an anxious desire to escape from its power and its condemnation, are indispensable requisites in the condition of him who would find the salvation of the Gospel.   2. That a deep sense of helplessness, of inability to obey the commandments and to keep the law of life, and a reaching upward to lay hold upon one that is mighty, to find a Redeemer, and to trust in him, is another essential requisite in the condition of the seeker after salvation. 3. That God does not intend that these spiritual exercises of the soul should expend themselves in indeterminate thoughts and feelings, which lead to no result, and are presently exchanged for other thoughts and feelings; but that, as man is composed of soul and body, so the plan of salvation, in correspondence with the nature of its subjects, has an external body in intimate connection with its spiritual truths.   Therefore, the kingdom of God is set up in the world, in visible opposition to the kingdom of evil.   This visible kingdom of God furnishes to those who think that they repent and believe, the opportunity of actualizing their spiritual states of consciousness.   By reducing these mental states to external acts, we are enabled at once to prove and to perfect them.

No man can be sure of the quality and value of any mere mental state, until he has the opportunity of translating it into action.   Every one thinks that he is exceedingly charitable, until the ability and occasion for the exercise of that feeling is presented, and then it is often found to have been but an unreal fancy.   No man ever believed that he would be a thief or a murderer, until the opportunity or the provo-

cation came.   Good and bad thoughts and emotions are
inchoate and imperfect until thus realized in action.

God has adapted revealed religion to the truth of our
nature.   The existence of His kingdom, with its Sacraments
and ordinances, enables every man to test the quality and
the value of his religious thoughts and affections.   If he
indeed abhors sin, and would forsake it, he may prove, while
he perfects, his repentance, by renouncing the powers of
darkness, and fleeing for refuge into the kingdom of light.
Baptism is appointed to be the exercise and realization both
of repentance and faith.   It is the actual renunciation of the
evil powers, thus consummating repentance..   It is the actual
entrance into the kingdom of grace and mercy established in
Jesus Christ, thus actualizing faith in the power of Christ to
save sinners.

The Sacraments of Christ's religion are no works of ours.
By no possibility can any merit be attributed to us from their
performance.   Their very meaning is an utter denial of all
merit or worth in us, and an entire reliance upon the mercy
of God in Christ the Savior.   Upon God's part they are
acts of grace.   Upon man's part they are acts of faith in
the necessity and power of that grace.   Sacraments are the
appointed channels of supernatural grace to us, and the instituted expression of our faith in God and in Christ.   By
them faith comes to Christ for salvation.   By them faith puts
forth her hand and lays hold on Christ.   Faith thus realizes
itself, and places him who has it within the covenant of grace
and mercy in Christ Jesus, and secures to him the adoption
of a child into the family of God.   When the heir of salvation is thus translated, by grace and by faith, from the
kingdom of darkness into the kingdom of light, the work of
salvation is but just fairly begun.   Then comes the life-long
discipline of Providence and of Grace, chastening, training,

strengthening, and perfecting the child of God by innumerable ministrations.

One great difficulty in the way of the popular reception
and appreciation of *the whole body of Christian truth*, is a too
general oblivion of the fact that the Church of Christ is an
integral and essential part of Christ's religion.

If Christian religion is simply the revelation of certain
abstract propositions, to be used and applied by men according
to their varying notions of fitness and expediency; if the
clothing and body of that religion, the Church, the Sacraments, and the Ministry, are mere human devices for the more
effective application of those abstract truths, then the whole
teaching of the Church for 1800 years has been one stupendous system of fraud and falsehood; then it is right for
every man, according to his own notions of fitness and expediency, to discard, retain, or modify any part of this human
device. Upon that supposition the external part of Christian
religion is just as much subject to human control as the rules
and regulations of a temperance society, and possesses just
the same kind of virtue and efficacy. To talk, then, about
any particular class of men being ambassadors for Christ
would be an absurdity; for, upon this hypothesis, either
there are no ambassadors for Christ, or all men are equally
so. Upon the same hypothesis, to require men to be baptized, or to receive the sacrament of the Lord's Supper,
would be an imposition upon human credulity, and an in-
fringement of individual freedom.

But, if the hypothesis from which these consequences necessarily flow be untrue, *if the Church of Christ is a part of the
religion of Christ*, if God himself has provided a Body for the
Spiritual truth which He revealed, thus adapting to man's compound nature the religion which He gave to man, then this appointment should be reverently received and faithfully obeyed.

If there is a ministry in Christ's Church of Divine appointment, if the Sacraments exist by Divine institution, if the Spiritual truth and the outward form of Christianity have been communicated to us as ONE REVELATION, then, surely, there is no human power adequate to the change or modification of the Truth, as *thus* revealed; there can be no right or prerogative, on the part of any of the subjects of this wondrous grace of God, to separate the things which he has joined together, and select one portion of the truth for their obedience, while they discard or modify the rest. If the same gracious Lord who required Faith, required, also, in the very same utterance, Baptism, as the condition of salvation to all to whom the Gospel is proposed—"He that believeth and is baptized shall be saved"—who shall dare to assume the place of the Almighty, and disjoin these conditions, and propose to man new terms of acceptance with God? If the life-giving Word which assures us of the availability of repentance, gives to us that assurance in the formula—"Repent and be baptized, every one of you, for the remission of sins," shall we harshly condemn the Church of Christ for her reverent submission to the very terms of salvation prescribed by the Author of salvation?

The case of the Episcopal Church is this: She professes to hold, and tries to maintain the Christian religion in its integrity—just as it was revealed, without change, addition, or diminution—as it was held and maintained for many ages after Christ. That Church regards Christianity as a Revelation made once for all, perfect and entire—the mind of God in regard to man. Man could not discover this truth, therefore it was *revealed*. Man can not improve it, therefore it was revealed in its *perfectness*.

CHAPTER IV.

COMMENCEMENT OF THE CHRISTIAN LIFE.

HAVING thus, in the most general terms, pointed out the way of salvation, we are prepared now to consider this great
§1. THREE GOS-   subject in a more detailed and systematic
PELS.   manner. If I were presenting these all-concerning truths for the first time to my readers, it would be very idle and improper to disturb their minds, and divide their attention, by the mention of diverse and conflicting views in regard to the way of life. But the existence of these variant and dissimilar views among Christians is a matter of unhappy notoriety. And many of the most formidable objections to the practical reception of Christianity, by vast multitudes, come from the confused perception of truth, occasioned by these jarring delineations. It will be best, therefore, to meet the real difficulties of the case, the difficulties which are actually in the minds of men, by a distinct statement and recognition of these variant systems. The truth thus presented in juxtaposition, and in contrast with opposing errors, will be more clearly distinguished and more perfectly understood.

Each one of the erroneous systems referred to has a basis of truth. In no other way could they have originated, or continue to be currently received. The denial, by each of these contradictory systems, of the truth upon which the other is based, helps to give currency and vitality to both.

It will be found that the actual truths contained in them all are recognized and provided for, in that which I shall first assume, and then prove, to be the system of the Bible and of the Church.

There are literally now, with regard to the beginning of a Christian life, three Gospels currently preached in the world. That Jesus Christ is the way, the truth, and the life, is indeed earnestly declared by nearly all who call themselves Christians. But with regard to the commencement of the Divine Life in the soul of man, there are, we repeat, three Gospels, or systems which profess to be such.

One is the Gospel of our Lord and Savior Jesus Christ, who came into the world, not to condemn the world, but that the world through Him might be saved. That Gospel teaches,

1st. That the entire race of man is by *nature* fallen, degenerate, dead. That each human being is so "far gone from original righteousness, as *of his own nature to be inclined to evil,*" so that "the flesh *lusteth always contrary to the Spirit,*" and "*is not subject to the law of God.*"   Art. 9.

2nd. That the Second Person of the adorable Trinity assumed our nature that He might become the Second Adam, and give to that nature a new and better life, and that the incarnate Savior suffered death upon the cross for the redemption of all mankind, and made there a full, perfect, and sufficient sacrifice, oblation, and satisfaction for the sins of the whole world.

3rd. That from the right hand of the Eternal Majesty, where He ever liveth to make intercession for us, He hath given gifts unto men, even the inestimable gift of His Holy Spirit, to be the Teacher, Monitor, and Guide of the souls for which He died; and to dwell in the hearts of men, the principle of a new and Divine Life, the bond of reunion between God and man.

7

4th. That this redemption and this consequent gift are as extensive and as universal as the previous condemnation which has come into the world by sin. Accordingly, we are assured that the Sacrifice of Christ and the benefits of that Sacrifice were made over to mankind—to the entire race of man—from the foundation of the world.

5th. The Divine Life thus given to every man is a germ, a seed, which does not necessarily, and by the force of the mere gift, destroy and take the place of the carnal nature, but co-exists with that carnal nature, and enters into conflict with all that is evil and depraved in the natural life; and, if properly entertained and nurtured, will ultimately overcome, mortify, and kill all the evil of corrupt nature, and substitute for that evil purity, goodness, and every Divine affection.

6th. The Church of Christ, with all its appliances of faith and holiness, has been appointed as the last, the fullest, and the most perfect of the means and instrumentalities for the nurture and development of the Divine Life, from its embryo existence as a power in the soul of man, through all the successive stages of growth, to the maturity of perfect manhood in Jesus Christ; and to be introduced into that Church by Baptism is the second birth—the birth of water and of the Spirit.

We design presently to offer the proofs of each of these propositions.

One of the other Gospels to which we have referred, teaches,

1st. That the Gift of God, the Holy Spirit, the Divine Life, is imparted only to the baptized. That it begins in Baptism, and is inseparably connected with that Sacrament.

2nd. That the Divine Life, by the mere gift thereof, effectually and at once destroys the carnal life—the whole evil of corrupt nature—remitting the subject of this gift to the state of Adam before the fall, making him pure, immaculate, without sin.

3rd. The same system teaches that this pure and spotless being may, nevertheless, fall, as Adam fell, by sin; in which case the Divine Life, before imparted, is in its turn utterly extinguished and destroyed; and the carnal life, by an anticipated resurrection, reappears in full strength and development, and resumes its previous sway and mastery over the soul.

4th. For this new and terrible incident of humanity, unknown to the true Gospel, and unprovided for there, the new Gospel has invented a Supplementary Sacrament of far more practical value and efficacy than the Sacrament of Baptism which our blessed Lord provided. For, according to the system we are now describing, the supplemental Sacrament of Penance reconveys the Divine Life to the soul in full maturity and strength, just as often as it may be forfeited and lost by sin.

There is yet "another Gospel," very similar in some of its features to the last mentioned, but differing from it in other particulars. It agrees with it in denying peremptorily that the Gift of God, the Holy Spirit, the Divine Life, is bestowed impartially upon all mankind. But instead of restricting this gift to the baptized, and looking upon Baptism as the instrument by which it is conferred, this other Gospel teaches,

1st. That the gift of the Eternal Spirit is bestowed only upon those whom it terms converted persons, and who have passed through certain experiences, and have been moved by a peculiar class of feelings designated as the New Birth.

So far the maintainers of this Gospel, which constitutes the popular theology of the day, go together in entire harmony of statement. But at this point two parties are presented to our view, who go as far asunder as possible. The smaller of these teaches,

2nd. That the converted persons, upon whom the Holy Spirit is bestowed, have been previously designated by an eternal decree; and that the recipients of this Divine Life can never lose it, or fail to secure the everlasting reward of the righteous.

The larger class of the adherents of the popular theology maintain, instead of the last proposition,

3rd. That men may fall from grace. That the Divine Life may be often lost and recovered; and that the way to recover it is to repeat the process by which it was first obtained—that is, by certain well known appliances, to stimulate the feelings, and to seek for the experiences which were at first regarded as the beginning and the assurance of the Divine Life.

This modification of the popular theology agrees, it will be perceived, with the Romish system previously described, in the principle that the Divine Life can be thus repeatedly and entirely lost, and as often and as suddenly regained. But it differs again from that system in this, that instead of going to the Priest to receive the Divine Life anew from him, *through the instrumentality of a newly invented Sacrament*, the devotee of the last system *waits upon the exercises of a protracted meeting*, until the desired point of excitement, that may be regarded as a Divine impulse, is reached.

It is not our purpose now to encounter or to expose either of these false systems—the human substitutes for the counsels of Heavenly Wisdom. The simple description of them in the plain didactic method which we have adopted, will enable every student of the Bible to perceive how far they deviate from that full and perfect standard of truth. And the positive proof which we intend to offer of the several propositions of the true Gospel will be the best refutation of these opposing dogmas. But as both these human systems derive a good deal of popular favor and apparent plausibility from a misapprehension of certain expressions in the Epistles of St. John, we will begin our examination by an attempt to ascertain the true meaning of those expressions.

As our fifth proposition provides for a perpetual growth of the Divine Life, from the first beginnings to the highest attainments of holiness, so it allows for the continued existence of the evil of corrupt nature, not yet subdued, in those who have received the Holy Spirit; and perhaps never to be subdued, on account of the faithlessness of the subject of this Divine grace. For as the evil nature and the Divine nature have entered into antagonism in the same person, the evil may be so entertained as to be always predominant, and ultimately to drive away the Spirit of life and holiness.

To this existence and possible triumph of a sinful disposition, in the subject of Divine grace, the expressions of St. John, before referred to, are objected. They are the following: "Whosoever is born of God doth not commit sin; for his seed remaineth in him; and he can not sin, because he is born of God." "For whatsoever is born of God overcometh the world." "We know that whosoever is born of God sinneth not; but he that is begotten of God keepeth himself, and that wicked one toucheth him not." (1st St. John iii, 9; v, 4–18.)

These are certainly very strong and emphatic expressions. But if taken literally, and apart from the purpose of the Apostle, they will prove too much for any system of theology. For thus taken, these expressions would prove that whosoever is born of God can *never, under any contingency,* commit sin. But this is directly opposed to universal experience, to the whole tenor of Scripture, to many positive declarations of the same Apostle, and to every theory of religion. The same system of interpretation would make this very Epistle a collection of contradictions. The Apostle positively declares that "whosoever shall confess that Jesus is the Son of God, God dwelleth in him, and he in God." (iv, 15.) Again, "Whosoever believeth that Jesus is the Christ, is born of God." (v. 1.)

The way to understand these and like expressions in the Epistle, is to look at its purpose. That purpose was principally to furnish to Christians a number of *practical and experimental tests of their continuance in the faith*, and of their perseverance in the way of holiness. Each one of these aphorisms is evidently designed for the use of the elect children of God, as a personal test for determining whether *they are practically living* to the new and Divine nature, or to the old and carnal nature. Interpreted by this obvious purpose of the Apostle, the whole Epistle coincides with the analogy of faith in assuming the fact of the co-existence of the good and evil nature in every man; and of the perpetual conflict between them until one or the other is subdued. Nothing in this Epistle, therefore, is at all repugnant to that which we have assumed to be the Church's teaching and the Gospel plan of salvation. The Apostle simply takes several distinct and separate results of the Divine Life on the one hand, and of the Carnal Life on the other, and applies each in turn to the determination of the question, whether the common subject of both is practically and habitually living to the one or to the other. "Whosoever is born of God," is therefore equivalent, for this purpose of the Apostle, to the formula— Whosoever is truly and faithfully living under the power and influence of the new and Divine Life. Such a one acknowledges "that Jesus is the Christ." He does not willingly and habitually commit sin, but strives against the sinful disposition. By prayer, watchfulness, the practice of repeutance, and other means of grace, he is gradually subduing the carnal nature, the tendency to sin; and the Divine Life is acquiring the entire mastery of his soul and body.

"The children of the Devil," on the other hand, in the sense of the Apostle, are those who submit themselves to the power of carnal nature—who, having received the Spirit of God, the new and Divine Life, resist that Spirit, live in continual opposition to His influence and teaching, and are thus gradually destroying the Divine Life in their souls.

Holy Leighton thus expresses the whole truth:

"The righteous be they that are students of obedience and holiness, that desire to walk as in the sight of God, and to walk with God as Enoch did; that are glad when they can any way serve Him, and grieved when they offend Him; that feel and bewail their unrighteousness, and are earnestly breathing and advancing forward; have a sincere and unfeigned love to all the commandments of God, and diligently endeavor to observe them. . . On the other side, evil doers are they that commit sin *with greediness;* that walk in it, make it their way, that live in sin as their element, *taking pleasure in unrighteousness,* as the Apostle speaks; their great faculty and their great delight lies in sin; they are skillful and cheerful evil doers. . . . . In a word, this opposition lieth mainly in the bent of the affection, or in the way it is set. The godly man hates the evil he (possibly by temptation) hath been drawn to do, and loves the good he is frustrate of, and having intended, hath not attained to do. The sinner that hath his denomination from sin as his course hates the good that sometimes he is forced to do, and loves that sin which many times he does not, either wanting occasion and means, and so he can not do it, or, through check of an enlightened conscience, possibly dares not do: the strength of his affection is carried to sin, as in the weakest godly man there is that predominant sincerity and desire of holy walking, according to which he is called a *righteous person*." (Com. on 1 Peter, iii, 12.)

Having disposed of this source of objection, we will look now at some of the proofs of those propositions in regard to the way of life, which we have affirmed to be the teaching of the Church of Christ.

§2. DEATH OF ALL MANKIND IN ADAM. The first proposition of the true Gospel—the foundation upon which the whole super-structure of a Christian life is built—declares that the entire race of man is by nature fallen, degenerate, dead. That each human being is so "far gone from original righteousness, as of his own nature to be inclined to evil;" so that "the flesh lusteth *always* contrary to the Spirit," and "is not subject to the law of God." (Art. 9.)

This proposition ought to be sufficiently proved for Churchmen by the above express declaration of the article to that effect. The language and spirit of all our formularies assumes this truth as a postulate: and the testimony of reason, observation, and Scripture, all concur in the same conclusion.

From the Scripture we learn that the original penalty of transgression affixed to the one positive enactment of the Paradisiac state was death—a dissolution of the original union between God and man. "In the day that thou eatest thereof thou shalt surely die." Accordingly, in that very day on which he sinned, the fallen rebel was driven forth from the place where that communion had subsisted; and cherubims and a flaming sword were stationed, "which turned every way to keep the way of the tree of life." The mortality of the body was involved in this death, as one of its ulterior consequences; but so far from constituting the principal burden of the sentence, it did not occur for several hundred years after the fall; and under the economy of grace it has been made a necessary means of relief from other consequences of the same judgment, and the passage from a world of tribulation to a heaven of glory.

It will be unnecessary to recapitulate the various familiar passages of Scripture which show the completeness and universality of the natural corruption of man. "Can a clean thing come out of an unclean?" is an interrogatory of Scripture which reason and observation answer unhesitatingly in the negative. As Adam essentially was, so his posterity must continue to be, unless the Almighty, by a further interposition, infuse a new element of life and character into His degenerate creature. To inform us of such an interposition on the part of our Heavenly Father, and of the manner of it, is the purpose of the blessed Gospel. "For as in Adam all die, even so in Christ shall all be made alive." And what constitutes this death in Adam and this life in Christ the Apostle plainly tells us. "For they that are after the flesh do mind the things of the flesh; but they that are after the Spirit the things of the Spirit. For to be carnally minded *is death;* but to be spiritually minded *is life* and peace. Because the *carnal mind* is *enmity* against God; for it is not subject to the law of God, neither indeed can be. So then they that are in the flesh can not please God." (Rom. viii, 5–8.) "If ye live after the flesh ye shall die; but if ye through the Spirit do mortify the deeds of the body, ye shall live." (Rom. viii, 13.)

Here it is abundantly affirmed that the natural man is really dead unto God, and to the things of God; that he is at enmity with God, and therefore hates and opposes Him and His will. That he neither *is* nor *can* be subject to the law of God; and therefore he is incapable of good in thought, word, and deed. For as the law of God commandeth the things which are good, in thought, word, and deed, he who *can not obey that law* must be under an inevitable incapacity to do, think, or speak, any thing that is good.

The same Apostle, in another place, states, in yet more startling terms, the utter degeneracy and deadness of mere human nature in regard to all that is good and pure. For he affirms that it is incapable of receiving or of knowing the things that are freely given to us of God—that is, all spiritual truth. "The natural man receiveth not the things of the Spirit of God: for they are foolishness unto him: neither *can he know them, because they are spiritually discerned.*" And he had previously illustrated this proposition by an argument derived from the nature of things. "For what man," he says, "knoweth the things of a man, save the spirit of man that is in him? Even so the things of God knoweth no man, but the Spirit of God." "Now we have received the Spirit of God, *that we might know* the things that are freely given to us of God." (1 Cor. ii, 12.) Again: "For we know that the law is spiritual; but I am carnal, sold under sin." "For I know that in me (that is, in my flesh) dwelleth no good thing." (Rom. vii, 14, 18.)

We have dwelt the longer upon the Scriptural testimony to this proposition, because a clear and full understanding of it is essential to a correct appreciation of all the rest of the Gospel system.

The formularies of the Church are equally full in disclaiming for the natural man all capacity for good, and in ascribing all the good of which we are conscious in ourselves to the immediate gift of God by His Holy Spirit. The Collect for peace in the evening service declares that "all holy desires, all good counsels, and all just works do proceed from God;" and can not therefore be the dictate of the natural heart, which is at enmity with God. The address in the beginning of the Baptismal Office says: "For as much as all men are conceived and born in sin, (and that which is born of the flesh is flesh,) and they who are in the flesh *can not please* God, but live in sin." In the Collects we find the following express, and many more implied, recognitions of the same truth. "Almighty God, who seest that we have no power of ourselves to help ourselves," (2nd S. in Lent.) "As by thy special grace preventing us, thou dost put into our minds good desires; so by thy continual help we may bring the same to good effect," (Easter.) "Who alone canst order the unruly wills and affections of sinful men," (4th af. Easter.) "From whom all good things do come, grant that by thy holy inspiration we may think those things that are good, and by thy merciful guiding may perform the same," (5th af. Easter.) "Because through the weakness of our mortal nature, we can do no good thing without thee," (1st af. Trinity.) "Grant to us the spirit to think and to do always such things as are right; that we who can not do any thing that is good without thee," (9th af. Trinity.) "Of whose only gift it cometh that thy faithful people do unto thee true and laudable service," (13th af. Trinity.) "Forasmuch as without thee we are not able to please thee," (19th af. Trinity.) "Who maketh us both to will and to do those things which are good and acceptable unto thy Divine Majesty," (Confirmation Office.) "The condition of man after the fall of Adam is such that he can not turn and prepare himself by his own natural strength and good works to faith and calling upon God: wherefore we have no power to do good works pleasant and acceptable to God, without the grace of God by Christ preventing us, that we may have a good will, and working with us when we have that good will." (Art. 10.)

To crown the whole of this testimony, the Christian Creed teaches us to believe in the Holy Ghost as the Author and Giver of Life. This, like all the articles of the Creed, is brief, but very full and expressive. If without the inspiration of the Holy Ghost there can be no true life, then the

mere carnal nature, *devoid of that Spirit,* must be altogether
dead unto God and the things of God : and therefore insensible to goodness, incapable of knowing God, of loving, fear-
ing, or obeying Him.

With this ample testimony of the Scriptures and the Church
reason concurs. For how can that being who is cut off from
all communion with God, the Source and Fountain of good,
and is at enmity with Him, be capable of doing good, or of
delighting in goodness? If man's nature is essentially corrupt, and inclined to evil, as universal observation attests, how,
but by the direct inspiration of the Almighty, can that nature
be turned to good, or be made capable of appreciating and
enjoying that which is good?

The doctrine thus conclusively proved by so many weighty
testimonies, is that which the Pelagian heresy vainly attempted
to overturn.   Very like to this Pelagian heresy, and as directly
opposed to this doctrine, and to the testimonies by which
it is established, is the notion that there were some relics of
the heavenly image left in Adam, and consequently in his
posterity, apart from Christ and independently of redemption,
by which men can perform some good things, and from which
are derived that amiability and nobleness of character by
which many persons are distinguished. On the contrary, it
has been fully proved that the natural condition of man is a
death, an utter insensibility to all goodness. There were
powers and faculties left in man by the fall; but these, being
cut off from the Fountain of goodness, were only and wholly
inclined to evil.   If, therefore, any good is found in man, its
source must be elsewhere than in his own nature.

The Gospel tells us whence that goodness proceeds which we
find every-where to co-exist with the evil in the heart of man.
And it further tells us how, and upon what inducement, that
new capacity for goodness came.

It is not intended by the terms of this first proposition to determine the mode of this vitiation. What is called by some the Catholic, in contradistinction to the Calvinistic theory, puts the effect of the fall in these terms.

"Man's Free-will is thereby weakened, and a bias toward evil established within him, and this to such a degree, that without Divine aid he can not attain to good."

This is the fearful consequence of that change of relations, that severance from God, which the Scriptures so emphatically term death. An established bias toward evil, to such a degree that man can not attain to good, is vitiation enough to satisfy the terms of this proposition, and the language of the Scriptures and of the Church which it embodies.

And here it is well to remember that the words Life and Death are but terms of relation. Natural life is to us the union of soul and body; natural death, the severance of that connection. Spiritual life is the union between God and man; spiritual death, the severance of that union. This spiritual death was the penalty threatened and visited upon the first natural head of the human race. The re-establishment of that union as a pure gift of God, so as to strengthen the Free-will and counteract the bias to evil, was the work of the Second Adam, "from the foundation of the world."

Bishop Seabury has admirably stated this meaning of Life and Death as terms of relation: "Death does not mean the end of our existence, but the end of a certain mode of existing. By death, in the ordinary sense of the word, we do not mean a ceasing to exist, but the ceasing of our present life. . . . . . Adam, therefore, really and truly died the very day he transgressed. He killed that nature and life which he received from God, and acquired a new nature and life, in which all his posterity have been born. He put an end to that perfect and holy state in which God created him; and he obtained, in the room of it, a state of error, and vice, and sin. Consider, now, what is necessary to be done for his redemption. That life which he acquired by his fall must be made to cease, and that life which he lost by his fall must be revived in him. . . . And whatever was necessary to be done for Adam in this case, was also necessary to be done for his whole posterity. Here the goodness of God prevented even his wishes. No sooner had man sinned than God *was in* Christ, *reconciling the world*—human nature—*unto Himself."* (Published in Amer. Ch. Monthly for May, 1858.)

§3. THE UNIVER-   2. The second proposition affirms the uni-
SALITY OF RE-   versality of redemption. "If any man sin, we
DEMPTION.   have an advocate with the Father, Jesus Christ
the righteous; and he is the propitiation for our sins; and not for ours only, but also for the sins of the whole world." (1 St. John ii, 1, 2.)

"In Him was life, and the life was the light of men." "That was the true light which lighteth every man that cometh into the world." "Behold the Lamb of God that taketh away the sins of the world." (St. John i, 4. 9, 29.)

"For as in Adam all die, even so in Christ shall all be made alive." "The first man Adam was made a living soul; the last Adam was made a quickening Spirit. Howbeit that was not first which is spiritual, but that which is natural, and afterward that which is spiritual. The first man is of the earth, earthy; the second man is the Lord from heaven." (1 Epis. to Cor. xv, 22, 45, 46, 47.)

"For the love of Christ constraineth us; because we thus judge, that if one died for all, then were all dead; and that he died for all, that they which live should not henceforth live unto themselves, but unto him which died for them, and rose again."

"God was in Christ, reconciling the world unto himself." (2 Cor. v, 14, 15, 19.) The first passage from 2 Corinthians illustrates a beautiful remark of Archbishop Sumner, that St. Paul never mentions condemnation, except as the subordinate correlative of redemption, and to show the quality and extent of redeeming love.

"As by the offense of one, judgment came upon all men to condemnation; even so by the righteousness of one, the FREE GIFT *came upon all men* unto justification of life." "That as sin hath reigned unto death, even so might grace reign through righteousness unto eternal life by Jesus Christ our Lord." (Rom. v, 18, 21.)

24. THE HOLY GHOST THE SOURCE OF LIFE. 3. From the right hand of the Eternal Majesty, where he ever liveth to make intercession for us, Christ hath sent His Holy Spirit to be the Teacher, Monitor, and Guide of the souls for which He died, and to dwell in the hearts of men, the principle of a new and Divine Life—the bond of reunion between God and man.

In the Scriptures, and in all Christian theology, the Holy Ghost is declared to be, since the ascension of Christ into heaven, the ever-present Minister of salvation, the Representative of the Father and the Son. The power of the Holy Ghost unites us to Christ, makes Christ to be present with us, forms Christ within us, gives efficacy to all the ministrations of the Gospel.

"It is expedient for you that I go away; for if I go not away, the Comforter will not come unto you; but if I depart I will send him unto you." (St. John xvi, 7.) "I will pray the Father, and he shall give you another Comforter, that he may abide with you forever." (St. John xiv, 16.) "It is the Spirit that quickeneth." (St. John vi, 63.) "Joseph, thou son of David, fear not to take unto thee Mary thy wife; for that which is conceived in her is of the Holy Ghost." (St Matt. i, 20.)

"I believe in the Holy Ghost, the Lord and Giver of Life." (Nicene Creed.)

§5. SPIRITUAL LIFE IMPARTED TO ALL.   4. This redemption from death, and this consequent gift of life, are as extensive and as universal as the previous condemnation which had come into the world by sin. For as the blessed Savior came to make an atonement for the sins of mankind, so likewise He is declared to be "the True Light which lighteth every man that cometh into the world." (St. John i, 9.)

The Apostle, indeed, makes this proposition to be the more certain and inevitable by arguing that it must, *a fortiori*, be so. He says, "If by the offense of one many be dead, *much more* the grace of God, and the gift by grace, which is by one man, Jesus Christ, hath abounded unto many." "For if by one man's offense death reigned by one; *much more* they which receive abundance of grace, and of the gift of righteousness, shall reign in life by one, Jesus Christ. Therefore, as by the offense of one judgment came upon all men to condemnation, even so by the righteousness of one the free gift came upon all men unto justification of life." "Where sin abounded, grace did much more abound; that as sin hath reigned unto death, *even so might grace reign* through righteousness unto eternal life, by Jesus Christ our Lord." (Rom. v, 15–21.)

It is this universality of redemption, and of the capacity of salvation, which truly entitles the revelation of Jesus Christ to be called the Gospel, or "glad tidings of great joy to all people." This was the description which the Angels gave of that which they came to announce, when at the birth of the Son of God they sang, "Peace on earth, good will to men."

But if the redemption which is in Christ Jesus was provided only for a few, and if the consequent salvation be possible only to that select number, then the message which the Angels brought would be bad news of great sorrow to all the rest of mankind: and that express declaration of the blessed Savior himself, that "God sent not His Son into the world to condemn the world, but that the world through Him might be saved," would be plainly and flatly contradicted. Our Savior commanded His Apostles to go into all the world and preach the Gospel to every creature; calling all men to repentance and remission of sins, and teaching every man to believe that Christ died for him. But if salvation be not possible to all men, then the ministers and ambassadors of Christ would stand in the name of the God of Truth with a falsehood on their tongues, with which to mock and delude the unhappy sons of perdition.

To this let us only add these Scriptures, "That He by the grace of God might taste death for every man." (Heb. ii, 9.) "I exhort, therefore, that first of all, supplications, prayers, intercessions, and giving of thanks, be made for all men; for this is good and acceptable in the sight of God our Savior, who will have all men to be saved and to come unto the knowledge of the truth." (1 Tim. ii, 1, 3, 4, 5.)

But if Christ died for all, how is the benefit of his death applied to all? We have before proved that man, of his own nature, is incapable of thinking, doing, or desiring any good thing; that he is dead to goodness and to God. Redemption from death, therefore, must be something more than the satisfaction made upon the Cross for the sins of the world. It must include the gift of life—the capacity to know, fear, obey, and love God. This life, this capacity for holiness, is a necessary part of redemption, and is therefore the gift of God to all who are redeemed, to every one for whom Christ died.

8

Unless this new life from God be a part of the redemption
that is in Christ Jesus, not only would the death and sacrifice
of Christ have been vain and idle, but it would be impossible
to bring men into judgment for their conduct in this life.
For trust or power, and responsibility, are commensurate and
inseparable.   Without the first there can be no such thing as
the second.   Responsibility for wrong necessarily presupposes
the capacity to do right.   There can be no moral evil where
the capacity to do good is denied.   This higher life, there-
fore--the power to apprehend, to love, and to do good—must
be superinduced upon human nature as a supernatural gift,
in order to make the judgment of men—the acquittal of the
righteous and the condemnation of the wicked—a possible
thing in the Divine economy.

How then is this new and Divine Life imparted?   The
answer to this question explains to us the reason for the revelation to man of the adorable mystery of the Holy Trinity.
As the Eternal Son became our Redeemer, Mediator, and
effectual Intercessor; so, to complete the work which He
began, to make effectual for our salvation His sacrifice, mediation, and intercession, the Holy Ghost was sent to dwell in
the hearts of men; to be the agent of reunion between God
and man; to be the source and beginning of that new life
from which comes the capacity of holiness, the power to know
and to love God, and to obey and love His commands.
Therefore the Christian Creed teaches us to believe, not only
in the Father Almighty, and in the Only Begotten Son, but
in the Holy Ghost, the Lord and Giver of Life.   Therefore
it was "*expedient* for us," that, when the sacrificial work of
the Son was finished, He should be received into the heavens,
and send down from thence, in newness and fullness of power
and manifestation, this Divine Source and Author of Life, to
abide with men, and to restore them to the lost image of God.

And, as in the counsels of the Divine economy, the Son was slain from the foundation of the world, that men might be pardoned and accepted for His sake, so was the gift of the Holy Ghost, the purchase of that Son's death and love, made over to mankind from the beginning, that in every man born into the world there might be a capacity for holiness and for heaven.

The Scriptural testimony to this great fact of the indwelling of the Spirit in the hearts of all men in all ages, is emphatic and conclusive. It is not probable that the wickedness of men has ever again reached the point which it had attained at the close of the Antediluvian period. And then, we are informed, that the Spirit had been unceasingly striving with men for their salvation; and that God was determined to cut off from the earth the hardened sinners with whom He would no longer permit that Spirit to strive and dwell.

That the same Spirit of light and life continued to dwell with men in the ages between the flood and the Advent of Messiah, is abundantly evident, not only from the necessity of the case, because essential to our probationary state, and from the fruits of the Spirit, which at all times were manifested by the sons and daughters of men, but likewise from numerous express notices of the fact in the Old Testament. "Thou gavest also thy good Spirit to instruct them," is the confession of all the people in Nehemiah ix, 20. "Take not thy Holy Spirit from me," "Stablish me with thy free Spirit," were the prayers dictated by that same Spirit for the use of every one of the people of God. See numerous testimonies to the same effect.

By the agency of this all-pervading Spirit alone can the declaration of the Apostle be true, "that Jesus Christ is the true light which lighteth every man that cometh into the world." St. Paul expressly affirms that "the manifestation of the Spirit is given to every man to profit withal." (1 Cor. xii, 7.)

"The grace of God that bringeth salvation hath appeared to *all men, teaching us,* that denying ungodliness," &c. (Titus ii, 11, 12.) "Of his fullness have all we received, and grace for grace." (St. John i, 16.) "This is the condemnation, that light has come into the world, and men loved darkness rather than light, because their deeds were evil. He that doeth truth cometh to the light that his deeds may be made manifest, that they are wrought in God." (St. John iii, 19, 21.) Here the principle is fully and plainly declared, that there is no condemnation except to those who turn from the light. And as the Apostle had previously announced that the True Light had enlightened every man that came into the world, so the condemnation is as universal as the love and choice of darkness. The parable of the talents conveys, in the most striking and forcible manner, the same great truth, that no more is required of any man than the use and improvement of that which has been given him.

In the Epistle to the Galatians, St. Paul thus describes the condition of every man that hath lived in the world: "The flesh lusteth against the Spirit, and the Spirit against the flesh: and these are contrary, the one to the other: so that ye can not do the things that ye would." He then enumerates the works of the flesh, some of which, in various degrees and proportions, have been exhibited in the life of every man. Afterward he tells us which are the fruits of the Spirit. And of these likewise it may be confidently affirmed, that some of them, as love, joy, peace, gentleness, goodness, meekness, &c., have been beautifully manifested in every human being that has lived. Every good and pure affection that moves the heart of man is the Divine testimony within him to the *New Life* which he has received; is the

earnest of his calling to be the child of God, and the inheritor of everlasting blessedness. If, as has been abundantly
proved, man can think, feel, and do no good thing without the
inspiration of God's Spirit, then every good thought, feeling,
and act, must of necessity manifest the presence and power
of that Spirit. And the condition of every man before God
is determined by the choice which each one may make to be
guided by the Spirit into all holy obedience, or to be led captive by the flesh in the way of sin and death.

The Scriptures not only in a few passages declare this truth,
but every-where assume it, by appealing to the capacity
which is in every human being to know, believe, and obey
the truth. "Grieve not the Spirit of God; quench not the
Spirit; harden not your hearts; resist not the Spirit;" is the
constant exhortation of the inspired Word. The same thing
is virtually and fully affirmed by every preacher of the Gospel in the world; for they exhort and beseech each man to
believe that Jesus Christ is his Savior; that He hath died
for him; and that He invites and calls this sinner to come
unto Him that he may be saved; and that if he perish it
will be his own fault for refusing to heed and obey this call.

This doctrine of the true Gospel, which we have thus
largely proved, alone worthily and sufficiently magnifies the
grace of God, "in that it wholly excludes the natural man
from having any place or portion in his own salvation, by any
acting, moving, or working of his own," but refers all to the
quickening and informing power of God's Spirit. And, "as
it makes the whole salvation of man solely and alone to depend upon God, so it makes his condemnation wholly and in
every respect to be of himself." No place is left by this doctrine for the intrusion into Christian theology of the Pelagian
and Socinian heresy, which exalts the light of nature, and
attributes so much power and influence in the guidance of

men to the natural conscience. We have seen that the light of nature in fallen man is nothing but gross darkness. That which has been falsely called such was the True Light, in whom is Life; "and the Life was the *light* of men; and The Light shineth in darkness; and the darkness comprehended it not."

The vice of Pelagianism, that which made this error to be a pernicious and deadly heresy, was its denial of one of the articles of the Creed, that the Holy Ghost is the Author and Giver of all spiritual life. By assuming for man, in his natural state, a capacity to hear, receive, and believe the Gospel, it discharged the Holy Spirit from His peculiar office and operation in the work of human salvation. The doctrine that the Holy Spirit is given to every man, is therefore the precise refutation of Pelagianism: because it takes the very same facts relied upon for the support of that error, and accounts for those facts by proving them to depend upon the gift of the Holy Ghost.

Neither is it the part of the natural conscience to be the *guide* or the *teacher* of men. The Spirit of Truth alone can exercise that prerogative. Natural conscience holds the office of a Judge, seated in the soul of man, and manifesting its presence and power only by producing a sense of complacence and pleasure when we do good; and by the application of a scorpion lash to the offender against a known law. But the conscience must itself be rightly instructed in order to know good from evil. This work of instruction the Holy Spirit performs for all men to a certain extent, using for that purpose various external agencies. One of these external agencies employed by the Holy Spirit is the traditional knowledge of right and wrong incorporated in the civil laws, and in the popular religions of all people.

But what is natural conscience? The blessed Savior

promising the Comforter, the Holy Spirit in the fullness of His power, said: "And when He is come He will reprove the world of sin, and of righteousness, and of judgment." (St. John xvi, 8.) There could not be a more accurate description of the known operation of conscience in our nature, in all ages and upon all persons, than is contained in these words. This would seem to show that conscience, that mysterious and transcendent power, seated in the human soul as a ruler and judge, is no integral part of our fallen nature, but is the witness and voice of God himself, dwelling in us by His Spirit, to govern and direct, yet in subordination to human will, all the faculties of nature. All of conscience that would seem to be left to mere nature by this description of the office of the Holy Spirit, is simple sensibility to the impressions and monitions of the Spirit.

The well known operation of conscience in redeemed humanity is to distinguish between vice and virtue, between sin and righteousness, and to testify of a coming judgment for these things. And this is precisely the work attributed to the Holy Ghost by our Lord. The subsequent words of the promise only indicate further a specific rule of the Spirit's action under the increased light of the Christian dispensation. He was specially to "convince the world of sin" under that brighter light, because men were so entranced by sin that they refused to recognize and believe in Jesus, the incarnate goodness, the highest manifestation of God. They were also now to be more effectually convinced "of righteousness," because the man Christ Jesus having gone away from them, the Spirit which He promised does actually impart to all who will be led by Him that same righteousness which Jesus manifested in His human life.

Again, under the new outpouring of the Spirit, the world is more powerfully convinced "of judgment," because the kingdoms of light and darkness are more strongly discriminated. The rulers and subjects of each are manifested in direct and irreconcilable antagonism. In the obscurer light of previous ages and of other systems, even the worshipers of God worshiped also the prince of this world, and all the powers of darkness, as gods. Now these powers are disclosed in their true character, judged, condemned, and execrated as devils.

This identification of conscience with the operations of the Holy Ghost in man, brings into beautiful apposition and accord some of the most startling phenomena of our nature, and some of the like startling declarations of God's holy Word.

We have all known and wondered at that strange phenomenon, a perverted conscience. We have seen, in society and in history, a conscience tampered with and its first pure whisperings disobeyed, turned to be the favorer and counselor of the most atrocious crimes. In exact accordance with this fact the eternal truth announces: "Thus saith the Lord God; Every man of the house of Israel that setteth up his idols in his heart, and putteth the stumbling-block of his iniquity before his face, and cometh to the prophet; I the Lord will answer him that cometh according to the multitude of his idols. . . . And if the prophet be deceived when he hath spoken a thing, I the Lord have deceived that prophet. . . . The punishment of the prophet shall be even as the punishment of him that seeketh *unto him;* that the house of Israel may go no more astray from me, neither be polluted any more with all their transgressions." (Ezek. xiv, 4, 9, 10, 11.)

A fearful instance of this method of dealing with men is prominently recorded in the Divine Word. Balaam received a clear and distinct command from God in regard to the subject of his inquiry. (Numb. xxii, *et seq.*) But he put the stumbling-block of his covetousness before his face, and went to inquire of the Lord again. And then God answered him according to his idols, and as plainly commanded him to do that which He had before forbidden, and which was directly opposed to His own will.

What is this transaction, and the corresponding principle of the Divine government announced to the prophet Ezekiel, but a translation into the plain language of revealed truth of those obscure and intricate mazes which we call the workings of conscience? It is in accordance with this teaching that the New Testament writers say so little about hearkening to the voice of conscience, and exhort so earnestly and continually to hearken to the Spirit, to be led by the Spirit, to grieve not the Spirit. For this language would seem to be simply the plain truth of those phenomena of our complex being, which, in all human disquisitions upon the conscience, are so obscure and difficult. And if this be a true account of conscience, then, of course, our fourth proposition is **proved**, yet again, by the conjoint testimony of Scripture and of **all** mankind.

26. THE DIVINE LIFE AND THE CARNAL LIFE CO-EXIST. THE CONFLICT BETWEEN THEM. 5th. Our fifth proposition affirms that the Divine Life thus given to every man is a germ, a seed, which does not necessarily, and by the force of the mere gift, destroy and take the place of the carnal nature, but co-exists with that carnal nature, and enters into conflict with all that is evil and depraved in the natural life; and, if properly entertained and nurtured, will ultimately overcome, mortify, and kill all the evil of corrupt nature, and substitute for that evil, purity, goodness, and every Divine affection.

The principle here announced is in direct opposition both to the Romish theory and to the popular theology before noticed. A correct apprehension of it will disabuse the mind of the fallacies of both systems. But it is with the latter

9

that the understandings of the people have been most seriously entangled. Each of these systems looks to a time and
place when the new Divine Life is infused into the soul in
fullness of strength and vigor; and this first creation of the
new man is represented to be coincident with the destruction
of the old and carnal nature. One system fixes the time and
place of this great change at Baptism. The other designates
the real or supposed conversion of the adult subject as the
precise period. The experience of universal humanity contradicts both systems, and coincides with the Gospel teaching,
that the carnal and the Divine Life co-exist in every human
being; that a struggle ensues between them, which results in
the gradual subjection and ultimate destruction of one or the
other; and that according to the issue of this conflict, upon
one side or the other, will be the destiny of each man for
heaven or for hell. For each man will go to that place for
which, by the character and the issue of this conflict, he is
fitted and prepared.

The Gospel conveys to us this all-important truth, in
many of its varied forms of instruction, by parable, analogy,
and didactic teaching. The Divine Life in the soul of man
is compared to the mustard-seed, which when first put into
the ground is less than the least of all seeds, but presently
springs up and becomes a tree in which the birds find shel-
ter. It is the little leaven hid in two measures of meal,
which gradually penetrates, and by and by leavens the whole
mass. It is every-where illustrated by the nature and condition of the physical system, commencing with an embryo existence, and passing through the varied stages of human
growth and development, to the stature and maturity of men
and women in Christ Jesus. So apposite is this illustration,
and so minutely is it employed, that the very food adapted to
the different stages of physical growth is used to designate

the kinds of instruction best fitted for the several stages of development in the Divine Life—as milk for babes, and strong meat for full grown men.

To the same effect are those comparisons of the Christian state to a race, in which the runner may be hindered, and fail to receive the prize; to a warfare and a battle, in which the champion may be worsted. But in the 6th, 7th, and 8th chapters of the Epistle to the Romans, St. Paul fully and plainly sets forth the whole matter. He there describes the condition of man with the carnal and the Divine nature struggling together within him for the mastery. And he refers the character and the issue of this conflict to the will of man made free by the Spirit of God to choose between good and evil; to submit to the lusts of the old and carnal nature; or to renounce that fatal subjection, and to follow the guidance of the Spirit of light and life. "Know ye not, that to whom ye yield yourselves servants to obey, his servants ye are to whom ye obey; whether of sin unto death, or of obedience unto righteousness." When we have made this good and wise choice of the Lord to be our God, and of the Holy Spirit to be our Guide and Teacher, then, mystically, and by profession, we are dead unto sin; and the mortification of the carnal nature begins and is carried on to its entire destruction. "For if ye live after the flesh, ye shall die: but if ye through the Spirit do mortify the deeds of the body, ye shall live. For as many as are led by the Spirit of God, they are the sons of God." (Rom. viii, 13, 14.)

On this, as on every other Christian doctrine, the language of the Prayer-Book is but the echo of the Bible. Article 9, "Of Original Sin," says: "This infection of nature doth remain, yea, in them that are regenerate." And Article 15 declares: "But all we the rest (although baptized and born again in Christ) yet offend in many things; and if we say we have no sin, we deceive ourselves, and the truth is not in us." In the Baptismal Service the prayer is made for the candidates, "that the old Adam may be so buried that the new man may be raised up in them: that all sinful affections may die in them, and that all things belonging to the Spirit may live and grow in them: that they may have power and strength to have victory, and to triumph against the devil, the world, and the flesh." The closing exhortation states: "Baptism representeth to us our *profession*, which is to follow the example of our Savior Christ, and to be made like unto Him; that as He died and rose again for us, so should we who are baptized die from sin and rise again unto righteousness; *continually mortifying all our evil and corrupt affections*, and daily proceeding in all virtue and godliness of living."

According to this service, every person rightly baptized is dead unto sin, just as Isaac was dead unto his father when bound and stretched upon the altar, and the arm of the faithful patriarch raised to execute the command of God. In this instance Isaac was dead in the purpose and intention of his believing father. He had been wholly and entirely given up. So when the world, the flesh, and the devil, are heartily and sincerely renounced in baptism, sin is dead to us in our will, purpose, and intention. We are no longer its servants; we no longer submit to its power. But we have chosen the Divine Life—the adoption to be the sons of God—for our condition; the Lord to be our God; and the Holy Spirit to be our Leader and Guide. And we have vowed to wage an unceasing warfare against the carnal nature, the body of sin, *with which we are still oppressed*. The *actual* death of sin results from the faithful discharge of this vow, from the successful conduct of this warfare. We must so contend as to "triumph against the devil, the world, and the flesh." We must "continually mortify all our evil and corrupt affections."

The business and the probation of every man in this world is to carry out, and to bring to full effect, this Baptismal profession; so that, by the mighty power of the Holy Ghost working in and with us, we may overcome, mortify, and kill, all the evil of corrupt nature; and substitute for that evil, purity, goodness, and every Divine affection; and become in all things like unto our Savior Christ.

The union of the baptized with Christ and His Church, and our consequent relation to God, as His children, and the heirs of eternal life, are all clearly set forth as *accomplished* in Baptism. But no mention is made, no hint is given, of any *moral* sanctification, any moral righteousness, effected, *or begun*, in baptism. On the contrary, the *stipulation* of the several parts of this moral change, to be accomplished *in futuro*, by the aid of the heavenly Grace first bestowed and now increased, and of the new relations now entered upon, *is the very condition imposed upon the baptized persons*. The whole office is framed upon the principle that one service is renounced, in will and profession, and another embraced; and that this renunciation on the one hand, and new allegiance on the other are to be made good by a severe and unintermitted contest. The evil of our own nature to which we were subject is indeed renounced, together with all other evil, in terms of present time. But so far is that evil from being destroyed, and substituted by true holiness and purity, that we only promise that, by "God's help we will *endeavor not to follow nor be led by it.*" And after the Baptism we pray that the baptized *may now* "crucify the old man, and utterly abolish the whole body of sin." And again, at the close of the office the baptized are solemnly exhorted—not to retain that which they have received—but, to spend the whole of their lives in striving after that which the Romish theory says has already been accomplished.

The Communion Office of the Church is constructed upon the recognition of the same immutable truth, of the co-existence of the carnal and the Divine nature in the regenerate. And it is utterly irreconcilable with the systems which deny that truth. For it requires every communicant to come to the altar of God with the most humiliating confession of personal guilt and unworthiness. If, therefore, men were made perfectly just and holy, immaculate and without sin, by the Sacrament of Baptism, by the pseudo Sacrament of Penance, or by the exercises of a revival meeting, then these righteous persons could not lawfully be admitted to the communion of the faithful. For, in order to join that communion, and to partake of the body and blood of Christ, they would be compelled to use a confession which in their case would be false and hypocritical. And all the Liturgies in the world are, and always have been, characterized by this same feature. The universal Church, therefore, has made no provision whatever for the entertainment on earth of this class of. persons; for it no where recognizes the existence of such a class. The true members of Christ's Church are adopted children of a Heavenly Father, who bears with their waywardness, rebukes their sin, chastens them in his love, instructs their ignorance, calls them to repentance when they go astray, and, while they submit to the guidance of His spirit, leads them from conquest to conquest over the evil of their nature, and thus reinstates them in the likeness of the second Adam, the Lord from heaven.

27. BAPTISM THE NEW BIRTH. 6th. Our sixth proposition affirms that the Church of Christ, with all its appliances of faith and holiness, has been appointed as the last, the fullest, and the most perfect of the means and instrumentalities for the nurture and development of the Divine Life, from its embryo existence as a power in the soul of man, through all

the successive stages of growth, to the maturity of perfect manhood in Christ Jesus: and to be introduced into that Church by Baptism is the second birth—the birth of water and of the Spirit.

A clear apprehension of this final proposition, taken in connection with all that has been heretofore proved, will put an end to several mischievous *isms* and logomachies, and will take from true Christian people the source of much painful jealousy and suspicion. But we have no thought of recommending this proposition in a spirit of compromise, as a means of reconciling contending parties. Truth can make no compromise. Unless this proposition be true, it ought not to be received for any purpose. But if it be true, then all should heartily receive it, and rejoice in this additional proof that the truth will make us free from many hurtful delusions.

The Church of Christ is represented to us in Scripture by all those varied figures and illustrations which convey the ideas of unity, nurture, and protection. It is a Garden, and a Vineyard, where the plants are cultivated and tended with unremitting care, in every stage of growth, from the planting of the seed to the fullest maturity of fruitfulness. It is a Sheepfold, where the kindest nurture is applied to the lambs of the flock, and where the care of the Divine Shepherd is manifested in the tenderest and most affecting manner. It is an Ark, in which a remnant is saved from destruction, and where the food which may sustain life for so long a period is amply provided. It is a Field, in which are the growing plants which have sprung from the seed, and are ripening for the harvest. It is, last of all, and chiefly, a Kingdom, in which is included every age and condition of humanity; and which is put at all points in direct antagonism with the world.

It will be observed that every one of these representations of the Church presupposes the existence of something which has life, to be the subject of nurture and protection. The Garden, the Vineyard, and the Field, are but the places where living seeds or plants germinate, grow, and are cultivated. The Ark does not produce, but merely secures and protects its living tenants. The Sheepfold, the City, and the King-dom, do not bestow life, but simply nurture, protect, and de-fend the subject of that life which is derived from a higher source. These representations, therefore, teach us that the Church of Christ is the appointed place in which the Divine Life in the soul of man is to be nurtured, developed, and brought to the maturity and perfection of Christian character, to the full proportions of a perfect man in Christ Jesus. To this effect precisely is the language of the Apostle, describing the purpose of the entire organization of the Church. "He gave apostles, and prophets, and evangelists, and pastors, and teachers, for the perfecting of the saints, for the work of the ministry, for the edifying of the body of Christ." (Eph. iv, 11, 12.)

Now as faith in Jesus Christ is the exclusive mean of sal-vation to those to whom the knowledge of Christ has been sufficiently proposed; and yet the Spirit of God may effect that salvation in some other way in those to whom this knowl-edge has not been brought; so the Church of Christ is the exclusive mean of salvation to those to whom it is sufficiently proposed; (he that believeth and is baptized shall be saved;) yet the same Holy Spirit may, without the Church, nurture and bring to full maturity the Divine Life in the souls of those to whom the Church, as Christ's institution, has not been sufficiently proposed. But when the Gospel defines the terms of salvation, it speaks, of course, and only, to those who hear the Gospel. It is not addressed to those who can not hear it; and says nothing, therefore, about the provision which in the Divine economy is made for them.

We are now prepared to appreciate the force, beauty, and expressiveness of the illustration employed by our blessed Lord in his conversation with Nicodemus, to explain the nature of the Divine Life, and the necessity for the introduction of the subject of that life into His Church or Kingdom, by a second birth. That illustration does not differ at all, in the sense and meaning intended to be conveyed, from all the other representations of the same subject which we have already examined.

We have seen that the analogy between the Divine and physical life of man, is frequently introduced in the inspired Word, and is carried out to the utmost minuteness of comparison. Now recollect that it has been fully proved that the Divine Life as a germ—the capacity for holiness, the power to know and to do good, to know and to love God—is the gift of God, through Jesus Christ our Lord, to human nature, to every soul that is born into the world. How this Divine Life is to be nurtured and developed, *so as to effect the salvation of its subject*, is the purport of our Lord's communication to Nicodemus.

To convey His meaning, the Savior here uses the illustration of the physical life of man, so frequently employed in other portions of the Bible. He tells the Jewish ruler that under the new economy, which he came to introduce, every man who would enter into the kingdom of God must · be born again; must be introduced into that kingdom as a little child, by a second birth—a birth of water and of the Spirit. The analogy is most forcible and expressive, and has been strangely misunderstood. In entire oblivion of the familiar facts of the case, the *birth* of a child has been confounded with its *life*, and our Lord's words interpreted as if these two things were one and the same. But we know that the birth of a child is the result and consequence of its previous life, not the occasion of that life. It is required to be born because it is a living creature, which, having passed through an embryo existence, must now, *by birth*, be placed in *new relations*, and under the power of new influences and agencies, *adapted to its further and full development and perfection.*

Our blessed Lord understood the force and meaning of the words and illustrations which He employed. When He speaks of a second birth, therefore, he evidently refers to something in the spiritual life analagous to the first or physical birth. As by the first birth the living creature, the natural man, is introduced into the world, in order that it may attain to the perfection of manhood; so, by the second birth, of water and of the Spirit, the new creature, the subject of the Divine Life, is introduced into the Church of God, there to be trained and nurtured, under fitting influences, to the perfection of manhood in Christ Jesus.

Under the Christian dispensation, this new birth of water and of the Spirit is just as essential to the development and perfection of the Divine Life in the soul of man, as is the birth of a child into the world, from the womb of its mother, essential to the development and perfection of the natural life. The still-born child is born indeed, but derives no benefit from its birth. Only the quick, the living child, must needs be born, in order that it may continue to live and grow by the supply of appropriate sustenance to every power and faculty.

It is strange that the force and expressiveness of this physical analogy should ever have been forgotten, when the very same distinction between *life* and *birth* was, by the Divine care, prominently set forth in the Christian Creed. In the very beginning all believers were taught that the blessed Savior "was *conceived* by the Holy Ghost, BORN of the Virgin Mary." To the pattern of His most holy life all Christian people must be conformed. The life of Christ can only be implanted in the nature of man by the sole operation of the Holy Ghost. The Christian man must thereafter "be BORN of water and of the Spirit," "into the Kingdom of God." The blessed Sacrament that brings the heir of salvation into the fold of Christ, into the Kingdom of God, is made by the joint operation of the outward element and the Holy Ghost, the blessed Spirit sanctifying that element to its instituted purpose, and renewing the vigor of the life which He had before imparted.

The efficient Agent in this new birth, this incorporation of the subject of the Divine Life into the body of Christ, is the Holy Spirit; "for by one Spirit are we all baptized into one body." (1 Cor. xii, 13.) The Holy Ghost is the ever-present and only efficient Administrator in all Christian ordinances. By the ministry of the Holy Ghost, the God-man, who has ascended into the heavens, is present nevertheless on earth in the assemblies of his faithful people; is formed in the heart of each believer; feeds, nurtures, and presides over His Church. In like manner the Holy Ghost is the true Minister in the mystery of the second birth. He gives authority to the human minister to act in the name of Christ. He sanctifies the water to the mystical washing away of sin. He comes with new power and more abundant grace into the soul of the new-born, enabling him to carry out the Baptismal profession, and to live according to God's law, and as the adopted child of a Heavenly Father.

When our Divine Master informed Nicodemus of the necessity of this new birth of water and of the Spirit, the Jewish ruler was confounded, as all his countrymen were. at a doctrine so disparaging to the Mosaic economy, and which evidently looked to a termination of the peculiar privileges of the Jews. As a child of Abraham, he was a member of that kingdom which God had heretofore established on the earth. In circumcision he received the effectual sign of his admission into that kingdom. He had grown up to be a scribe, and teacher, and ruler in the same. He understood very well how a converted Gentile might be born again into the family and kingdom of God. For such a new birth by baptism was familiar to all the Jews of that day. It was the established custom to receive proselytes into the Jewish Church by baptism, and this was called their new or second birth. But that Nicodemus, a Jew, and *a ruler of the Jews*, should be bound to submit to the same great change, seemed to him to be as strange and unnatural as for a grown man to enter the second time into his mother's womb and be born. The same humbling and most unexpected feature of the Christian doctrine, that in the new dispensation the peculiar privileges of the Jew were to be annulled, and that all men alike must submit to the same terms of salvation, hung like a veil before the hearts of the ancient people, and prevented them from seeing the glorious light that was shining in their midst.

It was necessary that all men, Jews and Gentiles, should be born again into the new kingdom of our Lord and Savior Jesus Christ, in order that the Divine Life in every man should be nourished by Divine grace conveyed to the soul through the instituted channels of that grace. In no other way, under the Christian economy, could that life be sustained, leveloped, and carried forward through all the stages of growth to the maturity of manhood, to the fullness of the stature of Christ.

In exact accordance with this plain and simple teaching of the Bible is the language of the Prayer-Book. Nowhere is the Divine Life said to be given or begun in Baptism. But the new birth—the introduction into the Church which is the body of Christ—the solemn adoption to be the children of God—is invariably made to be coincident with that sacrament. In Article 15, to be "baptized and born again in Christ," are used as equivalent terms. And instead of grace being then for the first time imparted, it is positively asserted, in the 27th Article, that then "grace is increased."

Such is Baptismal Regeneration, in the sense of the Bible and the Church. This meaning is the only one that satisfies the language used by our blessed Lord, and corresponds with the physical analogy by which He was pleased to illustrate the mysteries and the doctrines of His kingdom. This meaning, and this alone, agrees with the numerous similitudes in the inspired Word, already referred to, by which the Divine Life in the soul of man, and the relation of that life to the Church of God, are at large described. By every one of these similitudes the Church is presented to us as the place and the agency by which the Divine Life, previously received, is nurtured, sustained, and developed. This meaning alone concurs with the analogy of faith, leaving to every other truth of the Gospel its fit and appropriate place. Make the beginning of the Divine Life in the soul to be in Baptism, or at Conversion, and we will be forced either into Pelagianism—holding that man in his natural state, without the grace of Christ, can turn, repent, believe, and do good works acceptable to God—or into the most revolting form of Calvinism—believing that God created the greater part of mankind under a pre-ordained necessity of damnation, and that in His tenderest offers of mercy to these reprobates the Just and Holy One does but mock at the involuntary impotence and misery of His creatures.

Pelagianism must be a consequence of the first supposition, because where there is no spiritual life there can be no capacity to hear, receive, and obey the Gospel; just as where there is no natural life there is no capacity to receive impressions from external objects. "The things of God knoweth no man but the Spirit of God." "The natural man receiveth not the things of the Spirit of God; for they are foolishness unto him: neither can he know them, because they are spiritually discerned." (1 Cor. ii, 11, 14.) If, therefore, there exists in man a power to hear, receive, and obey the Gospel, *independent of the Divine Life imparted by the Spirit of God*, then such power must be inherent in the natural man—which is contrary to the Scriptures just cited, and to the Catholic Faith, and is the very proposition that constitutes the Pelagian heresy. But we know that this power both exists and is exercised in persons unbaptized. Therefore, either the Pelagian heresy must be true, or the theory which makes the beginning of the Divine Life in the soul to be at Baptism must be false.

The second alternative, fixing the beginning of the Divine Life at the *Conversion* of the adult subject, by inevitable necessity excludes the rest of mankind from the capacity to entertain the offers of salvation, which is the extreme Calvinistic theory. But both these dogmas are contrary to the Catholic Faith, and must be rejected along with the interpretation of Scripture which implies both or either of them.

Again, the doctrine of Baptismal Regeneration, as above explained, is the only view of this subject that corresponds with the phenomena of universal humanity. That the fruits of the Spirit, as enumerated by St. Paul, are exhibited by all men of every nation, at various periods of their lives, and *especially in childhood*, is a simple fact, which the experience of the whole world attests.* That the Gospel itself appeals

* This assertion has been denounced as extravagant and absurd, and the denunciation supported by citing the cases of Nero, Cæsar Borgia, &c. Yet surely

to every human being, with the assumption that he has previously received a spiritual power and discernment to hear,
feel, understand, and obey its admonitions, is apparent to
every reader of the Gospel. The Calvinist, indeed, manages
to account for these facts by a newly invented distinction of
his own between common and special grace; the former being
just sufficient to damn its subject, the latter enough to necessitate his salvation: thereby emulating or exceeding the impiety of those Corinthians who undertook to divide Christ
the Lord; for this system seeks to divide the Eternal Spirit!
But he who asserts that the Divine Life is first and only imparted in Baptism, has not even this miserable shift with
which to account for the facts that he can not deny.

The birth of water and of the Spirit, the introduction of
the subject of Divine Grace into the Church and family of
God, has been sneeringly called "merely a sort of *external* or
relative regeneration, a regeneration of *mere relations and
circumstances*," in contradistinction to "an actual regeneration."

Has the Church, then, the mystical body of Christ, fallen
so low in the estimation of any of her loyal children, that to
be made a member thereof, and the consequent recipient of
such great and precious privileges, is considered so slight a
thing, and that the words in which this event is described are
declared to be "a trifling with very solemn language?"

It is true, indeed, that the natural birth of a child is but

these monsters of iniquity were children once, *the selected emblems of innocence
and purity.* Have such objectors never paused to consider the profound Christian
philosophy of the history of Hazael, in the second book of Kings? "And
Hazael said, But what—is thy servant a dog, that he should do this great
thing?" Hazael was a heathen, yet the Word of God, and innumerable Christian writers and preachers—among them the sainted Bishop Wilson, of Sodor
and Man—have used his case as a most instructive instance of the progressive
power of evil in those who resist and grieve the Spirit of God. (See Bp. Wilson's
Sermon on "The sin and danger of grieving the Holy Spirit of God.")

a change of *relations*, but that change involves the continued existence and future well-being of its subject. To be changed from a servant of the devil and an heir of death into a child of God and an inheritor of the Kingdom of Heaven, *is a mere change of relations.* But those relations, on either side, are of the most awful character. Noah and his family, inclosed in the ark, were in a different relation to the deluge from the rest of the inhabitants of the earth. But *that relation involved the salvation of those by whom it was sustained.*

The truth is, the author of that sentiment did not know the proper, and original, and simple meaning of the word he was using. He conceived of that word only in the sense given to it by the popular theology of dissent. Hence he entirely misapprehended the doctrine of the Church. The principal error of the statement consists in the assumption that a change of relations is, of necessity, merely formal and external. Such an assumption involves a sad confusion of ideas. No real transaction in the Church of God, done by the command of Christ, and by the ministry of the Holy Ghost, *can be merely formal and external.* A Divine power, an influence for eternity, involving the issues of life and death, are inseparably attached to every sacrament and ordinance of our holy religion. To ascertain the precise virtue and signification of each one of these sacraments and ordinances, is not to eviscerate them of their force, but it is to recognize the sternest responsibility under which Almighty God has placed His creature man; to learn and obey the truth: soberly and diligently discriminating that truth from the fallacies on either hand with which the devil ever seeks to simulate and thereby to discredit and destroy it.

The doctrine of Baptismal Regeneration—that a man must be born again of water and the Spirit—that the Church is the appointed medium of salvation to those to whom it is proposed—is emphatically and specifically the great Church doctrine, in contradistinction to all the modern varieties of the loose theology of dissent.   In this doctrine is involved many of the contested questions between these two systems in relation to the Ministry, the Sacraments, and the nature of Faith.   It is therefore a fundamental verity—a mode of state-ment of a truth which is contained in more than one article of the Creed.   It asserts and maintains the union which God has established between the power and the form of godliness. It repels at once the wild fanaticism which affects to be so spiritual that it must needs despise and reject the institutions of the Almighty, and the cold rationalism which would dis-charge the Spirit of God from His effective and essential agency in all the work of man's salvation.   The doctrine of Baptismal Regeneration, truly understood, keeps together the things which God has joined; sets forth that, under the Gos-pel, the operations of the Spirit of God in man's salvation have been connected with the institutions of the Gospel.   He, therefore, who describes Baptism as nothing more than a form, or empty sign, as merely a thing of externals, insults and degrades the doctrine of salvation.

Baptism, 'ike all the other institutions of the Gospel, is both corporeal and spiritual.   It is "an outward and visible sign," "effectual" to the production of the thing which it signifies. For the Spirit is the true and efficient Administrator of the Sacrament.   The Spirit effects the new birth—incorporates the baptized into the body of Christ—bestows a larger meas-ure of His holy influences adapted to the state and circum-stances of the recipient, and continues to give power and efficacy to all the future discipline of the heir of salvation.

When a Churchman, forgetting the essential distinction be-tween Life and Birth, inadvertently confounds these two things, under the name of Baptismal Regeneration, and thus

10

admits in part the specific Romish theory of salvation, and
systematically adheres to this definition, he brings a new and
undeserved odium upon the truth; gives occasion to the enemies of that truth to triumph; and, if he continues to be a
Churchman, commits himself to many irreconcilable contra-
distinctions and inconsistencies.

But the admission of this one point of Romish doctrine
is very apt to lead to much further departures from the
truth.   The errors of Romanism, however inconsistent with
the truth held in connection with them, are very consistent
with one another.   They compose a logical scheme of falsehood, the parts of which are closely woven together.   This
doctrine, that the Divine Life is first imparted in Baptism,
is a seminal and prolific principle of error.   The earnest but
unbalanced mind, which is once thoroughly committed to the
belief of this principle, will be led on, step by step, to the
adoption of its dependent falsehoods, until, in despair of reconciling the supposed truths of God with each other, or with
the plainest dictates of right reason, the victim of. this delusion surrenders himself and all his heaven derived faculties
to the unresisted guidance of ignorant, corrupt, and unprin-
cipled men.

The doctrine of Christ is not so taught by the Church of
Christ.   That in Baptism the subjects of Divine Grace receive the seal of their adoption into the family of God—the
sacramental assurance of the remission of sins; that they are
thereby made the acknowledged children of a Heavenly
Father, entitled to all the privileges and graces of His household; that they then enter upon a Divinely established course
of parental training, by which the corruption of their nature
is to be purged away; by which, when they sin, they are to
be chastened, rebuked, and summoned to the healthful discipline of repentance, with the full and unqualified assurance

of the favor and loving kindness of their Heavenly Father
when they do repent: that the abiding presence and effective
power of the Holy Ghost to carry on this training, and
make it effectual to salvation, is abundantly vouchsafed to its
subjects: this is the teaching of the Church of Christ; this
is the way of salvation to which she points the redeemed of
the Lord; this is the blessed condition, the glorious distinction, of the baptized children of God.

The same Church calls upon every human being to hear
and obey the Spirit of God speaking within him. Every
good thought and desire, every pure and holy affection that
stirs the heart of man, is the witness of the presence of that
Spirit, and of his power to sanctify and save. He who refuses to be led by this Divine Spirit of light and life into all
holy obedience, fatally sins against the Holy Ghost, and consigns himself to the perdition that must ensue.

And now, dear reader, make this one practical and pregnant application of all that we have been learning together.
Remember that you are not to postpone the work of your
salvation until the Spirit is bestowed upon you at some future
period. For that Spirit, if not grieved away, already dwells
within you. Follow its guidance, and you shall be led to
holiness here, and to heaven hereafter. You are not to look
for a future beginning of the Divine Life in your soul.
That life exists already, rendering you capable of knowing
and of obeying the truth. That life, by your care and diligence in the use of the appointed means of grace, is to be
nurtured and nourished to the full maturity of the Christian
character, and to a meetness for heaven and eternal joys; or
by your neglect and sin, that life is to be extinguished, and
your soul sunk into the darkness of an endless death. If
heretofore you have refused to permit that life to be sus
tained by the heavenly nutriment of Divine grace, and have

suffered sin to remain in your mortal body, then you must be *converted* and live, or you must perish in your iniquity with an everlasting destruction.

§8. CONSIDERA-
TION OF OBJEC-
TIONS TO THIS
VIEW OF THE DI-
VINE LIFE AND
THE NEW BIRTH.
Most of the objections to the view presented in the foregoing discussion are founded upon various figures of speech employed in Scripture inconsistent with the language in which that view is presented. It is very strange that so large a portion of religious controversy consists of a determined effort to force together inconsistent figures of speech, and to make them agree as different parts of the same representation. If this is a vice in rhetoric, it is a much more serious wrong in argument. A large part of the Bible is necessarily a representation of spiritual truths by the aid of material and sensible images. A great variety of illustrations are employed for the purpose of conveying the same truth; and sometimes a single illustration is used in different places in order to convey different truths. The application of the figure must, in every case, be determined by the subject matter and by the context. But the figures, the illustrations, are not doctrines, are not truths, which must be made to fit together and adjust themselves into a consistent system. Different figures to express the same truth must necessarily be inconsistent and incongruous with one another, while the truths represented by those figures are identical. One of the passages adduced by several persons, as a refutation of the principle that the Divine Life is given to every man, presents a striking proof of the position just mentioned. "Awake, thou that sleepest, and arise from the dead, and Christ shall give thee light." Here, in the ardor of composition, the inspired writer throws together three utterly incongruous images, for the purpose of conveying two very important and perfectly accordant truths. First, the person addressed is

said to be asleep, which presupposes life; then he is described as dead; and after he has risen from the dead, he is told that he shall receive light. To reconcile these images would of course be impossible. To treat them as substantive doctrines, and try to compose them into a system, would make a wretched confusion. But there is no difficulty at all in apprehending the truths conveyed by this forcible and lively language.

The words Life and Death, and their cognate terms, as, to be begotten, to be born, to be crucified, to be buried, are all used in the Bible in a great variety of significations, and to express the most diverse truths. It is impossible to bring these figures together and make a good rhetorical sentence, or a consistent logical system out of them. They were not designed to be used in any such way. But it is very easy to ascertain the particular truth conveyed in each instance by the use of these terms, and compose these truths together into a consistent and harmonious system.

One object of the preceding discussion has been to ascertain the precise truth conveyed by our Lord, in his conversation with Nicodemus, under the figure of a New Birth. The great importance of that inquiry arose from the fact that the Church has incorporated the illustration, and the truth conveyed by it, together, into the most solemn of her formularies. For the ministers and the members of the Church to be constantly using these formularies, and attaching to them a different meaning, is a fruitful source of jealousy and suspicion. In ill governed minds, where passion and prejudice get the better of judgment and charity, these feelings frequently break forth into loud and angry denunciation, thus bringing scandal upon the Church and doing great injury to religion.

To determine the precise meaning which our blessed Lord, and the Church adopting his language, designed to convey by the image of a New Birth, does not fix the same meaning

to the same figure, when used in a different connection in
other parts of the inspired Word. On the contrary, it has
been shown that, to be born of God, is used elsewhere in a
very different sense, viz., to express that practical living under the power of the Divine Life, which by St. Paul is described as being "led by the Spirit." But to determine
accurately the sense in which this illustration was employed
by our Savior, and in which it has been incorporated by the
Church into her formularies, from the earliest time, does fix
the strict, theological meaning of this language; and this
meaning should be faithfully adhered to whenever those
formularies are examined or explained, if theological science
and parochial instruction are to be any thing better than a
Babel of confusion and of misconstruction.

The same principles of construction apply to those other
very common and emphatic terms—Life and Death. They
are used in the greatest variety of ways to express the most
opposite states. In the Epistle to the Romans this imagery
is lavishly employed in meanings which are constantly inter-
changing. Thus, the prevalence of a carnal life, the state of
a wicked man, is sometimes called death, sometimes life; and
the prevalence of the Divine Life, the state of a good man,
is called in one connection, death, in another life. The context determines the meaning in each instance. When in
any one of these instances we have ascertained the particular
truth announced by the apostle, it would be a very singular
objection to that truth to allege that the apostle had expressed a very different meaning by the use of the same illustration in another place! But this is the precise force of
the objection to the truths herein set forth concerning the
Divine Life and the New Birth.

The method which I have adopted in order to determine the
precise meaning of the phrase New Birth, as used by our

Lord, and in the formularies of the Church, was to prove *aliunde*, from other parts of the Divine word, and of the teachings of the Church, the truth of certain propositions. Then it was shown that the easiest, simplest, and most literal interpretation of the illustration under examination assumed a portion of these truths, and expressed the remainder. The sense of the illustration thus ascertained, was further shown to be closely analogous to the very purpose for which the same figure was familiarly employed by the Jews of our Lord's time; and that this same sense had been continuously given to it in every age of the Church.

This whole argument may be very faulty, and capable of easy refutation; but I submit that it is no answer at all to cite passages either from the Bible or from eminent Christian writers, in which similar imagery is employed to express other truths.

It is very true, as Hooker says, that "the first apparent beginning of life (spiritual life.) is in that Baptism which both declareth and maketh us Christians," just as the first apparent beginning of natural life is at birth. And this easily accounts for all the expressions that may be cited, re- • ferring to natural birth, and to new birth, as the beginning, respectively, of the natural and of the Divine Life. But this does not alter the fact that life existed in each case before; and that it was the assumed existence of that previous life upon which our Savior founded His illustration of a birth by water and the Spirit, of a child of God into the kingdom or Church of God.

I have acknowledged that it is incumbent on him who affirms the entire completeness and closeness of the analogy between natural and supernatural birth. to show, in some instances at least, the existence of the Divine or Spiritual life anterior to that "apparent beginning of life" which takes

place in Baptism.   That is, it must be proved that there is a
reality corresponding to this feature of the illustration.   If
this is shown, then the whole truth set forth by this ex·
pressive and beautiful illustration is fully maintained, and
one vicious theory is refuted.   If, again, it can be shown
that this Divine or Spiritual life exists anterior to what is
popularly termed conversion, then another mischievous error
is put aside.   The whole question then turns upon the truth
or falsehood of this proposition: "The Holy Spirit is given
to every man to be in him the principle of a new and Divine
life."   I must refer to the arguments already adduced in support of this proposition.   I will here only mention one or
two additional considerations.

By the Divine Life I mean a capacity given .by the
Spirit of God to discern, to love, and to do the things
which the natural man, according to Scripture, can neither
discern, love, or perform.   The existence of life can only
be shown by the phenomena of life.   In order to prove the
existence of life, it is not necessary that all the phenomena
proper to sound and vigorous life should be manifested.
The blind, the deaf, and the paralyzed are alive, although
some of the manifestations of life are wanting in them.   So
in regard to spiritual life.   The existence of any of the phenomena of which the natural man is said to be incapable, and
which are declared in the Scriptures of truth to be the fruits
of the Spirit, manifests the existence of Spiritual or Divine
Life.   What other test can we apply?   Must all the phenomena of healthful and vigorous life be exhibited in each
instance before we will allow that life exists at all?   Must a
sinner have perfected holiness before it is admitted that he
has received any portion of the Spirit of God?   If a man
has failed to subdue an unruly temper, shall we, therefore,
deny that he has received any grace?

The Scriptures affirm, generally, that the natural man is incapable of any good. It asserts, positively and unequivocally, that certain virtues are the fruits of the Spirit. Shall we venture to affirm, in direct contradiction to these declarations, that man is, by nature, his perverted nature, capable of good? Shall we say of those very virtues enumerated as fruits of the Spirit, that, nevertheless, they are not fruits of the Spirit, but the operations of a carnal and corrupted nature? Unless Scripture can be thus flatly contradicted, it must be held as demonstrated, that every man has received the Divine as well as the carnal life. For all men do both good and evil.* And the actual condition of every man is, according to the life he cultivates, a gradual progress towards the ascendency of the good or evil that is in him; until, in the one case, he is prepared for the communion of the just in heaven or, in the other, fitted for the society of the accursed in hell.

The affections of man are not like the instincts of brutes, fixed, unalterable, and destitute of a moral quality. When God bestowed upon the animal creation the affections essential to their being and enjoyment, He did not bestow likewise the moral freedom which could make them capable of

---

* The able author of an article in the *Edinburgh Review* for October, 1853, on " Church Parties," fully asserts this principle, and refutes an objection to it. Quoting the " Recordite Party," as maintaining, " If a man be not a believer his virtues are nothing better than splendid sins," the Reviewer says, in a note, " The Recordite Party justify this assertion by appealing to the 13th Article, which declares that ' works done before grace have the nature of sin.' But this proposition, if interpreted in the Puritanic sense, would contradict the inspired declaration that the prayers and alms of the heathen Cornelius were acceptable to God. (Acts x, 4, 35.) The true meaning of the Article is only that Divine Grace and Human Goodness are co-extensive; so that where there is no Grace there is no Goodness, and conversely, that wheresoever there is Goodness there is Grace. Thus the virtues of Socrates are not denied, but only ascribed to their true source. Whereas, in the Puritanic view, (which unhappily was adopted by some of the Continental Reformers,) they are denied to be virtues at all; and thus the very foundations of all religious evidence, the axiomatic ideas of mor ality, are cut away. (p. 145.)

11

responsibility, and enable them to pervert His gifts, and to forfeit His favor. These affections, therefore, are in them neither good or evil. But in man these same affections have a moral quality. They are either good or evil. These affections are to be brought into judgment—to be the subjects of reward or punishment. How the affections of a corrupted creature can be evil it is easy to understand. But the source of their goodness it would be hard to determine, unless we admit the Christian doctrine that this goodness proceeds from the Almighty—that it is the direct dictate and influence of God's Spirit bestowed upon every man as the inestimable purchase of Christ's most precious blood. Unless the Spirit of God be given to enable man to "do righteousness," how can he be judged for a failure to do that of which he is naturally incapable? If man has not received from God the power to do good, to walk uprightly, to obey the law, then there can be no moral quality in his actions. They are neither good or evil. This power must either be a natural endowment, derived from the original creation, and never forfeited or lost, or it must be a supernatural gift bestowed through Jesus Christ, for His sake, and on account of the virtue of His sacrifice and mediation. The first of these alternatives is the assertion of Deism and Pelagianism. The second is the Christian doctrine. I can see no room or place for any third alternative.

These are general considerations which coincide with all the Scriptural authorities to the same effect heretofore quoted. Let us see another Scriptural testimony to the same purpose. St. Paul frequently describes the most eminent operations of the Spirit as the "Circumcision of the heart." Now this very circumcision of the heart was a substantive part of that ancient covenant of which, not Baptism, but outward circumcision was the seal. "The Lord thy God will circumcise thine heart, and the heart of thy seed, to love the Lord thy God with all thine heart, and with all thy soul, that thou mayest live." (Deut. xxx, 6.) In the Epistle to the Romans this spiritual circumcision is plainly extended to the Gentiles. For although they had not been favored with the written law of Moses, yet they had a law written on their hearts, and they had received spiritual power to recognize and obey that law, as is fully implied by the apostle when he said, "Therefore if the uncircumcision keep the righteousness of the law, shall not his uncircumcision be counted for circumcision?"— for "circumcision is that of the heart, in the spirit, and not in the letter." (Rom. ii, 26, 29.) This is evidently the foundation of the previous declaration in the same chapter, that "the judgment of God is according to truth, who will render unto every man according to his deeds; unto them that are contentious and do not obey the truth, but obey unrighteousness, indignation and wrath, tribulation and anguish, upon every soul of man that doeth evil, of the Jew first, and also of the Gentile; but glory, honor, and peace, to every man that worketh good, to the Jew first, and also to the Gentile."

In the preceding chapter the Apostle affirms in three distinct places that the Gentiles had been "given up," or "given over," to a reprobate mind, because of their deliberate wickedness and impenitence. How could the Almighty "give up" those whom He had never tried to lead in the way of righteousness? How could He "give over to a reprobate mind" those who had never resisted His spirit? The apparent sense of the terms, and the analogy of faith, here equally impel us to the same conclusion.

When we add to all this weight of Scripture testimony the undoubted fact so dwelt upon and reiterated in the New Testament, that Cornelius had found favor with God, and

had manifested the most precious fruits of the Spirit before
he ever heard the Gospel; and that even the miraculous
gifts of the same Spirit were conferred upon him and his
friends before they were baptized, it seems to me that the
position now maintained is incontrovertibly established from
the Word of God.   And when again we find the great body
of heathen moralists using and anticipating the very language in which St Paul describes the conflict within himself, between the good and evil principle, between the
spiritual and the carnal nature, it is passing strange that
any Christian man should ever have questioned this proposition.   The authors of the Westminster Confession were
far too learned a body of theologians to attribute to the
natural man the good which they acknowledged to be in
all men.   They referred that good undoubtingly to the
Spirit of God; but, under the influence of their peculiar
views, they called it "some common operations of the
Spirit."

That Grace is given before Baptism generally in the case
of adults, is placed beyond a question by the united voice of
Scripture and the Church, requiring the most eminent fruits
of the Spirit as antecedents to Baptism.

The proposition thus fully proved that every man has received the Holy Spirit to make him capable of holiness, and
therefore responsible for unholiness, is a complete vindication
of the illustration used by our blessed Lord, and by the Church
continuously since, to express the operation and effect of Baptism, viz: that it is a New Birth, the introduction by water
and the Spirit of a living subject from the womb of nature
into the Church or kingdom of God.   This is precisely what
Hooker meant when he said: "Each Sacrament having both
that which is general or common, and that also which is peculiar
to itself, we may hereby gather that the participation of Christ

which properly belongeth to any one Sacrament, is not to be obtained otherwise than by the Sacrament whereunto it is proper." The 27th Article tells us what is that grace or "participation of Christ" which is *proper* to Baptism. "Baptism is a sign of Regeneration or New Birth, whereby as by an instrument they that receive Baptism rightly are grafted into the Church." Here "Regeneration," "New Birth," and "grafting into the Church," are used as convertible terms, and Baptism is declared to be both the sign of the thing thus represented, and *the instrument* by which it is effected. The remainder of the Article makes Baptism to be both a *sign* and a *seal*—that is, the assurance—of some other blessings. In Article 9 the Latin version uses the word *renatis*—reborn. The English version translates *renatis* by "baptized."

This ought to have prevented any question about the identity of the meaning of these words in the contemplation of the English and American Church. It has been often shown that they were used as synonymous by all Christian writers for fifteen hundred years.

It will not do to degrade this Divinely conceived and Divinely appointed institution, by calling it "a mere ecclesiastical rite, which man alone is quite competent to achieve." The Church is not a society of human appointment, but the mystical body of Christ, established by Grace. Union with this body can only be obtained by the operation of the Holy Ghost, whose power is in various ways exerted in order to constitute the Sacrament. And when this union is effected, the same Holy Spirit of life and light flows *through many channels* into the soul of the member of Christ. "*Man alone,*" therefore, can do nothing in regard to this Divine society. It is all of Grace. And on this account it is that the question of the *Divine* as opposed to the *human* institution of the

Church, its Sacraments, and its Ministry, is of such tran-scendent importance.

It is much harder to keep clearly in mind the important truth we have been considering than either of the vicious extremes between which it stands. And this is the condition of all truth. We are accustomed to speak of the simplicity of truth. But simplicity is no attribute of truth. Truth is always complex. It is composed by the meeting and ad-justment of various conflicting forces in nature, or proposi-tions in logic. The harmony of the universe is produced by the wise adjustment of many conflicting forces; the har-mony of truth, in every department of human learning, is produced by a like adjustment of many conflicting proposi-tions.

Error, on the contrary, is simple. It is, for the most part, a single, unqualified proposition. It is so much easier to ap-prehend such a proposition, and accept it with all its con-sequences, than to apprehend along with it many conflicting propositions, and bring them all together in a just and even balance, that men almost invariably take the former course. Hence the universal tendency to extremes. Of the different propositions which meet, and by their mutual compensation compose the truth, some minds seize upon one proposition and run it out to one extreme; other minds are more at-tracted by a different proposition, and with like recklessness carry that out to the opposite extreme. It requires rare qualities of judgment and temper to receive conflicting prop-ositions with equal favor, and to discern and firmly hold the truth which comes from their mutual adjustment.

This is the reason that simple despotic governments have been the common rule, and free, mixed governments the rare exception in all human history. A simple government, which is essentially a despotism, whether the ruler be one man or a few, or the multitude, is so much easier to understand, and to work, than the complicated system where freedom is secured by the just counteraction of many conflicting powers and interests, that the world has generally submitted to one or the other of these simple forms of despotism. The masses of mankind will not consent to exercise the intelligence and put forth the ceaseless energy required for the maintenance of those complicated governments where alone freedom can be found.

Hence, too, in the Church, the facility with which men accept wild licentiousness on the one hand, or Papal despotism on the other. Each is but a single idea, easily apprehended and easily submitted to. Whereas, the complex truth which constitutes the revelation of Jesus Christ is made up of many apparently discordant propositions, to be received with equal respect, and their mutual compensation carefully maintained. The reconciliation of Authority and Freedom, the right adjustment of the relations between the Scriptures, the Church, and the private Christian, demand the highest exercise of the best faculties that God has bestowed on man. But men are unwilling to respond to that demand. And so they indolently sink down into Popery, or Infidelity, or mere popular Protestantism, as circumstances may determine.

§9. PRACTICAL VALUE OF THESE TRUTHS. The conclusion at which we have now, by patient examination, arrived, is no mere abstract theory of religion for the exercise of the intellect, and for the gratification of idle curiosity. It is a practical truth of the most momentous consequence: a truth which is verified in part by the consciousness of every human being; and which is witnessed in all its saving and consoling efficacy, by all who have unreservedly submitted themselves to the power of God for their salvation.

I appeal, now, not to any external authority whatever, but

to the heart and consciousness of every man, and ask you, if you have not felt at all times the struggle within yourselves of the antagonist forces which we have been considering? Have you not experienced the power of corrupt nature inciting you to evil, and the gentle influence of a better monitor persuading you to resist the evil and to walk in the path of uprightness? We have seen that the Word of God, and right reason, combine to assure us that this better monitor dwelling within you, is the Holy Spirit of Life and Light— "the true light that lighteth every man that cometh into the world." You have therefore within you at once the sentence of condemnation against iniquity, and the earnest of your calling to a life of purity and to a heritage of bliss. The blessed Bible, in its highest meaning, is but the interpreter of these mysteries of your being. It is for you to confirm and ratify the sentence of condemnation which you feel within you, and which you read in God's Word, and thus to consign yourselves to an eternal night of hopeless woe; or, to make your calling and election sure, to own your adoption to be the children of God, and to live according to that high and holy relation, and thus to secure that exceeding great reward which your Father in heaven has promised to bestow.

By the recognition of these solemn truths, and by the faithful performance of your duty as created by them, you will at once obey the gracious exhortation, and prove the truth of the consoling assurance, so happily combined in the Word of God, "Work out your own salvation with fear and trembling, for it is God that worketh in you to will and to do of his good pleasure." That your salvation is the "good pleasure" of your Heavenly Father, He has declared with a soul-subduing emphasis of expression which infinite love and power could not surpass. The mission, the sufferings, the death of the Son of God, tell the story of redeeming love—declare the "good pleasure" of an Almighty Father whose compassions fail not, and whose tender mercies are over all His works. He, by his Spirit, works in you to desire and to will the accomplishment of "His good pleasure." But He does not work in you irresistibly. You must yield to His solicitations. You must submit to be led by the Spirit. You must work together with God. Then He will work in you to *do* as well as to *will.* Therefore, work out your own salvation with fear and trembling, indeed, lest you fail to do your part, but with joy and confidence, that it is God that worketh in you. That infinite love and almighty power are pledged to accomplish the "good pleasure" of your Heavenly Father, for all who work together with Him.

This work is no holiday pastime It is not the easy way of salvation, which encourages a man to continue in sin for the greater portion of his life, to add to the evil of corrupt nature the grosser evil of more corrupt habits; and then, when "a convenient season" arrives, when he is tired of the world, or the world begins to be tired of him, to leap at once from uncleanness to holiness, by the magical power of some wild, delirious excitement, or by a single effort of enlightened will.

To subdue the evil of corrupt nature, to reinstate man in that image of God from which he has fallen, is, according to the ordinary economy of Grace, the work and labor of the whole life. The Church, as represented by all the analogies which we have heretofore collected from the Word of God, as "the garden," "the field," "the vineyard," "the ark," "the city," "the kingdom," embraces the ordinary agencies and influences by which the Spirit works in us, and by which we work together with God for the accomplishment of this great result. Therefore it is that children should be brought to

Baptism in earliest infancy, because this blessed work of the soul's renewal in the likeness of God should be begun when corrupt nature can be taken at the greatest disadvantage. Then it is that the parent, by a holy discipline, must work together with God for his child, as in after life the child must work together with God for himself. And all who have studied the character of young children, know well that Grace is then most powerful to produce that purity of mind and holiness of affection which induced the blessed Savior to say, "Of such is the kingdom of heaven."

The mischievous theory which denies this work of Grace upon the infant mind, which turns the young heir of salvation forth into the world a stranger and an alien to its father's home, looking for grace only to some yet distant operation of the Spirit, gives time and opportunity for corrupt nature to rally. The Devil sees his advantage, and does not fail to profit by it. He comes and takes possession, and the result is that carelessness and impiety of a more advanced period of youth, which in so many cases is to ripen into the hardness and reprobacy of a settled, determined wickedness.

If that which we have seen to be the *ordinary* way of God's working for the salvation of His redeemed, be neglected or defeated by the unfaithfulness of man, then the difficulty and uncertainty of obtaining this salvation by other and extraordinary means, adapted by the Almighty to this exigency of our condition, are constantly increasing in a ratio which it is fearful to contemplate. Therefore, every one who desires to be saved, and who nevertheless refuses to begin to work out his salvation in the way that God has appointed him, is putting every day a stronger seal to his own damnation.

The account which has now been given of the way of salvation is the best refutation that I can make of that foolish, wanton slander, sometimes preferred against the holy Church of God, that she teaches men to rely upon the *mere formal* use of the means of Grace, having no regard to the state and affections of the soul, or to the transforming power of God's Holy Spirit. On the contrary, it has been shown that *salvation* and *holiness* are indissolubly bound together, and may be almost interchangeably used. And there is no vice against which our ministers so frequently warn their people as against that insidious and inveterate evil of the human heart, the tendency to rest in the *form*, without seeking for and securing the *power* of Godliness; telling them, that those who do so lightly and sacrilegiously trifle with Divine and eternal things, will but increase their own condemnation. We do earnestly teach them that the wickedness which is sought to be covered over by a loud and obtrusive profession of religion, is of all others the vilest and most loathsome.

Having thus presented to every man a motive to be instant and urgent in the work of his own salvation, I will now conclude by another practical illustration and application of the whole subject, in an address to parents from one of the best and most eminent of our early divines, the famous Bishop Jewell:

"Let us look upon our children as upon the great blessings of God. They are the Lord's vessels ordained to honor; let us keep them clean. They are Christ's lambs and sheep of His flock; let us lead them forth into wholesome pasture. They are the seed-plot of heaven; let us water them that God may give the increase; their angels behold the face of God; let us not offend them. They are the temples and tabernacles of the Holy Ghost; let us not suffer the foul spirit to possess them and dwell with them. God saith, 'Your children are my children.' They are the sons of God. They are born anew, and are well shapen in beautiful proportion; make them not monsters: he is a monster whosoever knoweth not God. By you they are born into the world; be careful also that by your means they may be begotten unto God. You are careful to train them in nurture and comely behavior of the body; seek also to fashion their mind unto godliness. You have brought them unto the fountain of Baptism to receive the mark of Christ; bring them up in knowledge, and watch over them that they be not lost. So shall they be confirmed; and will keep the promise they have made, and will grow unto perfect age in Christ."

CHAPTER V.

PROBATION AND REPROBATION.

TRUTH is always composed of antagonizing principles. The characteristic of all heresy is, to run out a single great principle, unchecked and uncontrolled by its antagonist principle, to the production of results that are monstrous and destructive. The Divine arrangement, and the human perversion of it, are finely illustrated by the muscular system of the human body. If but one set of muscles were kept in play, their action would produce only frightful deformity, and utter imbecility as to any useful purpose. But when the action of these is duly counteracted by the compensating force of antagonist muscles, the result of their combination is beauty, proportion, and strength.

Calvinism is an illustration of the vice just referred to. It takes a single truth, and runs it out very logically to the most disastrous consequences, without recollecting that the truth thus unreasonably pressed to such fearful consequences is, itself, controlled and modified by counteracting and antagonist truths.

The view which has now been presented of the Divine Life in the soul of man, shows the consistency and connection of the one truth of Calvinism with other great and important truths, thereby presenting the beauty and proportion of the glorious Gospel—the system in which the Church has ever instructed her faithful children.

It is true, as Calvinism asserts, that the death which sin brought into the world is a state of excision from God, the Fountain of all good, and may, therefore, very properly be called a state of "total depravity." The denial of this truth, by the opponents of Calvinism, is one cause of the continued vitality of that system. But Calvinism takes this one truth, and runs it out to conclusions as manifestly false as they are painfully revolting. Leaving out of view the connected truths which modify and control this single truth, it represents the *actual present condition* of all mankind as one of "total depravity," of utter incapacity to think or to do any good thing. But this conclusion is contradicted alike by the phenomena of universal humanity and by the spirit and the letter of revealed religion. The natural state of man is that, indeed, to which he reduced himself—a state expressed by the terms "spiritual death," "total depravity," or by any other equivalent terms. But man was not left in this, his natural condition of hopeless misery and ruin. Calvinism forgets that we are now living under the dispensation of GRACE. To the same common ancestor, whose transgression brought upon his race this death and this pollution of human nature, *was the promise made of Redemption through Jesus Christ*. It is the grace given, the new life imparted through this mediator—the second Adam—to co-exist with the old, and carnal, and corrupt nature which we derive from the first Adam, and to operate upon that nature, to the utter extinction of its vileness and guiltiness, that constitutes *the present condition of mankind a state of probation, of trial*.

Take away the fact that the Spirit of God imparts to the human race that spiritual capacity to know and to do good, which, in consistency with the illustration of the New Birth employed by our Lord, is, properly called, "the Divine Life,". and this world is no longer a place of probation—of trial for man. It can be regarded as nothing more than a sort of "prison-bounds," in which the reprobate are permitted to wander about, and to do as much mischief as they can, until God puts an end to this dreadful liberty.*

But the great truth of revealed religion, that which justly entitles the truth, as it is in Jesus, to be called THE GOSPEL —the glad news—is, that every man, through Christ, is in a state of probation, of trial, for heaven, or for hell. The corrupt nature and the Divine gift co-exist in every man, and by the choice which he makes and maintains, to be led by the one or the other, is his destiny for eternity determined. Calvinism and Universalism alike and equally deny the great truth of man's *probation in this world for an eternal state;* and both systems are therefore hopelessly at variance with Divine revelation, and with human consciousness.

By virtue of the dispensation of Grace, under which human nature is now placed—the gift of God in Christ operating upon corrupt nature—no man is "totally depraved" until he makes himself so by long continuance in sin, by deliberate rejection of the Grace of God, by driving from his soul the Holy Spirit, the source of all the good that is in man.

The early chapters of the Epistle to the Romans present to us a graphic account of Probation and Reprobation, as illustrated in personal experience and in the world's history. The endless controversy as to the character in which St. Paul speaks, "whether of himself or of some other man," and if speaking of himself, whether in his regenerate or unregenerate state, can only be disposed of by seeing that all these views are comprehended in the more general one, that the

---

* See a beautiful account of this world as a place of "probation" and not a "prison-house for man," in the work mentioned below. " Besides the traces of original beauty and subsequent destruction, there are proofs of Reconstruction o· Reorganization. (McCosh on the Divine Government, &c., pp. 78–85.)

Apostle is describing human nature in its many-sided aspects. The reconciliation of all the truth that is to be found in these conflicting statements will be apparent when we regard the Apostle as representing humanity—each single man and the whole race—and the development of this humanity under the operation of God's Spirit. That development proceeds, he says, in opposite directions, as men—whether "Jews or Gentiles"—yield themselves to be "led by the Spirit," or perversely refuse and reject that Divine guidance. It is first Probation for all, and abounding Grace, then Reprobation only for the obstinate despisers of that Grace of God that bringeth salvation. St. Paul includes in the very same condemnation, and for the same reason, the wicked Gentiles with the wicked among his own countrymen, of whom St. Stephen had said, "Ye stiff-necked and uncircumcised in heart and ears, *ye do always resist the Holy Ghost;* as your fathers did, so do ye." (Acts vii, 51.)

St. Paul exhibits the unbroken continuity of the one revealed religion, when he tells the Galatians "that the covenant" with Abraham, "that was *confirmed* before of God IN CHRIST, the law . . . can not disannul." (iii, 17.)

Christ, then, was the substance of the covenant with Abraham, and that was but a *confirmation of the previous covenant of grace,* with an added specialty, the sign of circumcision. The Christian covenant is thus expressly declared to be a continuation of the Abrahamic—the law having been interposed for a time—baptism being put in the place of circumcision And both the Abrahamic and Christian forms of the covenant are treated of by the Apostle as but renewals of the one original covenant of Grace.

To all who are not brought under the provisions of the Covenant *in its perfect Christian form,* by the preaching of the Gospel, that first gracious covenant in Christ yet remains unrepealed, the hope of all the ends of the earth, the one only ground and foundation of human probation—of this world's economy as a place and means of trial for man. The gift of the Divine Spirit to each one of the subjects of this covenant, to form in him a conscience, and to apply with effectual power the external truth which may be brought to his knowledge, is one of its essential and indispensable conditions.

I have already called attention to the fact that our blessed Lord describes the office of the Spirit, when He should come in largest measure and in fullest manifestation, to be identical with that which we ascribe to the natural conscience. "And when he is come, he will reprove the world of sin, and of righteousness, and of judgment." (St. John xvi, 8.) It is impossible to define the office of conscience more perfectly or more precisely. The Divine dweller in the souls of men, the eternal Spirit, had been executing this office from the beginning, just as Christ was "slain from the foundation of the world" for the salvation of the world, in the economy of grace. Afterwards, in the full light of the truth, for the manifestation of which there had been so many thousand years of preparation—that "God was in Christ reconciling the world unto Himself"—this same Spirit is poured forth in more copious effusion, thenceforth using specially the name and work, and righteousness of Christ as the instrument of His convincing, sanctifying, and condemning power.

That God did by His Spirit reprove the world of sin, of righteousness, and of judgment, in every age and in every nation, so that all have been without excuse, the history of the whole world and the consciousness of every human being have concurrently witnessed. The depth of wickedness to which all heathen nations have descended no more proves that they are not really the possessors of this one inestimable

12

talent, than the abounding wickedness of Christian nations proves that the three and the five talents of Gospel light and knowledge have never been imparted to them.   The fiction that is opposed to this truth, that God has ever and utterly abandoned nine-tenths of the human race to the unchecked and absolute dominion of the devil and their own depraved natures, is dishonoring to God, repugnant to the very instincts of humanity, and contradicted by the history and condition of all peoples.   This horrid fiction, if allowed at all, must include the children of these multitudes who die without actual sin.   For, if these children have only the depraved nature which they take from their parents, they must take the inevitable doom of that nature.   If they have received in no measure the Spirit of Christ, they are none of His, and therefore they can by no possibility be saved.

In the Epistle to the Ephesians St. Paul beautifully illustrates the glorious state and privileges of believers, as members of the Church of God—the body of Christ.   Yet, in this very connection, he sets forth that same process of gradual reprobation, more largely described in the Epistle to the Romans, by which the unbelieving Gentiles had resisted the Divine power that was in them for salvation.   And he expressly calls that power the "LIFE OF GOD," from which they had become "alienated" by this voluntary, and therefore criminal, submission to the evil of their nature.   "This I say, therefore, and testify in the Lord, that ye henceforth walk, not as other Gentiles walk, in the vanity of their mind, having the understanding darkened, being alienated from the life of God, through the ignorance that is in them, because of the blindness of their heart: who being past feeling, have given themselves over unto lasciviousness, to work all uncleanness with greediness."   (Ephes. iv, 17–19.)

Every expression here represents the unhappy results, in

those who love darkness rather than light, of the contest in each soul of man between the old corrupt nature and the Divine gift, "the life of God," which was in him. When their perverse choice of evil had ultimately extinguished all sense of a higher and better nature, then—"being past feeling"—they gave "themselves over unto lasciviousness, to work all uncleanness with greediness."

This process of reprobation may be going on without the exhibition of that recklessness of living described here by the Apostle. Men who refuse to recognize the Christ within them, and to nurture by a true faith the life of God in their souls, may nevertheless yield an outward obedience to most of the requirements of the Divine law. The law in such cases is simply an external rule, which the conscience confesses to be good, and to which custom, and civil law, and personal habit, produce a certain degree of conformity. A distinguished living Prelate has beautifully illustrated this sort of obedience by the similitude of a painter slavishly copying a picture set before him. Whereas, the true Artist produces from within, from the depths of his own soul, and realizes in the creations of the canvas, forms of beauty and loveliness. So the Christian, who has appropriated Christ by faith, who recognizes the life of God in his soul, and diligently nurtures that life by the heavenly food which God has provided, finds the law of God, not an external binding rule, but the very essence and principle of that life which is in him, and which he cherishes. The service of God is not then mere obedience, but the highest realization of liberty— the whole conduct and conversation in correspondence with the affections, and God's will the ruling, sovereign power in the soul.

This is the state which St. Paul describes in the words, "I am crucified with Christ: nevertheless, I live; yet not I, but Christ, liveth in me; and the life which I now live in the flesh, I live by the faith of the Son of God, who loved me, and gave Himself for me." (Gal. ii, 20.)

The Christian crucifies the old, evil nature, in will and intention, and relying on God's help, undertakes to do it effectually in deed, that so the risen Christ, formed in him by the Spirit, may be his true and better life, taking entire possession of his whole nature, and framing and fashioning it according to the perfect likeness of the new man, created in righteousness and true holiness. This life of Christ in the soul can only be sustained by faith, because faith is required to bring to the soul those continued supplies of grace ministered through the appointed channels of grace, by which that life is nurtured and developed. The Baptismal service puts the statement of St. Paul in other language—"Remembering always that Baptism representeth unto us our profession, which is to follow the example of our Savior Christ, and to be made like unto Him; that as He died, and rose again for us, so should we, who are baptized, die from sin, and rise again unto righteousness; continually mortifying all our evil and corrupt affections, and daily proceeding in all virtue and godliness of living."

Just here is one of the points of departure of the Calvinistic theology from the teaching of the Bible and the Church. That theology tells us that Christ has never been formed in the soul, has no connection with our humanity, until our own faith works the stupendous miracle of bringing Him into union with our nature, and that the union so formed is indissoluble.

Besides the many objections to this feature of the system which have already been mentioned, this particular form of expressing it is liable to the further difficulty that it destroys the very nature of faith, and makes faith to be the creator of the fact which it is called upon and professes to believe. The legitimate office of faith is, to believe and trust in the work which God has done for us and within us for our salvation; that so we may work together with God in the consummation of that salvation, by pleading urgently for more grace. But this system requires faith first to do the thing which it must believe that God has done, and thus to become the virtual author of our salvation.

True Christian faith, on the contrary, believes, appropriates, and concurs in the accomplished work of God, the Father, the Son, and the Holy Ghost, for our salvation. It recognizes the Christ formed in us by the Spirit, as the power of an ever-enlarging goodness, capable, by the diligent use of the "means of grace," of killing all vices in us, and of bringing us up from babes in Christ to the full stature of perfect manhood in Christ Jesus. This faith makes us earnest and watchful in the mighty work of our salvation. It keeps us near to Christ, in the Church, and in Providence, and helps us to aspire after the Christ in heaven, that "we may also in heart and mind thither ascend, and with Him continually dwell."

It is a blessed and transcendent mystery, this life of God, blending with the life of the human soul. And it is this life of God, in the very center of our being, that sin destroys. It is the God-man, formed in us by the eternal Spirit, whom we crucify afresh, by rejection of Him, by willful continuance in opposition to Him. Such is the force of the Apostle's expression above cited from the Epistle to the Ephesians, in perfect consonance with the entire spirit of God's Word. And what is the consequence of this war against the life of God in the soul? Gradually the perpetrator of this awful crime loses all feeling of good, all sense of shame and consciousness of wrong, and is "given over unto lasciviousness,"

and every other evil and base affection," "to work all uncleanness," and every vice of a malignant nature, "with
greediness." When we have consummated this double mur-
der of our own souls, and of the life of God within us, where
is to be our help and hope in eternity? And who will be
our helper? Has any revelation from Heaven proclaimed
another salvation? Has it told of another Savior, another incarnation, a more effective interposition between human corruption and human misery than the very life of God Himself,
communicated to us, dwelling in us, and forming in us the
sense and the love of goodness, purity, and perfectness?

In all these discussions I have assumed the universal Christian postulate, that the promise of the Holy Ghost by our
Savior Christ, and the glorious Pentecostal gift in accordance
with the promise, must be understood to mean the more
copious effusion of the Spirit, and the more perfect manifestation of His office, and of the work of Christ for our salvation; and not the gift of the Spirit for the first time, in any
measure. This last interpretation would make the Scriptures
self-contradictory, and every rational canon of interpretation,
therefore, requires the former sense. For innumerable expressions, and the whole tenor of the Old Testament, show
that the Spirit was given, and was recognized as given, to all
the people of God in all ages. The great Nonconformist,
Owen, who has written more elaborately and profoundly on
the work of the Spirit than any other person, thus expresses
the general sense of the Christian Church on this point:

"The *plentiful effusion* of the Spirit is that which was
principally prophesied of and foretold as the great privilege
of the Gospel State." "The work of Grace on the hearts
of men being *more fully revealed* under the New Testament
than before, and of the same kind and nature in every state
of the Church since the fall." "He is promised and given

as the *sole cause and author* of all the good that in this world
we are or can be made partakers of." "Although the work
of regeneration by the Holy Spirit was wrought under the
Old Testament, even from the foundation of the world, and
the doctrine of it recorded in the Scriptures, yet the revelation of it was obscure in comparison of that *light* and evidence
which it is brought forth into by the Gospel." (Vol. 1, pp.
126, 157, 159, 210.)

There is much more to the same effect. In one remarkable passage Owen clearly shows that nothing but his inveterate Calvinism, especially the dogmas of the irresistibility
and indefectibility of Grace, prevented his appreciation of
the glorious fullness and freeness of the work of the Spirit.
Arguing against the Pelagians, he says: "Now as we grant
that this spiritual renovation of nature will infallibly produce
a moral reformation of life, so if they will grant that this
moral reformation of life *doth proceed from a spiritual renovation of our nature*, this difference will be at an end, and
this is that which the ancients intended by first receiving the
Holy Ghost and then all graces with Him." (P. 219.)

Owen presents here the *gist* of Pelagianism, and shows
how that error is avoided by the doctrine that all "moral reformation doth proceed from a spiritual renovation of our
nature," and that this position is truly the doctrine for which
he so earnestly contends as against that heresy. It is need-
less to add that this position of Owen is the doctrine of this
work.

The mission of the Holy Ghost, previous to the incarnation, is more briefly and authoritatively stated in that form of
the ancient Christian Creed set forth in the Apostolical Constitutions. "I am baptized also into the Holy Ghost, that
is, the Comforter, who wrought in all the Saints from the
beginning of the world." (Book 7, chap. 41.)

Those who deny the universality of the Grace of God and of the Spiritual life which that Grace imparts, are accustomed to refer the manifest good that is in all men to what they style "*mere human virtues*"—carefully abstracting from the said human virtues all possible influence of the Grace or Spirit of God. Have these persons ever asked themselves what *virtue* is? Do they not know that all moralists and legislators have uniformly maintained that the knowledge of God and the capacity of obeying His law, is the foundation of all human obligation and of all human virtue? Human virtue is not a brute instinct. It is the conscious action of an intelligent being *doing right*, under a sense of obligation to God. It is no less than "the answer of a good conscience toward God." To affirm that a man can accomplish this without the Grace of God prompting and assisting him, is the precise expression of the Pelagian heresy.

The great English moralist, Bishop Butler, in the first three of his sermons, undertakes to tell us what may be known of the present actual condition of human nature, aside from any information derived from the Bible. He shows that there is in that nature a power to achieve all the goodness, both as to piety and morality, which Christianity requires or provides for, and that *the actual present condition of that nature is flagrantly violated*, when this goodness is not attained. This, he also shows, was the conclusion of the best heathen moralists, from the same premises. So, also, Sir Wm. Hamilton writes :

"For in man there are tendencies—there is a law—which continually urge him to prove that he is more powerful than the nature by which he is surrounded and penetrated. He is conscious to himself of faculties not comprized in the chain of physical necessity, his intelligence reveals prescriptive principles of action, absolute and universal, in the law of duty, and a liberty capable of carrying that law into effect, in opposition to the solicitations, the impulsions of his material nature. From the co-existence of these opposing forces in man there results a ceaseless struggle between physical necessity and moral liberty; in the language of Revelation, between the Flesh and the Spirit; and this struggle constitutes at once the distinctive character of humanity, and the essential condition of human development and virtue." (Metaphysics, sec. 2, p. 21.)

But this conclusion, unless taken in connection with the truths of the Gospel, as Bishop Butler intended it to be, is manifestly contrary to those truths. It is not for us to prove this here. The Church has decided it from the beginning, and that decision is sufficiently set forth in the 9th and 10th Articles. The 9th says:

"Original sin is the fault and corruption of the nature of every man that naturally is engendered of the offspring of Adam; whereby man is very far gone from original righteousness, and is, *of his own nature, inclined to evil,* so that the flesh lusteth *always* contrary to the Spirit."

And the 10th Article tells us that,

"The condition of man" is such that "we have no power to do good works pleasant and acceptable to God, without the Grace of God by Christ preventing us."

The Gospel truths, thus set forth, modify and explain the conclusion of Bishop Butler. They show the quality of man's present state, as the *fallen* but *redeemed* child of God. They point out the vitiation of his nature, by which that nature is only inclined to evil; and the gift of God's preventing Grace, by which man is enabled to resist the evil, to struggle against the flesh, to obey and love the Law of God. This is the present state of human nature, according to the greatest moralist of modern times, and according to the uniform decision

13

of the universal Church. This is the representation of human nature given by St. Paul in the first and second chapters of the Epistle to the Romans. He shows that the Gentiles were condemned because they held "the truth in unrighteousness." He traces the progress of their willful departure from God, just as we can every day see the same fatal descent, and the gradually attained supremacy of evil, in each soul of man who resists the Holy Ghost. He describes the process by which the whole Gentile world had gradually fallen into its actual condition, by sinning against light and truth, and the strivings of God's Spirit. The deterioration went on, says the Apostle, until "God gave them up to uncleanness," and "gave them up unto vile affections," and "gave them over to a reprobate mind." Just so God deals now with men. It is the same spirit, but divers ministrations.

The great Apostle to the Gentiles connects himself, in soul-stirring descriptions, with universal humanity. He stands before the world as a man; conscious of all that man had felt; and adopting for himself, and as the expression of his own experience, the very language of the great and the good men of all times, he sets forth the struggle between the good and the evil within us, which all could recognize, because all had felt it; and then he points to the Gospel of the Son of God as the necessary complement of humanity, as the effectual means of bringing this struggle to a glorious end, by giving a complete and final victory to the good over the evil. In the name of diseased manhood, as the representative of his kind, the Apostle exclaims, "O wretched man that I am! who shall deliver me from the body of this death?" Then, at this climax of the description of spoiled and perverted humanity comes from the lips of the same man, commending it to the hearts of all men, the sweet assurance of the glorious Gospel, "I thank God through Jesus Christ our Lord. So, then, with the mind I myself serve the law of God; but with the flesh the law of sin."

The Church, the visible kingdom of God, is an integral part of this blessed Gospel of Salvation. Man is born once into this world of sin and death with an evil nature, corresponding to his evil abode. Redeemed by the incarnation and death of the Second Man, he is quickened by the Holy Ghost given unto him; made alive unto God and to goodness; endowed with a capacity for holiness, with power to resist the evil of his nature and of the world, and to attain to a meetness for eternal joys. But this mere capacity of holiness, this spiritual power, this new life, which he receives *as a man* from THE MAN Jesus Christ, must, like all life, be nurtured, and developed, and trained, to its proper end and purpose, else it will become frustrate and perish. Therefore, says the blessed Savior, and therefore, says the Church, echoing her Master's words, "Ye must be born again, of water and of the Spirit." The child of God must be transferred, by the Sacrament of Baptism—by a second birth—from the world, where the evil nature alone is nurtured, into Christ's kingdom, where the new and spiritual nature may be nurtured and trained, and taught to overcome the evil, and to perfect holiness in the fear of the Lord.

This teaching of the Church is in consonance with the universal consciousness of men, and makes the Gospel to be, indeed, glad news of great joy to all people, because it shows how the struggle between good and evil, which is common to all men, may be brought in every man to a triumphant and glorious issue, "through Jesus Christ our Lord."

It is the conflict between these two powers, the earthly, sensual, and corrupt nature on one side, and the Divine Gift, the Third Person of the very Godhead, on the other, and the purposed design of this conflict—the conquest and extinction of the evil in man, and the complete triumph of the Divine, so fitting the redeemed child of God for an eternity of bliss—that explain and account for all the most striking anomalies of this strange, perplexing life of ours.

The loveliness and purity of a little child are emphatically and repeatedly employed by our Savior as the highest earthly image of a heavenly nature. But all Christian teaching, and all human observation, concur in the testimony that every child is born with a corrupt nature, the very nature that shows itself, in mature age, in the grossest forms of wickedness. Whence, then, its beauty of character, its loveliness and purity? These can only come from the fresh and full indwelling of the Holy Spirit, the author and giver of life, bestowed upon this child of Adam, to be unto it the power of a glorious immortality. There is, then, the same contest already commenced in the heart and nature of an infant of days which is to be the characteristic of its life-struggle, and the determining force of its eternal existence. To this conclusion we are shut up by the facts of the case, natural and revealed.

And this conclusion furnishes us with a full and joyous solution of one of the hardest problems of life, the sufferings of little children. Even the corrupt nature of these little ones, so blessed and so visited of God, must be purified and perfected by suffering; not for actual transgression, of which they are incapable, but that the moral nature may know, by trial and experience, the hatefulness of sin, and the pains that are inseparably connected with it. By this sharp but short experience of the dread penalty of sin, their eternity of happiness is augmented; they are washed in the same blood of the Lamb that taketh away the sin, the black, damning sin of the whole world that lieth in wickedness.

and are thus enabled to join in the song of the redeemed, "Worthy is the Lamb that was slain."

The recognition of the great gift of God—the Divine Life in the soul of man—rescues that important truth, the corruption of human nature, from the unhappy connections with which it has been too often confused, and by which it has been discredited. But unless we connect with that great Scriptural truth the *universal gift*, through Christ, of the spirit of life and light, to operate upon depraved humanity, we take away the only possible ground on which to base the appeals which the ministers of the Gospel are commanded constantly to make to the hearts and consciences of men, unconverted and unbaptized, to turn unto the Lord, to believe, to repent, to pray. We take away, at the same time, the only ground upon which the Savior of men can judge the world in righteousness, viz., that the subjects of His Grace have improved, or buried, *the talent entrusted to them.*

This universal gift is repeatedly mentioned by St. Paul in his Epistles to the Corinthians. The persons there addressed were quite as miscellaneous in their moral characters as any modern congregation that can be found. Many of them, therefore, yet needed conversion. And the sorrowing Apostle expresses his fears that after all his written exhortations he will yet be humbled when he comes to them by finding "many which have sinned already, and have not repented of the uncleanness, and fornication, and lasciviousness which they have committed." (2d Cor. xii, 21.) To a community comprising many such persons he appeals as follows: "Know ye not that ye are the temple of God, and that the spirit of God dwelleth in you? If any man defile the temple of God, him shall God destroy; for the temple of God is holy, which temple ye are." "Know ye not that your bodies are the members of Christ? Shall I then take the members of

Christ, and make them the members of an harlot?" "What! Know ye not that your body is the temple of the Holy Ghost which is in you?" "Know ye not your own selves, how that Jesus Christ is in you, except ye be reprobates?" (1st Cor. iii, 15, 16; vi, 15, 19; 2d Cor. xiii, 5.) These declarations effectually dispose of that branch of the theory which makes *Conversion* the starting point of spiritual life—the first introduction of Christ into the soul.

The "hypothetical theory" will not do here. St. Paul negatives that by describing the wicked lives of those whom he exhorts to repentance; and he urges them to repent because they are the temples of God, because they are members of Christ, and because the Holy Ghost dwells in them. The assertion that Christ is in them, and that the Holy Ghost is in them, are evidently used convertibly for the statement of the same fact. And this fact the Apostle says is true of all who are not "*reprobates.*" But by virtue of the dispensation of grace, under which human nature is now placed, no man is reprobate until he makes himself so, by deliberate rejection of the grace of God, by driving from his soul the Holy Spirit, the source of all the good that is in man. The actual present state of human nature, through the mediation of Christ, and by the gift of His Spirit, is that of Probation, not of Reprobation.

CHAPTER VI.

THE ROMISH DOCTRINE OF BAPTISM CONSIDERED MORE PARTICULARLY.

THE Papal religion is a new one, built upon the foundation of Christianity, and gradually, elaborately, and ingeniously constructed. The use made of Christianity by the defenders of this new religion is to employ the former as a support to the latter, to give it power, credit, and the apparent force of truth. One of the most common arts of Romish controversialists is to prove, with great force and vigor, some truth of Christianity, and then, under cover of that proof, put forward the modern corruption by which this very truth has been disfigured and overlaid. The Romish doctrine of Baptism is one of those first and easy departures from the truth which has been logically expanded into a formidable system of error. The following extracts from the decrees of the Council of Trent will exhibit this doctrine:

" Whoever shall affirm that the Sacraments of the new law do not contain the grace which they signify, let him be accursed." "Sacraments of the Church by which *all true righteousness is at first imparted*, then increased, and afterward restored if lost." "Whoever shall deny that the merit of Jesus Christ is applied, both to adults and infants, by the Sacrament of Baptism—that the guilt of original sin is remitted by the grace of our Lord Jesus Christ, bestowed in Baptism, or shall affirm that wherein sin truly and properly consists is not *wholly rooted up*, but is only cut down or not imputed, let him be accursed." "The causes of justification are these—the instrumental cause, the Sacrament of Baptism, which is the Sacrament of Faith, without which no one can ever obtain justification." "Justification is not remission of sin merely, but also sanctification, and the renewal of the inner man." "Therefore, when a man is justified and united to Jesus Christ, he receives together with remission of sins the following gifts bestowed upon him at the same time, namely: faith, hope, and charity." "Then, receiving in their regeneration true and Christian righteousness, as the best robe, white and spotless, bestowed on them through Christ Jesus instead of that which Adam lost by his disobedience, both for himself and us, *they are commanded to preserve the same*, that they may present it before the tribunal of our Lord Jesus Christ, and possess eternal life."

These passages contain the germ of that mystery of iniquity which has penetrated the whole Romish system, fructifying into the Sacrament of Penance, the doctrine of Purgatory and Indulgences, of Masses, and other satisfactions for the expiation of post-baptismal sin, and for the frequent restoration of the "perfect righteousness," and of the "spotless innocence" which were once bestowed in Baptism; but which, alas! are never retained by those who arrive at the age of accountability. Let us trace for a moment the progress of this unhappy growth.

If Baptism remits the party to the original state of Adam, then by a single sin he *forfeits that estate*, as Adam did; and his Baptism is no longer of any value or effect. He stands just where Adam did after his fall, and before his reconciliation to God. This consequence is seen and provided for. Upon it is founded the next step in this doctrinal system. The learned Moehler, the most profound of the recent theologians of that communion, speaking of post-baptismal sin, says, "Thereby is communion with God broken off, and the baptismal grace forfeited." (Moehler's Symbolism, p. 206.)

If the Church had not happily declared the repetition of Baptism to be sacrilege, before this doctrine was invented, the Mormon device of baptism once a week or once a month, might have been resorted to in order to restore the forfeited life in Christ Jesus. But as this Sacrament could not be repeated, the ingenious expedient was adopted of getting up a new Sacrament, to ·be in the place of Baptism, and to perform precisely the office of Baptism. Moehler therefore continues: "Hence if the sinner wish to be converted from his evil ways, he needs a new reconciliation with God, and *therefore another Sacrament;* and such a Sacrament is Penance." The Divine Sacrament is thus deprived of all real value, even while its supposed effect is so falsely magnified. It imparts but once an imagined grace, which is sure to be lost, while the human Sacrament is represented as imparting the same grace as often as it is needed. Thus the ordinary life of men is made to be a continued succession of deaths and births; of excision from the body of Christ, alternated with perfect holiness, righteousness, and purity. It is obvious that if a little discretion be observed in the administration of the supposed Sacrament of Penance, so as to repeat it in the article of death, and thus secure the new life and the perfect holiness which it confers, no man need fear the consequences of the sins and irregularities of his past life. And this acknowledged estimation of the value and effect of this rite does, in fact, account for the anomalies in the character of a Roman Catholic population.

Here is another branch of this evil tree. The pseudo Sacrament of Penance makes men righteous. And "the righteous can satisfy the Divine law by their own works, and may truly merit the attainment of eternal life," says the council of Trent.   And if these righteous persons choose to do works of supererogation, they may transfer this super- fluity of merit to less industrious sinners.   And so the "Catholic Manual" announces, "It is not less certain that the satisfactions of many saints were more than sufficient for their own sins, especially those of the Blessed Virgin Mother of God, who, although she never incurred the guilt of any sin, underwent the most exquisite afflictions and sufferings. Now the all good and just God could not allow those treas- ures of satisfactions to remain useless, which could be applied with great advantage to the other members of His Church. He therefore has given His Church the power of distributing to the faithful these spiritual gifts, according to their respect- ive wants and merits; and this distribution is effected by INDULGENCES, which therefore can be granted by him only who has received from Christ the government, and the care of the Church, together with the power of binding and loosing the faithful."

The same authority goes on to say that the Pope has been very liberal in granting indulgencies of late, "that as sin abounds grace might much more abound."   In point of fact, we know that every order and every society in that extended communion has one or more of these Indulgencies, as a part of its capital stock, which its members can apply to their own use, or to the benefit of others, for the remission of the pains of purgatory.   Thus the holiest and the purest Chris- tian acts, prayer and charity, are converted by this wretched corruption of religion into a base transaction of bargain and sale; so many prayers and so many good deeds being given for so much release of purgatorial torment.

But the notion upon which indulgences are founded—the conversion of repentance, good works, and providential suf-

ferings, into satisfactions for sin, is itself a subversion of the
Gospel; of the work of God in redemption, and of the work
of man as the redeemed child of God. It degrades the work
of God in redemption: for it essays to add to the infinite
satisfaction, which Christ has made for sin, the little and
miserably inadequate works and sufferings of men. And
God is made to stand toward his redeemed people not as a
reconciled Father in Christ Jesus, but as a rigid creditor and
judge, weighing our merits, and exacting the last farthing of
His due. To ascribe to any act or work of ours any power
to satisfy the Divine mind, as a commutation of the penalty
of the broken law, is that very heathen abomination which
degraded the majesty of the Eternal Father, and the sanctity
of His perfect law. To talk of man's satisfying a broken
law, by any thing short of its penalty, is an abuse of words
and a mockery of God. When the Almighty Father looked
upon our misery, and conceived the plan of our relief, He
did not come to the lost creature whom He was about to
save for the vindication of His justice, and holiness, and
truth. When the mercy of God moved in our behalf, it
moved with the power and infiniteness of its Divine source.
When Mercy triumphed, it triumphed wholly. Mercy found
the ransom for guilty sinners. "This is a true saying, and
worthy of all acceptation, that Christ Jesus came into the
world to save sinners." (1 Tim. i, 15.) It was only in the
infinite depths of His own nature that the Almighty could
find the price of man's redemption, and the fitting vindication of His own holy law. And there he found it perfect, sufficient, complete, wanting nothing, and incapable of addition.

This same corruption of religion perverts the whole idea
of the Christian life. It disposes of the sacrifice of Christ
as merely the cause of a certain determination in the Divine
mind, by which the Eternal Father has consented to open an

account current with His creatures, and to credit them with their penitence, their afflictions, their prayers, their works of mercy, as so much consideration paid, in part as a satisfaction for sins, and in part as the purchase of heaven. And the daily relation between God and man consists in the settling and adjustment of this account. This makes up the practical, every-day working of the system. And the great business of the minister of Christ under it, is to act as the factor between Almighty God and His guilty creatures; to settle the terms of this commerce in each particular instance; to receive the commutation, and to pass the receipts.

How different from this complicated device of priestly imposition is the Catholic doctrine, the teaching of the Bible and the Church. The Gospel of the Son of God proclaims that Christians are not enemies and rebels, who must pay the forfeiture of their crimes, but the ransomed of the Lord, the redeemed of the Holy One of Israel. The baptized members of the household of faith are no longer strangers and aliens, but children, adopted sons and daughters of the Lord Almighty. And they are not called upon to settle now the terms of their acceptance, to drive a huckstering bargain for the pardon of sin with their God and Savior. For reconciliation for iniquity has already been made. All their sins have been blotted out, all have been washed away in the fountain opened for sin and uncleanness. And now, all that they must suffer, and all that they must do—the varied dispensations of Providence, the pains of repentance, the exercises of charity, the consecration of the life to deeds of goodness and of mercy—are but parts of the healthful discipline, graciously appointed by a wise and indulgent Father to His children, to form and to mold their characters, to adapt them to their high relation, to qualify them for their station, to make them capable of that inheritance of everlasting glory to which they have been elected.

The maze of error which we have been contemplating springs from that early departure from the truth, that seminal principle of error, which represents Baptism as the beginning of the Divine Life—the first coming of the Holy Ghost, the Fountain of life, into the soul—and as the restoration of the baptized to perfect innocence, purity and uprightness.

If the first part of this proposition were true, men could not be brought to baptism at all, except upon the Pelagian hypothesis, that man retains such "relics" of his original goodness that he can love, believe, and obey the Divine Law. But this hypothesis discharges the Holy Spirit from all necessary agency in man's salvation, and was therefore by the whole Church rightly declared to be a deadly heresy. Leave out that hypothesis, and then, under this first branch of the Romish theory of Baptism, there could be no subjects for baptism at all, unless unbelieving and unrepentant sinners were dragged to the Sacrament, or brought, as the natives of East India actually were, by the Jesuit Missionaries, who surrounded them with soldiers and drove them to the Font.

CHAPTER VII.

PARALLEL BETWEEN BAPTISM AND CIRCUMCISION.

THE Covenant of Grace has been in operation ever since the first promise of a Redeemer. This covenant was made more specific in its form, and its character beautifully illustrated by the call and mission of Abraham. The same Covenant of Grace attained its full and glorious completion in Christ the Savior of the world. The peculiarity of the Abrahamic form of the covenant was the separation of that patriarch and all his successors in the faith from the world, by a solemn religious consecration and mark of difference. The visible Church of God, which before had contained the whole of mankind, was now restricted to those who received this mark of election and adoption. And because this characteristic feature in the constitution of the Church has been continued ever since, and is made perpetual under the Christian dispensation, Abraham, in whom it was begun, is called, by way of eminence, the Father of the Faithful—of all believers who are thus visibly separated from the world.

The purposes for which the Levitical law and the national covenant with Abraham had been superinduced upon the earlier Covenant of Grace, were all completed by the sacrifice of Christ. From that moment the subjects of that law were absolved from its obligations, and the former Covenant of Grace through faith, which had never been abrogated, remained, the common inheritance of Jew and Gentile. But the Jew of St. Paul's day, puffed up with spiritual pride, cast dishonor upon the God of his salvation, by rigidly restricting the grace of God to the subjects of the national covenant. According to him, circumcision was not the sign and seal of God's favor, and the introduction to peculiar blessings and privileges, but it was the actual and·exclusive bestowal of that favor of God which is life: and there was no favor, or love, or mercy, for the uncircumcised. This narrow, contracted, and technical system, the Apostle strongly reprobates in the Epistle to the Romans and elsewhere. St. Paul does not tell us that one technical and disparaging view of God's mercy had been abrogated, in order to make way for just such another. But he contends that the Jewish gloss upon the Divine institution was always untrue. He vindicates against that gloss the fullness and freeness of the Divine goodness as witnessed in the rite of circumcision, and emphatically derives the Christian Church from the Abrahamic form of the Covenant of Grace, and demonstrates the fullness and freeness of the Christian dispensation, because of the fullness and freeness of the Abrahamic.

Now, therefore, adopting the method of the Apostle, in his argument with the Jews, if we ascertain clearly the relation which our father Abraham bore to the rite of Circumcision, we shall at the same time have determined as clearly the relations which Christians bear to the Sacrament of Baptism.

1. Circumcision was the instituted way of initiation into a social body, elected to be the special people of God; and subsisting under the form, first of the family, and then of the nation. And it was to be indiscriminately applied to all males who were capable of composing a part of a family or of a nation. (Gen. xvii, 10–12.)

So Baptism is the Sacrament of initiation—the actual adoption—into the family and kingdom of our Savior Christ.

"Go ye therefore into all the world, discipling all nations, baptizing them," says the Divine commission. It is impossible for language to be more comprehensive than this.   "Discipling"—every one who has capacity to learn, in "all nations:" that is, every human being born into the world, and as soon as it is born; for then the capacity for instruction exists, and then the duty of instruction begins.   And all these, all capable of learning, in all nations, must be baptized; admitted, by solemn adoption, into the family of Christ; incorporated, by full naturalization, into the kingdom of Christ.

2. The sanction under which these related institutions were proposed.   See Genesis xvii, 14, for the sentence against those who despised circumcision: "That soul shall be cut off from his people; he hath broken my covenant."   In accordance with this we read, in St. Mark xvi, 16, "He that believeth and is baptized shall be saved."

But why, in the economy of salvation, were such tremendous sanctions attached to the performance of external rites so unimportant in themselves as Circumcision and Baptism? Salvation is a system of grace and mercy, adapted by Infinite Wisdom to man's nature and position.   It is a part of the Divine plan, contrived by this Infinite Wisdom, that all believers should be organized into that social body which God calls His Church.   The Church is an integral part of the revealed way of salvation.   It is a perpetual body corporate, organized with reference both to the spiritual condition of each believer, and to the accomplishment of the purposes of God in regard to the publication and perpetuation of the truth.   To adapt the economy of grace to man's nature, God requires the active labor and service of every man in the work of his own and of others' salvation.   And He commands every one, to whom the Gospel is proposed, to come into His Church and labor there in his appointed station, for

the fulfillment of the merciful purpose of God toward himself, and toward the whole world. To refuse, or to neglect
to do this, is to refuse or despise the mercy of God. It is
to reject the salvation of the Gospel.

3. The Prototype of Baptism, Circumcision, is called a
sign and a seal. It was a sign and seal of adoption into
God's family—of admission into His kingdom. Baptism is
just such a sign and seal. And in regard to this effect, the
Abrahamic and the Christian rite of initiation, produced the
thing which they signified. This results from the nature of
the institution and of the purpose to be effected by it. Just
as a deed is at the same time the evidence of a grant, and
the very grant itself, which passes the land, and invests the
purchaser with the title. Therefore, we say that Baptism
effects that New Birth into the kingdom of Grace, which it
witnesses, and of which it is the appointed sign.

But does Baptism actually thus accomplish all the other
things of which it is the sign and the seal? Does it confer
upon its recipient the favor of God, as well as certify that
favor? Does it recreate the heart? Does it infuse love into
the soul? Does it change a guilty sinner into a holy innocent? So says the mischievous theology of Rome. But we
have seen that this was the very corruption and degradation
of religion under the elder form of the covenant, as if its
sacraments were charms and sorceries, which St. Paul was
opposing.

Circumcision was, and Baptism is, the sign and seal of the
favor of God. But neither bestowed that favor in the first
instance, as is now strangely said. For Abraham had long
been pre-eminently in the favor of God before the appointment of this seal. Cornelius had found favor with God before he received the Christian seal of that favor. Circumcision
was, and Baptism is, the sign and seal of the imputation of

14

Christ's righteousness. "Cometh this blessedness then upon the circumcision only, or upon the uncircumcision also?" (Rom. iv, 8, 9.) The Apostle here, by a pregnant inference, affirms that this was imputed to the uncircumcised. Therefore, surely, to the unbaptized as well. Circumcision was, and baptism is, the sign and seal of the righteousness of faith; but neither bestowed that righteousness. For St. Paul expressly rules the contrary of the one: "He received the sign of circumcision, a seal of the righteousness of the faith which he had, yet being uncircumcised." (Rom. iv, 11.) And every Baptism of an adult person is a like demonstration in regard to the other. For there must be faith, formed and in exercise, as the condition of Baptism.

Thus we might go through the whole circle of Christian graces, and show that Baptism does not produce them, but witnesses the previous gift, and the continued promise, of that Holy Spirit from which they all proceed. It is the object of the Christian life so to follow the guidance of that blessed Spirit, given unto us, that all our powers and affections, all our appetites and passions, may be conformed to the will of God, and our whole nature transformed into the likeness of the Son of God.

A distinction is sometimes attempted between the participation of Christ, which is said to be the peculiar effect and operation of Baptism, and the other graces of the Spirit, which are admitted to have been given to God's ancient people, and to some unbaptized persons now. But this distinction will not stand when the test of Scripture is applied. For the Apostle tells us that all the members of the Church in the wilderness, good and bad, "did all eat the same spiritual meat; and did all drink the same spiritual drink; for they drank of that spiritual rock that followed them; and *that rock was* CHRIST." (1 Corinthians x, 3, 4.) And the same

Apostle adds, that the evil among them "tempted Christ." (Ib. 5–9.)

This parallel between the former and the later form of the Covenant of Grace leads us to the conclusion, so often reached before, that Christ is indeed the second Adam, the head and representative therefore, not of a few individuals, arbitrarily designated, either by a decree in heaven, or by a Sacrament on earth, but of the whole race of mankind: curing in that whole race, by supernatural gifts, the corruption of nature, so far as to place every man once more fairly in a state of freedom and probation. This is the great truth, the recognition of which, as the basis of all Christian doctrine, will most effectually remove the stumbling blocks which human systems have cast in our way.

This adorable mystery, the Word made flesh, is the connection of all humanity with Christ, in a union as close and as vital as that which subsists between the same humanity and the first Adam. As in the latter all the myriads who have succeeded him were included, and from him are derived, so to the Second Adam the same ALL of human nature is conjoined by the power of the Holy Ghost. In Christ is included the whole family of man for justification, *in the same sense and to the same extent*, in and to which they were included in the first man to condemnation. It is impossible otherwise to understand that continuously presented analogy between the two which runs through the whole history of salvation, and which is summed up by St. Paul in that profound and comprehensive summary of the mysteries of redemption, the 15th chapter of the 1st Epistle to the Corinthians.

This derivation of the spiritual life of Christ to the whole race of mankind, restoring men to freedom, and leading them to good, shows us how Christ hath bought us with His own blood; and yet we are permitted to choose whose servants we will be. This explains how we are freely justified; and yet by faith we are saved. How when we were enemies we were reconciled to God by the death of His Son; and yet we are continually entreated to be reconciled. How the Lord is our Righteousness; and yet without personal holiness no man can see the Lord. The resolution of all these apparent difficulties, which have so puzzled the makers of theological systems, is found in the fact that a glorious part of the work of Christ was performed for us, freely, without any agency, co-operation, or knowledge, upon our part. This is the work spoken of under various names, as the redemption, the atonement, reconciliation, justifying the ungodly, taking our nature into union with the Godhead, becoming the Lord our Righteousness. All this has been done for us, and without our agency.

But all this is not salvation, except in the case of those innocents, who, by the sole virtue of this redemption, are made holy by the inspiration of God's Spirit; and of whom it was therefore said by their Redeemer, the King of Righteousness, "Of such is the kingdom of heaven." In every other instance, all this glorious work of the Savior of men is not salvation, either to the few or the many. But it is the elevation of our common nature to the capacity of salvation; and the pledge of Almighty power to co-operate with every believer in making this salvation sure. The sole work of Christ places every man in a state of trial, and by the gift of the Holy Ghost puts him upon the vantage ground, in the contest for heaven and eternal life, against the forces of an evil nature, an evil world, and evil spirits.

This is the great central truth of Christianity, around which various systems of error have circled, each revolving in its own narrow orbit. Calvinism, Universalism, and

Romanism, alike, and equally, deny that *every man*, through Christ, is in a state of probation, of trial, for heaven or for hell. The maintainers of these systems forget that the whole race of mankind has been living ever since the fall under the dispensation of GRACE. To the same common ancestor whose transgression brought upon his race the death and pollution of human nature, was the promise made of redemption through Christ. It is the grace given, the new life imparted through this Mediator—the second Adam—to co-exist with the old and corrupt nature which we derive from the first Adam, and to operate upon that nature to the utter extinction of its vileness and guiltiness, that constitutes the present condition of mankind a state of Probation, of Trial. Reprobation is the inevitable consequence when men reject the terms of salvation, and sin away their day of Grace.

CHAPTER VIII.

TESTIMONIES TO THE UNIVERSALITY OF THE DIVINE LIFE.

EVERY age of the Church has exhibited something of that Jewish exclusiveness which held that the grace and mercy of God were restricted to their own communion, and that all the rest of mankind were only permitted to be born and to live in order that they might be the wretched subjects of the Divine displeasure. This spirit was not long in finding an entrance into the Christian Church, so that in the fifth century it was formally maintained by St. Augustine, that all heathens, and all infants dying unbaptized, were undoubtedly damned. Some persons in our day, whose principles would logically lead to this horrid conclusion, are happily enabled to supercede their principles by what they call a "charitable hope." But if that hope has no foundation in the Word of God, then it is illusory and vain; and to call it "charitable" is to arrogate to ourselves a charity beyond that of the Infinite Love. But if that hope has a firm foundation, then the principles that are against it had better be abandoned.

This severe exclusiveness is formally defended upon the ground that the Divine Word and the formularies of the Church, in stating the terms and conditions of salvation to those to whom the Gospel is preached, do not specially except from the binding force of these terms and conditions those to whom the Gospel has not been proposed. Yet such an exception is so necessary and so obvious, that the formal statement of it would seem to be improper and out of place. For the Gospel and the formularies of the Church speak only to and of those who have them.

There is one expression in our Catechism which, if rigidly and technically construed, without regard to the analogy of faith and to the most glorious truths of the Gospel, would inevitably conclude the revolting dogma of St. Augustine and his followers. The expression is, the answer of the child, that in Baptism he "was made a member of Christ, a child of God, and an inheritor of the kingdom of heaven."

Unquestionably there is a sense in which this declaration is true. The Church into which we are brought by Baptism is the mystical body of Christ. Baptism, therefore, *makes* us members of that mystical body, and, in a special and peculiar sense, *as such*, the children of God, and inheritors of the kingdom of heaven. Baptism is also the authoritative declaration, and *the specific grant to the individual recipient,* of all the benefits of Christ's incarnation, sacrifice, and mediation. So, Baptism is the solemn grant of remission of sins. But remission, or forgiveness of sins, being the mind of God toward the sinner, the sacramental or ministerial absolution is, of necessity, and by the nature of the case, but declarative— the Letters Patent—the authoritative declaration of the mind of God to the one subject of this Grace.

To make this recognition of a special relation to Christ, and this authorized grant of all the mercies of God in Christ Jesus to the recipient of Baptism, work a denial to all other persons of any participation of Christ, of any influence of His Spirit, of any filial relation to God, is one of those instances of literal and unreasoning technicality to which St. Paul seems to have referred, when he said, "the letter killeth, it is the spirit that giveth life." Such an interpretation places ecclesiastical Christianity at hopeless variance with the Bible, with the human consciousness, and with human experience.

All the parts of Revelation take for granted a certain previous knowledge among those to whom the Revelation is made. The Bible does not open with a statement of the being or attributes of God. It assumes this knowledge. So, because there is no formal statement of the immortality of the soul in the Old Testament, some theologians have strangely maintained that this truth was unknown to the ancient people of God, and that Divine revelation, before Christ, consisted only of transitory promises and threats. But if God's people had been thus ignorant, all the heathen nations would have shamed them, for this great truth ever remained an ineffaceable part of the convictions of mankind. The Old Testament simply assumes the knowledge of this truth—the universal truth which gives to the whole Revelation its meaning, force, and character. And this our Lord points out in His answer to the Sadducees.

In accordance with this mode of teaching, neither Testament tells any thing about the specific terms on which the Gentiles and the heathen, to whom the whole will of God has not been imparted, may nevertheless be partakers of the infinite mercy of the gracious and loving Father of all His children. Both Testaments assume the principle that God "is no respecter of persons; but in every nation he that feareth Him and worketh righteousness is accepted with Him;" "according to that a man hath, and not according to that he hath not."

Simply assuming this vital principle of the Divine government, without formally stating it, the Old Testament taught the Jewish Church that the Father of the faithful paid tithes to the Gentile Melchisedec, a Priest of the High God; that the wife of their law-giver, Moses, was a Gentile; that a Gentile Prophet had pronounced the most remarkable and glowing predictions concerning their nation and the Messiah; that from a Canaanite woman the Messiah was to come; that Jonah was sent to be a successful preacher of repentance to the Ninevites; that Cyrus was called to be an illustrious type of the MESSIAH—the "ANOINTED" of the Lord to bring deliverance to His people. The very dedication of the temple recognized the universal Fatherhood of God.

Notwithstanding the plain inference from these and like instances, that God was not the God of the Jews only, but the God of all the whole earth, and that His Gentile servants who used their one talent faithfully would not be unrequited, the Jews of our Savior's time had settled down into that state of odious ecclesiastical bigotry which He so frequently and emphatically rebuked.

Perhaps the most stinging of these rebukes is contained in the parable of the "certain man" who fell among thieves. The lawyer who was tempting our Savior had recited very correctly both tables of the law, according to their evangelic form, and then tried to elude the force of the injunction, "This do and thou shalt live," by raising a difficulty about the terms of the commandment. To remove this difficulty the Teacher from Heaven shows to the casuist his acknowledged neighbors, a Priest and a Levite, cruelly violating the commandment, resisting the Spirit of God, and quenching in selfishness and sensuality all His gracious influences; while the Samaritan, a man of the despised and hated race, manifests the graces and virtues of the same Spirit of love and holiness, in the most persuasive and engaging form, so that the soul of the bigoted Jew is taken captive, and he is obliged to confess that this hated alien is a brother to be loved, a child of God to be received.

Again, when the ten lepers were cleansed, how careful is our Savior to call attention to the fact that only one, and he

15

a Samaritan—a stranger—returned to give glory to God. The most illustrious instance of faith recorded in all the Gospels is by the Syro-Phenician woman, "the offspring of an accursed race," as Bishop Horsely emphatically remarks. The same blessed truth was taught by our Lord, when he reminded the Jews of the many widows that were in Israel in the time of famine, "but unto none of them was Elias sent, save unto Sarepta a city of Sidon, unto a woman that was a widow. And many lepers were in Israel in the time of Eliseus the prophet; and none of them was cleansed save Naaman the Syrian." (St. Luke iv, 25, 27.)

St. John, recording the unconscious prophecy of the high-priest concerning the efficacy of the death of Christ, speaks familiarly of "the children of God" beyond the pale of the visible Church, scattered throughout the world. The words are emphatic and very beautiful: "And this spake he not of himself; but being high-priest that year, he prophesied that Jesus should die for that nation, and not for that nation only, but that also he should gather together in one the children of God that were scattered abroad." (St. John xi, 51, 52.) And the blessed Savior Himself said to the Jews, "And other sheep I have which are not of this fold; them also I must bring, and they shall hear my voice; and there shall be one fold, and one Shepherd." (St. John x, 16.) And, refuting the Sadducees in regard to the resurrection, Jesus said, "For He is not a God of the dead, but of the living; for all live unto him." (St. Luke xx, 38.)

St. Paul, as we have seen, declares the reprobation of wicked Jews and wicked Gentiles in the same terms, and for the same cause. "Even as they did not like to retain God in their knowledge, God gave them over to a reprobate mind." (Rom. i, 28.) The same Apostle tells the Athenians that they are "very religious," and worship ignorantly the God whom he declared unto them.

The Primitive Church seems to have avoided the ecclesiastical intolerance so severely denounced by our blessed Lord. For Justin Martyr, in his Apology, speaking for the Christian people, declares their sense of the universality of the life of God in the soul of man. It appears that the heathen persecutors had attempted to defame the Christians by ascribing to them the belief that salvation was restricted to themselves. Justin replies in this memorable sentence:

"But lest any one should unreasonably object to what is taught by us, saying that Christ was born but a hundred and fifty years since, in the time of Cyrenius, and taught what we ascribe to him still later, under Pontius Pilate, and should accuse us of maintaining that all men who lived before that time were not accountable for their actions, we will anticipate and solve the difficulty. We have learned, and have before explained, that Christ was the first begotten of God, being the Word, or Reason, OF WHICH ALL MEN WERE PARTAKERS. They, then, who lived agreeably to reason were really Christians, even if they were considered Atheists, such as Socrates, Heraclitus, and the like among the Greeks; and among other nations, Abraham, Ananias, Azarias, Misael and Elias, and many others, the actions and even the names of whom we at present omit, knowing how tedious the enumeration would be. Those, therefore, who of old lived without right reason, the same were bad men, and enemies to CHRIST, and the murderers of those who lived agreeably to reason. Whereas they who ever lived, or now live, in a manner which reason would approve, are truly Christians, and free from fear or trouble." (Apology, sec. 61.)

Tertullian, in his treatise on "The testimony of the Soul," proves that God has taught to all men, of which they **give**

perpetual utterance, some of the most concerning truths of
Christianity. "These testimonies of the soul are as simple
as they are true, as trite as they are simple, as common as
they are trite, as natural as they are common, as divine as
they are natural. . . . Nature is the mistress, the soul
is the disciple: whatsoever the one hath taught or the other
hath learned, hath been delivered to them by God, who is,
in truth, the Master even of the mistress herself. What notion the soul is able to conceive respecting its first Teacher,
it is in thy power to judge from that soul which is within
thee. . . . Even when compassed about by its adversary,
it remembereth its Author, and His goodness, and His decree, and its own end, and its adversary himself. So it is a
strange thing if, being given by God, it teacheth those self-
same things which God hath given unto His people to know!
But he who doth not think that such utterances of the soul are
the teaching of a congenial nature, and the silent deposits
of an innate conscience, will say rather that the habit of such
forms of speech hath now become confirmed by the doctrines
of public books being wafted about among the people. Surely
the soul existed before letters, and discourse before books,
and the thought which is written before the writing of it,
and the man himself before the philosopher and the poet."
(De Testimonio Animæ, sec. 5.)

Bishop Harold Browne reports Clement of Alexandria as
holding "that God mysteriously worked in the Gentiles by
His Grace, using, as an external means, the imperfect instrument of their own philosophy. So that whatever good he
thought might have existed in heathens he still ascribed
to God's Grace, and therefore did not consider their goodness 'as works done before the Grace of Christ.'" (Browne,
art. 13.)

It was a sad declension from the purity of the early Church

which reproduced, in the fifth century, the intense bigotry of Jewish Pharisaism. Article 13, concerning merit *de congruo*, is directed against an awkward effort of the school-men to escape from the consequences of the Augustinian error which denied that "the Grace of God hath appeared to all men." That Grace is a free gift to all, and can not be merited or purchased by any.

Coming down to later times, we find the most influential man in the direction of the English Reformation—the martyr Ridley—declaring: "By the which oblation of Christ's body once offered up for all sinners, ALL were made perfectly reconciled, had forgiveness of sins, and were made beloved to God the Father, and heirs of his kingdom by Christ." "Seeing that some of the Gentiles, uncircumcised in the flesh, but circumcised in spirit and in heart, were of the elect people of God to salvation, we may gather that there may be of the elect of God amongst the Turks and Pagans, although they have not our outward Christian profession, as were amongst these Gentiles some better Christians than were many amongst the Jews." (Com. on Ephes.)

The good sense of John Calvin so far prevailed over his narrow system as to induce him to say: "The children of the faithful are not baptized for that reason that they may then first be made children of God, &c. But rather they are therefore received by that solemn sign into the Church, because they did before belong to the body of Christ by virtue of the promise." (Cited by Wall, vol. 4, p. 14.)

That eminent Divine, Dr. James M'Cosh, of the Scotch Presbyterian Church, quotes, with full approbation, in the paper formerly referred to, the following from John Calvin: "So often as we look into profane writers, let us be admonished, by that light of truth which shines forth admirably in them, that the mind of man, however much it may have fallen and been perverted from its integrity, is still clothed and adorned with excellent gifts of God. If we consider the Spirit of God *the sole fountain of truth*, we shall neither reject nor contemn that truth wherever it appears, *unless we choose to be contemptuous to the Spirit of God.* For the gifts of the Spirit are not reviled without contempt and opprobrium of the Spirit himself. What, shall we deny that truth shone upon those ancient jurists who set forth, with so much correctness, the order and discipline of civil life? Shall we say that philosophers have been blinded, both in their exquisite contemplation of nature and in their artistic description of her beauties? Shall we say that capacity was wanting to those who, elaborating the art of discourse, have taught us to speak in accordance with reason?"

This direct reference of all that is beautiful and true in human achievement to the immediate influence of the Holy Spirit, is an unexpected testimony from the stern but strong nature of the Genevan reformer.

Jeremy Taylor, speaking of the pardon effected by the death of Christ, thus discourses: "And this is not only a favor to us who were born in the due time of the Gospel, but to all mankind since Adam; for God, who is infinitely patient in His justice, was not at all patient in His mercy; He forbears to strike and punish us, but He would not forbear to provide cure for us and remedy. For, as if God could not stay from redeeming us, he promised the Redeemer to Adam in the beginning of the world's sin; and Christ was 'the Lamb slain from the beginning of the world.' . . . God had mercy on all mankind before Christ's manifestation, even beyond the mercies of their covenant; and they were saved as we are, by 'the seed of the woman,' by 'God incarnate,' by 'the Lamb slain from the beginning of the world,' not by works, for we all failed of them; that is, not by an exact obedience, but by faith working by love." (Sermon on the Miracles of the Divine Mercy.)

Bishop Horsley, discoursing upon that remarkable profession of faith made first by the woman, and afterward by the men of Sychar, says, "These Samaritans, who knew not what they worshiped, had truer notions of the Messiah's office, and of the nature and the extent of the deliverance He was to work, than the Jews had, who for many ages had been the chosen depositaries of the Oracles of God." And adds, "God had provided that something of a miraculous, besides the natural witness of Himself, should remain among the Gentiles in the darkest ages of idolatry. We shall find, if I mistake not, that a miraculous testimony of God, *as the tender parent of mankind*, founded upon early revelations and wide spread prophesies, besides that testimony which the works of nature bear to Him as the universal LORD, was ever existing in the heathen world, although for many ages the one was little regarded, and the other lay buried and concealed."

The discriminating sense and genial spirit of Olshausen often present to him a beautiful perception of the glorious fullness of redemption as disclosed in the Divine Word. But the influence of the reactionary evangelicalism of his time and country sometimes obscures those perceptions, and betrays him into gross inconsistencies. Here are some of his better utterances. On St. John viii, 30, 32, he thus writes: "It may, therefore, be said that the words, *to be in my word,* or, inversely, *my word is in any one,* are applicable to the most depraved person, when he experiences the power of God even against his will. *To be entirely free from the Word of God would be a predicate of the devilish.* But his gaining salvation from the Word of God depends entirely on his *remaining.* The depraved man seeks to get rid of the troublesome admonisher as soon as possible, and drives the Spirit of God away from himself."

Again, on St. John xv, 5, 8: "This idea is especially amplified in the verses now following, of which the words, *for apart from me ye can do nothing*, contain the central truth. If man could, whenever he pleased, and without the power of Christ, create in himself noble, holy inclinations and resolutions, then he could also act without Christ.   On the other hand, *οὐδὲν*, (*nothing*,) is to be taken as very emphatic. For if it be alleged that it is not absolutely all acting, but only what is good that is impossible without Christ, still it must be confessed that only that which is good is real, while evil is null and futile.   Or should it be said that man can perform *many kinds* of good actions without Christ—as, for example, the heathen did by nature the things contained in the law—it must not be overlooked that Christ, as the Logos from eternity, who *lighteth every man*, (John i, 9) is in all ages the power that excites to all good.   *Οὐδὲν*, therefore, maintains its widest signification.   No one is good but the one God, and he in whom God operates through the Son; there is none good *beside* him who is the only good."

Bishop Harold Browne, in his masterly work on the Articles, too often uses the common language in regard to Baptism, which makes it the only source and beginning of spiritual life, thus wantonly arraying universal observation and consciousness against Christianity.   But when he comes to put out of the way objections to the true doctrine of Baptismal Regeneration, he is compelled to see, and clearly states, the whole truth.   To the objection "that it is by faith we embrace Christ, and through faith receive the Spirit of God—that, therefore, to make Baptism the means of receiving Grace, is to put it in the place of faith," he answers: "It can not be that faith is requisite before any Grace can be given; for it is quite certain that there can be no faith unless Grace has first been given to generate faith. Otherwise we are inevitably Pelagians. 'The natural man receiveth not the things of the Spirit of God.' Therefore, it is quite clear that there must be some quickening from the Spirit before there can be any faith. To magnify faith so as to make it essential to the *first* reception of Grace, is to take away 'the free gift of God.' If God can not give till we believe, His gift is not free, coming down from the bounty of Him 'who giveth liberally and upbraideth not,' but is attracted (that we may not say merited) by our faith."

This, it will be perceived, refutes one of the false gospels of the day by the same arguments which I have already employed for the same purpose. I give the remainder of his reply to the same objection, because it introduces the condemnation of this opinion by two of the most eminent Reformers:

"Besides, this would go near to damn all infants. They can not have faith. Yet, unless they be regenerated, they are not within the promise of eternal life. (John iii, 3–5.) This is Calvin's argument against impugners of infant baptism. Infants, he contends, must be capable of regeneration, though they are not capable of faith; else they could not receive purgation from innate corruption. 'How,' ask they, 'can infants be regenerate who know neither good nor evil?' We reply, 'God's work is not of none effect, though not down to our understanding. It is clear that infants who are saved must first be regenerate. For, if they bear a corrupt nature from their mother's womb, they must be purged of it before entering God's kingdom, where nothing entereth polluted or defiled.'" (Institut., 4: 16, 17.)

Luther, who of all men spoke most earnestly of the importance of faith and its office in justifying, uses still stronger

language in condemnation of this opinion. He complains
that Papists and Anabaptists conspire together against the
Church of God, 'making God's work to hinge on man's worthiness. For so the Anabaptists teach, that Baptism is nothing
unless the person baptized be believing. From such a principle,' he says, 'it needs must follow, that all God's works are
nothing, unless the recipient be good.'"

In noticing the next objection, Browne puts an extinguisher
on the Romish theory of Baptism, and consequently on that
opinion which his previous loose language had seemed to
countenance.

"A fourth objection is as follows: In the case of adults it
is admitted that baptismal grace will not be bestowed on such
recipients as come in an unbelieving and impenitent spirit.
But if there be already repentance and faith, there must be
already regeneration, and therefore regeneration can not be
given in baptism.

"Here, again, the misunderstanding results from difference
of definition. The Church calls the grace of Baptism by the
name of regeneration, for reasons already specified; but she
does not deny that God may work in the souls of men previously to their Baptism. But that *spiritual life* she does not
call *the new birth*, till it is manifested in the Sacrament of
regeneration. We must remember that the terms *new birth*
and *regeneration* are images borrowed from natural objects,
and applied to spiritual objects. In nature, we believe life to
exist in the infant before it is born—life, too, of the same
kind as its life after birth. Nay! if there be no life before
it is born, there will be none after it is born. So, the unbaptized may not be altogether destitute of spiritual life; yet the
actual birth may be considered as taking place at Baptism;
where there is not only life, but *life apparent*, life proclaimed
to the world; when the soul receives the seal of adoption, is

counted in the family of God, and not only *partakes* of God's grace and mercy, but has a covenanted assurance and title to it." (Art. 27.)

The Fathers of the American Church, with that commanding breadth of intellect which belonged to the leading minds of this country at that eventful period, and with an intimate knowledge of the real thoughts and perplexities of educated men, not possessed by ordinary theologians, were far more distinct, clear, and Scriptural, in their conceptions and statements of the relation of Baptism to the way of salvation than their contemporaries elsewhere. They gave to the language of Scripture and of the Church, in regard to Baptism, a natural and consistent meaning, which does not involve the double absurdity, first of dividing children and men who think, feel, and act precisely alike, into two contrasted classes, the one having the life of God in the soul, the other utterly destitute of that life; and then calling upon the persons who compose the latter class to perform the very highest acts of spiritual life—to believe, repent, and turn with the whole heart to God.

I have formerly cited Bishop Seabury—the first Catholic Bishop in the United States—upon the meaning of the terms Life and Death, with special reference to the fall and restoration of man.

In one of his published sermons he says: "The first intimation of a Savior to deliver-man from sin and death was made to Adam when God said, 'The seed of the woman shall bruise the head of the serpent.' This promise being made before Adam had any posterity must include the whole human race." (Vol. 1, p. 96.) And in another place, "To this Baptism, and the regeneration therein signified, it was that our Savior referred, when he showed his surprise at the dullness of Nicodemus in not apprehending his discourse:

'Art thou a master in Israel and knoweth not these things'—
that Baptism is the figure of and represents a *new* or *second*
birth?" (Ib. p. 110.)

It is in the paper formerly quoted, and which remained
unpublished until 1858, that Bishop Seabury treats profoundly and thoroughly of this great subject. A few extracts must suffice us:

"No sooner had man sinned than God *was in* Christ, reconciling the world—human nature—*unto Himself*. . . .
The seed of the woman, said God, *shall bruise the serpent's
head*.

"If nothing more was meant by this expression than that
some great punishment should be inflicted upon the old
Serpent who had beguiled Adam, it would have had little or
no influence upon the recovery of mankind. Something
wanted to be done *within* man—*in the very center of his
being*—in order to save him. He had gotten a crooked, perverse, and serpentine nature, which required to be bruised,
crushed, brought to nothing in him, that the holy, heavenly
nature which he had lost might be renewed in him.

"Every word of God is attended with power. He that said,
'Let there be light, and there was light'—He now, as I take
it, imparted to Adam, and consequently to his whole posterity, a new principle, or sensibility of goodness, called *the
seed of the woman*—something of the holy nature of Christ—
in order to make it possible for Adam to recover again that
holy nature which he had lost. This shows how Christ was
the Savior of men before He personally appeared in the world;
because He was in them the Bruiser of the serpent, the Cor-
rector of their evil tempers and passions, and the Author and
Finisher *of all the virtue and goodness that showed itself among
men*.

"To cultivate and bring to perfection this principle of good-

ness, which was in man like a seed in the earth, was the end
and design of all the laws and religious institutions which
in different ages God gave to mankind, and which have varied
according as their exigencies required, till, in the fullness of
time—that is, when His infinite wisdom saw best—He sent
His Son really and visibly to take the fallen human nature
upon Him, in order to accomplish its redemption."

"I have already observed that a Divine Principle, or a
sensibility of goodness, was imparted to Adam when God
gave him the promise of a Savior, the Seed of the Woman.
This sensibility of goodness is the only foundation of virtue
and holiness in man. Without it he would have no capacity
of either. To bring this to perfection in man is the end and
design of all that Christ hath done.

"In the same proportion that this is cherished and attended
to it will grow and increase; and in the same proportion the
fallen nature will decline and die away. But if it be checked
and suppressed it will become weak, and the evil lusts and
propensities of our fallen nature will gather strength.

"This principle God always loves, and always elects,
because it is something of His own likeness and nature. He
can not turn away from it nor reject it. Its breathings after
Him He always regards, and always meets its tendencies toward Him."

"If we attend to the Scriptures, and study honestly our
own tempers and dispositions, it will be no hard matter to
distinguish what the influences of the Spirit are, nor to determine when we have them. *The fruit of the* SPIRIT, said St.
Paul, *is love, joy, peace, long-suffering, gentleness, goodness,
faith*—meaning, here, fidelity or faithfulness—*meekness, temperance.* Where these tempers and dispositions are, there
undoubtedly is the Holy Spirit; because He can not produce
these fruits where He is not. And if these virtues are the

fruit of the Spirit, then all wishes, desires, and endeavors after these virtues are influences from the Spirit. And, by parity of reasoning, all holy desires, and virtuous purposes, and pious wishes, are from the same Spirit. When we comply with them, and turn our minds to fulfill them, we co-operate with the Spirit, we are led by the Spirit. But if we check, and suppress, and turn away from them after evil purposes and designs, we quench, and grieve, and drive away the Spirit."

Tradition tells us that that man of wondrous power, Bishop Ravenscroft, of North Carolina, was especially clear in his teachings upon this subject. His few published writings contain only such general expressions as the following. In his answer to Dr. Rice, he said: "And I will here take leave to ask this learned reviewer, to what purpose he would press the doctrines and duties of the Gospel on, or in what method he would proceed to produce the conversion of a fallen being—absolutely unregenerated?" Again, he says: "Show us, if you please, upon what principle of reason or religion it can be said to any fallen creature, debarred of all benefit from the atonement of the Cross of Christ, 'believe in the Lord Jesus Christ and thou shalt be saved?'"

In yet another place: "Regeneration is a special grace, certified to us in the Sacrament of Baptism; conversion is a subsequent operation of the Holy Spirit upon the practical sinner, and it is inconceivable even without previous regeneration."

It will be observed that Bishop Ravenscroft, in both these places, uses the term Regeneration to express that universal participation of Christ, that spiritual life, which precedes the new birth in Baptism, as, he says, *it must precede conversion.*

One of the ablest theologians that the American Church has produced, Bishop H. U. Onderdonk, of Pennsylvania, treated of "Man's Infection of Nature" in three elaborate articles, of which the following sentences express the general conclusion upon the subject of our examination:

"But for Christ we should have no light in our souls, and be in entire depravity. Through Christ, however, a measure of light is restored to all men, the moral sense, moral obligation or conscience, moral ability; and thus in all men depravity is tempered with some degree of goodness. Nevertheless, our taint of nature is so inveterate that the carnal mind remains in us, even after it is overcome by the new and better mind produced by the Sanctifier; it remains in us, and wars mightily against His gracious workings. Only by His energetic, and constant, and unwearied striving is sin even then prevented from having dominion over us."

Upholding the agreement between Article 9 and "the deep and vital doctrine I have endeavored to secern from gratuitous error," the Bishop adds:

"Both phrases (in the Article) in the true doctrine of original sin, refer to what that inherent depravity 'the flesh,' man's 'corrupted nature,' is in itself, unaffected by the interposition of Christ: i. e. depravity, in or by itself, is nothing but depravity; and that mere depravity 'lusteth always against the Spirit,' it can do nothing better; and even when the Spirit conferred by Christ conquers it, it still remains through life a rebellious prompter. Through Christ and the Spirit it can be overcome and kept under; but without this Ransom and this Light, granted, however, to all, the moral infection hath no antidote, and can not be other than perpetually virulent."

It will be observed that all these witnesses in the American Church are especially clear and definite in the statement, that all goodness in man comes from the influence of God's Spirit—from that divinely assisted new nature in man which wars against the flesh—the old, corrupt nature This is the point in the conception of the Divine Life in the soul of man which has seemed to be most difficult of reception. A distinguished living Prelate, to whom I am indebted for many beautiful and forcible suggestions, says of this statement: "If so, there is no difference but in degree, none in essence and kind, between the goodness of the Saints and that which lingers in the most corrupt of mankind, and the line of separation in the day of judgment is only one of more, or less, of the *preponderance* of good or evil. This is my great difficulty in your work; and I suspect this is at the root of all the honest and unbiased opposition that it may have encountered."

To be so fully sustained against this fairly stated objection by the illustrious witnesses just referred to, and by the great moralists, Bishop Butler and Sir William Hamilton, is very gratifying. And all who are equally fair and candid as the kind objector above quoted, will, perhaps, be willing to concur in one conclusion, when they remember that all the statements of the Divine Word make the question of good and evil in men one of "degree," of the "preponderance of good over evil," *during the time of probation:* but that at the final judgment it is no longer a question of "more or less," but of the entire loss by the obstinately impenitent of all that made them capable of probation in this life.

The wise and the foolish virgins alike went out with their lamps lighted, and with oil of the same quality in their lamps. But the foolish made no provision for a future supply, and when the Bridegroom came their lamps were "gone out." The unprofitable servant who hid his lord's money, received a talent of equal value with each of those which had been delivered to his fellow servants. But the talent which he had failed to improve was taken from him, and *then* he was cast into outer darkness. And in the formal description of the last judgment, it is apparent that the righteous have fully exercised, and so developed into saintliness, those kindly affections which all admit to be the common possession of mankind: "Inasmuch as ye have done it unto one of the least of these my brethren, ye have done it unto me." While the wicked have so quenched in sensuality, selfishness, and crime these same affections, that God has withdrawn His Spirit, and given them over to a reprobate mind: "And these shall go away into everlasting punishment; but the righteous into life eternal." (St. Matt. xxv.)

I have the pleasure of presenting here the testimony of the late Rev. Samuel Farmar Jarvis, D. D., L. L. D., whose praise is in all the churches. In a letter to me, dated February 4, 1851, a few weeks before his death, and probably the last letter he ever wrote, he says:

"I am sure it will gratify you, as it has gratified me, to find that your views of the Divine life in the soul of man are fully supported in my history. Permit me to call your attention in particular to p. 12, that *all* the descendants of Adam and Eve WERE BORN UNDER THE GOSPEL COVENANT, and consequently had the Divine life given them through Jesus Christ; and to the striving of the Holy Ghost, p. 17, and note to Gen. vi, 3. I might refer to many other parts which support your doctrine fully; and, therefore, as far as history could with propriety enter into doctrine, will be found serviceable to you. Is it not strange to see how theories bias men's minds? Pelagianism denying the prevenient grace of God. Romanism doing in effect the same thing. Calvinism limiting the grace of God and the extent of human redemption. How admirably does the Catholic Church, as exhibited in the teachings of the Prayer-Book, show forth that clear and steady light of the Gospel which blends all into the harmony of truth."

16

The plain and perspicuous statement of the truth by this venerable and distinguished scholar but expresses the profound convictions of the able men of his day, the Fathers of the American Church.*

I will conclude this array of testimony with the language of another noble witness. When the first edition of a part of this work was published, in 1850, the current theories of the day on the subject of Baptism, hinging on the Gorham controversy, presented an apparent opposition between moral science and Christian truth. Such a discrepancy brought a heavy and undeserved reproach upon Christianity, of which we are still reaping the sad consequences. Soon after this publication the late Bishop Otey, of Tennessee, wrote to me, expressing his cordial concurrence in all the views I had presented. In this letter he says: "I am satisfied that the views which you entertain do away effectually with the whole difficulty between the Bishop of Exeter and Mr. Gorham. They are both wrong, in my opinion, and so I have said freely and repeatedly to my Brethren of the Clergy in Tennessee, and I was meditating a Charge to my Clergy upon this very subject when your essay appeared." To show the identity of his views with those of the essay, the Bishop then kindly furnished me with copious extracts from a Sermon which he had frequently preached, in and out of his diocese. Large por-

---

*The late Rev. Dr. Daniel Burrhans, of venerable memory, took the warmest interest in the effort of the Author to reinstate this great principle of the Gospel in its proper place in the estimation of Churchmen. At the age of 88 he commenced a correspondence with me on the subject, which was continued occasionally until his death. In one of these letters he says, referring to Dr. Jarvis: "That my late and venerable friend, of sacred memory, should set his seal, in the hour of death, to the truth of the Divine Life in man, I consider altogether Providential, and designed to disperse the intervening clouds that have obscured the Light of Lights. It is a truth that must and will prevail, to the sending back Calvinism to the shades of Manicheeism, from which Austin introduced it in his dispute with Pelagius."

This doctrine was powerfully expressed by the lamented Flavel Mines, in describing his own escape from darkness to light.

tions of this Sermon have been furnished to the public on several occasions. A very few passages will suffice for our present purpose: "To be cut off from all communion with God, the source of all goodness and happiness, is, to an immortal spirit, DEATH, in the most awful meaning of the term."

After speaking of the incarnation and sacrifice of Christ as the means of our restoration, he adds:

"And now, the very first blessing which results from this arrangement (the redemption in Christ Jesus) is, the *restoration of man's spiritual capacity.* There is that in him, *the gift of God in Christ,* which enables him to perceive, and perceiving, to love and venerate the perfections of God—which enables him to discern between good and evil—which qualifies him to receive instruction, and when instructed, and according to the measure of instruction, to determine in his own mind, at the instant of performing any action, whether he is doing right or wrong. This, by some, is called the Moral Sense; by others, Conscience; by Solomon, 'the candle of the Lord.' By whatever name you call it, it is that restoration of a spiritual capacity, by which the moral character of man is made susceptible of improvement, and it is the free, unmerited gift of God in Christ to man—to all mankind—to every human being endowed with a rational soul; and in this subordinate sense all men may be said to be regenerate. For thus argues the Apostle: 'By the righteousness of one, (that is Christ,) the free gift came upon all men unto justification of life.' He 'is the true light that lighteth every man that cometh into the world.' . . . And now, as the next step in the arrangement of Divine Wisdom for our recovery, we are to consider what purpose the Church answers for this end. You are to remember that the nature of man is yet sinful—his nature must be changed and made holy, otherwise the first step for his restoration avails him nothing."

He then refers to the office of Baptism:

"Here, first of all, an acknowledgement is publicly made of the interest which the child has in the salvation of Christ. Next the seal of the covenant giving assurance of that interest is affixed; and lastly, the benefit of this relationship is declared by the words, that the 'child is regenerate and grafted into the body of Christ's Church.'" . . . "Regenerate, not in the subordinate sense of which we spoke before, as applicable to all mankind in the restoration of their spiritual capacity by the undertaking of Christ, but *regenerate* as having received (more) grace in Baptism to exert an influence upon its moral character—as partaking (in larger measure) of that Holy Spirit which animates the Church as the soul does the natural body—as being placed in a state in which all needful helps are assured to it, to perfect holiness in the fear of God—where it may be guarded and protected from all the enemies of its peace, or strengthened against their assaults, and preserved to God's heavenly and eternal kingdom. Hence we say that the child or person baptized is translated from the kingdom of darkness into the kingdom of God's dear Son: and this change of state we denominate *Regeneration*. The term is used analogically, from the resemblances between the circumstances of the natural and spiritual birth."

The Bishop then traces the analogy between the natural and spiritual birth even more minutely than it has been already done in this work. The Bishop, in his letter, adds:

"The foregoing will suffice to show that we at least are perfectly agreed as to our views of this deeply interesting subject. Without these views I confess my inability to meet the Anabaptist in argument and defend infant Baptism

Under any other aspect of the whole subject I see no ; how from babes we are to attain the stature of men in Christ Jesus. There is one other analogy used by the Apostle upon the subject, very striking, which, if I mistake not, utterly overthrows both the opposing views of the Romanists and Calvinists. It is that of the graft. Now if the *graft be dead*, in vain may you attach it to the stock. It must have some life. And so the germ or principle of spiritual life must exist in the soul—planted there by God—before the dew of Divine Grace can impart its fructifying influence."

A living Prelate, another pupil of the great Ravenscroft, has expressed the same view, in a published sermon, in the most powerful and graphic form. And I might multiply these testimonies almost indefinitely. Enough have been given to prove that in this reconciliation of Christian doctrine with moral science and with human consciousness I have been guilty of no "private interpretation," but that this teaching is catholic in the truest and highest sense of the word.

The term, Divine Life, in contradistinction to corrupt nature, is employed to express the *spiritual capacity*, imparted to every man, to know and to do good, in precise conformity to the term NEW BIRTH, applied by our Savior and by the Church to Baptism. This use of the term Divine Life, in *this* connection, is necessary, in order to illustrate the meaning and to exhibit the force of the solemn assertion thus made by our blessed Lord, and repeated ever since by His Church.

Both these terms are almost indissolubly associated in the minds of many persons with other important truths as their legitimate expression. And words become sacred in their habitual association, and, as Bishop Browne observes, "we almost as readily part with a truth as with the word by which we have known that truth."

The misappropriation of these terms in the popular theology is another of the sad legacies which Protestantism has received from Romish error. For many ages the Church used the language of our Lord in its proper meaning, as one expression of the fundamental fact, that the Church of God is an essential part of the revealed way of salvation. But when Regeneration—the new birth in Baptism—came to be represented by the schoolmen as an infused grace, making the recipient pure, sinless, and holy, the continental Reformers, instead of returning to primitive usage, retained one-half of this Romish corruption and repudiated the rest. They continued to associate the terms Divine Life, Spiritual Life, Regeneration, and New Birth, with a highly exalted state of the moral affections, and dissevered them altogether from their original connection with Baptism. The result of this change was soon seen. Baptism became, in popular regard, a mere formal ceremony, of little or no value, and the Kingdom of God was utterly ignored as any part of the revealed way of salvation. The bitter fruits of this theology are but too apparent.

As long as we continue to use these words in the exclusive sense given to them by the popular theology, our minds will be more or less confused and bewildered in the mazes of that theology; and still more distracted by a different use of the same terms in the Scriptures, in the formularies of the Church, and in all Christian antiquity. Far better will it be to return habitually to that primitive use, and then express the truths which have been erroneously associated with these terms by their appropriate terms, as conversion, renewal, renovation, sanctification, growth in grace, Christian progress, holiness, righteousness, and such like.

Those indeed who adhere to the phraseology which separates the new birth altogether from Baptism, and identifies it with the conscious conversion of the adult subject, can not be reconciled to any other use of the related terms, Divine or Spiritual life. But all who accept the term NEW BIRTH to express the meaning given to it by our Savior and by the Church, will see that the use of this term to signify the introduction of a redeemed child of God into the kingdom of God by Baptism, requires, for the sake of congruity, that the corresponding and precedent truth—the quickening power of the Holy Ghost previous to Baptism—should be expressed by the related term, Divine Life, or Spiritual Life: and they will find no difficulty in adjusting all the views they have been accustomed to entertain of the life of God in the soul of man to this Scriptural phraseology.

CHAPTER IX.

JUSTIFICATION BY FAITH.

HERETOFORE I have described the beginning of the way of salvation without using that important but much abused expression, Justification by Faith. This omission has been intentional; because the phrase has been so tortured and misapplied that the use of it is calculated to produce confusion, rather than clearness of conception, in the minds of those who are trying to escape from the mist and darkness of much of the popular theology of our day. But having stated now, in other Scriptural language, what a man must first do to be saved, and distinguished that truth from some prevalent errors, my readers will be better prepared to appreciate the true meaning and force of this expression. It is important that the phrase should be understood; for it conveys a great truth, and is continually recurring in the Bible and in Christian theology.

Justification by faith only is often used by St. Paul in emphatic condemnation of that heathen corruption of religion which the Jews had imitated, and which was therefore almost universal. This corruption consisted in the conversion of the typical sacrifices, which foreshadowed the "Lamb of God that taketh away the sin of the world," into a real propitiation and satisfaction for sin; and in attributing a meritorious efficacy, deserving of eternal life, to those imperfect works of goodness which men are enabled, by the guidance of the Holy Ghost, to perform. To this gross corruption the whole tenor of revealed religion is opposed. St. Paul argues against it with impassioned vehemence, and frequently declares that Justification is the free gift of God to condemned and perishing sinners; and that it can be appropriated by faith only: that human satisfactions, and human merit, are ideas utterly incongruous with the actual relations between God and man.

But this corruption of religion springs from the deep-seated pride of the human heart, and is therefore constantly recurring. We have seen how prominent a place it occupies in the Romish system of Divinity. It pervades and characterizes every part of the new religion which, by that communion, has been built upon the old Christian foundation. The Reformers, therefore, were bound to protest most earnestly and vehemently against the prevalent and gross corruption of their own time. Thus the doctrine of Justification by faith only became the watch-word of the Reformation, and the sharpest weapon of offense against the heathenish abominations of the new religion. This naturally led to the use of this expression in after times, by many persons, as a mere party phrase, with little understanding of its real meaning, or of the corruption of religion to which it was opposed. One thing that has contributed to keep these persons forever reasoning in a vicious circle about the doctrine of Justification, is the fact that this word is employed in several distinct senses in the Bible. Without looking to the context to see, in each instance of its use, what is the precise meaning intended to be conveyed, the right meaning in one place is arbitrarily fixed upon, and all other passages of Scripture in which the word occurs must be tortured to bring out that same meaning. Precisely the same process is applied to the

17

other figurative terms of the Bible, leading in every case to like confusion and indefiniteness. As it is not probable that this abuse of Scriptural language will ever cease, and as different men will fix upon different meanings of Justification as the exclusive one, variant theories of Justification may always be expected. It will help us to a clear understanding of this subject to consider these different meanings.

Justification and its equivalent terms are indifferently applied in the Bible to three distinct classes of persons.

1. They are used to express the great act of redemption which was wrought for all humanity, and which entitles human nature to that gift of God—the Holy Spirit—from whose power alone every man derives a capacity for salvation. For, as the 10th Article says, no man can "turn and prepare himself, by his own natural strength and good works, to faith and calling upon God." "We are bought with a price," "justified freely by His grace," describes the glorious work of Christ, performed freely for all mankind, without any knowledge or co-operation on their part. Man is bought, indeed, with the precious blood of Jesus Christ. He is bought out of slavery, redeemed from the bondage of sin and death into the liberty of the children of God. By this purchase only does man re-acquire the freedom to choose between good and evil, between life and death. To this effect are such expressions as the following: "For as in Adam all die, even so in Christ shall all be made alive." "The first man Adam was made a living soul, the last Adam was made a quickening spirit." (1 Cor. xv, 22, 45.) "God commendeth His love toward us, in that while we were yet sinners Christ died for us. Much more, then, being now justified by His blood, we shall be saved from wrath through Him. For if, when we were enemies, we were reconciled to God by

the death of His Son; much more, being reconciled, we shall be saved by His life." (Rom. v, 8, 9, 10.)

In the last cited passage the words "justified" and "reconciled" are used convertibly to express the universal atonement; and this atonement is urged to prove that Christ will continue to be sufficient for those who trust in Him. The 18th verse of the same chapter is still more direct. "Therefore as by the offense of one, judgment came upon all men to condemnation, even so by the righteousness of one, the free gift came upon *all men unto justification of life.*" "God was in Christ, reconciling the *world* unto himself, not *imputing* their trespasses unto them." (2 Cor. v, 19.) And upon this foundation the Apostle beseeches the Corinthians "to receive not the grace of God in vain," saying, "Behold now is the accepted time; behold now is the day of salvation." (2 Cor. vi, 1, 2.) Upon this same foundation must every minister of the Gospel base the like exhortations to men.

The effect here expressed, not only by the word Justification, but by other kindred forms of speech, may be called, for the sake of distinction, the first Justification. With this man has had, and can have had, nothing to do. Faith here has no operation. It has been done for man entirely without his assent or consciousness—of the free mercy of God—free and universal as the act of creation.

2. There is a frequent application in the Holy Scriptures of the term Justification to a second class of subjects. For as the Justification already spoken of bestowed on man the supernatural power to work together with his Maker for his own salvation, so the very first, and altogether indispensable exercise of that granted power, must be faith in the reality and sufficiency of the provision made for salvation. This second Justification is offered to men upon condition that they accept it, and become parties to the covenant of grace,

of which it is an essential feature. Faith, therefore, not by any arbitrary appointment, but in the nature of things, is a necessary prerequisite in man, to enable him to become a party to this covenant. When we hear the glorious Gospel of the Son of God, and, with conscious mind, believe and trust in the way of life which it reveals, expressing our faith in the instituted Sacrament appointed for that purpose, then our formal adoption into the family of God, our admission, as His recognized children, to the unrestricted use of all the means of salvation, is called Justification.

This is Justification by faith only. "Therefore, being justified by faith, we have peace with God through our Lord Jesus Christ: by whom also we have access by faith into this grace wherein we stand, and rejoice in hope of the glory of God." (Rom. v, 1, 2.) Here man begins to concur with God in the matter of salvation. Faith had no part in the first mentioned Justification. But here it is essential, and it is, in one sense, alone. It is the only grace that is here required, or that can be exercised, in the very act of appropriating the merits of Christ. Faith is here the hand put forth to take the mercy that God vouchsafes. All personal merit is here disowned and worthless. Our sins and our ruin alone brought a compassionate Savior from the skies, to take upon Him our nature, that He might rescue it from pollution and sanctify it to God. A contrite sense of this our sin and utter ruin, is the only plea with which we can come before the Mercy Seat to receive the grace of pardon and adoption. The offer of any thing else—the tender of any righteousness of our own would be vain, impertinent, and presumptuous. It is this Justification by faith only which stands in direct antagonism to the heathen and Romish corruption of religion, that presumed to bring human merits and human satisfactions into the relations between a merciful God and pardoned sinners

In describing the instrumentality of faith in justifying the ungodly, I have passed by that most trifling of modern disputes, which attempts to get up an opposition between faith and its external expression in the Sacrament of faith. Baptism is the consummation, the completion of the act of faith. It is so appointed because man is composed of soul and body, and both must concur in all his actions to give them completeness and integrity. It has been seen that Justification is one of the terms of the covenant of grace. How must men become parties to that covenant? Almighty God has dealt with man, in this regard, according to his nature. In every covenant the interior consent of the mind of the parties is the principal thing. But in every covenant that which gives efficiency to the interior assent, is the external and appointed expression of it. So deceitful is the heart of man, so rapid, fleeting, and evanescent are the operations of his mind, that, until his purposes are made palpable, and reduced to some corporeal form and expression, he himself cannot be sure of their nature and efficacy ; and they are, in fact, inchoate and imperfect. So we determine, in regard to one another, in all the relations of life. So our Heavenly Father has determined for us, in regard to the various parts of the dispensation of grace. He requires the outward expression of the inward thought of the heart. Where, indeed, that outward expression cannot be made, the Just One will not require it. But where the opportunity of such expression is afforded He does require it, and it is for our benefit that He should do so. He has so condescended to our nature and to our infirmity, as to enter into covenant with each separate person, by a special and particular outward act.

God has not deemed it sufficient to make a general proclamation, once for all, of His mind and will with regard to the salvation of the human race ; but He has chosen and ordained

a class of men to stand forever as His representatives, and
upon His part, and in His name, to make, seal, and ratify,
with each man who will assent to the same, the precious covenant of grace and life in Jesus Christ. Shall man be too
proud to meet his MAKER in the like form of covenant?
Shall he requite the condescension of God by drawing himself up upon his dignity, and affirming that the interior assent
of his mind is sufficient, and should be satisfactory to the
Almighty?

This is the strange reasoning of some men. But is it not
apparent that the outward and instituted mode of entering
into covenant with God by Baptism never should have been
separated from the Faith, of which it is the ordained and
appointed expression? Baptism is not opposed to faith. It
is the instituted expression, at once of God's pardoning mercy,
and of the sinner's faith, humbly receiving that mercy. So
it is treated every where in the Holy Bible. So it was regarded in the Holy Church throughout all the world, until
a querulous disposition and a transcendental philosophy
began to corrupt this part of Christianity, and to sever the
things which God had bound together. St. Paul could not
make this separation. He says, "For ye are all the children
of God by *faith* in Christ Jesus. For as many of you as
have been *baptized* into Christ have put on Christ." (Gal.
iii, 26, 27.) Here Baptism and Faith are used as synonymous. They are different parts of one whole, and the word
which expresses either part is used for the whole. And in
this short, emphatic passage, each word is employed convertibly to designate the whole effect expressed by both.

3. There is a third legitimate application of this word
Justification and its equivalents to yet another class of persons. It is to those who, having been justified by faith only,
and received into God's family, go on to "lead the rest of

their lives according to this beginning." Or, if by any invincible obstacle some have been debarred from the instituted expression of their faith in Baptism, they at least strive to concur with the members of the household of faith in all things possible to them. All who faithfully endeavor to conform their hearts and lives to the principles and rules of the Gospel, using diligently all accessible means of grace and growth, seeking continually for more and more of the Holy Spirit as the power of God unto salvation, gradually put on holiness. Mortifying all their evil and corrupt affections, and daily proceeding in all virtue and godliness of living, they grow in grace, follow the example of their Savior Christ, and are made like unto Him. When these faithful souls come to appear before the bar of God they will be justified, because they have done the works of God; because they have improved the talent intrusted to them; because they have on the wedding garment of purity and love; because they are truly re-instated, by the operation of His Spirit, in the image of their Savior, the perfect Man.

CHAPTER X.

THE DOCTRINE OF ELECTION.

THE most profound mystery of natural religion is the apparent opposition between the omnipotence of God, determining all things, and the freedom of man. §1. DIVINE DE- This is a mystery of our being, and it presents CREES AND HU- itself as strongly to the simplest as to the MAN FREEDOM. most cultivated minds. It is a difficulty which occurs in our earliest conceptions of human nature, and remains in all its force to the latest moment of our lives. The minds of children are always confounded by this mystery; for it is presented to them as vividly as to the philosopher. No solution of this problem is possible to our present faculties. It is a mystery; and it must remain so until the powers of man are enlarged in a higher state of being.

But the mind of man is impatient of mystery. That spirit of inquiry, beneficently bestowed to enable man first to comprehend and then to control the hidden forces and capacities of nature, leaves its appropriate field of operation, and adventures here upon that mystery of Divine and human concurrence, where knowledge is unattainable, and where all human perspicacity is at fault.

Some minds, morbidly intent upon this inscrutable mystery, and unwilling meekly to acquiesce in an ignorance which is inevitable, become shattered and crazed in their earnest struggles to see light where God has not said that there should be light. Other minds, more superficial, but equally impatient of this Divine mystery, think that they have found a solution of it, and a final determination of the whole matter, when they make one of these truths override and destroy the other: when they make the Omnipotence of God, not to co-exist with, but to take the place of the freedom of man, by resolving all human actions into the decree of the Almighty. This is no solution of the mystery, although intended to be so. It is simply the denial of the existence of any mystery. It is an entire leaving out of one of the terms of the problem. It is a subversion of a first truth of our being. Instead of a deep philosophy, as it calls itself, it is but a specimen of the facility with which men can be put off with a show of reason, in place of reason itself. This is the way in which whole nations, and many hard and seemingly profound philosophies and systems of religious metaphysics, have disposed of this mystery.

This pretended solution of an insuperable problem has exercised the most pernicious influence upon vast multitudes of people in our own country. It is a difficulty which is presented with equal force to all minds. The easiest way of getting rid of it is to acquiesce in that delusive determination which makes it no difficulty at all, and at the same time takes away from human nature the *oppressive sense of responsibility*, by resolving all events into the predestination of the Most High. Many persons are actually presenting this vain speculation as an excuse to themselves for the neglect of the plainest and simplest duties of religion.

The common use which is made of this pernicious philosophy is a sort of half conscious resting upon one or both of these fancies. 1. That blind and undistinguishing trust in the mercy of God, which takes it for granted that he will not arbitrarily determine other than an easy and tolerable condition to the creatures He has made, and over whose destiny he exercises unlimited control. 2. That if God should intend our condemnation, we at least would be consoled by the thought that the result was one which we could not avoid. These fancies might be correct enough if they were at all applicable to our case. Revealed religion shows that they have no sort of application to human condition or destiny.

§2. THE GOSPEL DOES NOT ENTERTAIN, MUCH LESS DECIDE, THIS PROBLEM OF NATURE.
The way in which revealed religion deals with this deep mystery presents another beautiful instance of that analogy between the Word and the works of God, which shows the identity of their origin. Nature offers no solution of the problem. But every man of sound mind is compelled, by his moral constitution, to lay the problem aside, and to act, in all the practical conduct of life, as if there were no such mystery. The most determined fatalist takes care of his own life, of his own health, of his own well-being in every respect, just as if he had never heard or dreamed of a Divine decree. The ordinary course of nature and the constitution of the human mind absolutely require that every man should ignore the imagined existence of any compulsory Divine influence over his actions. This is one revelation of God's will in regard to our practical entertainment of this mystery.

The Gospel is another revelation of the will of God in regard to the practical conduct of human life. Like the natural revelation, it says nothing about the mystery involved in the co-existence of Divine predestination and human freedom. It leaves that mystery untouched and unconsidered, and simply points every man to his duty, assuming for him a power to perform it. The whole Christian dispensation is founded upon the postulate of human freedom, just as the whole course of the world, in the Providential government of man, is founded upon the same postulate.

Christian religion assumes in every man a WILL, enslaved indeed by nature, but made free by the inspiration of the Most High, through the redemption that is in Christ Jesus; and which may now, therefore, turn to good as well as to evil. It recognizes the natural impotence of man to keep the moral law. But revealed religion is a plan of intervention between the Divine law and our impotence. It is an elaborate system of *means* skillfully and wonderfully adapted to our enfeebled and depraved condition; designed to remedy the evils, and to remove the corruption of that natural condition, and to restore man to the capacity of obeying perfectly, in the strength of Christ his Savior, the law of life and happiness.

The most striking representation of this meaning of Divine Revelation is conveyed to us in those numerous parables by which our Lord illustrated the nature of His kingdom of grace. They all announce and confirm the same great truth; but that truth is perhaps most clearly and emphatically expressed in the parable of the talents. The wicked and slothful servant in this parable probably represents the very class of persons who allege the Divine predestination as a reason why they should do nothing in the work of their own salvation. These people say that they can not fear, and love, and trust in God, as the Divine law requires, and therefore they think it will be unjust for God to condemn them for not doing those things which He gave them no power to do, and which had been already fixed by His predetermination. The parables referred to very plainly expose the futility of this objection, by showing that the things in regard to which we allege a want of power, are not the things for which we shall be judged at all.

Christian religion is the revelation of Divinely efficacious

means and instrumentalities for the removal of human infirmity, for the cure of human corruption, for the recovery
of an apostate creature to the favor and likeness of his Creator.   The means and instrumentalities thus offered to us by
revealed religion are the talents bestowed upon every man to
whom this religion is proposed.   When we come to give an
account of ourselves to God, the question will not be, whether
we have kept the whole law? but, how have we employed the
talent absolutely given to us?   How have we acted in regard
to those things which were clearly within our power?   There
will be no place for controversy about Divine predestination
or human infirmity.   For the only question will be as to the
employment of means over which we have the same control
as we have of our daily locomotion.   We will not be asked
whether we love God with all our hearts; but whether we
have been accustomed to kneel down to pray to Him for His
grace; whether we have obediently submitted ourselves to
the teachings and strivings of God's Holy Spirit, which has
so often urged us to consider our ways, to repent us of our
sins, and to come, through Jesus Christ the Savior, to the
throne of grace for pardon and acceptance.

The opportunity and the power to do these things are the
talents for which we will be called upon to give an account.
These talents have been given.   They are certainly, by our
own undoubted consciousness, as entirely under our unlimited
control as are the movements of the hand and arm.   To go
to church is as much within our power as to stay at home or
to walk about the streets.   To kneel down and pray to God in
His house is as certainly within our control as, indolently
and irreverently, to retain our seats during the time of prayer.
It is clearly by a determination of our own will whether, at
lying down to rest or rising up to labor, we will recognize
our consciousness of a God, and humbly commit ourselves to

Him, or whether we will be as the Atheist, who knows no God. These are the things, in regard to which we will be questioned; and it will be vain and impertinent, upon such an arraignment, to allege our opinions about the Divine decrees, or to complain of the imagined hardship of the Divine government. The slothful servant in the parable tried this evasion: but out of his own mouth his Lord condemned him. He was only inquired of as to the talent that had been given to him. In his very plea he confessed to the fullness of his power over that talent. He had hid the talent in the earth, of his own will, contrary to the interest and intention of his Lord. The same will, rightly exercised, would have put out that money to the usurers, for the benefit of his Master. So, our refusal to use the means of grace is, itself, evidence enough that we had the power to use them.

The Universe is composed of minute and insignificant atoms. The mightiest results are made dependent upon the concurrence of the most trifling causes. So it is in nature. And so in Grace. The Savior of the world has opened for man a way of access to heaven, to happiness, and to God, which consists of successive steps on our part, each of them minute, and of little seeming consequence. Each of these steps, in its order, is placed entirely, and beyond all question, within our own power, and subject to our free and unrestrained action. The power to take the first, and any successive one of these steps, is the talent given to us. No person in the world ever entertained a doubt about his absolute control over the doing or the leaving undone these little things. The consciousness of every man has assured him of his unqualified freedom in these particulars, with a certainty which all the reasonings in the world cannot confute. Instead of employing the talent certainly committed to us, we fix our attention upon the great results of the Christian life—love, holiness, purity—and say that we cannot accomplish these great things, that God has predetermined these mighty results. But the Judge before whom we are to appear will not institute the slightest inquiry about those things, in relation to which we ever alleged a want of power to compass them. The only account demanded of us is, in regard to our performance, or neglect, of those little and easy duties which were certainly within our power. The talent given to us, our use or abuse of that, alone will be inquired of. God's destined purpose, in appointing the varied means of grace, will not be required of us at all. That is His own work, and He will see to its accomplishment. The result of the means we are commanded to employ is indeed beyond our control, and therefore we will not be questioned at all in relation to it. Where we have no power there will be no accountability. But an account must be rendered of those things over which our power is known, by ourselves, to be supreme. We must give account of our use or neglect of those means and instruments of grace which are placed as entirely within our control as are the means and instruments of our daily calling.

This does not authorize a merely formal and perfunctory employment of the means of grace, resting in them as an end. Although we cannot command the result of those means, which is God's own work, yet to use them, without reference to that result, is no faithful use of them at all. As moral beings we must work together with God in the whole business of salvation. And God works effectually in us, only when we use the means of grace, with a constant and earnest looking to, and striving after, the end which they are designed to accomplish—the sanctification of the soul. This is the Christian's life work. And to this sanctification he must be continually reaching forward. This is the mark of his high calling, toward which he must press with earnest longing.

There was, in our Lord's day, a Jewish doctrine of election, very different from the metaphysical dogma we have been examining, and just as far from the truth. This maintained the absolute and unconditional election of the Jews to eternal life, as the peculiar and favorite people of God—the circumcised members of His Church. Many of the parables of our Savior are directed against this doctrine of election.

§ 3. Jewish Doctrine of Election.

But there is a true doctrine of election, of which the Scriptures make frequent mention. There is an election, in the economy of grace, corresponding with that in the economy of Providence. Here again the two kingdoms of nature and of grace are alike, because they proceed from the same infinite Fountain of goodness and truth. This true election, in either kingdom, is, to privileges, to honor, to dignity, to station, and to responsibility commensurate with the gifts and advantages bestowed.

§ 4. The Bible Doctrine of Election.

By the dispensation of Providence one man is elected to encounter the trials and temptations of wealth ; another to the harder estate, but not to the sorer trials and temptations, of poverty. The election of one man puts upon him the obligation to make a right use of a large fortune ; keeping and disbursing it in the fear and to the honor of God. The abuse of this trust causes rich men to be proud, sensual, vain, selfish, and atheistic. The poor man, who must struggle through life for the means of living, is disciplined to hardness, and to a certain strength of character, apart from his own exertions. The abuse of his position is apt to produce envy, discontent, dishonesty, groveling thoughts, feelings, and practices. Which of these two classes of evil affections produce the greatest degree of unhappiness it would be hard to say. Thus, in the necessary inequalities of the social scale, there are, as the Scripture phrases it, vessels to honor and to dishonor. The election of Providence determines to a large extent the position which each one is to occupy: but each place and each station has its own duties, its own responsibilities, and its own rewards.

So precisely in the Kingdom of Grace. The election here, for which God has given to His creatures no account, and no reason, determines whether we shall be born in a Christian land, of Christian parents, and placed by Baptism in the fold of Christ. But there is no such irrespective election to eternal life. The spirit and the letter of Divine Revelation assure us that eternal life is dependent upon the use which men make of the means of salvation accorded to them. The election is, to the possession and enjoyment of more or less of the instituted means of salvation. It is an election to privileges, to honor, and to responsibility. And that which ultimately equalizes this distribution of the Divine favor, and vindicates His government as without partiality, is the principle, that unto whom much is given of him only will much be required; that the possessor of five talents must render a just account of each one of the five and of its increase; while the man with one talent will only be held accountable for that one and its reasonable increase. Many of the parables, as we have seen, illustrate the principle, that the use which men make of the privileges to which they are elected, and not the extent or value of those privileges, will be the measure of their reward.

The Jewish doctrine of election has been reproduced in the Christian Church, and may always be expected, because it springs from one of the most powerful tendencies of the natural heart. This is the tendency to seize upon externals, rest in them, and worship them. It displays itself universally. The rich man fastens his affections upon his wealth, regards it as an end—the great end of human life—and not merely as the means of doing good. He looks upon him-self, not as the steward and trustee of this wealth, but as its sovereign owner, unaccountable to any power in heaven or in earth for its employment. And he very often magnifies him-self, and worships himself, as a God, by reason of his uncon-trolled possession of this instrument of power.

So again in the kingdom of Grace. Men look upon their privileges, their election to honor and responsibility, as an end, rest in that supposed end, and magnify themselves for these privileges, forgetful of the only purpose of them. This is in truth to destroy the whole character and value of the means of Grace. Their character and value consist in the fact that they are *means*, instruments, of Grace. They are the agencies by which God's Holy Spirit works in us and with us, to recreate us in the Divine image. To divorce this purpose, this end of these appointments, from the means of Grace, resting in them as an end, is to annul their virtue and efficacy.

Christian people are "elect through sanctification of the Spirit, unto obedience, and sprinkling of the blood of Jesus Christ." (1 St. Peter i, 2.) Their election is "unto obe-dience," and that application to their souls of the blood of Christ, by which God has been reconciled to them, vouchsafed to them the pardon of all their sins, and adopted them into His family as His dear children. This election "unto obe-dience" places its subject in a condition to heed the exhorta-tion of the Apostle: "Work out your own salvation with fear and trembling, for it is God which worketh in you both to will and to do of His good pleasure" (Phil. ii, 12–13.)

God works in us, but He works in us as intelligent crea-tures, who must work together with Him for the accomplish-ment of the same glorious end. That end is to make us

18

"new creatures in Christ Jesus," by "mortifying and killing all vices in us," by subduing every unholy affection, and re-instating us in the image of Christ our Savior. To leave out of view this end of Christian life, not to reach continually forward toward the attainment of that end, to be satisfied with a mere perfunctory performance of the routine of external religious acts, is to degrade religion to a sort of mechanism, and fatally deceive the souls of all who are guilty of this desecration. This resting in the form of Godliness, while regardless of its power, is a most obstinate as well as a general disease. It is hard to remove, because it is so congenial to the heart of man. It satisfies the mere religious instinct, and puts a quietus upon the conscience, while it leaves the passions to seek their gratification in unrestrained indulgence.

CHAPTER XI.

THE BAPTISM OF INFANTS, AND THE NURTURE CONSEQUENT THEREON.

THE subject last considered forms an appropriate introduction to that view of Christian progress which must now be presented. In Baptism every child is taught to say, that he "was made a member of Christ, a child of God, and an inheritor of the kingdom of heaven." They were made members of Christ, because they were, by Baptism, incorporated into "the Church, which is His body, the fullness of Him that filleth all in all." (Ephes. i, 22, 23.) The members of Christ are necessarily, by virtue of that relation, the children of God; "and if children, then heirs; heirs of God, and joint-heirs with Christ." (Rom. viii, 17.)

I shall not attempt a formal refutation of that pernicious and destructive heresy which denies the seal of God's covenant of love and mercy to the most precious subjects of that covenant—the dear children for whom Christ died. The word heresy is advisedly applied to this corruption of religion, because it directly contradicts and annuls, in regard to more than one-half of the subjects of redemption, that article of the Christian Creed which teaches us to "believe in one Baptism for the remission of sins."

It is true that God, of His infinite goodness, does not tie His mercy to His sacraments; and so, the children of His

love, dying in infancy, are saved by the blood of Christ,
notwithstanding the folly of those natural guardians who
withheld from them the blessed sign and seal of this saving
mercy.   But God does tie us to His appointments ; and
thus to set aside the most solemn of those appointments can
only be excused upon the ground of invincible ignorance.
The plea that the child may be saved without Baptism is
but a limited application of the Quaker argument, which
puts away the Sacraments entirely, and of the Infidel
argument, which dispenses with the whole Christian revelation.   God, by His Spirit, can cleanse the soul, says
the Quaker, without these external agencies.   God can be
merciful, says the Infidel, without the instrumentality of a
Christ, or of a revealed religion.

If God has appointed " one baptism for the remission of
sins," original and actual, Christians have no alternative
but to apply that Sacrament to all the subjects of redemption who are capable of it.   Now, as we have seen, Baptism
is the seal of the forgiveness of sins, and the actual adoption of the baptized into the family of God.   Children are
not only capable of receiving these benefits, but they are
the best and fittest subjects of them.   They are *capable*
of receiving the inestimable benefit of adoption or new
birth into God's family, just as they were capable of birth
into an earthly family ; because the common object of the
first and of the second birth is, that the children may receive that tender nurture which is necessary to their well
being.   And young children are the *fittest* subjects of the
new birth, because the nurture thereby secured to them
will be much more effectual to its destined purpose, the
formation of a Christ-like character, than the same nurture
applied to the adult subject, whose habits and affections
are fixed in enmity to God and goodness.

In the kingdoms of nature and of grace alike parents and children are bound together by the strongest and tenderest ties. As parents give to their children a sinful nature, so every child of man has been *born* under the covenant of grace in Christ Jesus. And during the earliest Patriarchal dispensation, the first-born of every family was, by that mere primogeniture, consecrated to the Priesthood. (Numbers iii.)

When it pleased God, in His infinite wisdom, to restrict the visible Church to a single family and nation, the Sacrament of initiation into that Church was specially appointed to be administered on the eighth day after birth. And the Sacrament then to be administered is emphatically called in the New Testament " the seal of the righteousness of faith." The Apostle tells us that the GOSPEL was preached " unto Abraham, saying: In thee shall all nations be blessed." . . . . . " That the blessing of Abraham might come on the Gentiles through Jesus Christ." (Gal. iii, 7, *et seq.*)

Now, one part of the blessing of Abraham, to which we are heirs, was to have his children visibly and sacramentally united with him in the covenant of redemption. By what enactment of Christ was this precious part of the blessing of Abraham taken away from us, his Gentile children? How and when were we disinherited as to that blessing? For many ages the children of Abraham enjoyed the inheritance in full as one nation.

When our Savior came to fulfill the promise to Abraham in its fullest extent, " In thee shall *all nations* be blessed," He uses in the great Charter of the kingdom the very terms of the promise: " Go ye, therefore, and disciple ALL NATIONS, baptizing them."

It is strange that any one, with this Charter before him, should ask for an express command to baptize infants. The command here is just as express as language can make it.

The command is precisely the same for infants as for men and women. The word nation includes them all alike, and the command applies with the same force to each one of these essential constituents of a nation. That the Apostles and their successors for fifteen hundred years so understood the commission, is certain ; for in all that time the Christian people continued to use and enjoy this portion of their inheritance, " the blessing of Abraham," without question, by the baptism of their children with themselves into the fellowship of Christ's body.

Suppose it had been otherwise, and that the Apostles had so grossly misunderstood the commission of their Lord as to exclude the children from His earthly kingdom, and to refuse to them the seal of adoption and favor. The New Testament tells us how bitter and relentless were the Jews in their opposition to the infant Church. Besides this, it informs us of a jealous and active party of Judaisers in the Church itself, urgently insisting upon the requirements of the ancient law. Now, if the Apostles had been guilty of an innovation so great, and shocking alike to natural feeling and to the religious convictions fostered by their whole national history, as, for the first time in the economy of redemption, to exclude the children of believers from the kingdom of grace, what excitement, what clamor, what stern conflict, would the innovation have occasioned ! The hostile Jews would have used this strange and unnatural feature of the " Galilean heresy " as the most potent weapon with which to overthrow it. In the Church itself innumerable complaints and questions would have arisen out of the same novelty. The New Testament, and early ecclesiastical history, would have been burdened with the discussions necessary for the settlement of this vital point. We find them full of questions about the terms of social intercourse between Jewish and Gentile converts, about days, and meats, the eating of blood and things strangled, but not a whisper about the exclusion of children from the kingdom.

Is not this silence of Scripture upon such a subject the strongest practical demonstration that such exclusion was never known or thought of in the Christian Church, until in the twelfth century one Peter de Bruis, a crazy fanatic, held that those who died in infancy could not be saved, and therefore ought not to be baptized?

Even if it were possible to suppose that the exclusion of children from the kingdom of God could have been effected, without the slightest intimation of such a change in the writings of the Apostles, and in early ecclesiastical history, how are we to account for the unanimous return to the ancient economy of that kingdom, by the sacramental admission of the infant heirs of salvation to the fellowship of the kingdom, without controversy, and without objection? When "infant sprinkling," as they classically call the baptism of children, first commenced, where were the Baptist preachers to sound the alarm, and fill the world with their indignant remonstrances? Ecclesiastical history, the whole range of Christian literature, give no sign. Such a class of people as Baptist preachers had never been heard of for fifteen hundred years after Christ. The men and their notions arose together, at Munster, in Germany, as a part of the froth from the seething caldron of excitement and frenzy in the sixteenth century.

The other fancy about Baptism, which originated with the same parties, that it can only be administered by putting the whole body under the water, is sufficiently disposed of by a single fact. Baptism, as a ceremonial purification, was the daily practice of the whole Jewish people. It was ordered, in a vast number of instances, by the Divine law, and still more largely used by the people as a voluntary service. The Priests, ministering at the temple, were obliged to be baptized twice every day; and the people, on every return from the market, or other place of concourse, where they might have contracted ceremonial uncleanness, baptized themselves at the door of their dwellings before they entered the house. Of this we have frequent mention in the Gospels. Not one of these innumerable Baptisms was by immersion. There were no facilities for such a practice, and the thing was both repugnant to the Divine law and unknown to the people. The baptism of the Priests in the temple service was effected by turning a cock, from which the water flowed upon their hands and feet. The baptisms constantly recurring at private houses were performed in the same manner from water-pots of stone, conveniently placed for that purpose. (St. John ii, 1–10.)

When, therefore, our blessed Lord, as the predicted PURIFIER, who should " sprinkle many nations," (Mal. iii, 2, 3. Is. lii, 15. Ezek. xxxvi, 25, 26,) adopted this familiar ceremonial of purification, as the sacrament of initiation into His kingdom, He must have been understood to mean those modes of baptism to which the people were accustomed. And all the subsequent notices of baptism in the New Testament—as of the baptism of three thousand persons in a few hours—correspond with this conclusion, and cannot, without violence, be reconciled with any other. The prevalence of immersion in after ages may have arisen from the same feeling which led the Church at Corinth to celebrate the Lord's Supper by eating and drinking to surfeiting and drunkenness. That is, that, if water is good for purifying, the more we have of it the better. The application of this fancy in regard to one Sacrament was made in time for an Apostle to rebuke it. The Jewish converts in every city probably prevented for a long time any innovation upon the established mode of Baptism. That this innovation was not so early as is generally supposed, may be inferred from an expression of Eusebius, Anno 324, describing the spacious baptisteries, in which large classes of candidates for baptism were instructed. He says: "Which buildings were erected for those who require yet the purification and the sprinklings of water and the Holy Spirit." (Ecclesiastical Hist., Book 10, ch. 4.)

The fancy of these good but misguided people about the exclusive validity of one mode of baptism, is a small matter compared with the fatal heresy which strikes at the very foundation of the kingdom of God, and at the deepest meaning of the Gospel, by excluding from the Church those infant subjects of redemption, which are the Church's hope and her most inestimable treasure.

To refuse the Sacrament of adoption to the children of God and the fellow-heirs with Christ; to withhold the seal of the covenant of grace from the recipients of grace; to deny the outward token of reconciliation with God to those who are partakers of the nature of Christ; to shut out from the kingdom, as strangers, aliens, and enemies, those who were appointed to be fellow-citizens with the saints; to exclude from the family and household of God, and from the holy nurture and the succors of heavenly grace there provided, the youngest and feeblest members of the family; to fence off from the fold of Christ the lambs of His flock, is a sub-version of the Gospel plan of salvation at its foundation—is a virtual surrender, as far as one false principle can go, of the most impressible and helpless portion of Christ's redeemed, to the dominion of sin, and to the power of the Devil. St. Paul tells us (1st Cor., x, 2) that all the Israelites were baptized in the cloud and in the sea; but according to

19

this theology, the children should have been left on the other side, to become the unresisting prey of Pharoah and his hosts.

The Church which has preserved and transmitted to us the Holy Bible, the Sacraments of Christ's institution, the Ministry of His appointment, and the Faith "once delivered to the saints," has always joyfully complied with the command of her Lord to "suffer the little children to come unto ME, and forbid them not, for of such is the kingdom of heaven." Gladly she receives them, and earnestly she exhorts the godfathers and godmothers of these heirs of salvation, diligently and faithfully to bring them up in the nurture and admonition of the Lord. She puts upon these guardians the charge, so to inform and cultivate the minds, and so to guide and chasten the affections of Christ's loved ones, that, at the appointed age of discretion, they may be brought, with a glad and willing mind, "to the Bishop, to be confirmed by him." The effect of a true Christian culture will be, to induce the children to offer themselves a living sacrifice to God, renewing in their own persons their vows of allegiance, and receiving anew, with new succors of heavenly grace, the assurance of the forgiveness of all their sins, and of God's fatherly love and goodness toward them.

Christian nurture is always at first successful. I have never known the child who had been taught the elements of Christian knowledge, who was not religious—who did not show a tender susceptibility to the influences of religion. But religion is a life. And the unfailing law of all life is progress or decay. There is no such thing as a stationary point in the natural or in the spiritual life. Those who do not go forward will inevitably go backward. Growth or decline are the only alternatives.

CHAPTER XII.

CONFIRMATION.

THE Apostolic rite of Confirmation tells the Church's estimate of the necessity of progress in personal religion. It is appointed for all who, having been born again in Holy Baptism, of water and of the Spirit, have arrived at the age of discretion, and have been growing hitherto. It thus marks distinctly a stage in the heavenly progress of the soul. It tells of the new dangers and of the increased responsibilities of the heir of salvation, in the new career which a new period of life ushers in. It teaches, therefore, the necessity for higher and further helps and assistances of the Holy Spirit, for this new position. And it provides those succors of Divine Grace for the pressing exigency of the occasion. It warns most faithfully against the danger of ceasing to go forward, or of thinking to stand still. The folly and impossibility of this position are involved in the very issue then presented by the Church to her children. For, when the question is thus distinctly put to each one, Will you engage now to serve your God, or will you turn from that service? Will you acknowledge your Creator and Redeemer, or reject Him?—the negative answer to these inquiries exposes at once the backward and downward course which the soul is taking. The refusal to go forward is a deliberate self-devotion to go down, on that facile and slippery descent, which stops for a time at simple irreligion, and terminates at last in apostasy and reprobation.

The Church thus presents to her younger members a blessed opportunity, at this crisis of the religious life, to try themselves, to see what manner of spirit they are of, to ascertain what progress they have made, and if they find themselves careless and indifferent about this holy rite, and their soul's condition; or if their hearts are averse to it, and to its solemn vows; then they have reason to be greatly alarmed at their state.   Their only safety is to be thus faithfully warned of their danger, and to fly from their impending doom, to the refuge set before them in the Gospel.   Their dreadful fate, if being warned, they will not turn, is no contingency.   Their punishment is involved in their crime.   If they will not go forward to heaven, they are assuredly going backwards to perdition.   Progress is the law of the religious life.   That law must be obeyed, or its penalty is sure.

Confirmation, or the " laying on of hands," takes its place in beautiful symmetry in the Scriptural order of Sacraments and Ordinances.   Baptism is the sacramental recognition of the whole, undivided Trinity, when the children of God are formally adopted into His family, and made citizens of His kingdom, by the invocation of His mystic and blessed Name, Father, Son, and Holy Ghost.   The Eucharist — the Lord's Supper—is the special recognition and constant memorial of the person and work of the adorable Being designated as the Second in this mystic name, the eternal Son, our blessed Savior and Redeemer.   In like manner, Confirmation specially witnesses and sets forth the Person, work, and office of the Holy Ghost, in the Divine economy of man's redemption. Leave out this special recognition of the Holy Ghost, and you see how sadly marred is the symmetry of the Divine institutions.   But the Divine care did not permit it to be left out. St. Paul, in that sublime epistle in which he treats of the deepest mysteries of religion, places this Divine institution in the very place in the circle of Christian verities which it would most appropriately occupy, and which all the other Scriptural notices of it show that it did actually occupy — that is, immediately after Baptism. " Therefore," he says, " leaving the principles of the doctrine of Christ, let us go on unto perfection, not laying again the foundation of repentance from dead works, and of faith toward God, of the doctrine of baptisms, *and of laying on of hands,* and of resurrection of the dead, and of eternal judgment." (Heb. vi, 1, 2.) That the laying on of hands in ordination is not here meant, is certain, from its position among the most elementary truths common to all believers, and from the fact that the Ministry or Priesthood is one of those profounder mysteries of the Gospel to which the body of the Epistle is devoted. That the doctrine of laying on of hands is an elementary principle, compared with the doctrine of sacrifice, as contained in the Lord's Supper, is also shown by the elaborate exposition of that doctrine of sacrifice in this Epistle. In accordance with this arrangement, we find all the incidental notices of Confirmation in the brief, inspired record of the first planting of Christianity. Every-where it follows Baptism, either immediately, if an Apostle is present, or as soon afterwards as an Apostle visits the place where believers have been baptized. For, uniformly, it appears that ordinary ministers might baptize, but only to the Chief Ministers was committed the duty of performing this holy rite. And the Holy Ghost emphatically sealed, with the Divine sanction, all that was thus done, by restraining the fullness of His gifts until this part of the counsel of Heavenly Wisdom had been fully obeyed. Confirmation, like Baptism, was an ancient practice in God's earthly kingdom, under the former dispensation, adopted by our blessed Savior as a part of the orderly arrangement of His Church in the new dispensation. It is another testimony to the fact that such external order is essential to the right working of every institution which is to operate effectually upon mankind. In the eighth chapter of the Acts of the Apostles, verses 5, 6, 7, 8, 14, 15, 16, and 17, we have the first account of the Christian administration of this solemn ordinance. In that passage we see that the newly ordained Deacon, St. Philip, went abroad, preaching the Gospel, working miracles in attestation of its power, and baptizing all who believed. The Holy Ghost was the necessary and efficient Agent in all this work. But He did not visit these converts in the plenitude of His power until the Apostles at Jesusalem, hearing of this success of the Gospel, sent some of their own number for the purpose of completing, by an act which belonged only to their own office, that which had been so well begun.

That we must interpret the expressions here, and elsewhere in the New Testament, in relation to the gift of the Holy Ghost, as referring only to that plenitude of the Spirit's power, and fullness of His manifestation of the truth, which are peculiar to the Christian dispensation, and especially connected with this Christian ordinance, is very certain. For to give to these expressions a more stringent meaning, and to consider them as affirming that the Spirit of God was now, for the first time, bestowed in any measure upon men, would make them contradict the whole tenor of the Divine Word, and put them into direct conflict with the faith. That faith teaches us that all the true piety which had ever existed in the world had proceeded from the inspiration of the Spirit. There is no canon of interpretation more important or necessary than this, that all the parts of a document must be taken together, and each part so modified by the rest that a proper meaning may be given to the whole. These very passages illustrate strongly this principle. For, without going beyond them to the other parts of the Word, they contain within themselves the necessary and intended limitation of the general expressions employed. According to the analogy of faith, the persons upon whom the Apostles laid their hands could not have exercised repentance and faith so as to have been proper subjects of baptism, without the previous gift of the Holy Ghost. We are absolutely compelled then to understand the gift of the Holy Ghost at Pentecost, and after the "Laying on of Hands," as a larger measure of His influences, and a more glorious manifestation of His power.

There is another instructive account of this rite of Confirmation in the Acts of the Apostles, xix, 1, 2, 3, 4, 5, 6. In this passage, also, a mistake has been made by some intelligent persons in relation to the formula of Baptism, from a neglect of the canon of interpretation above mentioned. Because the historian tells us that these disciples of John the Baptist were now "baptized in the name of the Lord Jesus," it has been strangely assumed that this holy name alone was used in the administration of this baptism. But this would be to suppose the Apostle, and those who were with him, to have violated, deliberately and wantonly, the very commission from which they derived their authority. The truth is, that St. Luke, *writing for the Church and to Christians,* who understood that faith in the Lord Jesus necessarily included faith in the undivided Trinity, simply uses this expression to let us know that Christian Baptism was then administered in the only authorized formula by which it could be administered.

The beautiful and expressive rite of Confirmation is religiously practiced by all the Christian people in the world, except a few Protestant denominations. And of the Christian bodies who, from various causes, but principally from their want of the Apostolic Order of the Ministry, have lost this Divine institution, all of any note have expressed, in some form, their sense of the Divine authority of the ordinance, and their desire for its restoration. The Rev. B. Wistar Morris has published a very curious and valuable little book, containing a number of these testimonies. Few works could be circulated with more advantage than this little volume.

If God has graciously deigned to make this and other provisions for our salvation—thus wisely adapting the plan of salvation to the nature of its subjects—shall we insultingly say, "It is unnecessary, we will obtain this salvation in some better way?" The Holy Spirit, given unto us, and given according to the established provisions of the economy of grace, is the sole efficient Agent of salvation. This has been true under every dispensation. And so the Prophet Zechariah announces, "Not by might, nor by power, but by my Spirit, saith the Lord." (Zech. iv, 6.) "There are diversities of gifts, but the same Spirit." And "the manifestation of the Spirit is given to every man to profit withal," says St. Paul. (1 Cor. xii, 4, 7.) God and man, co-workers in the great business of salvation, characterizes the whole mediatorial scheme. The whole work of Christ was performed by the union of God and man. The entire work of human renovation is performed by the union of God and man. God, the Holy Ghost, the efficient power in the soul; not taking the place of human nature, but making that nature free, free as a child of God, free as the servant of truth, and aspiring to that perfection and happiness which God will bestow upon His faithful children. To accomplish this glorious result, man must work together with God. Man can do nothing here by himself. God will do nothing, beyond the first gift of spiritual life, without the consent and the co-operation of man. For the freedom to be attained is moral freedom, the victory to be achieved is a moral conquest, the work to be done is the conversion of the will and of the affections to God. God gives by His Spirit the power to resist evil, to withstand temptation, to choose and maintain the right, to love and follow after goodness, to be the free, cheerful, happy doers of His will. But men must exercise this granted power. They are free now by the inspiration of the Spirit. God does not drag His people to heaven in chains. Christ leads them there as the Captain of their salvation, as His brethren in arms. Whenever, therefore, men cease to perform their part in this work, when they refuse to be led by the Spirit of God into all holy obedience, when they neglect to resort to the instituted channels of grace, when they no longer strive against the world, the flesh, and the Devil, then the work of salvation is at once arrested, growth ceases and decay begins. The corruption that remains in the regenerate is the power of an endless death, until it is entirely removed, until the soul is purified from the last dregs of this infection. It is this fearful truth, and the natural indolence of the soul in all its conflicts with sin—the fatal tendency to rest satisfied with present attainments—which makes it absolutely necessary to be pressing continually forward, and which induced the Apostle to rouse the Christians of Ephesus by the stirring exhortation, " Awake, thou that sleepest, and arise from the dead, and Christ shall give thee light." (Ephes. v, 14.) The disease of the soul is not superinduced upon previous health, but it is congenital—born with us—and infecting every power, and faculty, and feeling. This world and this life are the time and opportunity of extirpating that disease. Jesus Christ is the great Physician who alone can cure.   Whenever we cease to call upon Him for aid, and to use the prescriptions by which He works our cure, the ravages of the disease are resumed, and will terminate in the death that never dies.

CHAPTER XIII.

THE APPLICATION OF THE GOSPEL TO ADULT PERSONS WHO ARE NOT CHRISTIANS.

IN the foregoing sketch of Christian progress from the Baptism of the infant to the Confirmation of the intelligent
§ 1. PRACTICAL EVILS OF THE THEORY WHICH REFERS THE BE- GINNING OF SPIR- ITUAL LIFE TO THE PERIOD OF CONVERSION.
believer—the young, but well trained soldier of the cross—we have presented the ordinary plan of salvation, according to the design of its Author. But that Divine plan is thwarted and defeated at innumerable points by its willful subjects.

That theory of religion, which refers the beginning of spiritual life to the Conversion of the adult believer, has operated with most pernicious influence upon the popular mind. Intimately and legitimately connected with this theory is the denial of Baptism to the larger part of the redeemed children of God—the infant portion of the race. Many of those who have adopted this mischievous theory of the religious life, inconsistently retain the Sacrament of Baptism, according to the institution of Christ; administering it to all the heirs of salvation. But to baptize any person, infant or adult, who is destitute of spiritual life, who is not connected with Christ, the Source of life, is a mere form, and consequently a solemn mockery.

The persons who thus inconsistently administer baptism to

infants, are induced by their theory so to disparage and un-
dervalue the sacrament, as to deprive it of all its moral
power and influence upon the life. Baptism passes for
nothing at all—a mere ceremony—and the error is deeply
fixed in the public mind, that the spiritual and religious life
is yet to be begun, and completed too, by a great change in
the feelings and convictions of the soul, *at some appreciable
moment*, after the period of childhood has passed.

I have stated the fact, so irreconcilable with this malign
theology, that young children, who receive any fair degree
of religious instruction, are always religious. But this state
does not last long under the ordinary culture of the society
in which we live. The social feeling which denies a Christian character and Christian nurture to children, quickly
destroys this healthful state. The law of progress and its
penalty operate with tremendous power here. The child who
does not go forward in the Christian life, goes backward,
until all religious sensibility is lost, and we behold the pre-
cocious unbeliever, cold, callous, sneering, blaspheming.
Evil example and evil companions have wrought this ruin.
It is horrible to think of, but too true, that, sometimes, one
or both the parents, by their own irreligious lives, have led
their children away from God into this loathsome pit of
darkness and death. The very power of filial reverence and
love is used by parents to the destruction of their children.
Thus the tradition of ungodliness descends, with increasing
force and volume from generation to generation, until now a
boy or young man, even if properly educated, must possess
an unusual force of will, and heroic constancy, to be able to
resist the current.

In consequence of this unhappy condition of things, the
ordinary economy of the kingdom of grace is no longer applicable to the salvation of the great mass of the community.

That ordinary economy is set forth in the Divine injunction: "Train up a child in the way he should go, and when he is old he will not depart from it." (Prov. xxii, 6.) And in that Divine commendation of the Father of the Faithful: "For I know him, that he will command his children and his household after him, and they shall keep the way of the Lord, to do justice and judgment." (Gen. xviii, 19.)

In direct contradiction to this ordinary economy of salvation, children are taught by the generally received theory, that they have nothing to do as yet with religion—that they are strangers and aliens from the household of God, and can do nothing good or acceptable unto Him, until they pass through some mysterious change and transformation of character, variously styled regeneration, the new birth, conversion, and justification. In the mean time, until this mighty change comes, the natural corruption of the heart, and the overwhelming current of ungodliness in social life, concur to stimulate the deluded. children of the promise to serve the world, the flesh, and the Devil, with all their heart, with all their mind, and with all their strength.

Thus the forming period of life, the time when character is most surely developed and most firmly fixed, when the disposition is determined, and when the affections receive their permanent impress and direction, is taken away from God and devoted to impiety. Can we wonder at the difficulty of persuading men, after this, to become Christians? The work of changing a corrupt nature into a holy nature is hard enough when performed at every advantage, when all the precious means of grace are employed from the dawn of existence unintermittedly to the end of life. But when that corrupt nature has been cultivated and hardened into fixed habits; when the affections have been taught to flow, in deeply worn channels, at enmity with the truth; when the

Gospel must change the long established current and purpose of the soul, the difficulty of its successful operation is
almost infinitely increased.   And so the strong, unbroken,
and fast flowing stream of ungodliness that is rushing over
the land plainly testifies.   Not many of the vast multitude
become nominal Christians in mature life.   Not so many
become real Christians then in heart and life.

§ 2. REPENT-
ANCE, FAITH,
AND CONVERSION,
AS APPLIED TO
THIS CLASS OF
THE SUBJECTS OF
REDEMPTION.
The Gospel of Salvation has made provision for this, and for all other exigencies of
human position, produced by human willful-
ness and wrong.   The Church must not cease
sternly to rebuke the doctrinal error out of
which so much of this evil has proceeded.
But she must also faithfully apply to this wound of humanity the healing balm which the great Physician has placed
in her keeping.   Repentance and Conversion are the first
and the indispensable remedies for this inveterate sickness
of the soul.   Or, as the same thing is convertibly expressed
by St. Paul when he described his own full publication of
the Gospel, "Testifying both to the Jews, and also to the
Greeks, repentance toward God and faith toward our Lord
Jesus Christ."   (Acts xx, 21.)

Let it not be understood that these health-giving medi-
caments of the Gospel are applicable only to the condition
which we are now considering.   They belong to the whole
Christian life in all its states and varieties.   Faith, informed
by the Holy Spirit, is the continuing power and the ever
present guide of the Christian life.   Repentance is the chastening discipline by which at all times corrupt nature is to
be purified and brought to healthfulness.   Conversion is that
gradual and ceaseless change of the renewed soul, by which
all the powers and affections of man are transformed into
the image of Christ.   And this is the appointed work of the

whole life of man in this world, of the whole allotted period of probation.

But these words, and especially the term conversion, have a more precise and emphatic application to those persons who have surrendered themselves to the dominion of sin, and have been living without God in the world, when they would turn and be saved. They must be CONVERTED, as some of the Jews were who had crucified their Lord and Master; as St. Peter was, who had denied him; as St. Paul was, who had persecuted Him; as the Prodigal Son was, who had left his father's house and wasted his substance in riotous living. That is to say, these sinners must see the error of their way, and turn from it, confessing and bewailing their sins, and seeking earnestly of God pardon and forgiveness, through the blood of Christ. They have been walking hitherto in one direction, and in one path—downward to eternal ruin. To be saved, they must reverse their steps, they must leave that path, they must find the way of life which Christ has marked with His own footsteps, and resolutely walk therein, upward to God. This change of direction and of pathway is Conversion, in the sense of that term as applied to this class of persons. Again, these persons have been long estranged from God, they have been living in utter disregard of Him and of His laws. They have been serving with all their might the enemies of God and man. To be convinced of the wickedness, danger and folly of this course, to renounce with all the heart this fatal subjection, to turn with the whole soul unto God for pardon and reconciliation, this is Conversion.

§ 3. POPULAR FALLACY IN REGARD TO CONVERSION. But even here the popular theology has made an issue with the Bible, and with the ordinary consciousness of men, which puts a new obstacle in the way of the sinner's return to God. The theory which makes Conversion to be the beginning and almost the consummation of spiritual life—the first access of the Holy Ghost to the soul, changing at once all its perceptions, thoughts, feelings, and desires—so magnifies this change, speaks of it in such mystical and exalted strains, and so leaves out of view all its necessary antecedents, that plain men, who can not be controlled by imagination, and are not easily brought under the mesmeric influences of a revival meeting, are unable to recognize any thing of the sort in their own experience. They, therefore, conclude that they have not yet been effectually called of God to His service. With some little tinge of incredulity, perhaps, they rely upon the faithfulness and sufficiency of their guides, and easily accept an agreeable delusion, which enables them to enjoy the pleasures of sin, while they throw upon their Maker the responsibility of their own delay and the whole care of their conversion.

This popular offspring of modern sectarianism, by substituting certain vague, indefinable and fantastic notions and sentiments, for the simple faith and the humble obedience of the Gospel—insisting upon the former as the only tests of true religion, and depreciating the latter as worthless and deceptive—has confounded the minds of many honest and intelligent persons. Deluded by the oft-repeated phrases of this indefinite system, these persons have come to look upon practical Christianity as an unreality, with which they can have nothing to do until God shall please to perform in them a new miracle and to make to their souls a new revelation. It is obvious that such a system is admirably fitted to encourage self-deception in the sickly and imaginative, and to serve as a cover for the hypocrisy of the vicious, while it discourages and repels the honest, the intelligent, and the plain dealing.

In contrast with this whole system of errors and ambig-
uities, the Bible and the Church, as has been largely proved,

§ 4. THE BIBLE REPRESENTATION OF THIS GRACE. assure us that "the manifestation of the Spirit is given to every man to profit withal," that "by one Spirit we are all baptized into one body," that spiritual life has been imparted in Christ Jesus to every soul of man, to co-exist with the carnal life, as the only means of trial and the only ground of the judgment of men. The probation of every man, therefore, con-
sists in the choice of the emancipated will to be in subjection to the flesh or to the Spirit, to be led by the one or by the other. The Bible and the Church, therefore, speak to all men alike, telling them not to wait for the Spirit yet to be given, but to hear and obey the Spirit that is already in them, sealing and confirming upon the heart the external truth which the messengers of God proclaim. The Bible and the Church say to all men that the Spirit of God has been poured upon all flesh, (Acts ii, 17;) That God hath sent forth the Spirit of His Son into the hearts of all the redeemed. (Gal. iv, 4, 5, 6.) And they exhort all men to grieve not the Holy Spirit of God, (Ephes. iv, 30;) To quench not the Spirit, (1 Thess. v, 19;) To stand fast in one Spirit, (Phil. i, 27;) To be filled with the Spirit. (Ephes. v, 18.) To "walk in the Spirit and ye shall not fulfill the lust of the flesh. For the flesh lusteth against the Spirit, and the Spirit against the flesh: and these are contrary the one to the other: so that ye can not do the things that ye would. But if ye be led by the Spirit, ye are not under the law." (Gal. v, 16–18.) "He that soweth to his flesh shall of the flesh reap corruption; but he that soweth to the Spirit shall of the Spirit reap life everlasting. (Gal. vi, 8.)

When Christ calls us by the external Word and by the
20

external ministry to come unto Him, He has already given to us grace sufficient to enable us to obey the call, and truly to come to Him in soul and in body. For Christ calls the whole man, and demands the allegiance and the service of soul and body alike to Himself. The soul must come by the action of the enlightened will, fleeing for refuge from the vengeance of insulted mercy, " to lay hold upon the hope set before us " in the Gospel. And this determination of the will must be made effectual and complete by bringing the body to enter visibly into the covenant of grace, or to return to obedience to that covenant, by confessing Christ before men, by diligent use of all the appointed means of Grace, by taking our allotted station and performing our whole duty in the ranks of Christ's militant Church, by laboring faithfully in the vineyard of the Lord ; " for with the heart man believeth unto righteousness, and with the mouth confession is made unto salvation." (Rom. x, 10.)

Those who refuse to obey the call of Christ, do it freely, to their own wrong. They choose their own state, and, consequently, affix the sentence of condemnation upon themselves. There is no mysticism and no mystery about this part of Christianity at all. It is a plain question of choice between one service and another; between the carnal and the Divine life ; between sowing to the flesh and sowing to the Spirit; between being led captive by the lusts of the flesh, or being led by the Spirit into the glorious liberty of the sons of God. The Spirit of God within them, the Divine life of the soul which they have been trying to extinguish by sin, gives to every man the same power to make the better choice, which the old carnal nature gives to make the worse. The will, by the inspiration of the Spirit of Christ, is free—perfectly free—to make the one choice or the other ; except in so far as it has been brought again into bondage by indulgence in sin, by men's own previous voluntary submission to the dominion of sin.

This additional enslavement of the will, and consequent diminution of its power to turn to good, is a párt of the penalty which every man is accumulating upon himself every day that he continues to be the servant of sin. ·But until he becomes reprobate, until he is utterly abandoned of God — as long as the Holy Spirit stays with him, giving him any inclination to good, and love of good—the possibility of freedom, the capacity to turn to God and to do works meet for repentance remains. A harder struggle and a stronger effort will be required, in proportion to the time during which men have submitted themselves to the power of evil; but when the awakened soul feels the faintest desire to be free, and will manfully resolve no longer to earn the "wages of sin," but anxiously to seek for "the gift of God," the Spirit of the Most High will be found sufficient for the exigency and the mighty power of God unto his salvation, if the sinner will be faithful to himself.

§ 5. A POPULAR OBJECTION TO SUBMITTING TO THE TERMS OF THE GOSPEL. It is an entire departure from the terms of the choice freely offered to us between good and evil, between the service of God and the service of the Devil, to allege, as is often done, that we cannot fulfill the whole law, that we do not love God with all our heart, or our neighbor as ourselves, or hate all sin with a perfect hatred, and therefore to conclude that we have no right to come to Christ for salvation, to enter into His vineyard, or to enlist in His army.

This is a mistake which produces an infinite deal of mischief. The law is not a part of the covenant of grace, but the end of that covenant. If men could perfectly obey the law of life and happiness there would be no necessity or place for Christianity. But because the law of life is to us sinners a law of condemnation and death, Christ came to fulfill the law for us. Now then, says St. Paul, we "are not under the law, but under grace." (Rom. vi, 14.) "The law was our schoolmaster to bring us unto Christ, that we might be justified by faith." (Gal. iii, 24.) And the same law remains a schoolmaster, the standard of Christian attainment, the unrepealable condition of eternal life and happiness, to keep us near to Christ, abiding in Him, trusting not in ourselves but in Him, seeking for more and more of His Spirit, laboring in His strength, "growing up into Him in all things," going from grace to grace, "till we all come in the unity of the faith and of the knowledge of the Son of God, unto a perfect man, unto the measure of the stature of the fullness of Christ." (Eph. iv, 13.) Then, when we have attained this fullness of the stature of Christ, we shall be enabled like Him to obey perfectly the law of life and happiness. Whether this consummation of grace is reserved for the reward of the faithful soldier of the Cross in the article of death, or when it is given, we are not informed. Certain it is that St. Paul had not reached to this summit when he wrote the Epistle to the Philippians, for he says there, "Not as though I had already attained, either were already perfect: but I follow after, if that I may apprehend that for which also I am apprehended of Christ Jesus. Brethren, I count not myself to have apprehended: but this one thing I do, forgetting those things which are behind, and reaching forth unto those things which are before, I press toward the mark for the prize of the high calling of God in Christ Jesus." (Phil. iii, 12, 14.)

To allege then our inability to keep the whole law, or any part of it, as a reason for declining to accept the terms of the Christian covenant, or to come to Christ for salvation, is a flat contradiction of the very sense and meaning of the

Gospel. Christ came to call, not the righteous, but sinners, to repentance. If men could keep the law they would not need Christ; but because they cannot keep it, they must come to Him for salvation, and be found in Him, or perish in their sins.

What is really wanted to bring the sinner to Christ, is a sufficient and proper sense of sin, of our own guiltiness before God, of our inability to walk in the law of the Lord, and a sincere desire to escape from the power and the condemnation of sin, joined with so much knowledge of the Gospel as enables us to believe and trust in Christ as the Savior from this power and condemnation of sin. That sense of unworthiness which men sometimes offer as an excuse for staying away from Christ, so far from being a valid apology, is, if deep and real, the very condition, and the indispensable condition, of their coming to Him acceptably. A true conviction of sin is the passport of the sinner to Christ. This, with trust in Christ as the Savior of sinners, and a full determination to accept the salvation of the Gospel upon the terms of the Gospel, is all the qualification that can ever be attained for entering fully and unreservedly into the Gospel covenant.

If these feelings have been awakened in the soul in a faint degree, like the grain of mustard seed to which our Savior likens the kingdom of heaven, they are the witnesses there of God's Spirit striving with us. They are the remaining manifestations of that spiritual life which Jesus gives to all His redeemed, in order that by the sympathetic power of that hidden life He may draw them all to Himself, and conform them all to His perfect nature. Do not rudely stifle or banish these precious feelings, these blessed manifestations of the Divine life in your souls; but cherish them, nurture them, follow their guidance, go with them to Christ, from whom they came, and they will prove to be the power of an endless life with God. For, however faint and feeble they may be now, their existence proves their vital power. It is the essential quality of all life to grow under proper culture. The physical and the spiritual kingdoms are identical in this. The feeblest beginnings are slowly developed into the mightiest results. The flower and the fruit are in the little, dried seed. But the flower and the fruit will never be produced unless the seed be placed in the earth, where it will be kindly nurtured by the dew and the rain and the sunshine of heaven, and be allowed gradually and silently to expand and grow.

So of the Divine life in the soul of man. God gives just enough grace to bring every poor sinner to Christ for more grace. To demand that God shall give this additional grace before we use the grace already given by coming to Christ for all we need, is a foolish delusion. It is an idle and thankless attempt to substitute our wisdom for the appointments of God, and can end in nothing but disappointment and destruction. The same principle applies to every stage and period of the Christian life. When we no longer come to Christ for grace we receive no more, and the spiritual life is starved and will ultimately be destroyed. When men cease to work with God in the matter of their salvation He refuses to work with them. Salvation is all of grace, but it is grace given to those who will receive and use it.

If the feeble stirrings of spiritual life in the soul be repressed for any cause, or upon any plea, the poor sinner, at each repetition of the folly, writes his own doom, pronounces his own sentence of condemnation. He thus consigns himself to the darkness and corruption of his natural state and willingly accepts the eternal death, which consists in entire separation from God and utter destitution of the happiness

which God alone can give.   Our merciful and long-suffering
Savior does not, indeed, often take the deluded servant of sin
at his word when first he is guilty of this wrong to his own
soul.   He permits His Spirit of light and life to abide in us
still.   Again and again the word of reconciliation, the blessed
Gospel of the Son of God is heard.   And again and again
the Spirit of Christ in the soul moves and stirs within us to
produce conviction and obedience.   If all these efforts for
our salvation are through life resisted the Spirit will leave us,
all spiritual life will be extinct, and the soul will be given
over to the corruption it loved and to the death it has chosen.

§ 6. PHYSICAL   The external and material world is the type
ANALOGIES TO   and expression of the inner and spiritual
THE DIVINE LIFE   world.   The Scriptures copiously employ the
IN THE SOUL OF
MAN.   analogies of nature as representative of spiritual truths.   The physical life of man in every possible
variety of illustration is made to symbolize the Divine life in
the soul.   Birth, infancy, growth and maturity, all find their
counterparts in the spiritual man.   And the death of the
body is the loathsome image of spiritual death—the separation of the soul from God by sin.   So the economy of
nature in the life and germination of seeds and in the nourishment, growth and fructification of plants; the care and
diligence of the husbandman in preparing the ground, in
sowing the seed and in gathering the harvest, are continually
used to image the spiritual life of the soul.   There are, indeed, a few expressions apparently inconsistent with these
numerous and constantly recurring delineations.   Such are
those expressions which represent the souls of wicked men
as dead, as if life was utterly extinct, or had never existed
in them.   But these comparatively rare instances are easily
reconciled with the general teaching of the Bible by a reference to the *usus loquendi* of Scriptural language, which sel

dom employs our degrees of comparison, but signifies the diminution or lesser degree of a thing by its absence or negation. Numerous instances of this familiar form of speech will occur to all who are acquainted with the Bible.

By this Scriptural standard then, employing so profusely the analogies of nature to explain and illustrate the spiritual life of man, we can test the truth of those conflicting views of the religious life which have been now considered.

Does man himself, the noblest of these types, come into the world full grown and amply endowed with strength and wisdom? Does the majestic forest rise up at once in its glory and grandeur by the one fiat of the Almighty? Let us go where the Bible sends us, to the fields and to the woods, for instruction. We behold a glorious harvest. Did it come there of itself? Did it grow up in a day? No. Its beginning was a parcel of dry and apparently lifeless seed. If the seed had been really, as well as apparently, lifeless, there would have been no harvest now. There was a hidden life in each one of those dry grains. That living germ is so small that you can not see it. And when the germ is first developed into the young plant, how feeble, how tender is its life. It grows, but so gradually, so insensibly, that you can not see it grow. We often say, after a succession of warm showers in the genial month of May, that we can *almost* see the plants grow and the flowers unfold. But we never did see them. Their life is too mysterious, too hidden; their growth too gradual and insensible for that. Yet they grow on to the consummation of their glory.

Behold the image of the spiritual life in every fruit and forest tree. In the winter you can hardly see the little bark-covered germ of leaf and flower. The warm sun of many spring days has gradually swelled them, and very slowly the buds opened and tiny leaves were half expanded, giving early promise of beauteous foliage and of grateful shade. But a rude and comfortless north-easter has been blowing for several days, and the whole process of expansion and growth has stopped. Every thing remains stationary, as if suddenly petrified in that precise stage of development which it had reached before this wintry storm. The sun and the warm south wind must return to nurture these buds of promise or they will perish.

So it is with the spiritual life, the life of God in the soul of man. It is implanted there at the very dawn of existence to be the power of an eternal life. It is the consequence of the connection of our manhood with Jesus, the Son of God. It is a life hidden and only to be gradually and insensibly developed into visible results and into glorious fruition by the agencies of grace, by the power of the Holy Ghost, operating through accustomed channels, and by preconstituted instrumentalities. If men perversely refuse to employ the agencies graciously established for the nurture of the spiritual life, that life must of necessity perish; and they will be driven away to the everlasting perdition which their sin and folly have provoked. Christian religion, therefore, addresses its invitations and its warnings to all men alike, because all have a Divinely imparted capacity to hear and obey the Gospel. By reason of this gracious gift every man must act in the great matter of religion at his own peril. For the judgment day will but proclaim the decision which each one has made and re-affirm the sentence which each one has pronounced upon himself.

§ 7. COMMON EXCUSES FOR REFUSING TO ENTER UPON A CHRISTIAN LIFE. Many persons who undoubtingly believe the whole Christian revelation are deterred from a manly and open following of Christ, in an obedient submission to all the institutions of the Gospel, by various popular excuses for the neglect of a

21

plain duty. One of the most common of these, an alleged sense of unworthiness, has been already considered and disposed of. It was not the worthiness of men that brought the Son of God from heaven for our relief. As sinners we were redeemed, and as sinners we are called to a participation of the benefits of redemption. What we really want, to qualify us for a joyful acceptance and a faithful use of the means of salvation, is a sufficient sense of the fact that we are sinners, and that only by the mercy of God in Jesus Christ, and in the way in which He has promised to dispense His mercy, can we be saved from the everlasting destruction which our sins deserve.

Another common apology which men offer for this species of impiety is the inconsistent lives of many of the professed Christians around them. But what has a man who believes in Christianity, and is seeking the salvation of his soul, to do with the faults or with the hypocrisy of those who call themselves Christians? If this religion had never produced any fruit of holy living, such a failure of what ought to be its effect might be a reason for refusing to believe its Divine origin. But this allegation has never been made by the bitterest enemies of Christianity, and it is contradicted by the personal knowledge of every man who has lived in a Christian community. Besides, every one who has studied this religion sees plainly that its principles and precepts, if carried out, tend to produce the sublimest virtue of which human nature is capable.

What then does the objection amount to? Simply to these two positions: 1. That many of those who are honestly using this exalted rule of life have not yet succeeded in reducing their corrupt natures and their vicious habits to conformity with this perfect standard. 2. That some Christians, while they profess to live according to the Gospel rule, are in fact living according to some other and lower rule. Both these cases are expressly mentioned and provided for in the Gospel, and are only proofs of the extent and inveteracy of that corruption of human nature which Christian religion proposes to cure, and which must be cured to make men capable of eternal felicities in the presence of God.

Is the dishonesty of this latter class of Christian professors any reason at all why we should not honestly try to do what they only pretend to do? Because there are failures and false pretences in every business of life, is that any reason why we should refuse to use any of the means of earning an honest livelihood? If an idle vagrant were to allege the large amount of fraud and cheating in the ordinary trades and occupations as a justification for his not working for his daily bread, would we admit the excuse? What a miserable self-deception then it is, when we allege a reason precisely equivalent to this for refusing to use the means of salvation—for neglecting to labor for the bread that cometh down from heaven?

Another way in which men excuse themselves from a performance of the external duties of religion is by a complacent estimate of their own moral character. They flatter themselves that persons so just and exact in the performance of the relative duties of life need have no fears of the eternal wrath of the Almighty. Now, put this standard of morality, so far as our fellow men are concerned, as high as we please, and supposing that we come up to it, making no allowance for self-deception in the measure of ourselves by this standard, what does this boasted morality of ours prove? Why, that the Christianity, a large part of which we practically reject, has so forcibly impressed itself upon the public law and the public sentiment of the age and country in which we live, that its moral precepts have become the common rule of social life, and are incorporated into the civil law and into a controlling public opinion. To this rule we have become habituated by education, and we are retained in the observance of it by self respect, by regard to our reputation, and by the love of that virtue which we have thus actually found to be a source of the purest pleasure.

If we are thus indebted to Christianity for all that is most ennobling in our character and position, how can we justify our neglect of that more important portion of the same system which determines our relations to God, and which provides the only sanction by which any part of this vital element of human society can be maintained? Out of his own mouth, therefore, is the man condemned who puts his morality in opposition to Christianity. The thing in which he prides and exalts himself is but the faint reflection of Christianity itself; and in magnifying this morality he but testifies to the inestimable value and necessity of the whole religion that God has revealed for the salvation of men. For a man to allege his accidental obedience to a portion of this saving and ennobling truth as a reason for his contemptuous disregard of the rest, is a poor self-deception. Besides, the morality of the Gospel only impressed itself upon the world so as to become the law of the land, and the law of public sentiment, through the power of the Gospel as *an institution*, openly professed, and daily exhibited to men. Upon the principle of action which dispenses with that institution, the morality of the Gospel would have died with its promulger, and civilization, and all that adorns, refines and ennobles human life and human society would have been banished long since from the earth.

These, and all other difficulties which men permit to hinder hem from the practical acceptance of the salvation of the Gospel upon its own terms, are evasions and sophistries, which have no foundation in common sense or in the Word of God. God made every man to be saved, and no truth can stand in the way of that salvation. God and truth are one. God can not contradict Himself. Whatever then contravenes His design for our salvation is not a truth, but a falsehood. Only let men act in this most important matter in character with themselves as reasonable creatures, and the result is certain. They will accept the invitation of God's love and mercy. They will at once begin, and diligently continue, trusting only in Him for strength, to do their own part in the mighty work of salvation.

CHAPTER XIV.

WORSHIP.

TRUE Religion and Idolatry are opposites, in perpetual conflict in the human soul, in human society, and in every *§ 1. ITS NA-* stage of human history. Out of this conflict *TURE.* come the most concerning phenomena of personal, social, and national life. Man is so essentially a subject creature, so essentially religious—that is, *bound* to the service of a superior—that he must have a God to believe in and to worship. If he does not know the true God, or will not own or worship Him, then he must find or make a God. It is not at all necessary that the false God should be carved out of wood, or stone, or metal. That is but a refinement of idolatry, a sort of liturgical development, to aid in the worship of the God first framed by man's device out of his own nature. We can see then how universally practical, how grandly philosophic, are the Old Testament Scriptures, in representing all the phenomena of false religion, in every aspect and under every variety of form and fancy, as simple idolatry.

Man must believe in something, and worship something, a God or a Devil, a lust or an idea. Fond and foolish therefore is the conceit of those vain-glorious people who boast of their freedom from all religious restraint. The service of God is perfect freedom, because it is the full, healthful, and right action of all the powers and faculties of man, issuing in true enjoyment, real happiness, the highest good of our nature and condition. The man who will not serve God is under service, nevertheless. And his service is bondage, a degrading servitude, not in accordance with the right action of his faculties, but contrary to that right action; and the issue is, not happiness, not well being, but discontent, misery and ruin.

The varieties of idolatry are: 1. The worship of an evil Spirit. 2. The worship of some creation of a superstitious fancy; under which may be ranked all the things natural or artificial which have been ignorantly worshipped as gods. 3. The worship of some lust, more or less sordid and degrading. 4. The worship of some conceit or diseased fancy of our own, or of the leader whom we follow. The lives and actions of all men, in all ages, may be reduced under one or other of these five heads: the service of God, which is freedom; or one or more of these four varieties of idolatry, which is slavery.

Take any passage of life or of history, and you will be at no loss under which head or heads of this classification to place it. The common language of mankind makes the application for us. The expression, "slaves to lust," tells of a whole troop of cruel and relentless masters, under whose subjection men have suffered and groaned, and sacrificed their peace and happiness and manhood, from generation to generation. Sordid avarice, bloody ambition, emasculating licentiousness, tyrannous hate, gnawing envy, fierce revenge, and drunkenness, which, alas! needs no appellative: what real horrors, beyond all human imagining, have signalized the destructive power of these hideous forms of idolatry! For examples, on a scale of terrific magnitude, of the worship of our own conceits, take the history of fanaticism every where, and in every form, religious or atheistic. See it in the chronic horrors of the Inquisition, in the massacre of St. Bartholomew's, in the purple gore which ran down the streets of every city in France, as an offering to liberty, equality and reason.

Worship is the devotion of the whole man, body and soul, to the Deity we serve. When we have chosen an idol for our Deity there seems to be little difficulty in rendering this worship, because such devotion runs with our corrupt nature and speeds its downward course. But the worship of the true God, the devotion of the whole man to Him, is against that corrupted nature, and is always a hard and difficult ascent.

There must be continual acts of faith, reverence and devotion, to keep God in our mind and to urge us to our duty. And because this is necessary, God has made it imperative by express command, and by restraining His gifts of grace to our obedience to that command.

It is a sad confusion, which some persons have fallen into, in representing prayer as having no other virtue than to work in ourselves the feelings which it expresses. It is true enough that there is no *natural* efficacy in prayer, so far as we can understand, to act upon the purposes of the Almighty God. And true enough it is, also, that there is a natural efficacy in prayer to nurture in those who make it the feelings and desires it expresses. We see this effect continually in children. They often ask for a thing almost idly, with little care or desire for it. But the mere request suggests the object more prominently, and the mind dwells upon it, and the desire for it increases. And as the petition is repeated, the urgency of desire grows, and becomes importunate and troublesome, both to child and parent, until it is appeased by gratification.

This would be the natural effect upon the soul of real prayer offered to God. Those who fancy that this is its only effect and meaning, seem to have left out of view, altogether, the wisdom and goodness of God, in adapting the *positive* laws and ordinances of religion to the actual nature of the creature He had made. Because He knew the natural fitness of prayer to act thus beneficially upon our nature, He enjoined it as a duty; and to make it an intelligent and a real act, He has ordained the faithful use of this medium of access to Him as the condition of those renewed supplies of grace which we continually need. For, observe, a child would not seriously ask its parent for that which it knew could never be obtained for the asking. The child knows, by nature and experience, the efficacy of prayer in moving the earthly parent, and therefore he prays truly, really, urgently, and with the expectation of receiving because of his prayer. The same thing is true of prayer to the heavenly Father. On the supposition that prayer, or other worship, is only intended to operate on ourselves, our worship would not be real, it would be a mere "make-believe," a sort of pious mockery.

To make prayer real, and so to accomplish its saving purpose, God has appointed, as a part of the economy of redemption, that it shall be efficacious, and the indispensable condition upon which He will minister His grace and mercy. And He has revealed this gracious provision, in some way, to all souls, and it is a part of all religions. It is the instinctive cry of the human spirit in the urgency of need and of distress. The whole animal creation has been framed in intimate sympathy with this yearning and trusting faith of the human soul. As the Divine Word beautifully expresses it, "God feedeth the young ravens that call upon him." And with what variety of tender and striking representations does our blessed Savior make known to us the efficacy of prayer, and the method of it, in the economy of redemption.

§ 2. PUBLIC WORSHIP. A LITURGY. As we have already seen, God could not be kept in memory by such a creature as man without continually recurring and formally expressed acts of faith, reverence and adoration. And man is so essentially a social being, that to make these acts effective to their purpose, to give to them sufficient animation, earnestness and power, some of them must be social, common and public; else they would exercise little or no influence upon mind, character, or conduct. Therefore, in revealing Himself to man, the Almighty Father has always accompanied the revelation with a prescription of some definite time and method for the exercise of these necessary acts of faith, reverence and adoration. This Divine prescription has been the foundation—the starting point—of all the Liturgies, or forms of public worship, that have prevailed in the world. By the Divine appointment, all other acts of worship were attached to the sacrifice of material things, formally offered to God upon an Altar. It is a strange mistake to suppose that Altar and Sacrifice belong only to animal and bloody offerings. On the contrary, as we shall show hereafter, all material offerings to God, animate or inanimate, in all religions, were sacrifices, presented upon an Altar, and are themselves but symbols, as needful helps to our infirmity, of that higher and truer sacrifice which we are required to make of ourselves to God. In that elaborate ritual which God gave to Moses there were Altars upon which no animal sacrifices were ever to be made; and there was one—the Golden Altar of Incense—upon which nothing but incense from fragrant herbs was offered. And this incense only symbolized the prayers of the assembled congregation, which began to be uttered simultaneously with the burning of the incense. (Exodus xxx, 1–10; xxxvii, 29.) (Lightfoot's Temple Service, ch. 9.)

St. Paul refers to the Golden Altar of Incense, on which only "sweet spices" were offered, when he tells the Phillippians that their gifts sent to him were "an odor of a sweet smell, a *sacrifice* acceptable, well pleasing to God." (Phil. iv, 18.)

From this Divine foundation there arose by gradual accretion in the Jewish Church a grand and noble Liturgy, to which Prophets, and Kings, and Psalmists successively contributed, as the ages passed along. This Liturgy was in constant use in our Savior's time, and we see, from incidental notices in His life, that none were more devout than He in the employment of it. How touching and instructive is that wonderful and reverent exclamation of the God-man, in reference to one prominent portion of this Liturgy, "With desire I have desired to eat this passover with you before I suffer." (St. Luke xxii, 15.)

In reorganizing His kingdom under its Christian form, the blessed Savior instituted Baptism as the substitute for all the sacraments of purification, and the oblation of bread and wine as the substitute for all the sacrifices, bloody and unbloody, of the dispensation that had passed away by His fulfillment of it. These Sacraments are in their nature social and public, and to consecrate more effectually the principle of common worship, under the new economy of grace, the great Head of the Church promises His especial presence only to the assemblies of His people: "For where two or three are gathered together in my name, there am I in the midst of them." (St. Matt. xviii, 20.) This necessity in human nature for public worship, so emphatically recognized by the Divine prescription, is but one feature of that more general necessity, which required the establishment of the visible kingdom of God, as the conservator of all religion, "the pillar and ground of the truth." (1 Tim. iii, 15.) Henceforth, around the Christian Sacraments were all the acts of faith, and penitence, and prayer, and praise, to be grouped, as their center. At once the most delightful portions of the Jewish Liturgy were adopted and transformed into vehicles for sending up on high the Christian sacrifice of confession, supplication and praise. Unquestionably the Apostles, and their immediate successors, used the liberty which belonged to their office and their work, by giving to each Church such a rudimental Liturgy as was best adapted to the situation, knowledge and circumstances of that Church. Hence, we find in the earliest ages four distinct types of the Christian Liturgy. "The first may be entitled the *great Oriental Liturgy*, as it seems to have prevailed in all the Christian Churches from the Euphrates to the Hellespont, and from the Hellespont to the southern extremity of Greece. The second was the *Alexandrian*, which from time immemorial has been the Liturgy of Egypt, Abyssinia, and the country extending along the Mediterranean Sea toward the West. The third was the *Roman*, which prevailed throughout the whole of Italy, Sicily, and the civil diocese of Africa. The fourth was the *Gallican*, which was used throughout Gaul and Spain, and probably in the exarchate of Ephesus until the fourth century. These four great Liturgies appear to have been the parents of all the forms now extant, and indeed of all which we can in any manner discover; and their antiquity was so very remote, their use so extensive in those ages when Bishops were most independent, that it seems difficult to place their origin at a lower period than the Apostolic Age. The liberty which every Christian Church plainly had and exercised, in the way of improving its formularies, confirms the antiquity of the four great Liturgies; for where this liberty existed, it could have been scarcely anything else but reverence for the apostolical source from which the original liturgies were derived that prevented an infinite variety of formularies, and preserved the substantial uniformity which we find to have prevailed in vast districts of the primitive Church." (Palmer's Origines Liturgicæ, vol. i, p. 8.)

A precomposed Liturgy is an essential of public or common worship. If each person in such an assembly were to make aloud his own prayer, and sing his own hymn, instead of the beauty of rational worship, there would only be the discord and confusion of a disorderly mob. Those mistaken persons, therefore, who have such a horror of Liturgies, and declaim so vehemently against forms of worship, as cold, lifeless and unspiritual, have, in truth, and from the necessity of the case, but exchanged a full, expressive, and well-composed Liturgy, the ripened product of the learning, taste and piety of successive ages, for the crude and indigested forms which the leader of the congregation may happen to compose. For, be it remembered, that the utterance of the Minister, in a congregation which fondly fancies that it has never used a Liturgy, becomes the precomposed form of prayer for all the people who receive and use it, as it flows from the lips of this extemporized prophet. It is the prescribed form for them, and they must take it as it comes, with all its defects of language, of propriety, and of affection, and with all its unseemly conceits, political, fanciful, or inhumane, and appropriate it as best they can.

Fortunately for these good people, they have not entrusted their worthy minister for the time being with the office of extemporizing for their use, at each occasion of public worship, the poetry and music in which they sing the praises of God. So much of a duly prepared liturgy they have happily retained. In this better custom they are inconsistent with their avowed principles; but inconsistency in folly is always a benefit.

It will hardly be contended by the most earnest advocate of extemporized devotions that the psalms and hymns they are accustomed to use are less hearty and less spiritual than the rest of their worship. On the contrary, all feel that this is the most animated, stirring, and inspired department of worship. And in the congregations which flatter themselves that they are too spiritual to worship out of a book, the very portions of the service which are supposed to be extemporized, are, of necessity, *precomposed* for the people, and *prescribed* to them, as the form of prayer which they must use on that occasion, or else refuse to join in common worship.

The question then of a Liturgy resolves itself, by the necessity of the case, into the issue of better or worse: a liturgy well or ill composed, carefully expressing the needs of all hearts and adapted to all estates and conditions of men—or the hap-hazard efforts of adventurous sciolism; a liturgy reverently constructed by a succession of great and godly men, in perfect accord with the analogy of faith—or the ever changing reflection of the thoughts, passions, conceits, and partyisms of individual men in each passing week.

To make the decision upon this issue more emphatic, let it be remembered that a proper Liturgy, starting from the Divine prescription, and built up by the successive contributions of holy men, in jealous adherence to the "proportion of faith," is absolutely necessary as a preventive of the worst form of Idolatry. For, when the human minister can pray as well as preach what he pleases, he will presently transfer the formal worship of the assembly to his own ideas, his own cherished idols. He will gather all his whimsical or fanatical conceits into one monstrous conception, and make the people worship it with him as their God. Such an idolatry as this would be far more fatal in corrupting and debauching the consciences of men than any other idolatry that has appeared in the Christian Church. This is not a merely speculative assertion. The assertion has become fact, over and over again, in most of those Christian bodies which have tried the hazardous experiment of dispensing with an established Liturgy, and have committed the awful realities of religion to the sole disposal of the transient impulses and fluctuating opinions of their human guides.

The extent of this departure from the worship of the true God may be seen in the fact that some of these errorists have openly clamored for a new Bible, while others have more covertly tried to impair the authority of the old one, because that Bible revealed a God altogether different from the fantastic or ferocious idol of the imagination which they were accustomed to worship.

A Liturgy, like all living things, must grow. It cannot be struck off at a single heat, from a single mind. It starts from the Divine prescription of Sacramental acts and words, and is adapted to the continued progress of society by the piety, taste, and learning of successive generations, under fixed and unalterable laws.

The Liturgy of the Protestant Episcopal Church is not faultless. But it is almost universally confessed to be the most perfect of human compositions. The English-speaking nations enjoy an inestimable blessing in the fact that the Bible and the Prayer-book were rendered into the common tongue just at the time when the language was in its purest and best state, and when the agitations of the world had raised up a generation of men of unsurpassed power, wisdom and greatness. Hence the simple majesty of the language of the Prayer-book, embodying thoughts so full, so pure, and so touching, and beautifully expressing all human needs, affections and aspirations. The variety attained in this Liturgy is another of its distinguishing excellences. All the parts of public worship are so skillfully disposed that neither mind nor body can become wearied by the continuance of any one affection or posture, before the congregation is called to refreshment and renewed ardor in this heavenly service by the transition to some other exercise of devotion.

"It ought to be mentioned, also, in passing, as a real though not a principal element of spirituality in the prayers of the Prayer-book, that they are written prayers, prepared with forethought, and, in their language, familiar to the mind of the person praying. Because it is this, and nothing short of this, which can set the spiritual faculties wholly free for their appropriate work in the act of devotion. It is this which disengages all those inferior ingredients that bring themselves into what is popularly called worship—all intellectual entertainment and criticism, all the pleasures and disgusts of taste, all surprises, wonderments and apprehensions at the choice of an extemporizer's expressions—drops all these clear out of mind, and leaves the worshipper but a single occupation—that of sending up his own soul as an offering on these wings, which are then as free as they are familiar, and which have been lifting the Church below into communion with the Church above ever since the Apostle called them both 'one family.' "*

Public Worship alone will not serve the exigencies of the

---

* The Rev. F. D. Huntington, D. D. Sermon on The Spirituality of the Liturgy. The volume of Sermons on the Liturgy, from which the above extract is taken, came into my hands since this chapter was written, and I cannot forbear the opportunity of entreating such of my readers as are not familiar with it to procure it for themselves as a household book, and to distribute it freely as one of the best missionaries of the Church.

Christian life. Without that, indeed, there would be no
other true worship of God, for without it there could be no
§ 3. FAMILY true religion, to keep in mind the true God
AND PRIVATE and the duty of worshiping Him. But pub-
WORSHIP. lic and sacramental worship cannot be used
with such frequency and regularity by the people, even under
the most favorable circumstances, as to answer their needs.
Besides, there are vices of human character which public
worship, if separated from all other worship, would fatally
nurture. This was shown by the miserable hypocrisy of the
Pharisees in our Savior's time, who made all their prayers
only to be seen of men. Therefore, the Divine prescription
has always required Family and Private Devotion. The Old
Testament is full of the Divine care for the exercise of religion in the Family. Even the greatest national festival of
the chosen people, the Passover, was ordered to be cele·
brated as a Family Service, in the house, and by the household, with the head of the family as the officiating Priest.

The consecration of the family relation is even more perfect
under the Christian than under the former dispensations.
Our Savior carefully removed from the fifth commandment
all the glosses by which the Jews had tried to diminish its
import. The increased sanctity of the marriage tie, the
many exhortations to children to love, reverence and obey
their parents; and to parents to bring up their children in
the nurture and admonition of the Lord, show very plainly
the mind of the Spirit in regard to this sacred relation.

The family is the foundation of the Church and of the
State, and if this primeval institution be dissolved or loosened,
human nature must deteriorate, and all other interests of
mankind be irreparably injured. The general disuse of the
family altar—the banishment of religion and sanctity from
the family by the refusal of its head, God's anointed Priest,
22

to offer up the spiritual sacrifices of prayer and praise for his household, and with them—is one principal cause of the social evils with which our unhappy country is afflicted.

The Divine Life in the soul of man requires more continual nourishment from its heavenly source than either of these forms of social worship can supply. Here, again, the analogy is close between the physical and the spiritual creation. The growing plant must receive continued nourishment. The animal body must be supplied with more than daily food. These are the necessary conditions of health and life. So the Spiritual life of the soul must be constantly sustained. Prayer is the medium by which the soul procures this continued nourishment. Prayer performs, in the spiritual economy, the office assigned in the vegetable economy to the minute radicles which are spread out to be the purveyors of nutriment for the whole tree. Isolate these radicles from the source of supply, even for a short time, and the tree must perish. Let daily prayer cease, and spiritual life will soon wither and die. Therefore, private prayer has been the practice of God's people in all ages. And our Savior, warning his disciples against that flagrant sin of the Pharisees in making even their private prayers, if they could be so called, "in the synagogues, and in the corners of the streets, that they may be seen of men," gives this direction for our private devotions: "But thou, when thou prayest, enter into thy closet, and when thou hast shut thy door, pray to thy Father which is in secret; and thy Father, which seeth in secret, shall reward thee openly." (St. Matt. vi, 5, 6.)

The power and efficacy of prayer are largely declared in God's blessed word. And the experience of all good men has beautifully attested the faithfulness of their heavenly Father in these declarations. The three great forms of this holy exercise, Private, Family and Public Prayer, belong to- -

gether, and must support and help each other. Prayer is thus the strength of man in each of the leading aspects of his nature, as an individual, as a portion of the family, and as a member of society.

The ministration of the Holy Ghost employs every part and incident of human life, and all the Providential government of the world, as means of Grace and helps to salvation. Health and sickness, joy and grief, pleasure and pain, wealth and poverty, are all, when sanctified by faith and prayer, instruments of holiness. They are a part of the healthful discipline which God uses to prepare a people for Himself. The heir of salvation must work together with God here also. He must strive to make each of these estates and incidents of life an occasion for the exercise of those affections toward God, which they respectively require and which they are designed to produce. And, to consecrate the whole life to God, the heir of salvation must earnestly strive to obey the Apostolic injunction to "PRAY WITHOUT CEASING."

CHAPTER XV.

THE LORD'S SUPPER.

ALL the views which have been presented of the requisites
for Confirmation, and of the necessity for perpetual progress

§ 1. A MEANS
OF GRACE AND
NOT A TESTIMONY
OF HOLINESS.

in the Christian life, apply to that most solemn
of all the ordinances of Christ's religion—the
Sacrament of His body and blood.   In all
that has been said of the means of grace, and
of their value and importance, reference has been intended
to this, the most eminent of them all.   This Sacrament is a
means of grace, appointed for our benefit, and adapted to our
exigency.   It is therefore a superstitious error which looks
upon this Sacrament as too holy for the uses of any sincere
and humble believer.   The Christian who would interpret his
access to this sacred feast as a testimony to his own sanctity
is sadly mistaken.   It is, on the contrary, another and the
strongest possible testimony to his sinfulness, and to his need
of a better righteousness and greater strength than his own.
The Church provides that none shall partake of this benefit
but those who come with the most humbling confession of
sin and of their own unworthiness.   It is in truth one of the
gracious opportunities which Christ has provided for communicating Himself to His redeemed people, for enduing
them with His Spirit, with His purity, with His strength.

The misapprehension just mentioned has arisen in part

from not understanding the words of St. Paul: "He that eateth and drinketh unworthily, eateth and drinketh damnation to himself, not discerning the Lord's body." (1 Cor. xi, 29.) But St. Paul is speaking of those who had changed the Lord's Supper into a drunken feast. His condemnation of that iniquity is just as applicable to the hypocritical or the sensual abuse of any of the institutions of the Gospel. Every reason that exists for the use of any of the appointed means of grace—every reason for Baptism, for Confirmation, for public and private Prayer, is a reason, of the same force, for the coming of all adult persons to this Sacrament. It would be a mere repetition, therefore, of much that has been already said, to urge the importance of this duty. If it is essential that the Christian should grow in grace, then it is necessary that this most eminent means of grace should be faithfully used.

As many erroneous views, and some gross corruptions of religion, have clustered around this holy Sacrament, a distinct statement of its nature and meaning will be a help to those for whom this work has been prepared, by removing some of the stumbling blocks which have been placed in the way of life by the mischievous ingenuity of men. The intimate connection of this great Sacrament with other parts of the doctrine and institution of Christ, will make this explanation a proper opportunity for the consideration of some of these connected truths.

There are two great errors in regard to the nature of this Sacrament. One of these degrades it from the most eminent of the means of grace, or mysteries, by which Christ is communicated to us, into a mere commemoration, having only a natural effect. The opposite error equally degrades the Divine institution by changing it into a silly and blasphemous fable. These two errors will be sufficiently exposed by a simple exhibition of the true meaning of the Sacrament. But between these vicious extremes there are a great many conflicting views and statements, which have been the occasion of much angry controversy and gratuitous abuse. Of all these last mentioned diversities, I do not hesitate to say that they are for the most part the merest logomachies, or word disputes. The only real ground of controversy in regard to them is, that the parties will not condescend to agree upon the meaning they attach to the words which they use in common. Of course such a controversy can have no end, and no result but anger and bitterness.

The Communion Service of the Church presents this Sacrament to us in two principal aspects. First, as a Eucharistic and Commemorative Sacrifice. Secondly, as a participation of Christ. Under these two aspects we will consider it.

§ 2. A EUCHAR-
ISTIC AND COM-
MEMORATIVE
SACRIFICE.
    The prayer of consecration applies to the Sacrament the specific title—"Sacrifice of praise and thanksgiving"—which is the meaning of the popular name of this Sacrament— The Eucharist. Eucharist means praise, gratitude, giving of thanks, and the prayer calls the Sacrament, "this our sacrifice of praise and thanksgiving." The other title, a Commemorative Sacrifice, is not precisely used in the Communion Office. But the commemorative character of the Sacrament is shown in every part of the Service, and is not by any one denied; and all the terms applicable to a sacrifice are applied to this "perpetual memory" which we make before God. Its character is plainly designated by such terms as "Consecration," "Offertory," "Oblation," "Invocation," "Holy Mystery," and by the care which is taken to restrict the power of administering this Sacrament to those who have been solemnly admitted to the order of Priesthood.

It can hardly be doubted that this statement has already

excited in a few of my readers a host of prejudices, the cherished growth of some of those logomachies to which reference was just now made. I have only to ask that these prejudices may be held in abeyance until we can agree upon the meaning which should be given to the words of the Prayer-book just now cited. It will then be clearly seen that I do not differ in this statement from any candid and intelligent Christian who thoroughly eschews the two great errors already mentioned.

The plain derivative meaning of the word sacrifice is, any thing made sacred, holy; any thing devoted, offered, or dedicated to God. The popular use of this important and familiar word corresponds precisely with the derivative sense. In this same latitude and comprehensiveness of meaning is the word used in every part of the Bible. This is the one common idea, which belongs to the word wherever it appears. Every thing is called a Sacrifice which includes this idea, and nothing else is so termed. A great many different kinds of Sacrifices are mentioned, but always the particular sort intended must be ascertained from the context. The first sacrifices of which we have any account were of different kinds. Cain brought of the fruits of the earth, an Eucharistic offering. Abel offered the firstlings of his flock. St. Paul says, that "Abel offered unto God a more excellent sacrifice than Cain." (Heb. xi, 4.)

In the Old Testament there is more frequent mention made of the sacrifice of animals, because the typical nature of the former dispensations made the greater part of the external observances of religion to consist in these lively representations of the LAMB OF GOD that was slain from the beginning of the world. But there were many unbloody sacrifices under those dispensations, and the word is just as familiarly and as properly applied to the Sacrifice of righteousness, of thanksgiving, of joy, of praise, of a broken spirit. These expressions occur frequently in the Old Testament. When the typical dispensations were superseded by a higher and better one, the use of the word without reference to blood-shedding is still more frequent. "Present your bodies," says St. Paul, "a living sacrifice, holy, acceptable unto God." (Rom. xii, 1.) He speaks of himself to the Philippians, as being "offered on the sacrifice of their faith," and of the gifts they had sent to him as "a sacrifice acceptable, well pleasing to God." Again he says, "We have an ALTAR." "By Him, therefore, let us offer the sacrifice of praise to God continually." "To do good and to communicate forget not, for with such sacrifices God is well pleased." (Heb. xiii, 10, 15, 16.) St. Peter says we are to "offer up spiritual sacrifices, acceptable to God by Jesus Christ." (1 St. Peter ii, 5.)

The word Sacrifice is applied just as literally and as appropriately to one of these kinds of sacrifice as to another. The primary idea, which gives to any of them the name of sacrifice, is as fully preserved in the one as in the other. There is no more figure in the one application than in the other. A sacrifice is an offering made to the Lord, no matter of what. If there is any figure in the use of this word in any of the modes already cited, that figure must be found ιn its application to brute and inanimate things. If one use of the word is more literal than another, it is its application to the souls and bodies of men, to the powers of the mind and the affections of the heart. These are the offerings upon which the Almighty does indeed place a value. These are the things He desires. The offering of the fruits of the earth, and of living animals, can only be regarded by Him as the external expression of the real sacrifice of the heart, and mind, and life, which these offerings represent. If, therefore, there is any figure in the use of this word, it is in its application to the outward emblem rather than to the thing signified. But, in truth, there is no figure in either case. Whatever is offered to the Lord is a Sacrifice.

To adapt religion to the compound nature of man, as composed of soul and body, it was from the beginning appointed that the spiritual sacrifices of faith, and penitence, and praise, and love, should be embodied into certain prescribed external rites and actions. Under the law, besides the sacrifices of the Patriarchal dispensation, there were a great many ceremonial offenses, the guilt of which could be taken away by a ceremonial atonement. This appointment was designed to keep more constantly in the mind of the people, by scenical representation, the real guilt and defilement of human nature, and the *propitiatory* sacrifice of the blessed Jesus, by which the sins of the whole world were to be taken away. But the Lamb of God, offered upon Calvary, was the only real *propitiatory sacrifice* ever made. This was the only true satisfaction for sins ever offered to the Divine Majesty. It is only through the mediation and worthiness of that Sacrifice that every other sacrifice unto God has been made acceptable to Him.

§ 3. Priest and Priesthood. These words, and the equivalent Greek and Latin terms, are inseparably connected with the idea of sacrifice, and they all have the same general meaning with the word sacrifice. The Latin, *Sacerdos*, is a derivative from the same root with sacrifice, and the Greek, Ιερεύς, has precisely the same derivative meaning, viz, "sacred, consecrated to God." The general idea intended to be conveyed by all these terms is that of a person having a right to come before God and to offer unto Him holy gifts.

By transgression Adam became the enemy of God and a rebel against His just authority. This enemy and rebel could therefore render no service to his Maker, but such as

23

would be an abomination in the sight of the HOLY ONE. And this is the natural condition of all the descendants of the first man.

But the state of Grace, which was provided for man's necessity as soon as the state of nature became so dreadful, changes entirely these relations between sinful men and the Holy God. The Lamb of God, slain from the beginning of the world in the purpose of the everlasting Father, became at once the Mediator, through whom the Eternal Presence was again accessible to man. Through the effectual mediation of Christ's all-atoning blood, man could come before the Mercy Seat and offer to God the sacrifice of faith and love, of praise and thanksgiving. The blood of Christ thus again *consecrated* human nature to the service of the Divine Majesty; and men became Priests unto God, privileged to offer gifts and sacrifices, both spiritual and material. The latter were merely ordained as representative of the former. Thus we find the two first sons of Adam offering sacrifices as Priests unto the Lord. This Patriarchal Priesthood continued through the period of the first and second of those fearful apostasies which attested the deep corruption of our nature.

When the second apostasy became universal, God was pleased to call out from this degeneracy one family, to preserve the true notion of the Priesthood, and to offer acceptable sacrifices to Him, through faith in the blood of the everlasting covenant. And when this family became a great nation, God emphatically declared of them, "Ye shall be unto ME a kingdom of PRIESTS and a holy nation." This appointment was made under circumstances the most solemn, and in a manner the most imposing. It is recorded in the 19th chapter of Exodus, as the fit preparation for the second publication of the law, to those who were thenceforward to be the consecrated witnesses and keepers of the truth. Thus we have the proper application and the comprehensive meaning of the titles Priest and Priesthood, solemnly affirmed by the mouth of the Lord. These titles comprehended the whole people of Israel, who were consecrated, set apart, made holy for the service of Jehovah.

The same grace and wisdom which called the people of Israel to this high and holy estate, deemed it right and proper that out from this holy nation, this kingdom of Priests, there should be taken a smaller body, to be more especially the Ministers of religion. From this latter body again was chosen a still smaller number to be yet more solemnly devoted to the service of God for special acts of worship. And from this last body one was ordained to be the High Priest. The terms Priest and Priesthood are frequently applied, in a restricted sense, specially to these several orders, to whom the duties of the Priesthood were more specifically committed. This gradation of rank and division of offices, because it offended the pride of some, the Lord of Hosts was compelled to vindicate by the most fearful sanctions.

Men were made Priests, and empowered to offer acceptable sacrifices to God, by virtue of the *purpose* of His coming, who, as an atoning Priest, was to offer Himself a sacrifice to God. By the *actual* sacrifice of this glorious High Priest the consecration of humanity to the service of God was consummated and perfected. For sin itself, for the real guilt and corruption of human nature, there never was but one atonement, but one propitiation, but one satisfaction. Access in his own right to the presence of God, to offer gifts and sacrifices as a Priest, was never enjoyed but by one man— the Man Christ Jesus. By virtue of their union with this great High Priest alone have men been authorized to come into the presence of God, and offer before Him the sacrifice of their hearts and lives. So that Christ is emphatically all in all; the beginning and the end; the first and the last.

In precise accordance with what would seem to be the position and relations of Christians, is the language of the New Testament concerning them. St. Peter says, "Ye also, as lively stones are built up a spiritual house, a holy priesthood, to offer up spiritual sacrifices, acceptable to God by Jesus Christ." (1 Peter ii, 5.) In the 9th verse of the same chapter he uses almost the very language employed by the Almighty to His ancient people. "But ye are a chosen generation, a *royal priesthood*, a holy nation, a peculiar people; that you should show forth the praises of Him who hath called you out of darkness into His marvelous light. Which in time past were not a people, but are now the people of God." St. John declares that Christ hath made us "Kings and Priests unto God and His Father." (Rev. i, 6.) Thus the Christian Church occupies precisely the place, in regard to these particulars, which the ancient Church had occupied. The members of both constituted a holy Priesthood unto the Lord, privileged to come before Him to offer gifts and sacrifices.

As the Jewish and Christian Church alike was a polity, a social body, designed to have within itself the power of self-perpetuity, and compelled by the very purpose of its being to perform the most important and concerning functions of a social body politic, it was necessary, in either instance, that there should be a regular and distinct organization, and subordination of office and authority, else the Church would have been no better than a disorderly mob, unable to perform the functions of a social body, and incapable of providing for its own preservation. Therefore, distinction of office, and social subordination, were essential ingredients in the constitution of the Church of God, under the former and the latter dispensation; "for God is not the Author of confusion," says an Apostle.

As God, of His mere mercy and goodness, conferred the Priesthood, in its most general and comprehensive sense, upon the whole nation of Israel, and upon all Christian people, so He could parcel out the several offices and degrees of that Priesthood in such manner and to such persons as to Him might seem most conducive to the accomplishment of His purposes of beneficence and love. We have seen how the Lord was pleased to distribute the duties of the Priestly function under the old law, and with what imposing sanctions He maintained the integrity of this arrangement from impertinent violation by any who would presume to intrude into the performance of parts and duties not assigned to them by the Divine order. Speaking of this very subject in the Christian Church, St. Paul inquires, "Are all Apostles? Are all Prophets? Are all Teachers?" (1 Cor. xii, 29.) Afterwards he adds, "For God is not the Author of confusion, but of peace, as in all Churches of the saints. (1 Cor. xiv, 33.)

The teaching under the new dispensation is not like to that under the old, in systematic arrangement and particularity. The reason is, that the new dispensation presupposes the continuance of the former one, in those respects in which it is not done away by the principles or the injunctions of the new. Therefore the sanctions by which the Almighty was pleased to ratify and confirm the distribution which he had made of the duties and offices of the Priesthood, under the old law, should be regarded as decisive indications of His purpose that Christians should respect any distribution of the same duties which He has been pleased to make under the Evangelical economy.

Our Church determines that God has appointed an order

of men out of the general Christian Priesthood, to be especially engaged in the sacred functions of that Priesthood, and that He has ordained a subordination of rank and authority in the order thus specially set apart. As all Christian people are Priests and a Priesthood, so the ordained Ministers of the sanctuary are more especially so, *in so far and in such particulars* as their office and authority to minister in holy things exceeds that of the people at large. Their Priesthood differs, not in kind, but in degree, from that of the Christian community. For all are sanctified, all are set apart, and permitted to offer sacrifices unto the Lord. But whatever the Minister may do which the private Christian may not do, in that particular does the Minister exercise the Priestly function in a more eminent manner than the layman. And, therefore, according to that accommodated use of language which prevailed under the old dispensation, and has been perpetuated under the new, those who are appointed thus specially and eminently to exercise Priestly functions may be termed, by restriction, Priests; and their order, the order of Priesthood.

But in strictness of speech, the Priesthood belongs to all. In every act of sacerdotal function the people participate with the Minister. They are joint offerers. The Sacrament of Baptism is not ordinarily to be administered without the congregation, which unites with the Minister in the dedication of the child and in the invocation of the Holy Ghost, although the Minister alone is authorized to affix the seal of God upon the subject. So in the Eucharist, the prayer of consecration and the entire service are said in the common name of the whole congregation, except the absolution and the benediction, in both of which the Minister assumes the exclusive character imposed upon him to speak in the name and by the authority of Christ.

Slight as is the distinction between the offices of the Priesthood, common to the whole people, and those appropriated to a particular order, very important consequences have been made dependent on its maintenance, and God requires us to respect His pleasure and His wisdom in ordaining that distinction. The plea of necessity is often urged as a reason for setting aside the appointments of God. That this plea may be justly urged, in cases where individual preservation is in conflict with some provision of ceremonial law, is taught us by the example of David, who was permitted to eat the show-bread. This instance comes under the principle that God will have mercy rather than sacrifice. But where the alleged necessity is only a supposed danger of religion itself; where one positive institution is violated in order to preserve another positive institution, which is supposed to be in danger, there the case of Uzzah seems to have been recorded for our instruction and warning. (1 Chron. xiii.) This man verily thought that the Ark of God was about to be overturned. Now all the sacredness of the Ark was derived from God's positive institution. There was nothing to be hallowed in it but the integrity of that institution. The apprehension of Uzzah proceeded from distrust of the Providence of God in the preservation of His own appointment. In order to supply this supposed deficiency of Divine care and power, the officious servant breaks the institution of the Almighty in one point in order to preserve it in another. He put forth his hand, not consecrated to that service, to save the ark from falling. His presumption was punished with instant death. This single instance effectually disposes of all those undiscovered islands which have been ingeniously suggested as a sufficient apology for the violation of one of God's positive appointments in order to maintain another. Baptism and the Lord's Supper derive their whole efficacy from the positive institution of God. They have no natural or inherent power to do good. Their virtue depends upon the integrity of the institution. Where the Author of that institution has not provided or allowed to us the means for its preservation, He does not require it at our hands, or restrain His grace to these ordinary channels of grace. The same Divine power that ordained the Sacraments can sanctify and save us without them, where the institution can not be maintained in its integrity. For one, unauthorized by the Divine appointment, to administer these Sacraments, because the proper Minister can not be obtained, is the very presumption of Uzzah. God has the positive institutions of religion in His own keeping and under His own care. All that He requires of any one of us is obedience, and fidelity, and zeal, and earnestness, in the discharge of that ministry to which we have been respectively called. He will not hold us responsible for the administration of functions not committed to our charge, and He will not lightly look upon our intrusion into offices to which we have not been appointed.

It is urged as an objection to the views above presented of Sacrifice and the Priesthood, that some theological writers arbitrarily restrict the meaning of these titles to a *propitiatory* sacrifice, and to a *propitiatory* Priest. But we have seen that, in this sense, there never was but One Sacrifice and One Priest. We have seen also that this restricted sense is not the proper or the derivative meaning of these words; that this is not their Scriptural use, or their popular use.

Again, it is said that Romanists use the words in this restricted sense, and that to be as unlike them as possible we must not use these words at all, even in their proper and legitimate sense. But this canon would require us to give up the Bible itself, and a great many other good things which Romanists have perverted and abused. The words, in their true and legitimate meaning, have been so incorporated into the common speech of men, and are so prominently used in the very charter of our salvation, that it is idle to think of removing them from the language. They are appropriate and significant, and they will be employed in the language of religion as long as there is any religion. Let us not aid the adversary of men, in his effort to confound truth with error, by permitting these words of universal use and acceptation to be identified with the most stupid of the errors which have disgraced the heathen and the Romish apostasies.

§ 4. THE POW-
ER OF ABSOLU-
TION COMMITTED
TO THE PRIEST-
HOOD.

The power of Absolution conferred upon the Ministry of reconciliation is more specifically set forth in these remarkable words than elsewhere:

"And when he had said this he breathed on them, and saith unto them, Receive ye the Holy Ghost. Whosesoever sins ye remit, they are remitted unto them; and whosesoever sins ye retain, they are retained." (St. John xx, 22–23.)

The conflicting views which have prevailed upon this subject present another instance of the tendency of the human mind, on account of its fondness for simplicity, to run out a single truth into grievous error, rather than be at the pains to combine into harmony several apparently conflicting truths.

One party maintains, or seems to maintain, that the power of the Priest to forgive sins is plenary and absolute, and that his act is final and conclusive. Another party, knowing that God alone can forgive sins, that forgiveness is of necessity the mind and act of God toward the sinner, and shocked by the presumption and impiety of the claim of the Priesthood, as above stated, vehemently affirm that the Ministry has nothing to do with the matter, and that the forgiveness of sins is purely a transaction between a man and his God.

Of course, this latter assertion denies all sense or meaning to the solemn declaration of our Lord just quoted, and is inconsistent with other parts of the Divine word. Let us try to harmonize the truth that is in these opposing assertions.

Forgiveness is essentially the mind and act of an offended party toward the offender. None but God, therefore, can forgive sins against God. But the whole Gospel of salvation is a declaration of the forgiveness of sins, through Jesus Christ, our Lord. This is. its distinguishing and glorious feature. This Gospel every where treats man according to his nature, a being composed of soul and body. Its saving truths are not conveyed in abstract propositions merely to the intellect. They are embodied into sensible forms, living and enduring facts, which the whole man, sense and spirit alike, may perceive and recognize.

The great truth of the Gospel—the forgiveness of sins—is contained and authoritatively set forth and effectually conveyed in both the Sacraments, Baptism and the Lord's Supper. The Ministers of Christ are the authorized administrators of these Sacraments, and the power of absolution is, therefore, an essential part of their official duty.

So important and all concerning in the economy of redemption is this great fact of the forgiveness of sins, that the blessed Jesus deemed it wise, even beside the institution of the Sacraments of remission, to make it a special and prominent part of the commission to His ministers. These ministers thus become the living, visible representatives of the mercy of God in Jesus Christ. The pardoning grace of God is embodied in that living Ministry, so that men may continually see, hear, and feel the truth, in the very presence, the words, the actions and the influence of this order of men, whose perpetual existence in the world is promised by Him who cannot deceive.

Yet absolution, either in its most solemn and authoritative form by the Sacraments, or otherwise, is of necessity but declarative. The act of any ambassador can be no more than an authorized declaration of the mind and purpose of his government. And Romish theologians admit this consequence by affirming that the absolution is null and void if not accompanied by the required conditions of faith and penitence on the part of the sinner.

The commission is given in full and confiding terms, without the expression of those exceptions which, as they grow necessarily out of the relations of the parties and the nature of the case, are inevitably implied and did not require to be expressed. The commission assumes common honesty and fair intelligence on the part of those who exercise the ministry of reconciliation. These will ordinarily enable them to discriminate between the sincere seekers of God's favor, the hypocritical pretenders, and the self-deceived; so that they may comfort and guide the first class, repel the second, and strive to tear away the veil from the hearts of the third. That Ministry thus shows forth, in living forms, and in indissoluble association with human sympathies and human intelligence, the goodness and mercy of God in the forgiveness of sins through Him who taketh away the sin of the world. The man who, having heard the Gospel, refuses to receive the pardoning grace of God through the appointed channels of that grace, despises the Author of salvation, and must perish in his presumptuous pride.

That fearful abuse of this gracious provision for our necessity, which relies upon the mere Priestly declaration of pardon, as sufficient and effectual, without the essential conditions of penitence and faith, we have considered in a former chapter, when treating of the pseudo-sacrament of Penance. The necessary qualification of the power of absolution, admitted by Romish theologians, allowing it to be null and void when unaccompanied by faith and penitence, makes the absolution just that which we have described it, the authorized declaration of the great purpose of the Gospel, and so satisfies the more intelligent members of that communion; while the general claim, in its most unqualified form, imposes upon the ignorant and becomes a potent instrument of Priestly domination over the masses of the people.

§ 5. INSTITU-TION OF THE LORD'S SUPPER.   All the bloody sacrifices of the old law were commemorative of the *promise* of redemption, and faintly shadowed the real *propitiatory* Sacrifice, by which redemption was to be made. By the living victim offered up and slain, and by the blood of the victim poured forth, the GREAT ATONEMENT was typically represented. When Messiah came He thereby determined and put an end to the memorials by which His coming had been prefigured. A new kingdom of Priests was about to be established, chosen out of every nation, and consecrated by the blood of Christ to offer sacrifice unto God. Jesus chose twelve men, "whom also He called Apostles," to be the chiefs, and after Him the founders of this new kingdom. With these twelve the blessed Savior, on the very day in which He was to fulfill the former dispensation and accomplish the whole system of types and shadows, engaged in keeping the paschal feast. This was the most eminent of the typical representations of Himself; the Paschal Lamb signifying the body and the blood of the promised and only true expiatory sacrifice for sin.

While they were feasting upon this Sacrifice, the real Priest and the real Victim, so faintly represented by it, instituted, in place of this and of all the bloody sacrifices of the law, the Sacrifice and the Memorial, thenceforth to be made under the new dispensation. For, "as they were eating

Jesus took bread, and blessed it, and brake it, and gave it to the disciples, saying, Take, eat, THIS is my body, which is given for you; DO THIS in remembrance of ME. Likewise after supper He took the cup; and when He had given thanks, He gave it to them, saying, Drink ye all of this; for THIS is MY Blood, of the new testament, which is shed for you, and for many, for the remission of sins; DO THIS, as oft as ye shall drink it, in remembrance of ME."

The Paschal Lamb was no longer to be killed in anticipation of the death of Christ, the true Passover: for He, the very Paschal Lamb of God, was now about to be slain. The blood of immolated victims was no longer to represent the precious blood of the Savior of sinners. But *this bread* henceforth shall represent the body given for the life of the world. *This cup* henceforth shall represent the all cleansing blood of the Son of God. Christians were hereafter to *do this*, to offer bread and wine to God, and to feast upon them, as the only instituted memorial of the death of the one only satisfaction for sin. And from the day of Pentecost to this hour, Christian people have made this memorial before God. By doing that which He commanded, by this sacrifice, they have "showed forth the Lord's death" till now, and they will continue to do it "until He come."

By this instituted action Christians do continually manifest their faith in the great atonement and their reliance upon it; and they thus plead before the Mercy Seat of the Eternal Father the all-sufficient merit of the one perfect sacrifice for sin made upon the Cross. The meritorious sacrifice, thus represented to the Divine Majesty, God has ever been graciously pleased to accept, and to knit together by His Spirit into the one mystical body of His Son all who faithfully and devoutly make this memorial which He hath commanded.

This Sacrament of the body and blood of Christ is a true Sacrifice, because it is an offering of the fruits of the earth to God. These gifts are consecrated, made holy, made a sacrifice—all which are equivalent expressions—when they are presented by the Christian people as an oblation to the Lord.

This Sacrament is a true Commemorative Sacrifice, because when the words of institution are pronounced by the lawful Minister, these fruits of the earth, these gifts which we have first offered to the Lord, are changed from their original character into real and effective representatives of the body and blood of Christ; and in that new relation are again presented to our Heavenly Father, as a more acceptable oblation, as a sweet smelling savor, as a precious memorial before God of the meritorious sacrifice of His Son, our Lord.

This Sacrament is a Eucharistic Sacrifice, because it contains within it the solemn oblation to God of the worship and obedience, of the praises and thanksgivings, of the hearts and lives, of the souls and bodies, of all who are engaged therein.

The Sacrifice having been thus made complete, then, according to the blessed and gracious institution of Christ, the worshippers are invited to draw near, to feast upon the sacrifice, to partake of the gifts which they have offered unto the Lord. Thus they enter anew into covenant with God— thus they are admitted into the most perfect, intimate and endearing communion with Him whom they worship and adore.

In each part and stage of this sublime institution the Holy Ghost is the present and effective Administrator. He puts it into the hearts of the people to offer. He consecrates them, and the gifts which they bring, to their respective offices. He changes the elements from their mere natural character into their instituted meaning and significance. He makes the reception of the bread and wine by the faithful to be the communion of the body and blood of Christ, in all their saving power and efficacy. "Having, therefore, brethren, boldness to enter into the holiest by the blood of Jesus, by a new and living way, which he hath consecrated for us, through the veil, that is to say, his flesh, and having a High Priest over the house of God, let us draw near with a true heart, in the full assurance of faith, having our hearts sprinkled from an evil conscience and our bodies washed with pure water." (Heb. x, 19–22.)

§ 6. THE RO-MISH DOCTRINE OF SACRIFICE. Bloody sacrifices were first instituted as types of the one atonement to be made upon Calvary, and as expressions of the faith of men in that promised atonement. But the institution was soon perverted by the foolish hearts of men into an imagined *propitiation* for sin, the offerings being supposed to have an intrinsic value in the sight of the Deity. This perverted notion led at last to the sacrifice of men and of children, as the most costly and acceptable offerings. Even the chosen people were often guilty of this great abomination, for which they were severely reproved.

In spite of the emphatic warning contained in the heathen apostasy, and in direct opposition to many strong declarations of the New Testament, affirming that but one propitiatory sacrifice for sin · has ever been made, the new Romish creed asserts that "In the Mass there is offered to God a true, proper and propitiatory sacrifice for the living and the dead." —Creed of Pope Pius IV.

The doctrine thus broadly stated in the Creed of Romanism is the precise form of the ancient heathen apostasy from the truth. It attempts to change the Memorial which God has instituted of the One Sacrifice for sin, which He had provided, into that One Sacrifice for sin. The heathen, by stupidly supposing the instituted types of the promised Atonement to be a real propitiation and satisfaction to the Divine Majesty, degraded the character of the Supreme Being by representing Him to be such an one as themselves, capable of being appeased with the fat of fed beasts. The Romish corruption does the same thing in a different way. In order to make the commemorative sacrifice of the One Atoning Sacrifice, itself a propitiation and satisfaction for sins, the theory stultifies human nature, and thereby insults and degrades the Divine Majesty, for man was made in the image of God. This theory, which goes under the name of transubstantiation, declares that the bread and wine of the Sacrament are "truly, really and substantially the body and blood, together with the soul and divinity of our Lord Jesus Christ," so that the things which seem to be bread and wine are no longer so; but "that there is made a conversion of the whole substance of the bread into the body, of the whole substance of the wine into the blood."—Creed of Pius IV.

To believe this is to contradict the evidence of all the senses, and thereby to destroy the only means which God has given us of knowing any thing. If we are not to believe the concurrent testimony of all the senses, then the foundations of faith, as well as of science, are taken away, and all truth and all knowledge are at an end.

One of the most familiar and profitable parts of the Romish religion is founded upon the dogma above cited, that, "In the Mass there is offered to God a true, proper and propitiatory sacrifice for the living and the dead." At the death of every Romanist all the feelings of affection and piety of the surviving relatives are excited, to bring this dogma into play, for the release of the soul of the deceased from purgatory by the purchase of a sufficient number of masses to be said in his behalf. This is the known and admitted consequence of the dogma, familiarly practised upon without scruple or doubtfulness every day. Such a consequence is evidently destructive of all correct notions even of natural religion, and confounds all reasonable apprehensions of the relations between God and His offending creature. But if this doctrine of sacrifice in the Mass and the corresponding doctrine of transubstantiation be true, then it is certain that every sale of a Mass, however disguised, is an actual sale of the Lord Jesus Christ, and every Priest who offers the sacrifice of the Mass for a reward re-enacts the part of the traitor Judas, and receives for his wages the price of blood.

§ 7. THE SACRAMENT OF THE LORD'S SUPPER IS THE PARTICIPATION OF CHRIST.
Jesus Christ, being God and Man, is the medium of reunion between the Divine and human nature. The Divine Life which men receive to make them the children of God and the heirs of heaven, is bestowed by the communication to them of the Divine and human nature of their Lord and Savior. Christ himself has ascended into heaven, and He declared that "it was expedient" for us that He should go there, in order that He might send the Holy Ghost to be the effective Agent in the commencement and consummation of the union between Christ and His people. We know from many places of the Divine Word that Christ is to remain at the right hand of God, to be our High Priest and effectual Intercessor until He shall come again to judge the world in righteousness. Until this second Advent of Christ, the Spirit is the sole efficient minister of Christ's kingdom in the world. By the mysterious oneness of the Divine nature, where the Spirit is, there also is the Father and the Son. Through the Spirit the Father and the Son take up their abode, as Christ has promised, with those who love Him. (St. John xiv, 23.) By the Spirit is the blessed

24

Savior always with the Ministry He has established. (St. Matt. xxviii, 20.) By the Spirit is He present with the two or three gathered together in His name. (St. Matt. xviii, 20.) By the Eternal Spirit, sent into our hearts, is that mysterious union effected between Christ and His people, which constitutes the hope and the life of man. Many are the ways by which this union is begun, strengthened and completed, but in all of them "worketh that one and the self-same Spirit." (1 Cor. xii, 11.) It is the Spirit which broods over the waters of Baptism, and incorporates the child of Adam into the body of Christ. (1 Cor. xii, 13.) By the ministration of the same Spirit we continually receive the communication of the body and blood of Christ to nourish our souls and bodies to everlasting life. For He saith, "I am that bread of life. He that eateth me even he shall live by me. Because I live ye shall live also." (St. John vi, 48, 57; xiv, 19.)

This is a declaration of the simple truth of the provision made for our salvation, without any explanation of the mode of the Spirit's operation in the production of these Divine effects. This revelation of the fact is enough for faith, which implicitly relies upon the word of eternal truth. The plain manifestation of a fact is all that men require in regard to the phenomena of external nature. But the vain wisdom and the licentious curiosity of men disdain the humble and appropriate faith in religion which they are content to exercise in nature. By the effective ministration of the Spirit the same Christ, who is our life, becomes our spiritual food and drink in the Sacrament of His body and blood. Here is a deep mystery—the mode of the spiritual communication of the body and blood of Christ is hard to understand. And forthwith, out of this difficulty there arise two schools of theology, each one seeking in its own way to remove the difficulty.

A mistake is sometimes made here by the defenders of the truth, in regard to the place in this transaction wherein the mystery lies. The mystery consists in the communication of the life of Christ to men. This mystery pervades the whole scheme of redemption. St. Paul assures us that the members of the ancient Church "did all eat the same spiritual meat, and did all drink the same spiritual drink: for they drank of that spiritual ROCK that followed them; and that ROCK was CHRIST." (1 Cor. x, 3, 4.) It is only the same great mystery which reappears in all its force and offensiveness to human pride, in each one of the appointed agencies and channels for its accomplishment. How Christ can be formed in our hearts by the Spirit, and how the life, thus derived, can be fed and nourished by the body and blood of Christ imparted in the Sacrament, are only parts of the same continuous and ever recurring mystery which runs through the whole plan of salvation. The mystery does not lie at all, as we shall see, in the plain and simple words of Christ when He instituted this Sacrament. These words are familiar, intelligible, and of universal use; and nothing but the merest wantonness of interpretation can find any difficulty in them. The real difficulty and mystery lie behind the words, in the fact that any material agency can be the means of conveying the life of God and the nourishment of that life into the soul of man.

One of the schools to which I have referred disposes of this whole mystery of salvation by quietly resolving all the expressions which indicate it into mere Eastern metaphor and hyperbole. The Sacrament of the Lord's Supper, they say, is nothing more than a memento to put us in mind of the event which transpired on Calvary eighteen hundred years ago, and to assist us to apprehend the reality of that event.

An opposite school proposes a theory of the *mode* of the communication of the body and blood of Christ to us, and thereby reduces a sublime spiritual mystery to an absurd, bungling and contradictory physical hypothesis.

I have said that the words of institution of this Sacrament present no difficulty and involve no other mystery than the general one, that the life of our souls is derived solely from union with the Divine and human nature of Christ, and that it must be nourished and completed by *constituted external agencies.*

The symbolical delivery of a thing, as being effective to pass the possession and property of that thing, has been common in all nations and ages. The delivery of a key, when so expressed, is a delivery of the house. The delivery of a little twig becomes, by positive institution, the delivery of a whole tract of land. Every day the entire property and full possession of landed estates are given, in this country, by the delivery of a piece of paper, called a deed. To this universal custom of mankind all language has been framed, and no one ever thinks of misunderstanding the person who calls the instituted symbol of a thing by the name of the thing itself. So we perfectly understand the Apostle when he says, "that Rock was Christ." So our Savior spoke, in precise accordance with the universal language of mankind, when delivering the new symbols of His body and blood, He said, "THIS is my body," &c. The words were the plainer because they had just been engaged in feeding upon the instituted symbols of the same body and blood under the economy then about to be terminated. By the mighty power of the Holy Ghost, the instituted symbol becomes, to the worthy recipient, the communication of the body and blood of Christ. Human incredulity will not receive this Divine mystery unless it can understand *how* the communication is effected. Therefore it invents the debasing hypothesis that the symbol is actually destroyed, and that the flesh, and blood, and soul, and divinity of the blessed Jesus are in the paten and in the chalice, in place of the symbol, although all the appearances of bread and wine remain.

This extravagant conceit, by which the nature of a Sacrament is entirely overturned, was at first but a wanton speculation of the schoolmen. In the gradual progress of corruption it has become, with a large sect, an article of faith, to be held on pain of damnation.

By the universal construction of human language, the words of our Lord were always plain and simple; but the usages of modern society make them even more familiar and intelligible than formerly. Take a bank note, promising to pay five dollars. We call it five dollars; and it is five dollars, in virtue and effect. But why do we call it, and why is it, virtually, five dollars? Because, being a genuine document, issued by competent authority, it truly represents five dollars. It has the power and worth of five dollars wherever the drawer is known. Instead of its being an abuse of language to call this paper five dollars, it is the most common and approved, and universal form of speech, and every one understands the meaning of that form. But here comes in the theory of transubstantiation, and kindly undertakes to explain to us why it is proper to call this note five dollars. To make this language correct and intelligible, it says, you must believe that the paper and the engraving, and the signatures, are all gone; the accidents of these things indeed remain, but the substance is gone; what you really hold in your hand now is five round pieces of silver, with the United States stamp of one dollar on each! Such stolid folly was bad enough when considered merely as the trifling of literary and scholastic subtlety; but what shall we think of it when such fantasies are made first the watchword of a party in the Church of Christ, and then the symbol of a sect which imposes this as an article of faith essential to salvation!

If we apply this same illustration to the first mentioned process of getting rid of the mystery in the Lord's Supper, which is known by the name of the Zuinglian hypothesis, we shall find our bank note to be neither five silver dollars nor the effective representative of that sum, but merely a memento to put us in mind of five dollars.

The subject of religion is so awful and overwhelming that there is constant danger of allowing the reason to be put in abeyance by loud and boastful pretenses, and by imposing assumptions. All that God has revealed, as well as all that He has made, is above our reason. Nothing that He has revealed or made is contrary to it. Our Heavenly Father appeals to the reason of His children for the manifestation of the truth. The religion which He has revealed leads to the highest cultivation of the reason; and if that religion stultified the nature it has so highly exalted, it would be self-contradictory.

It is a blessed and glorious truth, that Christ in this Sacrament does, by His Spirit, impart Himself to His people, and give to them the saving might and purifying excellency of His body and blood. Because this is a spiritual operation it is not the less, but the more real. No carnal union could be so perfect, or so enduring, as the spiritual union which is thus effected. The actual union of the corporeal elements with our bodies—the type of the spiritual union between Christ and the soul—is itself but transient. The spiritual union is for eternity. How this miracle of grace is accomplished, how the Spirit acts here, as in all other instances of His ministration, faith asks not, but meekly receives the benefit and humbly adores the Savior God, whose infinite bounty bestows this wondrous gift.

The qualifications of persons to be admitted to this Sacrament are precisely the same as for the admission of adults

§ 8. QUALIFICATIONS FOR PARTAKING OF THIS SACRAMENT. to Baptism and Confirmation. These several institutions are all designed to be, on our part, a full, entire, and hearty submission of ourselves to the service and obedience of Christ. The natural effect, independent of the supernatural grace, of such a solemn, external and public confession of Christ, and pledge of fealty and obedience to Him, is, in each one of these instances, to increase, strengthen and deepen the feelings thus strongly exercised. In regard to this important natural effect, the Lord's Supper has a very great advantage over its connected institutions, in that they are to be used but once, while this must be continually repeated. To the question, "What is required of those who come to the Lord's Supper?" the Catechism answers, "To examine themselves, whether they repent them truly of their former sins, steadfastly purposing to lead a new life; have a lively faith in God's mercy through Christ, with a thankful remembrance of His death, and be in charity with all men."

Any one can see that such a self-examination as this, continually recurring, and faithfully conducted, under the influences of this most solemn institution, and issuing in a renewed public self-dedication to the cause of Christ and of righteousness, is the most effectual natural means of improvement and of moral progress that can be conceived of. To secure the full benefit of this natural efficacy of the institution, the Minister is required to give notice of the Communion upon the Sunday or other Holy-day preceding, and to exhort the people to a due preparation for this Holy Sacrament. The searching and comprehensive language of the two exhortations in the Prayer book, appointed for this purpose, make one of the best manuals for the assistance of those who are preparing for the Holy Communion. But the general principles therein set forth are carried out into minute details, and very important and valuable directions, in many other private manuals which holy men have prepared and published from time to time. Some one of these should be the closet companion of every communicant.

When we add to this natural effect the supernatural grace that is surely pledged to every faithful receiver of these holy mysteries, every Christian must see how he wrongs his own soul, and keeps up the barrier between himself and heaven, by neglecting to avail himself of every opportunity of using this Divinely provided appliance for his salvation. The great end of this, as of all the doctrines and institutions of Christian religion, is to produce in each subject of redemption the mind and character of Christ. Our distance below this exalted standard of excellence is infinite. How foolish and sinful then the waste of time and opportunity which will neglect this most eminent means of grace and growth, which God, of His infinite mercy, has provided for our necessity!

CHAPTER XVI.

THE CREED.

THE Bible emphatically announces that "There is One Body and One Spirit, One Lord, One Faith, One Baptism, § 1. ONE FAITH. One God and Father of all, who is above all, and through all, and in you all." (Ephes. iv, 4–6.) This is St. Paul's beautiful summary of the religion he preached. The same blessed unity is virtually contained in the great Charter of salvation, proclaimed by our Lord just before His ascension into heaven. That Charter reveals Father, Son, and Holy Ghost—One God; commands one baptism in that mystic NAME, thereby constituting One Body; and demands a true faith in the Divine Persons represented by that august name, as the triune Authors of our salvation, thereby requiring One certain and definite Faith, and not a multiplicity of variable or discordant beliefs. We are now to examine the provision made by the Divine care for this prescribed unity of faith.

It is plain that the prescription, "ONE FAITH," demands that the Faith should be the same for each believer, and the same in every age, from the beginning to the end of this dispensation. One faith for the man of learning, and another for the unlettered man, would be in direct conflict with this Divinely ordained unity. So, one faith for the first century, another for the fourth, and another for the nineteenth,

25

does not meet this requirement, but is a flagrant subversion
of it.

To solve these, and some other difficulties, we must recollect that Christian faith is not that which a man may believe,
or which he ought to believe, but—*that which he must believe
in order to be saved.* A man may and ought to believe
whatever seems to him to be true. As there are incalculable
diversities of knowledge among men, and a constant progress
of knowledge in successive ages, the ordinary beliefs of men
are almost infinitely varied. And this is true, to a large extent, in the kingdom of grace as well as in the kingdom of
nature. The two. books of God, by which He speaks to
man—the world of nature and the Holy Bible—convey a
vast and comprehensive learning, extending from the beginning of the creation to the end of time. The faith of those
who look into each of these Divine records necessarily differs,
according to the opportunity of each one to study, and the
capacity of each to comprehend, the facts and mysteries contained in them. The belief of the man of science, in the
department of natural phenomena, differs immeasurably, in
quantity and quality, from the belief of the plodding plow-
man. The knowledge conveyed by that other Divine revelation, the Holy Scriptures, requires for its complete mastery
a vast array of subsidiary learning and a large expenditure
of time and intelligence. The belief of the theologian, who
has devoted to the study of the Scriptures this learning, time
and intelligence, of necessity embraces a large body of particulars which the unlearned Christian has never heard of,
much less believed. Now, how are these two classes of Christian people to have ONE FAITH? The answer to this question
solves several theological puzzles, and settles some inveterate
controversies.

The correct answer to this question determines, by a logical necessity, the mooted point of essentials in religion. Some Romish theologians, and several popular denominations, to sustain their common denial of the sufficiency of the ancient creed, undertake to maintain that there are no essentials in religion to be distinguished from the whole body of revealed truth. The learned Palmer, in his laborious collections upon this subject, unhappily confuses it. His own declarations seem to be at variance with important principles which he had elsewhere established, and exhibit an unaccountable avoidance of the real question. He says: "We cannot, without temerity, divide the doctrines which He has revealed into those which may be denied, and those which may be believed. Independently of the rashness and folly of such a distinction, made without any authority of Revelation, its impiety is manifest, as it in effect constitutes man the judge of God himself." (Palmer on the Church, vol. i, p. 101. American edition.)

The Church of Christ, ever since her foundation, has been guilty of this alleged impiety, and Mr. Palmer, as one of her Ministers, has officially enacted it every time that he administered the Sacrament of Baptism. For the only faith which he is permitted to require of any one, as the condition of admission into the kingdom of heaven, is set forth in the question, "Dost thou believe all the articles of the Christian faith, as contained in the Apostles' Creed?" The Church has thus, in the sphere of the *Credenda*, the things to be believed, decided the question of essentials in religion, authoritatively, and as a public fact, to be known and observed of all men. The Christian faith, as contained in the Apostles' Creed, or in its equivalent, the Nicene Creed, has been thus prominently distinguished from all other revealed truths, from the beginning, by the whole Church. And this, not arbitrarily, but by the express command of her Lord in the great Charter of her foundation. "He that believeth and is baptized shall be saved: he that believeth not shall be damned."

This command raised the question, *then once for all* to be authoritatively decided by the Church, *what must be believed under this awful sanction?* Not surely the whole Divine Revelation, which had been accumulating for so many thousand years, the greater part of which was then locked up in a dead language, and another large portion of which was not contained in any writing until many years after the Church had executed all over the civilized world her commission to baptize into the required belief. To have demanded such a belief as this would have been an impossible condition of salvation to the mass of mankind. Only a very few of the very learned could have attempted a compliance with it.

The previous words of the charter define the designated object of belief. "Disciple all nations, baptizing them in the name of the Father, and of the Son, and of the Holy Ghost."

But these names would have had no intelligible meaning without an explanation. To tell who was meant by Father, Son, and Holy Ghost, and what each one of these Divine Persons had done "for us men, and for our salvation," was a duty imperatively imposed upon the Church by her Lord, in order to make this belief a real and intelligent act. To make the same belief also a common act, adapted to all classes and to all grades of learning and capacity, this information must be expressed in such plain, comprehensive and brief terms, that all could learn and retain it, as the ever present object of faith, the firm rock on which the soul could rest and be at peace, undisturbed and unmoved by the changes and vagaries and surging billows of the tempest-tossed world.

Such a brief formula of the saving faith, which all—learned and unlearned alike—could commit to memory, and constantly retain as the object of belief, is the perfect and the only possible solvent of the problem involved in the Divine prescription of ONE FAITH. The profession of this faith *by all believers*, leaving outside of it that variable and indefinite number of beliefs which belong to diversities of learning and capacity, is thus a logical sequence of the Divine requirement of "One Faith," and a necessity of that requirement. The same fixed and determined faith is contained, by a like logical necessity, in the Charter, commanding the Apostles and their successors to baptize into a belief. Unless the belief attached to this solemn Sacrament was positive, ascertained and definite, the whole transaction would have been an idle superstition, a mockery of God and man.

By an equal logical necessity the terms of the Charter involve the conclusion that the faith in every age must be the same with the faith of the first age. Each Apostle was, therefore, compelled by his commission to give to every Church which he founded a formula containing this one faith, to be used by that Church and transmitted as a sacred deposit.

The necessary oneness of the faith did not require a literal, but only a substantial sameness. If there were no evidence upon the subject, it would be a fair presumption that the Apostles used the same freedom and adaptation to circumstances in the preparation of the Creed as in the composition of the Gospels. But the evidence of primitive antiquity is conclusive that the Apostles did use this freedom, securing substantial sameness with considerable diversity of language and method. For, as it is the distinguishing excellence of the Christian Creed that it consists of facts, and not of speculations, so the existence of the Creed is *itself a fact* which every particular Church in the world witnesses.

Now, in the earliest ages we find, besides other literal variations, two distinct and clearly marked types of the common Creed. For the practical and little learned Western nations the twelve facts contained in the Creed were set forth in the plainest and fewest words. While for the Eastern nations, familiar with the subtleties and refinements of many elaborate systems of theology, and distracted and wearied by their complications and uncertainties, the same facts are couched in terms more expressly meeting and denying these visionary schemes.

It is true that in the scanty remains of the earliest Christian antiquity which have come down to us, the notices of the Creed are but incidental. Sometimes only one or a few Articles are cited. Frequently the Articles given are accompanied with a running commentary. But the fact of the existence of the Creed itself, and its paramount importance in every Church, every where appears. And there is no difficulty at all in recovering from these incidental notices the two forms of the Creed which we now possess, and which are known as the Apostles' Creed and the Nicene Creed.

These are the unquestionable facts of Christian history in the ages preceding the first General Council. When heresies began to arise, when the subtle and restless Eastern mind began to work upon the Christian Revelation, and when in the recklessness of partisanship men tried to corrupt both the Scriptures and the Creed, a Council of all the Bishops was called to assemble at Nice in the year 325. Few of the Western Bishops attended this Council. It was mainly an Eastern Council to consider and rebuke an Eastern heresy. It has been too often said that this Council made a new Creed, or enlarged the old one, to meet this exigency in the history of the Church. The Nicene formula is by some considered and called an *exposition* of the Apostles' Creed, then for the first time prepared and published. All the facts of the case are against these assertions.

Instead of being a new Creed, or an exposition of the old one, the Nicene formula is simply a critical revision, and a condensation rather than an enlargement, of the Creeds which we know to have been before immemorially professed in the Eastern Church. The history of the Council shows that the Bishops presented the Creeds of their respective Churches as their testimony to the ancient faith. These the Council seems to have examined and compared together, selecting from each the strongest, the most comprehensive, and the most fitting expressions of the common faith which they concurrently witnessed. Theodoret, one of the historians of the Council, tells us, "The Bishops did not invent any expressions themselves, but having received the testimony of the Fathers, they wrote accordingly." He reports the Bishops as saying, "The faith which we hold is that which we have received from the Bishops who were before us, and in the rudiments of which we were instructed when we were baptized. (Theod., B. i, ch. 8, 12.)

All the early Councils having thus, as witnesses, authoritatively settled and published the most perfect form of the ancient Creed, they then, as composed of Doctors and Pastors set for the defense of the truth, proceeded to make an authoritative *exposition* of the Creed, and refutation of heresies; not by another Creed, but by a series of Definitions, by formal Propositions, by elaborate Decrees, and by Synodal Letters.

The duties of the General Councils of the Church were various.

1. They were assembled witnesses of the ancient faith of the Church. 2. They acted as a general legislature, to provide for the pressing administrative exigencies of the Church

in their days. 3. They were judicial bodies, acting as a court of last resort. 4. As a body of learned teachers well practised in the controversies of the times, they were exceedingly competent to define and explain the terms of the Creed, and to expose the injurious consequence in regard to the integrity of this faith of certain opinions and speculations which had been put forth by different persons.˙ This last important office each of the Councils performed by embodying the opinions of its members in a variety of documents— synodal letters, formal definitions, &c.

In the first character, as assembled witnesses of the Christian faith, they simply declare and transmit to us that testimony to the faith which the Church was divinely commissioned to give to all generations of men. The same testimony might have been given without the intervention of any Council, as has indeed occurred by the uncorrupt transmission of the same faith in the Western Church in the Apostles' Creed. But that testimony is yet more satisfactorily given in the unanimous concurrence of so many early assemblies of the representatives of the Church.

The articles of the faith thus witnessed are the only part of the acts of the Councils which are bound upon the consciences of all men to be believed as THE FAITH. Tho explanations and definitions of this faith, put forth by the Councils, carry the very highest persuasive authority to all; but only those few persons are bound to believe them whose learning and acuteness enable them to perceive that they are eliminations brought out, by a practised mind, of the contents of the several articles of the Creed. These definitions and distinctions, suggested in the first place by a great variety of heresies, stand like a firm intrenchment around the faith, a defense against every open and secret assault which the ingenuity of future errorists may induce them to make.

Every one of the early heresies arose from the attempt to press a particular truth too far. They were not bald and naked falsehoods, but were one-sided propositions. The disproportioned statement of one truth overturned by consequence some other truth. The subtle definitions of the Fathers, following and closely tracking the subtle distinctions of the heretics, point out the evil consequences of each successive error. So perfect and complete is the circle of these definitions, that it would be almost impossible now for human ingenuity to originate a plausible heresy which has not been already indicated and condemned by some one of them.

A perusal of the acts of the several councils will show that the Fathers understood the different relations in which they stood to the Church, precisely as I have just stated them. The third General Council, held at Ephesus, A. D. 431, put forth many very refined definitions of doctrine in the solemn form of anathemas. Yet, because some one had presumed to alter that part of the Creed which was collected and published by the Fathers at Nice, the Council clearly discriminates between its own definitions of the Creed and the Creed itself, by enacting this canon: "These things having been read, the holy Synod has determined that no person shall be allowed to bring forward, or to write, or to compose any other Creed besides that which was settled by the Holy Fathers, who were assembled in the city of Nice with the Holy Ghost. But those who shall dare to compose any other Creed, or to exhibit or produce any such to those who wish to turn to the acknowledgment of the truth, whether from Heathenism or from Judaism, or any heresy whatever, if they are bishops or clergymen they shall be deposed."

No definitions of faith, however solemn, are ever called by these Councils THE CREED, or placed upon an equality with these immemorial confessions of the faith by the universal

Church. The doctrines of the Creed, and they alone, present us with a full, natural, and connected sense for the whole Bible. Each of the articles of the Creed is thus proved by the Bible, more certainly and conclusively than by the citation of single texts of Scripture in its support. Take away any doctrine of the Creed from Christianity, and the Bible can no longer be fully understood. Hence the learned and ingenious effort to explain away or to get rid of portions of it. On the other hand, if any pretended article of the Creed could not be proved from the Bible, it would be certain that such article was surreptitious. By this very process the Fathers were aided in exposing the fraud of those who had altered the ancient Creed. The Creed is the key which exactly fits and adapts itself to all the wards and divisions of the Word of God, and unlocks and brings to light the full, and glorious, and life-giving meaning of the whole of the Divine Word. Just as true Christianity, thus expounded and thus thoroughly understood, adapts itself to all the parts of our complex human nature, admitting all, allowing for all, and providing for all. This full and entire adaptation of Christianity to man proves that they are the common production of one Almighty Author, and that they were designed by Him for each other. So the fact that the doctrines of the Creed explain, illustrate, and give effect to all the parts of the Bible, proves that they are but varied representations of the same Divine truth, and that each of these representations came from the inspiration of Him who is all-wise, and who thus provided for bringing the whole of His redeemed people to the perfect knowledge of the truth.

The importance of a correct appreciation of the position of the Creed in Christianity, and the constant recurrence of errors upon this subject, make it advisable to examine a little further into its character and history.

Christianity is essentially the revelation of God, and of His relations to us in the matter of salvation. The Creed simply embodies this revelation, in briefest terms, and in a concrete and intelligible form. This summary of Divine Revelation does not tell us about the abstract Infinite and Absolute, the ONE, or the ALL, of which philosophy talks; but of Deity, as related to man: of God MANIFESTED, in His works of Creation, Redemption, and Sanctification; a real and possible object, therefore, of human cognition, affection and worship.

One of the most important issues now before the world is between the fact of one full and perfect Revelation of the truth, given by Christ and His Apostles, and the notion of a continuous inspiration and ever changing revelation, of which the Revelation contained in the Bible was a mere starting point. Romanism, Mormonism, and the latest Infidelity, assume the latter position. The Catholic Church has ever held, in her standards, the former alternative in this momentous issue. She maintains that the religion delivered to us by Christ and His Apostles is a perfect and finished revelation, sufficiently attested, by a CONCURRENCE of Divine Witnesses, to enable every man to know, with certainty, the things which he must believe in order to be saved. These Witnesses are, the Holy Scriptures; the Church, delivering to us now the same testimony in the Creed which she gave in the Apostolic age; and the Sacraments. Each one of these parts, muniments and witnesses of Christianity, stands upon the same foundation, and is sustained and assailed by the very same arguments. Christian writers give a mortifying advantage to infidelity when they gratuitously surrender the Divine authority of any one of these connected but independent witnesses to the truth.

The truth, thus revealed in its fullness, is adapted to all

minds and to all stages of cultivation, to be continually the elevating power of humanity. The objective truth is one and unchangeable, yet boundless in its reach. It is so grandly simple as to be intelligible to the most ordinary capacity, thus raising the lowest stratum of society to a higher level; while it is so sublime and comprehensive, that the most advanced minds may be carried forward to a more exalted position in an indefinite progression. The only development known to Christianity is in human nature itself, under the operation of the truth. There may be, and there ought to be, a continued development, in successive ages, of the capacity to apprehend and appropriate the one objective truth, by the subjects of its quickening power. And this result is shown very clearly by the most accomplished enemies of Christianity. Many of the speculations of these boasters of an enlightenment beyond the mark of Christian revelation, are but the revival of philosophic theories long ago tried and abandoned as worthless. But take their best achievements in religious and moral science, their truest and most beautiful thoughts, and they are either copies from the old Bible, or they are surpassed by the utterances of the Book of God on the same subject.

§ 2. THE BIBLE NOT A CREED.   The rash and rhetorical assertion of the great Chillingworth—"the Bible, the Bible alone, is the religion of Protestants"—has been abused and travestied into many grievous forms of error, utterly abhorrent to the declared principles of the illustrious author of this sentence.

One popular denomination in America has carried this notion apparently to its furthest extreme of irrationality, by maintaining that the Bible is the Christian Creed. We have already seen that the Bible is unfitted for such a purpose. The multifariousness of the contents of this inspired volume;

the appalling apparatus of varied learning and capacity required for its complete comprehension; the innumerable questions to be determined in regard to the genuineness and authenticity of every book, and of every verse of every book; the impossibility, on the part of the majority, of reading the Scriptures in their original languages, and the necessity of deciding upon the faithfulness of different translations: these, and many other insuperable difficulties, make it plain that the Bible is not and can not be a Creed, and was not intended to be that precise and definite proposal of certain truths, upon which every soul can repose for salvation.

§ 3. THE BIBLE NOT THE ONLY WITNESS OF THE CREED. Perhaps, in contemplation of these difficulties, the maintainer of this opinion may say, that he only meant that his Creed consists of those plain and simple truths which every man can find for himself in the Bible. This would be an abandonment of the fundamental principle of the denomination referred to, and is the prevailing notion of the members of all the popular denominations. It has its own difficulties.

Many things will appear plain and certain to one class of minds which to another are obscure and doubtful. There results, therefore, from this rule, as many diversities of faith as there are varieties of learning, candor and discrimination among men.

This conclusion, however, is controlled by another fact, viz, that men do not really as well as professedly go to the Scriptures with unoccupied minds to find a faith there. Those who renounce the authority of the Catholic Church are nevertheless under the influence of some sect, and they go to the Scriptures with the prepossessions fostered by the sect, and they are very apt to fancy that they find the doctrines of the sect very clearly revealed in the Scriptures.

Such a principle as this, even with the modification just

mentioned, making the Scriptures seemingly to reveal, with
equal clearness, so many opposing dogmas, shows that the
Scriptures were not intended to be alone in witnessing to the
saving truth which they reveal, and vindicates the wisdom
of God in constituting other and concurrent witnesses to the
same truth, against the folly of those who have despised the
Divine provision and profanely put asunder the things which
God had joined together.

This concurring but subsidiary testimony of the Creed
does not place it upon an equal footing of authority with
Scripture, as has been objected. The Creed is not proposed as a separate revelation from the Scriptures. It is
the dogmatic decision of the whole Church, declaring the
same saving truth so largely and variously revealed in the
Scriptures. It comes to us with Divine authority, because
the Church pronounced it, *by the Divine command*, while yet
inspired men were the earthly rulers of that Church. If the
Church did not act in this determination of the things to be
believed with Divine authority, then her refusal to admit
into the way of salvation all who do not profess this faith
has been a cruel and impious usurpation of the Divine prerogative from the beginning until now. Instead of imputing
this wrong to God's own institution, we must see and admire
in this provision the Divine care which has placed the faith
of every child of God upon a basis which cannot be moved,
and saves every faithful soul from the uncertainties, contradictions, and impieties which have resulted from the neglect
of this provision of infinite wisdom and goodness.

§ 4. THE CREED
NOT AN ECCLESI-
ASTICAL DEVEL-
OPMENT.
The principle of ecclesiastical development
has been freely applied to explain the for-
mation of the Creed. The persons who hold
this theory differ very widely in its practical application.
One very liberal school of its maintainers says, that the

development may be made by any sect, or by a single person, and that the development may be by taking away as well as by addition. Another school contends that the development may be made by any number of Christians who can procure the concurrence of the Pope of Rome in their determination, and that the development must always be by addition. This only differs from the last mentioned school by providing for an accumulation of doctrines, and by restraining infallibility to one man at a time, instead of allowing it to all claimants.

There is a third school among the holders of the theory of development, which limits the power of the Church to develop articles of faith to the first four or five centuries. But even if the development is thus, arbitrarily, or in any other way, stopped at the fourth century, all the objections to that theory remain in as strong force as against a development extending through all the ages.

All that has been said already about the Creed is properly an answer to this theory. These considerations, and some additional facts and reflections, may be summed up as follows.

§ 5. THE THE-ORY OF DEVELOP-MENT INCONSIST-ENT WITH "ONE FAITH." The theory is in direct violation of the Divine prescription of "ONE FAITH." This theory opens a wide door, not only to diversities of faith, but to the wildest excesses of speculation, confounding all real distinction between truth and error.

Some respectable Christian writers have carried this notion of development so far as to assert that a profession of belief that Jesus was the Christ, the Son of God, was the only faith required in the first age of the Church. For this opinion they allege such passages as the confession of the Eunuch: "I believe that Jesus Christ is the Son of God. (Acts viii.

37.) "Believe on the Lord Jesus Christ, and thou shalt be saved." (Acts xvi, 31.) "When they heard this they were baptized in the name of the Lord Jesus." (Acts xix, 5.)

Surely this is a strange wresting of the Scriptures, thus to derive from isolated expressions a meaning which directly contradicts the most solemn teaching of the Divine Word. The first and the most important canon of interpretation is, that the whole of any document must be taken together, and each part understood so as to be in correspondence with the apparent meaning of the whole. Now, if the Bible is God's Word, it is one connected document, and reveals one system of truth. Therefore, every single expression in the Bible derives its meaning in part from the whole Bible. The words mean what they are used to express in that place, and in connection with the accompanying truths to which they belong.

It is not necessary, however, to go beyond the simple commission to baptize, from which the Apostles derived all their authority in the premises, to rescue these passages from this false application. By the plain direction of that commission there could be no such thing as Christian Baptism, except in the entire name, Father, Son, and Holy Ghost, and upon confession of the whole faith included in that name. In the cases before us, instruction in the Messiahship and work of Jesus was the principal matter to be added to the knowledge which the parties already possessed, and a confession of faith on that point is therefore recorded as equivalent to a confession of the whole Christian faith. What the use of such forms of expression by the Evangelists does prove, is, that they were writing to Christians who would understand all such expressions according to the analogy of faith, *of which they were in full possession*, in that orderly arrangement of the facts of Christianity, the Creed.

One of the passages above cited makes this conclusion inevitable, even from its own immediate context. Certain disciples were found at Ephesus, of whom St. Paul inquired, "Have ye received the Holy Ghost since ye believed?" The Apostle probably wished to ascertain whether these disciples had received the laying on of hands in Confirmation, for the full Christian measure of the gift of the Holy Ghost, that so he might impart to them that gift if they had not yet received it. Their answer informs the Apostle that they had not yet received even Christian baptism. "We have not so much as heard whether there be any Holy Ghost." The next question of the Apostle evidently implies that there could be no Christian baptism except in the name and upon belief in the Holy Ghost, for he asks them, "Unto what then were ye baptized?" Upon receiving the answer, "Unto John's baptism," he instructed them in the whole mystery of salvation by Christ, after which they were baptized and confirmed. All this instruction, with the account of the Baptism and Confirmation, St. Luke condenses into three verses. Was it to be expected that he would formally recite the whole formula of baptism in that brief account?

The expression, "they were baptized in the name of the Lord Jesus," and all similar declarations, are simply a mode of saying that these persons received Christian Baptism, which would be the modern mode of expressing the same facts. Nor ought it to have been supposed possible that any Christian man would infer from this narrative that St. Paul neglected to instruct these ingenuous disciples in the very point on which he had first ascertained their ignorance; or that he would throw contempt upon his own Divine commission by baptizing them in any other name, or in any less faith than the name and belief of Father, Son, and Holy Ghost.

26

There was an *a priori* necessity that the whole saving faith of the Gospel should be gathe.ed into a short formula, to be distinctly recognized and confessed by the first converts to Christianity. The institution of Christ makes Faith to be the mean of salvation, and commands all men to be baptized into a Faith. What faith? Christian religion does not treat men as idiots, or as the subjects of a sort of necromancy. It treats them as intelligent beings, who must know and profess in whom they trust, and what they believe.

§ 6. THE APOSTOLICAL ORIGIN OF THE CREED CAN BE PROVED BY THE NECESSITY OF THE CASE.

The Faith is nowhere collected into a compact formula in the Scriptures, but it is scattered miscellaneously through the whole volume in the forms of history, prophecy, song and parable. Why this omission to gather up these scattered truths, if the Author of the Scriptures made no provision by which this most needful task should be accomplished, under such sanction, as to satisfy all fair and ingenuous minds of the truth of the faith which they were required to believe? A distinguishing glory of the Christian religion is that it consists of facts. It is a fact that the Author of the Bible instituted the Christian Church before He caused the New Testament to be written. He commanded that Church, then, to baptize men in a certain faith, and He called the same Church "the pillar and ground of the truth." (1 Tim. iii, 15.)

This Divine provision furnishes a complete answer to the question just proposed. The articles of faith are not collected in the Bible, because the Author of the Bible made ample arrangement for their collection in another way. Men were to be baptized into a belief. Christianity is a religion addressed to the reason and intelligence of men. *Ex necessitate rei*, therefore, the terms of that belief must be stated to the catechumen in *a form of words which he could learn and understand.* This is necessary now. How much more necessary was it before the New Testament was written; long before it was collected; and for the ages during which, as a book in manuscript, it was utterly inaccessible to nine-tenths of the Christian people?

There was an *a priori* necessity for the existence of a Creed in the beginning on another ground. The Sacraments, which symbolically set forth the faith to the eye and in action, would be mere enigmas if unaccompanied by a verbal formula explanatory of the mysteries contained in them. Some writers contend that the words of institution in Baptism constituted the whole of the Creed for some ages. But these words, taken by themselves, have no apparent meaning and no rational purpose. They do not propose an intelligible faith. To make the Sacraments and the use of the words of institution *intelligent acts*, the believer must know and confess who is the Father, who the Son, who the Holy Ghost, and who that Lord whose death he is commanded to show forth.

§ 7. THERE ARE EXPRESSIONS IN SCRIPTURE WHICH PLAINLY REFER TO THE CREED. St. Paul says to Timothy, "Hold fast the form of sound words, which thou hast heard of me, in faith and love, which is in Christ Jesus. That good thing which was committed unto thee keep by the Holy Ghost which dwelleth in us. . . . And the things which thou hast heard of me among many witnesses, the same commit thou to faithful men, who shall be able to teach others also." (2 Tim. i, 13–14; ii, 2.) That which Timothy was to hold fast, and to commit to others, and they again to others, in regular succession, was not a sentiment, or a feeling, or a doctrine, but a "Form." It was a FORM OF WORDS: a "FORM OF SOUND WORDS." Could the Christian Creed be described in words more definite and expressive? What other meaning can be given to the Apostle's language? They certainly are emphatic words, and describe something deemed by the Apostle of great concernment in the Christian religion. Nothing that we can find answers to their meaning but the Creed, and we are therefore almost compelled to assign to them that meaning. This conclusion becomes more certain when we find in the next succeeding ages that the Creed is familiarly spoken of in the very language here used by the Apostle, as something very precious "committed" by the Apostles to the Pastors of the Church, with the charge to hand it down in perpetual succession to their successors, as a sacred deposit. One of the common names of the Creed in those early ages was the *Depositum*—the thing "committed" to the Church.

The existence of the Creed seems to be irresistibly concluded by St. Paul, in his extraordinary charge to the Galatians: "Though we, or an angel from heaven, preach any other gospel unto you than that which we have preached unto you, let him be accursed." To make this declaration more emphatic, he immediately repeats it, with slight variation: "If any man preach any other gospel unto you than that ye have received, let him be accursed." (Gal. i, 8–9.) How could these new converts test the doctrine of an Angel, or of the very Apostle who had taught them, by the Gospel which they had first received, unless the truths of that Gospel were embodied in a "form of sound words" which had been committed to them, and which was then in their possession? How else could they measure a subsequent teaching? Were they to place their frail memory of the Apostle's Sermons, years ago, against the solemn declarations of an Angel, and of the same Apostle now? The Apostle clearly implies that these Christians had received and retained the Gospel which he preached, in such a connected and available form, that they could use it as the standard by which to determine the soundness of any preaching which they might afterwards hear.

Again, St. Paul writes to the Christians at Rome: "Having these gifts differing according to the grace given to us, whether prophecy, let us prophesy according to the proportion of faith." (Rom. xii, 6.) This exhortation, requiring all Christian teaching to be according to the proportion of faith, evidently implies that the whole saving faith was already ascertained for these Roman Christians in a form of such ready access, or so familiar, that they could adjust all their own deliverances to this healthful proportion. I see not how else they could understand "the proportion of faith," and keep to it in all their utterances.

The known existence of this Baptismal confession of faith, one of the chief articles of which was "the resurrection of the dead," furnishes the only clear meaning yet proposed to those words of St. Paul in his great argument for the Resurrection: "Else what shall they do which are baptized for the dead, if the dead rise not at all? Why are they then baptized for the dead?" (1 Cor. xv.)

St. Paul was writing to the baptized members of the Church at Corinth, who, still retaining their Christian profession, were perverting the faith. To other masterly arguments he therefore joins this, an appeal to the confession of faith, which was a part of that baptism that made them Christians. They were baptized in this faith of the resurrection of the dead, which he, by an ellipsis, called "baptized for the dead." If there was to be no resurrection that Article of their faith was a falsehood, and their profession of it a mockery. His question puts strongly before them the alternative, that they must either renounce their Christian profession, which they had no mind to do, or abandon their sophistical objections to the doctrine of the resurrection of the dead.

§ 8. THE EX- Strong as is the foregoing testimony of
ISTENCE OF THE Scripture to the existence of a formula of
CREED CAN BE
PROVED AS A Faith in every Church, that testimony is fixed
FACT IN ALL THE decisively to this meaning, by the fact that
ANCIENT
CHURCHES. all the remains of early Christian antiquity
speak of the Creed as a common fact in every Church. They
call it by the emphatic names—Symbol, Canon, *Regula fidei*,
or Rule of Faith. And many of them refer to it in the very
words applied by St. Paul to the "form of sound words,"
which he had committed to the Churches.

Irenæus, just after the Apostolic age, mentions the Creed
as "the unalterable canon or rule of truth which every man
received at his baptism." "This faith," he says, "is the
same in all the world. . . . Nor did the most eloquent
ruler of the Church say any more than this, (for no one was
above his master,) nor the weakest diminish any thing of
this tradition. For the faith being one and the same, he that
said most of it, could not enlarge it, nor he that said least,
take any thing from it."

Tertullian recites the substance of the Creed in several
places, and calls it "the one only rule of faith, which admits
of no change or alteration." "*Sola immobilis et irreforma-
bilis*" are his strong words. The same testimony comes from
every quarter of the Church in all the ages, before and after
the Nicene Council. The learned Bingham, from whom the
above citations are made, collects all these testimonies in his
tenth book of "The Antiquities of the Christian Church."
After a full consideration of the whole subject, he comes to
the conclusion which I have already expressed, that the symbols thus held by the different Churches were identical in
doctrine, but indefinitely variant in expression, and that there

are two general types of these formulas: The Western, now called the Apostles' Creed, and the Eastern, now called the Nicene Creed. He also concludes that these variant types of the Creed are of equal antiquity.

The general uniformity of the symbols of faith held in the Churches gave rise in the fourth century to an opinion that the Apostles composed one common formula before their separation. But the substantial sameness and circumstantial variety of these symbols negative that opinion, as well as the fancy that they were composed in any age subsequent to that of the Apostles. For, if the Apostles had composed one formula for all the Churches, there could have been no variety of method or expression. It is plain, therefore, that the Apostles acted in this matter as they did in composing the books of Scripture. That is, each one gave to the Churches he founded such a form of Confession of Faith, comprising all the facts, as was best suited to the capacity and circumstances of the people. Hence we find the two general types already mentioned—a shorter form for the ruder Western nations, and a more elaborate statement of the same truths for the Eastern nations, who were familiar with the refined and subtle philosophies of the Babylonian, Greek, and Persian sages.

On the other hand, it is impossible to account for the substantial sameness, and especially for the selection of the same facts, by so many distant and separated nations, except upon the supposition that the Apostles, or others from their dictation, gave to the churches which they respectively founded this summary of all that was necessary to be believed. A practical demonstration of this conclusion has been given in modern times by the innumerable varieties, inconsistencies and contradictions of sectarian Confessions of faith. And however widely they differ from each other, they differ still

more widely from the simple statement of facts which constitutes the Apostolic Creed.

When the Fathers of Nice assembled to consider the
opinions of Arius, they evidently spoke, in setting forth the
Creed, as witnesses merely of the ancient faith. Their office
in regard to the early confessions of faith was the very same
which many of the Fathers discharged in reference to the
canon of Scripture. That is, they bore testimony to the facts
as they had received them.

It is true, as we have seen, that the Creed is older than the
New Testament. For Churches were founded, and were in
full working order, long before the New Testament was composed. That which the Churches possessed then, as essential
to their foundation, was what the blessed Savior called "the
New Testament in my blood"—the Gospel contained and set
forth in the Sacraments of Baptism and the Lord's Supper,
and in that "form of sound words" which was the necessary
explanation of these Sacraments, and a full confession of the
faith by which they were to be saved. So much was absolutely necessary to the first foundation and continued existence of any Christian Church, and therefore no part of the
Church could ever have been without the Sacraments and the
Creed. To these were subsequently added the written Gospels, the Epistles, and the revelation of St. John. Each
inspired writing was jealously retained and guarded by the
Church to which it was first directly addressed, or given, and
then diligently dispersed, in multiplied copies, among all the
Churches in the world. The Canon of Scripture was thus
really formed by each Church for itself, from near the close
of the first century onward. And the uniting testimony of
so many distant Churches was the strongest that could be
imagined. The Canon of Scripture was never enough disputed to require the intervention of a General Council.

Particular Fathers, and at last the Provincial Council of Laodicea, gave historic voice to the concurrent and consentient testimony of all the Churches.

What a Provincial Council did for the canon of Scripture, the General Councils did for the universal confession of faith. They simply placed their solemn seal, as the august representatives of all the Churches, and therefore as unimpeachable witnesses, upon the common confession of them all. At the Council of Nice this conciliar examination and publication only extended to the part of the Creed which had then been brought into controversy. But *we know* that **the** articles subsequently examined and published by the Council of Constantinople formed a part of the very Creeds which had been submitted to the Council of Nice. For the history of this Council recites at large the Creeds presented by some of the Bishops as the ancient Creeds of their respective Churches; and these Creeds *have all the articles subsequently passed upon by* the Council of Constantinople. The inference, therefore, is irresistible, that those Creeds were used *entire*, before and after the Council of Nice, *upon the ancient authority by which they had been transmitted to the several Churches;* and that the office of the Council was nothing more than to compare them together, reject those which had been fraudulently altered to suit a purpose, and authenticate the true and genuine.

The Councils, in the form of their several acts, mark the distinction, as strongly as possible, between their office as witnesses of the ancient faith, and their office as interpreters and expositors of the same faith. In the first character they simply recite the Creed; in the second they explain and defend its articles by the most subtle and elaborate definitions. The Council of Ephesus, which put forth a great many of these definitions, expressly denounces the penalty of depo-

27

sition against any clergyman who should propose to a catechumen any other than the Nicene Creed as a Confesssion of
Faith.

Now, as the Creed recited and used by this very Council
of Ephesus contained all the Articles not authenticated by
the Council of Nice, it is demonstrable that the decree of the
Council of Ephesus included, *as one common confession of
faith*, that part of the Creed authenticated at Nice, and the
whole ancient Creed of the Church.

§ 9. THE
ATHANASIAN
CREED.
The so-called Athanasian Creed is simply
a digest of the decrees, definitions, anathemas
and synodal letters of the General Councils,
by which these representatives of the Church undertook to
explain and defend the ancient Creed. This masterly compilation was made by some scholar in the Latin Church in
the early part of the fifth century. The action of our
Mother Church of England in treating this valuable document as a Creed, and in failing, in this one particular, to
recognize the essential distinction between any such collection
of truths and the primitive Creed of the Christian Church,
has been an unhappy source of confusion, and has opened
the door to many and fatal errors. For, if we are to receive
a new Creed compiled in the fifth century, why not another,
and another, put forth in the increasing light of the sixteenth,
seventeeth and nineteenth centuries? The Synods of Trent
and Westminster, and popular Sectarianism ever since,
answered this question in the affirmative, to the infinite injury
of religion, the destruction of unity, and the utter loss from
the public mind of the first principles of Church authority.

The Athanasian formula consists of those very definitions
and subtleties which the General Councils deemed important
as *muniments* and *explanations* of the Creed, but which they
expressly refused to insert in the Creed. This refusal to

issue these propositions of their own, as parts of the Creed, must have proceeded from one of two causes. Either they knew that they had no authority to issue them in this form, which is the apparent reason; or, if by possibility, they could have fancied that such authority was vested in them, they refused to exercise it on the ground that these subtleties of elaborate controversy were not the proper articles of a Creed for the universal mind—for that solemn confession, expressed or implied, which is an essential constituent of all Christian worship. In either case the decision of the Councils is clearly and positively announced against these articles as the Christian Creed. In precise conformity with this decision, Bishop Harold Browne informs us that for some time after its compilation, this formula was called an *"Exposition of the Creed;* which is the proper title for the work in question, a work which was rarely called a *Creed (Symbolum)* by the ancients." (Art. 8, sec. 4.)

The American Church has but ratified this authoritative sentence of antiquity by striking out that formula from every part of the liturgy, and from all ecclesiastical recognition as a Creed.

This minute and perhaps tedious examination of the history of the Creed seems to me to prove conclusively that in both its forms it is as old as Christianity; and that the Nicene Creed was not a development of Christian doctrine, originated in the fourth century, but is one form of the ancient deposit of the faith, "committed" by the Apostles and Apostolic men to the Churches which they respectively planted. The existence of such a Creed in the first age of the Gospel is as clearly made out as any Christian verity can be. Certainly the evidence is not stronger for the canon of Scripture, and I do not see how any historical testimony could be made stronger.

Objectors to the Catholic doctrine of the Trinity have expended a great deal of ingenuity in special criticism upon
§ 10. THE   isolated texts of Scripture which are con-
DOCTRINE OF   sidered as favoring that doctrine, trying to
THE TRINITY AS
SET FORTH IN   explain away some of them, and rejecting
THE CREED.   others as spurious. The main force of these
criticisms comes from a previous conclusion, supposed to be
historically deduced, affirming that the doctrine of the
Trinity did not originate with Christ or His Apostles, but
was a product of the Platonizing tendency of the third and
fourth centuries.

This supposed historical conclusion is contradicted by all
the actual facts of the case. The uniform position of
the ancient philosophies and religions to Christianity was,
for a long time, simple and fierce antagonism. No efforts
at reconciliation or compromise were made on either side.
The Church, both from choice and necessity, held itself aloof
from all association and sympathy with the enemies against
which it was compelled constantly to contend, resting all the
time upon the traditional faith which it had received. The
early Christians possessed neither the disposition, the motive,
nor the ability to accommodate the faith to the religious and
philosophical opinions by which they were surrounded.
That faith was, from the beginning, so carefully embodied
into independent formularies—Scripture, Creed, and Sacraments—that it could not thus be tampered with. It is true,
and this only strengthens the conclusion at which we have
arrived, that for a long time there was not that sharpness of
statement, and subtlety of distinction, which afterwards characterized theological doctrine. The various heresies which
successively arose, requiring each a distinct denial, led to this
subsequent characteristic of Christian dogma. The first
Christians simply held, with unquestioning faith, the broad,

general statements of Scripture and the Creed, without attempting to explain or modify them.

The first symptom of the inter-action of Christianity and the ancient systems was the attempt of Eastern Gnosticism to engraft upon itself many of the Christian truths. This only called forth strong opposition from the Christians, and a more tenacious adherence to the traditional faith. Long after this Platonism and the other Greek philosophies continued to treat Christianity with bitter enmity and unmitigated scorn. And it was only when the Christian faith had virtually conquered the intellect of the world, that Neo-Platonism, a conglomerate of Christian dogma and the debris of the ancient philosophies, undertook, in its short but brilliant career, to revivify the old heathen mythologies.

When these philosophies ceased to be merely antagonistic, and attempted to influence and modify the Christian faith, their only effect was to form heretical parties, which the Church had acquired firmness and vigor enough to exfoliate from her body as corrupt and dangerous excrescences. Then indeed began in Christian teaching that sharpness of statement, that subtlety of distinction, which were required in order to eliminate the falsehood of these various heresies assailing the truth from every side. These eliminations and denials of successive errors were made by successive Councils, in the shape of decrees, formal propositions, and synodal letters, forming when completed, a firm barrier around the old Creed, which remained unchanged and unchangeable.

Suppose now that we grant to the enemies of the Catholic faith all that they claim in the way of Scriptural criticism? Suppose we give up every disputed passage, and decline to insist upon what seems to us the fair meaning of all the rest, except that single one, THE GREAT CHARTER, of which the Creed is the primary and Apostolic expansion?

"All power is given unto Me in heaven and in earth. Go ye therefore and disciple all nations, baptizing them in the name of the Father, and of the Son, and of the Holy Ghost; teaching them to observe all things whatsoever I have commanded you: and lo, I am with you alway, even unto the end of the world." (St. Matt. xxviii, 18–20.)

From this Charter alone, about the genuineness of which no dispute has ever been raised, the whole Catholic faith necessarily emerges.

This charter or commission evidently contains the fundamental idea of Christianity as a religion. The fundamental idea of any religion is faith in a Deity—one God or many. Christ commands His Apostles to disciple all nations into a religion, a faith. What religion? what faith? What Deity must all nations be taught to know and to worship? The answer is, "baptizing them in the NAME of the Father, and of the Son, and of the Holy Ghost." They must be taught to know and believe in, and be enrolled into the service of the Being or Beings represented by these three titles, as the Christian Deity.

Do these three titles represent one God, or three Gods? If three Gods, then we have Polytheism, with all its absurdities and contradictions. If, of these three titles, thus placed in co-ordinate rank and authority, we say that one represents the Supreme God, and the others two created beings, then Christianity is but a modification of the heathen mythology, with its graduated scale of Divinities. The only remaining alternative is the Catholic faith, so simply set forth in the primitive Creed. That faith is, that there is one only God to be believed in, worshiped and served; that in the essential unity of His nature there is a distinction which He has been pleased to represent to us under these mystic names or titles; and that this distinction has been so positively and clearly revealed, because each of the hypostases represented by these titles sustains to men, in the economy of redemption, a distinct and separate office, in which offices men must intelligently co-operate, for the furtherance of their salvation, with these Divine Persons.

The objection to the recognition of this essential distinction in the Divine nature, that we cannot comprehend it, is surely the idlest of all idle words. Can man comprehend the essential nature of any created thing? How then can he comprehend the Creator, either as simple Unity, or as Trinity? Man may comprehend the essential nature of any thing that he has made, as of a watch, or a steam engine. But he cannot comprehend in like manner the meanest of the works of God. All that we know of natural objects is just their effects—phenomena. All that we can know or believe of God is just what He tells us of Himself, and what we see of His workings.

Simple being is itself the mystery of mysteries, awful and unfathomable, which accompanies and includes all other mysteries, and banishes utterly from the sphere of rational inquiry the strange objection to any special mode of being that it is incomprehensible.

Simple being, Being uncaused, eternal and infinite, so far transcends the powers of the human mind, that it is palsied and overwhelmed by the attempted contemplation of it. Yet this mystery, in all its inconceivableness, is a necessary conclusion of the same overpowered mind, a conclusion which is at the foundation of all religion, and of all knowledge. The Christian Revelation can not increase this mystery, for that is, in the nature of things, impossible. Nor does it pretend to diminish or unfold the mystery; but leaving it in all its awfulness and unapproachable grandeur, the Revelation does, for the sublime and precious uses of religion and wor ship, bring the First Cause, the Eternal Being, within the range of human apprehension, by manifesting Him in personal relations to us, under the mystic, yet familiar and endearing titles, Father, Son, Holy Spirit.

The kingdom of God, which Christ established in the world, is founded upon that mystic name of God. So the great Charter runs. The salvation proffered in that kingdom to all believers flows from the personal relations of God to man designated by that mystic name. The recognition of this name of God, and of the relations therein contained, is no theory, no private fancy, no human speculation, no sect dogma. It is authenticated to every man as Divine and true by an accumulation and concurrence of testimonies which exclude all place for reasonable doubt. Let us enumerate them in one view.

1. The great Charter, as we have just seen, establishes the Church, and the whole saving truth that the Church dispenses, upon the simple revelation of this name of God.

2. Every baptized person, ever since the publication of that Charter, vows allegiance and service to God under this name, and receives the seal of pardon and adoption under the same name.

3. Another Divinely instituted Sacrament, celebrated continually from the beginning, formally sets forth the work and redeeming love of the Second Person of this adorable Trinity.

4. Yet another Divine institution, Confirmation, exhibits the office and work of the Third Person described by this mystic name.

5. The Holy Church, from the Apostles' days, has, in the Creed, uninterruptedly confessed this mystery, and required this confession from all who would enter into the appointed way of salvation.

6. The BIBLE—both Testaments—in its whole spirit, tone, symbolism, and type, and in many express declarations requiring painful violence to wrest them to any other meaning, corresponds to the mystery contained in this name of God.

Ten thousand analogies in the works of God illustrate without explaining this mysterious distinction in the Divine nature. Brute matter curiously organized, an animal life or soul, and an intellectual soul—"body, soul, and spirit," St. Paul terms them—make the one composite creature man. Do we comprehend the mode of the union, or the essential nature of either of the constituents of this complex whole?

Away then with such an objection to any Revelation which God has been pleased to make of Himself. The God whom we could comprehend would only be such a God as we could make. He would be less than ourselves, less than the meanest of God's creatures.

CHAPTER XVII.

REVEALED RELIGION AN APPEAL TO HUMAN REASON.

CHRISTIANITY is a reasonable religion, and God addresses it to the intelligence, as well as to the affections of His reasonable creatures. Corrupt human nature, on the contrary, inculcates the principle that it is easier and better for each man to take his religion upon trust; that it is impossible for the reason to decide between so many conflicting claims; and so the Pagan clings to his idols; the Mohammedan swears by his Prophet; the Papist submits his neck to the yoke of a heathenized and grossly corrupt Christianity; the Skeptic denies that there is any truth; and the scoffing unbeliever loudly proclaims that nothing is certain but his senseless negations.

But when God addresses His truth to the reason of men, He does not appeal to mere unassisted reason. He furnishes aids, helps and facilities to the private reason, by the right use of which the few and simple facts that constitute the saving truth of God may be ascertained. And each man is responsible, not only for the exercise of his reason in searching after truth, but for the faithful use of those helps to the reason which God has provided.

This principle is not only assumed in the whole character of Divine Revelation, but was specially determined by a very remarkable transaction, recorded in the early part of our Savior's ministry:

"Now when John had heard in the prison the works of Christ, he sent two of his disciples, and said unto Him, Art thou He that should come, or do we look for another? Jesus answered and said unto them, Go and show John again those things which ye do hear and see: the blind receive their sight, and the lame walk, the lepers are cleansed, and the deaf hear, the dead are raised up, and the poor have the Gospel preached. to them. And blessed is he whosoever shall not be offended in me." (St. Matt. xi, 2–6.)

The truth emphatically set forth by this narrative is, that God appeals only through the reason of men to their faith. He demands faith in things supernatural and entirely beyond the power of reason to comprehend. But the evidence upon which He makes this demand, the proof that the things to be believed are revealed by Him, He submits exclusively to the reason He has bestowed. Unreasoning credulity is inconsistent with the exalted nature which Christianity recognizes and aims to cultivate in man.

The message sent by John the Baptist to our Savior required a plain, categorical answer to the question, whether Jesus was the Messiah. An answer was desired which might relieve John and his disciples from all painful doubt, and from all laborious and earnest exercise of their own minds upon the evidences of truth. Like our modern seekers after an infallible tribunal, who want to be relieved upon the whole subject of religion from the painful discipline of uncertainty, and from the hard task of thinking and reasoning, if Christ had complied with their request, and given them the affirmative and positive answer they required, they would have been abundantly satisfied. But He, who came to exalt and ennoble all the faculties of man, refuses to minister to the intellectual indolence, or to pander to the simple credulity of men. He furnishes to these honest inquirers ample materials for the exercise of their own reason in the determination of the two questions, His Divine Mission, and His Messiahship.

The answer, as an appeal to human intelligence, is wonderfully full and comprehensive. In this brief compass it contains a pregnant reference to all the great branches of the Christian evidences, external and internal, miracles, prophecies, the adaptation of this religion to the character of God, and to the necessities of man. From a diligent comparison of what they now saw and heard with the Old Testament Scriptures, the inquirers are told to determine for themselves the question which they had proposed to our Lord.

God does not appeal to the reason of His creatures without furnishing to that reason abundant materials for its faithful exercise. He furnishes a concurrence of testimonies to the truth, the meeting and blending of which in one conclusion give sufficient reasonable assurance of the truth to all who will honestly use these varied helps. These testimonies are: 1. The witness of God in the works of Creation. 2. The witness of God's Spirit in the soul. 3. The Scriptures of the Old and New Testament, containing the truth in the historic order in which it was revealed. 4. The Church keeping the same Scriptures and setting forth a brief compendium of the faith which they contain. 5. The Sacraments of Baptism and the Lord's Supper, in which the same faith is visibly and symbolically represented.

In these Sacraments each Christian man is continually required to become an *actor* in holy offices, which witness, in the most impressive manner, to the senses, to the understanding, and to the heart, the truths of redemption and the way of life.

The glorious purpose of the true religion is to elevate the

whole nature of man. This higher position can only be reached by exertion, by the faithful exercise of all human faculties. To this exertion of the higher powers of his nature man is disinclined, and therefore he prefers to take his religion, or his irreligion, upon trust, upon the bold assertion of a man or a party. God will not indulge this indolence and simple credulity, for such indulgence would counteract His design for the improvement and exaltation of human nature. It would appear, therefore, that the true religion must always be in charge of that small number of persons who will consent to have it on the required conditions of examination and judgment. The majority must take the penalties of the falsehood they love or supinely acquiesce in.

God's overflowing economy of mercy and grace doubtless provides for the eternal salvation of multitudes who passively receive these defective or perverted systems, and who, in other respects, try to fulfill the obligations of the truth that is to be found in most of them. But the Divine method of educating the world, and progressively elevating the actual standard of human attainment, requires, as we see, that these false systems should utterly fail to preserve the health and purity of society, or to save the human mind from that degradation which has seemed to render a despotism, a government of brute force, a dreadful necessity in nearly every age and country of the world. The experience of the past connects with this darkness one cheering gleam of light. The same gracious Providence which permits the evil that men do, and the consequences of it, seems to have placed, for ome nations at least, a limit to the process of degradation; and by preserving, in His own Word and institutions, the uncorrupt truth, stimulates, ever and anon, to healthful and purifying reformations.

The progress of modern society has brought out in bold relief the issue between the true religion, appealing to human reason, as that reason is enlightened by God's Holy Spirit and aided by all the helps which He has graciously provided, and various human systems, either discarding human reason altogether from the sphere of religion, or exalting that reason into the place of God and defiantly rejecting every Divinely proffered aid to the reason.

Dreamy, imaginative men, like the two brothers, Francis and John H. Newman, with sufficient sharpness of intellect to see all the difficulties of Christianity, and without force or breadth of mind to solve or to rise above those difficulties, drop down into one of two fearful depths.

The representative of one class arrays his bare reason, the illogical conclusions of his small mind, against the testimony of nature and the conscience of mankind, and boldly asserts that Atheism, or Pantheism—another name for the same thing—is the necessary conclusion of human reason.

The representative of the other class, virtually admitting the same conclusion, but too instinctively religious, too strongly bound by affection, fear, and a sense of dependence, to venture forth into the cold and darkness of Atheism, deliberately renounces the exercise of reason in religion, and passively submits to the most exacting and obtrusive authority that comes in his way. The recent revelations of J. H. Newman, in his *Apologia*, describe this latter class precisely, as the experience of his own mind and history. His equally fanciful and sensitive brother Francis, it is known, belongs to the former class.

A comparatively small part of the visible Church, since the Apostolic age, has humbly submitted to God's plan of making religion the great educator and enlightener of mankind, by diligently applying human reason, Divinely assisted, to learn, receive and obey the truth which God has revealed.

It is in perfect consistency with the fitness of things, that the bitter enemies of Christianity should take the part of Mr. J. H. Newman in his assault upon the Church of England, and echo his declaration that the position of that Church, reverently holding in their original integrity the word and all the institutions of God, repelling from co-equal authority with them all human speculations and devices, is a mere theory; while the Papal Church, with its portentous corruptions, is termed, in flattering distinction, a great fact. (Westminster Review, October, 1864: Art. 5.) Thus, these two rival adversaries of God and man, Atheism and Superstition, work together, as they have ever done, in antagonism to the truth, to cast dishonor upon God, and to thwart His gracious purpose for the elevation of the human soul in dignity and worth. Thus, all practical falsehoods, however seemingly opposed, work together, rendering needed aid and succor to each other, in a common enmity to truth and righteousness.

God's actual method of educating mankind, by His Providential government and by supernatural revelation, alike disproves and rebukes both these falsehoods. In nature, no truth, no knowledge, no valuable result can be secured, except by the exercise of reason, assisted in innumerable ways.

The teaching of the supernatural revelation is precisely the same. By a concurrence of Divine testimonies it is essentially an appeal to human reason. God has not furnished one all pervading "fact which shall be to men as constant a quantity as the air they breathe" to overwhelm the reason and to take the place of testimony and proof. So far as this result has been accomplished it has been purely the creation of human pride and fraud. Paganism, Buddhism and Mohammedanism are greater and more overwhelming "facts" than the Papacy. The whole tenor of revealed religion, and many express declarations of the Divine Word, teach men the truth by commanding the highest exercise of reason as the indispensable condition of knowing that truth.

Besides the remarkable reply of our Savior to this effect to the disciples of John the Baptist, already cited, the same method of teaching is emphatically stated in the exclamation to the two disciples on the way to Emmaus, "O fools, and slow of heart to believe all that the prophets have spoken!" (St. Luke xxiv, 25.) The signal discomfiture of the combined Pharisees and Herodians by the demand, "Shew me a penny; whose image and superscription hath it?"—His like refutation of the Sadducees—His constant teaching by parables: all concur, with the whole analogy of Revelation, to prove that God will not permit any man to decline the responsibility of using the noblest faculty He has bestowed in His service. He will not accept driveling superstition, or listless unbelief, in place of intelligent faith. He will not allow men with impunity so to frustrate His gracious plan for the education and exaltation of the nature He has essayed to redeem and save.

An imperfect appreciation of this great fact in the dealings of God with man, that Revelation is emphatically an appeal to human reason, is the source of much of the feebleness and indefiniteness of Christian faith in the present age. The advocate of Papal infallibility boldly denounces reason as the antagonist of religion, and declares that God has ordained their opposition. He says that the "all corroding intellect" must have in Authority "a face to face antagonist." "It is the vast Catholic body itself, and it only, which affords an arena for both combatants in that awful, never dying duel." (Apologia, p. 276.) "There are but two alternatives, the way to Rome, and the way to Atheism." (Ib., p. 236.)

We have seen how eagerly the enemies of Christianity have accepted this issue. Even some of the friends of revealed religion, in commenting upon this declaration, concede that there is a conflict between reason and dogma. (North British Review, August, 1864.) And there is unquestionably an uneasy feeling in the popular mind, produced by such oracles as these; a painful suspicion that there is a real and fatal discrepancy between reason and Revelation.

If the writer last referred to means by "dogma" something imposed by mere human authority, and witnessed by no Divine attestation, the dictum is true enough. But if he means the truths which are sufficiently witnessed to the reason by Divine testimonies, then the dictum is untrue and mischievous. And it is just this uncertainty and indefiniteness of much of the language of educated men which is inflicting irreparable injury upon the general mind and conscience.

The Papal authority—for Mr. Newman is fully sustained by Papal edicts, the last issued in 1864—arrives at its conclusion, insulting alike to God and to regenerate humanity, by confounding two very different contests now waging in the world. One is the perpetual conflict between corrupt humanity in all its departments, and the life giving truth from heaven which seeks to cure that corruption. The other is a salutary and vital antagonism between enlightened and regenerate reason, and a usurped human authority inimical both to reason and to religion. Unhappily, where this usurped authority is inextricably mingled with the only religion that the people see or know, this necessary self-assertion of reason becomes an awful warfare against religion so

28

disguised and corrupted. This lamentable modification of the conflict is between different sides of the same humanity, and it is death-dealing on either side.

The Papal authority urges, on its own behalf, in this destructive conflict, that "no truth, however sacred, can stand against it (human reason) in the long run; and hence it is that in the Pagan world, when our Lord came, the last traces of the religious knowledge of former times were all but disappearing from those portions of the world in which the intellect had been active and had a career. And in these latter days, in like manner, outside the Catholic Church, things are tending, with far greater rapidity than in that old time, from the circumstance of the age, to Atheism in one shape or other." (Apologia, p. 269.)

This is Mr. Newman's idea of Atheism, as the necessary result of the human intellect, unless reason is restrained by an arbitrary human authority.

Lord Bacon puts the case very differently: "God never wrought a miracle to convince Atheism, because his ordinary works convince it. It is true that a little philosophy inclineth men's minds to Atheism, but depth in philosophy bringeth men's minds about to religion; for while the mind of man looketh upon second causes scattered, it may sometimes rest in them and go no further; but when it beholdeth the chain of them, confederate and linked together, it must needs fly to Providence and Deity."

The zealous advocate of Papal pretension forgets that Superstition and a corrupt Priesthood—a usurping human authority—had first changed, travestied and degraded the primitive truth, before human reason began to discard it. And even then the highest reason, in a few, still clung to that truth, dimly discerning it among those base corruptions.

The like corruptions of a usurped human authority have

reproduced in the Christian Church a too faithful image of that degenerate age. It is in Popish countries that Atheism has most prevailed. The ignorant adhere, indeed, tenaciously, and sometimes ferociously, to their superstitions, while almost the entire educated class is confessedly and recklessly unbe lieving.

In God's economy of the world, the proper antagonist of Darkness is LIGHT. The real and only "face to face antagonist" of ignorance, and pride, and self-will, is reason, enlightened and elevated by God's objective truth.

The real conflict that God has ordained is between life-giving truth and all the depravity of fallen human nature. In this endless conflict God summons human reason—the Divinest faculty in man—to be on His side. And, as one means of securing that result, He addresses Revelation to the reason, by making its testimonies to be just such as that reason recognizes to be sufficient in all human transactions. That which satisfies the reason in all the most important affairs of life is a concurrence of independent testimonies. God enables the reason to apprehend the constitution and properties of external nature, not by the testimony of one sense, but by the concurring testimony of several, distinctly witnessing to the same thing. How deceptive the testimony of a single sense, unaided and uncorrected by others, is familiar to all. How practically infallible is the concurring testimony of all the senses is equally well established.

So in regard to human testimony. One witness, unsustained by other witnesses, or by circumstances, furnishes no ground for a reliable conclusion. But a number of independent witnesses to the same fact supplies to reason a ground of certainty absolutely overwhelming and practically infallible.

Precisely thus does God address revealed religion to human

reason, and so demands the joyful service of that reason to the truth. By at least three distinct witnesses, sent and authenticated by Himself, differing in their nature, and variant in their mode of testifying, but concurring in their testimony, He conveys to the reason all essential, saving truth. He speaks at once by His Church, by His written Word, by His Sacraments; all alike Divinely empowered to utter, in dissimilar ways, the same life-giving truth. That truth is more distinctly and formally embodied in the Creed, at first and continuously ever since imposed as the confession of all believers. These witnesses not only utter the same truth, in these distinct and variant forms, but, by that variety of utterance, they mutually explain and illustrate each other.

Human reason, accrediting the essential truth thus concurrently witnessed, is practically infallible—just as infallible as in the determinations made, in accordance with an equal force of testimony, in any department of human knowledge. The assurance thus produced, besides being the assurance of man's highest faculty, is, even for the repose of the soul, far above and beyond that which can result from the assumption of an extraneous and artificial infallibility, not proved, but simply supposed to be necessary as the antagonist of reason. The truth, thus sufficiently witnessed to the reason, is the firm rock on which every believer may stand in conscious security, and against which "the gates of hell shall never prevail." Falsehood will constantly assault it, and will marshal against it all the force of perverted intellect. But no legitimate exercise of human reason can ever impugn this truth. No real discovery of science can shake or disturb its solid foundations. After every conflict it will remain more evidently stable and enduring than before.

Beyond the essential truth, so securely guarded and so

sufficiently witnessed because the knowledge of it is necessary to all, God has been pleased to leave a large domain of
religious truth, natural and revealed, on which the human
mind may expatiate at will, and arrive innocently at different
conclusions, so that the saving faith is untouched.

The history of the Church in all her contests with error
has amply proved the sufficiency of this Divine appeal to
human reason for the vindication of the truth. No matter
how arduous the struggle, or how popular the error, the continuing and concurring testimony, of the Church in her Creed,
of the Written Word, and of the Sacraments, defeated every
assault. The most illustrious Prelates might be carried away,
different Councils might pronounce contrary decisions for
awhile; but the OBJECTIVE TRUTH, enshrined in these
Divinely ordained forms, and continually appealing to human
reason, finally prevailed. Even Romish advocates innocently
argue that Papal infallibility never speaks until the case has
been thoroughly argued and the mind of Christendom firmly
settled. This is, of course, to reduce that imagined infallibility to the uses of a fifth wheel to a wagon, for any beneficial purpose, leaving it powerful only for mischief, as an
instrument of imposition upon the weak and credulous.

The influence of OBJECTIVE TRUTH, sufficiently witnessed
to the personal reason, is God's method of educating man,
of elevating and purifying the human soul, of advancing in
a continued progress the human race. OBJECTIVE TRUTH—
a reality outside of us and independent of us, the food of
the soul and not its own subjective state—is the instrument
with which God works for the benefit of mankind. It is so
equally in the realm of nature and in the sphere of Revelation. In nature some truths are so essential to the welfare
of all, that they are witnessed in a way which enables all
alike to apprehend them. Other truths, less necessary, con-

stituting the gradual discoveries of science, are more obscurely witnessed, and are yielded up as the rich rewards of patient labor and generous exertion.

It is precisely the same in the kingdom of grace as in the kingdom of nature. Some revealed truths are so essential to all, because all must receive and act upon them, that they are witnessed to the personal reason, with such reiteration, and in such variety of form, that all who will can recognize and confess them. Outside of these fundamental verities there remains a vast number of truths, less clearly attested, to exercise the powers and to reward the diligence of successive generations.

Each body of truth alike appeals to the reason, and demands the highest exercise of that Divine faculty: for so God educates his children; and in the very act of communicating the knowledge of salvation, elevates their nature and prepares them for the enjoyment of salvation. The testimony of God may therefore be neglected or turned aside, and men may choose darkness rather than light, ignorance rather than knowledge, proud unbelief instead of intelligent and adoring faith.

Now let it be distinctly noted, that this Christian mode of educating the individual and the race is simply A FACT. Instead of being a theory, or a paper system, it has been strangely overlooked by theorists of all sorts, and by the authors of theological systems. At all times the superintending Providence which guides and controls the Church has maintained in living action this Divine method, when, very often, the private opinions of a whole generation proposed a different method.

In all the ages the Church has stood before the world a great corporate body, the witness of her own Divine institution. In all the ages that Church has administered to all believers the Sacraments of Baptism and the Lord's Supper as "generally necessary to salvation." In all the ages the Church has imposed that faith which is contained in the old Christian Creed, *and no more*, as the condition of admission to these Sacraments, and consequently as the condition of salvation. In all the ages the same Church has held, and borne witness to, the Holy Scriptures, as the full record of Divine revelation, containing not only the truths set forth in the Creed, but a vast body of additional truth, serving for edification, and offered to the study and examination of all who have the means and opportunity of such study and examination.

These are facts, notorious and incontrovertible. For many ages these facts existed simply, and acted on the world, without any exception or complication from inconsistent facts. All apparent exceptions and complications have come from mere fractions and dissevered parts of the Church. Even to this day the whole Church has never concurred in a departure from the Divine method of teaching the world, set forth in the facts above recited. Even to this day, these are the only facts in which the whole Catholic Church concurs; and in these facts the concurrence has been perfect, in all times, as well as in all places.

The profound influence of the Divine method of education in elevating and purifying the nature of man may be feebly estimated, when we consider the preparation of mind and heart required for a due reception of the Sacraments, and for an intelligent and *ex animo* confession of the articles of faith contained in the Creed. And with all the obstacles which human wilfulness and pretended "Authority" have opposed to this method, its power and efficacy may be seen in the elevation of Christendom over the rest of the world.

CHAPTER XVIII.

CHURCH AND STATE.

THE relations of Church and State have been perplexing and complicated at all times.   The fact that the same persons are oftentimes members and officers of these two perpetual corporations ; the points of conscience and conduct at which their respective jurisdictions necessarily meet ; and chiefly, that love of dominion which is inherent in our nature, and which induces every holder of power to desire its extension, are sufficient causes of this complexity, and of continually recurring confusion on this subject.

The uncertainty and continually varying condition of these relations all over Europe, the recent startling developments in regard to the true nature of those relations between the State and our mother Church of England, and the anxious fears and earnest inquiries awakened by those developments, make this to be one of the most interesting and concerning questions of our age.

A few years ago, however eagerly we might have entered into the consideration of this question on account of the vast consequences depending upon it to the Church at large, we would hardly have esteemed it a practical question for this portion of the American Continent.   The common impression among us has been, that here, at least, a final settlement of the whole matter had been made, by the entire separation of Church and State, and that no question in regard to the relations between them could ever again arise. But the complete secularization of the leading denominations ; the attempt of so many ecclesiastical bodies to regulate the polit- ical opinions and conduct of their members, the conversion of the Pulpit into a political rostrum for the fulmination of decrees for or against the Cæsar of the day—the civil authority of the time—the natural interference of that civil authority, when so provoked or invited, with ecclesiastical affairs; and the manifest absence of all definite conception of the nature of these relations on the part of the general public, prove that this impression was a mistake ; and that it is necessary here, as elsewhere, to go back to first principles, and to the ordinance of God, in order to ascertain the right and the safe course.

It is not wonderful that this confusion and indefiniteness exist. For ever since the complete establishment of the Christian religion as the law of the Roman empire, a continuous struggle has been going on—the civil rulers striving to use the Church as a department of the State, and ambitious Churchmen to treat the State as the rightful servant of the Church. The essential independence of each has hardly ever been realized as a fact, and seldom even recognized as a principle. One invariable result has attended this con- tinuous struggle. Whichever party triumphed, the Church and religion suffered loss. Both were sacrificed upon the altar of secular ambition.

One great source of confusion and difficulty in the Christian mind, on this subject, is the fact, that the Jewish State was a Theocracy, Church and Commonwealth forming one indi- visible polity. This fact is the foundation of the whole argument of Hooker's eighth book. But the application of

29

the fact to the Christian Church was a sophism pregnant with mischief and disaster.

The only sound argument, as it seems to me, for that union of Church and State which has subsisted so long in England, and elsewhere, is the simple fact that such is the actual state of things, and that the people, representing both parties to the alliance, have been and are satisfied with it. This was a part of the established order which the Reformation seems nowhere to have disturbed, or even brought into serious question. The Presbyterian Scotch Confession of Faith really gives over to the civil authority the entire administration of the kingdom of God, except a few merely functional acts, which are reserved to the ordained ministers. The Confession, Chap. 23, Sec. 3, says:

"The civil magistrate may not assume to himself the administration of the Word and Sacraments, or the power of the keys of the kingdom of heaven ; yet he hath authority, and *it is his duty* to take order that *unity* and peace be preserved in the Church, that *the truth of God be kept pure and entire*, that all blasphemies and heresies be suppressed, all corruptions and abuses in worship and discipline prevented or reformed, and *all ordinances of God duly settled, administered and observed*. For the better effecting whereof he hath power to call Synods, to be present at them, and to provide that *whatsoever is transacted in them is according to the mind of God*."

This surrender of all real authority in the Church of God to the civil magistrate evidently proceeds from the confused notion that every Christian State is just such a Theocracy as God established for a temporary purpose, in one family, before the coming of Messiah. The authors of this sweeping article "of faith" probably expected that they would be virtually rulers both of Church and State.

The one ancient Theocracy—Church and State not united

but essentially one—was appointed for a special purpose and for a limited time. That purpose was accomplished, that limit reached, when Christ uttered from the Cross the crowning exclamation, "It is finished," and "the veil of the temple was rent," and the Catholic Church received its great Charter, "Go ye into all the world, discipling all nations." The condition of the Catholic Church, as a spiritual kingdom in all the world, composed of all nations, having its seat in the heart of every kingdom, utterly forbade its identification with any earthly kingdom, or with all of them, as a sheer impossibility.

The same facts equally forbid any connection between Church and State except that of mutual recognition, and, on the part of the Church, passive obedience in all things not contrary to the Divine law. For this kingdom of God is made up of the members of every earthly power, and those members, in their civil character, owe allegiance to the civil government of the place in which they reside. The members of this kingdom, therefore, owe equal allegiance to all the civil governments in the world, without any respect to their endless variety of form, character or legitimacy. The Church, as such, must recognize and submit to the *de facto* government, every-where. She can ask no questions and enter into no discussions. Democracy, Monarchy, Autocracy, Legitimacy, Usurpation, are all the same to her, from the necessity of her constitution. These are questions for her members, in their character as citizens, and in common with other citizens, to ask, discuss, and determine. She has but simply to accept the actual conclusion which she finds as a fact, in each country, at any specified time. The members of the Church in their civil capacity may be loyal or disloyal to an earthly government. The Church, as a corporate body, cannot be either. The terms are misplaced when applied to her. By her normal constitution she is required to recognize and obey

29

all earthly governments alike, in the place where she may be, which is utterly inconsistent with the conception of allegiance or loyalty to any. Only citizens or subjects owe allegiance, and for disloyalty they must be called to account.

This great change in the condition of the kingdom of God is not only contained in its constitution, as the ONE Catholic Church of all nations and all ages, but is often specially mentioned by our Lord and by His Apostles.

The blessed Saviour said, "I appoint unto you a kingdom, as my Father hath appointed unto me." (St. Luke, xxii, 29.) And again: "My kingdom is not of this world: if my kingdom were of this world, then would my servants fight, that I should not be delivered to the Jews; but now is my kingdom not from hence." (St. John xviii, 36.) And yet again : "Man who made me a judge, or a divider over you." (St. Luke xii, 14.)

"Render therefore unto Cæsar the things which are Cæsar's, and unto God the things that are God's." (St. Matt. xxii, 21.) "Seek ye first the kingdom of God and his righteousness." (St. Matt. vi, 33.) The Apostolic writings are full of references to this kingdom as one entirely distinct from the kingdoms of this world, while they carry out their Master's injunction, "Render unto Cæsar the things that are Cæsar's," by repeated commands to the Christian people to obey the civil authority, in all things not contrary to the law of God, or in conflict with the higher allegiance which they owed to Christ.

The close of the Jewish Theocracy was characterized by one remarkable incident, full of instruction and warning for the people of God in all ages, and closely bearing upon the subject of our present inquiry. Before the consummation of that dispensation, and while yet the Theocracy was the kingdom of God on earth, and its rulers and people His liege subjects and representatives, this appalling scene occurred.

"The Jews cried out, saying, If thou let this man go, thou art not Cæsar's friend: whosoever maketh himself a king speaketh against Cæsar."

"Pilate saith unto them, shall I crucify your king? The Chief Priests answered, We have no king but Cæsar. Then delivered he him therefore unto them to be crucified." (St. John xix, 12, 15.)

These pregnant passages describe the final apostasy of the ancient Church, as precedent to the re-establishment of the kingdom of God in its latest form. The then rulers of the kingdom, for worldly ends, denied their King, and deliberately abdicated their seats of power in the spiritual kingdom which God had set up in the world to be the light of the world. Therefore they were removed, and the curse of apostasy fell on them and on their children.

For many ages the Christian people were scrupulous in their fidelity to Christ as King; and discriminating in their recognition of the obedience which they owed as subjects to the civil rulers on the one hand, and of the relations they sustained to the kingdom of God on the other. All the early persecutions were founded upon this fidelity and enlightened discrimination on the part of the Christians, and on the obtuseness of the popular mind in refusing to recognize or permit this distinction. In one of the persecutions recorded in the Acts of the Apostles, the Jews and "certain lewd fellows of the baser sort" whom they "gathered into a company and set all the city on an uproar," thus accused St. Paul and his companions: "These all do contrary to the decrees of Cæsar, saying that there is another King, one Jesus." (Acts xvii, 5, 7.)

Unquestionably this accusation was true in both its parts. They did say that there was "another King, one Jesus," and they did refuse to obey those public laws which required them to renounce their allegiance to this King of kings, by sacrificing to the statue of the Emperor, or to any of the popular Deities. We know that every subsequent persecution found its pretext in the same truthful allegation, that the Christians professed to be citizens of another kingdom than the Roman Empire, and to owe allegiance to another King than Cæsar.

These two jurisdictions ought never to have been in conflict, for their nature and their aims are entirely distinct. The one is an earthly kingdom having in charge only earthly interests and duties. The other is a spiritual kingdom, having in charge the interests of men in eternity, and the duties which they owe to God.

The decrees of Cæsar, determining the manner and the objects of religious worship, were always presumptuous violations of the rights of conscience, and wanton invasions of the spiritual kingdom of the Lord of hosts. The attempt of the Church of God to manage the secular affairs, and to regulate the political conduct or principles of the people, is a like wanton intrusion upon a jurisdiction which belongs to another, a criminal invasion of those earthly kingdoms which God has committed to earthly rulers.

Alas! the bloody history of the world and of the Church has been, for the most part, a history of the mutual conflicts and usurpations of these two diverse kingdoms, each claiming the jurisdiction, and seeking to exercise the prerogatives of the other. Romanism and Puritanism, however opposed in other respects, are identical in this, that they are essentially politico-religious institutions. Each is an attempt to confuse and to blend together secular and spiritual jurisdiction, the earthly and the heavenly kingdom. And most of the miseries of mediæval and of modern society have come from this profane attempt to join together the things which God has strongly separated.

Romanism is avowedly a kingdom of this world: wielding

the two swords of secular and spiritual dominion; loudly and earnestly protesting, that the former is essential to the full exercise of the latter, and anathematizing all who contradict that claim, or who declare that the secular arm should not be used for the enforcement of spiritual jurisdiction. The Encyclical of 1864 re-asserts these and other Papal prerogatives of the darkest ages; and a Priesthood jealously separated from the ordinary sympathies of social life—its members bound only to their Superiors—and armed with the most effective appeals to superstitious terror, is ready at all times to enforce these vaulting claims.

Puritanism was conceived, born, and nurtured in political agitation, and through all the moods of its ever changing faith it has religiously retained this one tradition. Some of the Puritan fathers left England for Holland, professedly in search of religious liberty. They found there all the liberty they professed to seek, but not that which was indeed the liberty they wanted, viz., the power to control the faith and practice of all other people. They ingenuously give as their reason for leaving Holland, that "in ten years' time, whilst their Church sojourned among them, they could not bring" the sturdy Hollanders into "their way."* These uncompromising lovers of unlimited control in Church and State therefore left the old world in disgust, and founded in America a stern imitation of the ancient Jewish Theocracy. The milder influence of the British Government at first, and the shock of the American Revolution afterwards, dissolved the Puritan Theocracy as a formal establishment. But this principle of Puritanism has injuriously tainted, not only the Congregational Societies, but most of the religious denominations of our country.

Romish Priests and Puritan Preachers may be and have

* See Coit's Puritanism, p. 106.

been successful Politicians.   But they are not Statesmen.
And all their efforts at State craft, and their mingling of
worldly and spiritual powers, have been injurious to the people
and destructive of religion.   Out of this darkness one bright
hope arises.   The strength of character which, turned to Puritanism, has been so fruitful of mischief, when re-appropri-
ated by the Apostolic Church, will be equally efficient for
good.   In testimony whereof witness the history of Episco-
pacy in Connecticut.

The small body of persons in this country who are neither
Romanists or Puritans, and who profess to be members of
the Holy Catholic Church, have this among other solemn
duties to perform, viz., to bear a constant and emphatic testimony to the essential diversity, the Divinely ordained separation, between the kingdoms of this world and the one
kingdom of our Lord and Savior Jesus Christ.   It is true
that these very distinct kingdoms must meet and interpenetrate, because both are in this world and the same persons
are the common subjects of both.   But this meeting should
be like that of land and water, of earth and air, each retaining
its identity and diverse nature, and performing only its own
appointed function.

Surely the rulers of an earthly kingdom are competent, in
their civil capacity, to the management of its affairs, without
the dictation or guidance of the confessional or the pulpit.
In point of fact we know that the interference of these alien
powers has been productive only of mischief and misrule in
all lands.

In their official capacity in the kingdom of Christ, the
ministers and members of that kingdom can rightfully have
no politics, be of no party, have no opinions and no convictions.   One comprehensive duty, _ passive obedience in all
things not contrary to the law of Christ, expresses the whole

relation which the members of Christ's kingdom, as such, sustain to the State. The Church can entertain no question as to the respective merits of different forms of government, monarchial, republican or democratic. All that she has to do is to accept and submit to whichever may be established. Her only King has laid down the law for her as for Himself: "Man, who made me a judge, or a divider over you?" (St. Luke xii, 14.)

These same questions properly belong to the members, and even to the Ministers of Christ's kingdom, in their other relation, as citizens or subjects of an earthly kingdom. The distinction, when once clearly apprehended, is easily retained, and may be fully acted upon. Men find no difficulty in distinguishing between their duties as members of half a dozen civil corporations. The same persons may sustain the most intimate relations to these different corporations, but there are properly no relations at all between the several corporations as such. So the Christian people owe true allegiance to the State, and the State owes protection to its subjects in all their rights, including their religious rights. But between Church and State, as distinct kingdoms, there is properly no relation but that of mutual recognition, as great and all concerning facts in the Divine economy of the world, and the duty of submission and protection above mentioned. That both Church and State recognize God and His Providence, and the moral law which He has impressed upon man's nature, derogates not at all from the rightful independence of each. Composed of the same persons, and dealing with many of the same subjects, they necessarily, as before remarked, meet and interpenetrate. But the instant that the two jurisdictions are confounded, and either attempts to perform or to dictate the duties of the other, wrong and injury are the only and the necessary results. The well-being of the State, and of the

Church alike, especially in this land, require that the essential distinction between these two kingdoms, and their mutual independence, be clearly understood and jealously maintained.

In the progress of modern society the Periodical Press has become a mighty power for good and for evil. The Church of God has deemed it expedient to employ this strong agent of influence in the service of the sacred interests committed to her keeping. To make that agency either safe or effective, every Periodical professedly published in the interests of Christ and his Church, should observe, with jealous discrimination, the Divinely ordered distinction between the earthly and the heavenly kingdom. It is true that these Periodicals are individual enterprises, but they rely for their support and existence entirely upon the devotion and Christian feeling of the members of the Church. As such, their supporters are of every shade of political opinion and principle. They sustain these Church papers, not to learn their politics from them, but that they may be influential advocates of the Church and her interests. Many thousand secular papers, many hundred professedly religious papers of the various denominations, take care of the interests of the State. Is it too much to expect that three or four Church papers should esteem it their sufficient and noble work to take care of the interests of God's kingdom? Shall they be driven from this glorious advocacy, and from their undivided fealty to King Emanuel, by the popular cry, "Thou art not Cæsar's friend?" The dangers and momentous issues of the passing time, and the vast responsibility resting upon the Church of God in this almost heathen land, should induce all Church people to require this exclusive devotion to the kingdom of God on the part of the Church press. Else that agency will be shorn of all its power for good, become the pliant representative of one and another faction, the supple follower of every popular vagary, and the victim of every popular excitement.

This necessary rule for the conduct of the Church Press does not at all affect the right of the Editors to submit their views to the public on every political question. Their rights and duties as citizens or subjects of an earthly kingdom are not taken away by the relations which they sustain to the kingdom of Christ. The secular papers, the public meeting, the lecture-room, are open to all alike in the former relation. The mischief to be avoided is, the confusion of the relations which we respectively sustain to these two very distinct and utterly diverse jurisdictions. The Altar, the Pulpit, the Church Synod, and the Church Press, as agencies and representatives of the kingdom of God, should be exclusive in their devotion to the interests of that kingdom. Those who serve in these capacities can owe, as such, in their official capacity in the kingdom of God, no allegiance but to the glorious King Eternal whose servants they are. This allegiance is due and is the same every-where, in every nation. But each member of the kingdom of Christ, in the relation of citizen or subject, owes another allegiance to the particular civil State or kingdom to which he may belong; and the State claims that allegiance from each person, as citizen or subject, and not as a member of the Church of God. Vast are the interests which depend upon the intelligent recognition and practical observance of this distinction.

CHAPTER XIX.

CHRISTIAN UNITY.

1. *Cause of Divisions.*

THE basis of Church Unity has been shown in the chapters on The Kingdom of God and on the Creed. What will now be added as the conclusion of this work, is with continual reference to the principles and facts set forth in those chapters. The divisions among Christians have been an injury to the cause of truth, and a pain and grief to ingenuous minds from the beginning of Christianity. The blessed Savior foresaw this evil as the greatest obstacle to the progress of the Church and to the saving power of the truth. And He prayed for unity with all the fervor that Divine love and a perfect knowledge of the disastrous consequences of the evil could inspire. But the source of this wrong is in the very nature which Jesus came to change and purify by the life-long discipline of his religion. Therefore, even if the Church while militant on earth had been designed to be composed only of sincere and faithful men, all that the blessed Savior could do, in accordance with the Divine method of salvation, was to warn His people against this sin as against all other offenses, to pray for them, and to provide such correctives of the evil that, as one of the "gates of hell," it should never prevail to the destruction of His Church. And when we remember that besides this essential imperfection of the soundest members of the Church, the Divine arrangement contemplates the co-existence of the tares and the wheat, the bad and the good, in that Church, it is obvious that this evil is a necessary concomitant of the Divine constitution of the Church. Accordingly, the later Scriptures exhibit it to us, in a slight degree, even in the Apostolic College, and, most injuriously, in the life-time of the Apostles, in all the Churches which they founded. And ever since, this evil—the efflorescence in the Church of many of the worst passions of our nature—has been operating disastrously to religion, perilously to souls. The sin had surely reached its extremest limit, when, in our day, it was wantonly called good, and defended as the true and healthy state of Christ's kingdom.

The formal provision made by the Divine care against the destructive excesses of this spirit of discord, was to place the unity of the Church upon such a broad foundation of fully accredited facts, that "all who profess and call themselves Christians," of every variety of mind, learning and character, might stand together upon that foundation in fraternal and persuasive union.

We have seen that the appointed witnesses of revealed religion are the Scriptures, the Church, and the Sacraments, all Divine Facts, distinct in their nature, but bound together by the Author of Salvation, as concurring and mutually sustaining witnesses to the same life-giving truth. Only the perversity of man has separated these witnesses, and out of that separation worked the evil of prevalent unbelief.

The same great facts, viewed in a different aspect, are at the foundation of Christian Unity. The Church is ONE, and brings into the Divinely ordained unity all her members, by maintaining unimpaired her own Divine constitution; by administering the Sacraments ordained by Christ her Lord; by confessing the One Faith once for all delivered; by the

348 DIVINE LIFE AND NEW BIRTH.

exercise of her office as the keeper and witness of Holy Writ, in which, as the original record, is contained the Divine warrant for all that has been revealed.

All these constituents of unity are simple facts, offering themselves as facts to the observation of all Christians in all ages. They are virtually expressed in that brief but wonderfully comprehensive "form of sound words," the Catholic Creed. The fullest form of that Creed teaches us to believe in One Holy, Catholic and Apostolic Church. But the Church could not be either One, Catholic, or Apostolic, if it departed from the constitution which the Apostles established by the inspiration of the Holy Ghost; or rejected the Sacraments which Christ ordained; or ceased to guard and reverence the Scriptures which the Apostles gave and sanctioned as God's Holy Word.

These "Notes of the Church," as they are called, are virtually contained in the very nature of the Church, as a real entity—a body corporate. As such, it is essentially ONE; by its constitution it is CATHOLIC—"Go ye into all the world, discipling all nations;" by its purpose and by the spirit with which it is endued, HOLY. Therefore, some of the early Creeds expressed this Article simply by the words, "and in the Church." The Nicene Creed, as the fullest expression of the universal faith, gathered up all the terms by which this essential nature of the Church was described in the prevailing forms.

The term Catholic, in this description of the Church, has a definite and recognized meaning, derived from the history of the kingdom of God. For a long time, by the Divine appointment, that kingdom was confined to a single nation, and its most solemn rites restricted to a single place—the temple at Jerusalem. In direct contradistinction to this temporary arrangement of the kingdom, the commission of the Christian

Church sends it into all the world, and commands the administration of its holiest offices in every place where believers can be gathered. This is the Catholic constitution of the Church. And that Church being, as we have seen, essentially ONE, the feature of Catholicity necessarily attaches to the element of time as to that of space. As certainly as the Church, at Antioch, at Ephesus and at Rome, was one with the Church at Jerusalem, in the first century, so certainly must the Church in the second and all following centuries be one with the Church in that first century. And in all the Divinely ordained constituents of unity, the Church did continue one, until the general breaking up in the sixteenth century. And even since that time nearly all Christians have retained those essential constituents of unity, thereby making a Christendom, although they are lamentably and criminally divided on other and lesser points.

In recent times the most criminal of all the parties to this division has undertaken to give a new sanction to its usurped authority by a new definition of the title Catholic, resolving that time-honored name into a mere designation of an accidental or enforced majority of voices in any passing age.

This novel definition overturns the very nature of the Church, as ONE in all ages; and changes the objective truth given to men, which they must receive, and by which they must be saved, into the subjective fancies and conceits of the "popular Christianity" that may happen at any time to prevail. The contradiction of all historical fact by this theory, and its fatal influence upon the very life of Christianity, are its sufficient refutation.

This question of Unity carries us back again to God's gracious provision of objective truth, given to man, as the savor of life, and the only corrective of human error, frailty and passion. The Church, as originally constituted, the

Sacraments once ordained, the Faith once delivered and continuously imposed, the Holy Scriptures intrusted to the same guardianship, these are the Divinely appointed bonds and essential constituents of Unity, which are outside and independent of us, above and beyond our fancies, conceits and speculations. These stand firm, immovable and unchangeable, their own witnesses, clearly defining every departure from themselves, marking the distance of that departure, and continually calling back all Christian people to the same sure foundation.

As was said a little while ago, between those who retain these constituents of the Unity that Christ ordained, there necessarily subsists a real and effective unity, which they should cherish and gratefully acknowledge. Human shibboleths, making divisions, sadly mar the effects of this essential unity, but in spite of these divisions, the cheering fact remains, that nearly all who profess and call themselves Christians, are ONE in some or all of these grand constituents of unity. The Christian people who are so happy as to possess all the materials of unity just enumerated require no more. These are the elements of the real unity that God ordained in His Church. Unity in the kingdom of heaven does not melt all minds into one, nor enjoin a slavish and crushing uniformity of opinion and action, any more than the necessary unity of an earthly kingdom demands this result. To be one in submission to the Divinely appointed rulers, in the use of the same sacraments, in the confession of the saving faith, and in the acknowledgment of the Divine Word, leaves a vast field for the exercise of individual opinion, preference and practice. The universal Christian heart feels and recognizes this unity as something above and beyond all the dissensions and variations of sectarian animosity. It is this substantial unity, on the only Divine foundation, which constitutes, as we have said, a Christendom. And when the members of that Christendom meet in heathen lands, then the divisions which separated them at home are lost in the greatness and preciousness of the bonds that make them Christians.

When these bonds of unity subsist in their integrity, and yet Christian communities are divided from each other, the fault may be on one or both sides. Both may have established unauthorized terms of communion, confounding their party symbols with the Divine basis of unity. In such cases the return to unity requires that both parties should recede from this confusion of things so different. It is not necessary that the party symbol should be absolutely abandoned by either, but simply that it should be removed to its proper place, as an opinion which may be entertained by those who like it, or think it true, without the violation of communion with those who reject it.

2. *All Truth objective and independent of Human Conceptions.*

It can not be too often repeated that the truth consists of facts external to us, outside of us, and independent of our conceptions; submitted indeed to our examination, but existing just the same whether we take cognizance of them or no, and however faulty may be our conceptions of them.

Thus the world revolved on its own axis and around the sun in its present orbit, producing day and night and the succession of the seasons, although for ages and ages men supposed it to be a stationary, flat surface.

Thus also the moral law contained in the Ten Commandments was the constitution and the authoritative rule of man's spiritual nature at all times, notwithstanding the

30

false and varying standards of morality which have from time to time prevailed.

Both in the physical and the moral sphere the *Facts*, the objective truth proceeding from God, were permanent and unalterable. The human, subjective conceptions of those facts varied with the changing conditions of human life and character. It is the failure to perceive this distinction which impairs the value and poisons the quality of Mr. Lecky's laborious and interesting collections.

Precisely the same principle and the same distinction must be recognized in religion. There is the objective truth, eternal, unchangeable, revealed from heaven. There is the human conception of that truth, variable, uncertain, indistinct; producing theories, speculations, systems of divinity, often false, fanciful, variant, and mutually antagonistic. The failure to recognize this principle and to act upon it is the most prolific source of the innumerable evils of a divided Christendom.

Look now at the objective truth, *the great facts of Christianity*, and contrast the certainty, simplicity, and permanence of this truth with the shifting varieties of human opinion which have assumed its place and have been imposed upon the souls of men.

When Christ, the Lord and the King, at the close of His earthly ministry, gave to His ancient kingdom a new charter and a new organization, He commanded the Officers of that kingdom to *baptize* all nations into a certain *belief*. In this one declaration, therefore, He gave to His kingdom a Sacrament and a Creed. He had previously committed to that same kingdom another Sacrament, of His Body and Blood, showing forth the Lord's death and the meaning of it till He come.

The Creed committed to the Churches long before any

of the books of the New Testament were written is that compendium of the faith, that authoritative standard of truth, to which the writers of those books repeatedly refer. I know of no argument which has been so effective against Christianity and so fruitful of corruption as the statement incautiously admitted by Christian people that the Eastern form of this Creed authoritatively witnessed and set forth by the Council of Nice was a new and enlarged formula of the faith originated by that Council. The facts, on the contrary, are that this Nicene type of the Creed, long before the Council of Nice, was just as familiarly known and professed, from immemorial antiquity, in the East as was the Apostles' Creed in the West. Both types indeed are found with verbal variations in different Churches, but for substance the several copies of each are the same. Epiphanius, after reciting the Creed, says, "This is the faith which was delivered by the holy Apostles and received by the Church in the Council of Nice, where three hundred and eighteen fathers were present." The learned Bingham, speaking of the omission of the concluding articles of the Creed from the Nicene formula, says, "It plainly appears from most of the forms before recited that several of the articles which follow after the Holy Ghost were always a part of the Creed; and the reason why the Council of Nice repeated them not was only because there was then no dispute about them, and *they only rehearsed so much of the former Creeds as there was then occasion for to oppose the heresy of the Arians, leaving the rest to be supplied from the former Creeds, then generally received in the Church.*" He afterward adds, "Therefore it is plain the Nicene Creed was only one part of the ancient Creed that was used at full length in baptism, though not here so recited." (Bingham, Book X, ch. 4, secs. 14, 15.)

It is simple matter of fact, therefore, that the Creed in
one or other of the two forms which we now call respectively the Apostles' Creed and the Nicene Creed was for
substance held and taught by all Christian Churches
wherever planted from the Apostles' age downward.

Furthermore, while these first depositories of the truth,
the Apostles of the Lord, were still engaged in the fulfillment of their high commission, the same Power which
had sent them forth inspired some of their number, and
some of their disciples under their direction, to commit to
writing in varied forms, historical and didactic, the whole
body of truth which it was important that the Church
in all ages should know, and which might take the place
of the personal testimony of these Apostles.

Here then we have in the very beginning of Christianity,
and *constituting that Christianity*, these facts: First, The
Church or Kingdom of God fully and Divinely organized;
second, The Creed; third, The Sacraments; fourth, The
Written Word. This is absolutely all that we know any
thing about as constituting the Christianity of this first age
and of several succeeding ages. Speculation and theory,
of course, began at once, for these are necessary results
of the constitution of the human mind; and as long as
speculation and theory were in harmony with these facts,
they were harmless; but if they overturned the Sacraments, or impugned the Creed, or changed the constitution
of the Church, or contradicted the Written Word, they
were to be indignantly rejected as pernicious errors.

3. *The Church the Pillar and Ground of the Truth.*

St. Paul declares one of these great facts, "the Church
of the living God," to be *"the pillar and ground of the
truth."* (1 Tim. iii, 15.)

Now see how the Church has fulfilled and is fulfilling to-day in all the world this grand purpose of her being. That same objective truth which she received, those grand facts which we have been contemplating—her own being and Organization, the Sacraments, the Creed, and the Written Word—she held and taught in the first age, and she has held and taught the same in every succeeding age. Torn and divided and convulsed as she has been for many centuries, each part of this Church which retains the Divine organization still, by the overruling Providence of the Divine Master, perseveres in holding and teaching this same objective, immutable truth, enshrined in the same ancient forms. Thus the Church of all ages and of all nations—which is the proper definition of the Catholic Church—concurs in holding and teaching the one truth once for all received. And this is the only thing in which these torn and divided fragments do concur. And alas! by large sections of the Christian body these eternal truths are only formally held and taught in the ancient formularies, while a new and alien body of fable and cunning superstition is ardently cherished and earnestly inculcated as the practical religion of the people.

Each generation since the fourth or fifth from the Apostles has thus displayed upon the surface its own special conceits as the true Gospel, while the old objective truth was imbedded in the foundations. But this surface religion, this superficial drift overlying the old objective truth, has never in any case been the teaching of the Catholic Church, the Church which is "the pillar and ground of the truth." For by the very terms of the proposition the teaching being not that of the first age, it is not the teaching of the whole Church, but only of a fragment in time of that Church.

It is certain, therefore, that the Church of our time or of any age since the Apostles fell asleep, *viewed as separate from that first age*, is not the Catholic Church, the one Body of Christ. The Divine promise of indefectibility, the sublime trust to be "the pillar and ground of the truth," were not given to any of these dissevered portions, but to the whole Church. The peculiar teaching, the new surface religion, of one of these parts is not the teaching of the Catholic Church. The old objective truth taught in the first age and continuously ever since alone is that teaching, and has remained in its integrity, unchangeable like its Author, to be the standard by which to detect, to measure, and happily in many instances to correct the successive deviations and departures from that truth.

The fallacy we have just examined, which puts a part of the Church for the whole and calls that one part the Catholic Church, is the favorite sophism of Romish controversy, and has deluded many unstable souls into the embrace of the mother of Schisms.

4. *The History of Corruptions.*

The first formal alliance of the Church with the world engendered, as we have seen, Arianism, with all its brood of successive errors, pretenses, and persecutions. By the middle of the fifth century the Church had emerged from this fiery trial, with its faith unimpaired, and each Article of the Creed successfully vindicated against every assault, and fenced around with an impenetrable hedge of definitions and distinctions, meeting and repelling all the subtle heresies by which it had been impugned.

Presently we behold another portent of evil from the same unhappy alliance. The triumph of the Church, inviting the caresses of the world, brought in upon Christianity as a flood the most seductive forms of the ancient Paganism. The Christian sacrifice of commemoration and of praise and thanksgiving for the one all-sufficient atonement of Calvary was perverted in the imaginations of men into a propitiatory sacrifice for the living and the dead.

The Pagan Pantheon, with its crowds of gods and goddesses, was reproduced in the Christian Church without a change, except in the mere names and titles of the objects of worship. And parallel with the heathen apotheosis of men to the rank of Deities we find the corrupt Christian designation of a vast multitude of men and women blasphemously pronounced to be transferred from Paradise to Heaven, as effectual Mediators, to whom is ascribed the Divine attribute of ubiquity, and to whom it is declared lawful to address religious adoration.

In place of the ancient discipline, which repelled from the communion or imposed other penances upon public offenders, and then upon sufficient evidence of true repentance remitted the remaining part of such punishment, the heathen conceit of temporal and purgatorial torments after this life was boldly foisted upon Christianity, together with the assumed power of the Priesthood to abridge or terminate those torments by the hired performance of masses or by the more summary process of a Papal Indulgence; and the mercenary traffic in these masses and indulgences became for several ages the popular, practical religion of Western Christendom.

5. *The English Reformation an Appeal to the Catholic Church.*

The glaring contrast between such a heathenized religion and the old objective truth, which every part of the same Christendom still faithfully held and professed to revere,

at last aroused the slumbering conscience of mankind
and produced that mighty spiritual awakening which we
call the great Reformation. Whatever may have been
the faults or excesses of that Reformation, its guiding
principle, certainly in England, was the grand assertion
of St. Paul, "The Church is the pillar and ground of
the truth." From the testimony of the local Church of
their own generation, sanctioning and commending profane
travesties of religion and the grossest popular delusions,
the Reformers appealed to the testimony of the Catholic
Church—the Church of all the ages—and found clearly
witnessed in that testimony the old objective truth once
for all revealed from heaven, still guarded and treasured
in its own sacred forms, the Creed, the Sacraments, the
Written Word, and the CHURCH itself in its Divine constitution.

Here was the sufficient test, measure, and standard, Divinely given and preserved, by which to try and determine
the quality and character of all else that claimed to be a
part of Christianity. By the application of this Divine
test and measure of truth abuses and corruptions were discovered and put away, while all those details of worship,
doctrine, and discipline which accorded with the essential
truth, and tended to edification and to the meet array of
the Bride of Christ, were retained.

6. *Formation of the Romish Sect.*

After this reformation the multitude who loved and
adhered to the corruptions of mediæval Christianity became organized as a Sect, upon the avowed principle
that the testimony of any body of persons in communion
with the Bishop of Rome, in any age, is to be received
in place of the testimony of the Catholic Church, and is

sufficient to authenticate as true and Divine any proposition which may be so announced. In other words, they forged a new definition of the Catholic Church, making it to consist only of those who may concur in the vagaries of this one Bishop, and cutting off from it all the myriads who had gone before, and all living in each generation who will not substitute these profane novelties for the old truth.

Under the operation of this principle all the popular conceits of mediævalism were embodied in the Trentine Creed, and so was ratified the union between that part of the Church and the world, securing to this communion a large plurality of the nominal Christians of the world. But from this mongrel Christianity the educated intellect of each of the countries in which it was established has utterly revolted, presenting the painful contrast, in the different classes of the same society, of a mocking and atheistic unbelief, and of a superstition passively recipient of every Priestly dogma and actively obedient to every Priestly command.

The logical consequence of the Roman Sect principle—that the Catholic Church consists only of those, *few or many*, who may concur in the dogmatic utterances of the Pope as Divine truth—really made that one Bishop the Catholic Church, and his decrees infallible and equal to the voice of God. The Jesuit party, which has long ruled in the Romish Court, was not slow to avail itself of this logical advantage. In vain the great lights of that communion, from Bossuet and his illustrious compeers in the last century down to Strossmayer and Döllinger in our own day, have protested and argued and appealed to the plain testimony of history and of the Catholic Church in magnificent bursts of generous eloquence. Inclosed in the
31

logical vice of the monstrous principle of the Sect, their
writhings have been all in vain, and the year 1870 witnessed the formal installment of one man in place of the
Catholic Church, and the substitution of his voice for the
voice of God.

In the ruthless execution of this fatal consummation
of what must now be called the Papal religion the leaders
of the Jesuit party, conscious of the alienation of the intelligence of mankind from the religion which they have
long proposed as Christianity, seem deliberately to have
resolved to make that alienation more complete and final,
and to throw themselves unreservedly upon the superstitious credulity and enthusiasm of the masses.   The calculation is not a bad one for Jesuit morality, for they know
too well that if they can secure these masses they can
safely count upon at least the passive acquiescence and
sometimes the active aid of the interested intelligence of
the nations.   For a long time in America, and recently in
France and England, the soundness of this calculation and
its complete success have been abundantly proved by the
obsequious subserviency of the Politicians of every party
to that Romish Priesthood which by a word to its retainers
can turn the scale in so many elections.

7. *All Christians bear Testimony to the Objective Truth.*

And now amid this fearful apostasy of many, this din
and diversity of all, where is God's eternal and unchanging
truth, and how are men to know it?

That truth is now, as ever, where its Almighty Author
placed it, unchangeably preserved in the Divinely chosen
forms in which He first enshrined it.   There it is in the
Creed, in the Sacraments, in the Written Word, in the
unadulterate Testimony of the *whole Church*, its own wit-

ness and the witness for God to all nations and to each inquiring soul.

And here behold the wonder of God's Providence in the government of men, by which He makes the folly as well as the wrath of man to praise Him. Each one of these separated and jarring branches of the Church yet retains through all its own changes and diversities these same Divinely-given, objective forms of truth, and all witness to them with consentient testimony as the deposit once received. In their departures from this old objective truth each division presents its own peculiar form of error. *Only in the truth is their testimony one.* In their variations from the original deposit — in their denominational principles, as they call them—they differ; and they wrangle over these differences continually. To an outside observer these differences would seem to be the greater part of their religion, and with the naturally combative portion of each of these communions it is even so. The main stress of their thoughts and the force of their minds are expended on these distinctive dogmas, but with the great body of the truly devout in each it is not so. The real substantial basis of the religion of these earnest followers of Christ, in all forms of Christianity, is the old deposit of fact and faith given for the life of the world. This Catholic Christianity is the operative power on their souls, the power of God unto salvation, sanctifying and purifying their whole nature.

It is because our branch of the Church *as a Church* cleaves only to this Catholic truth, held in common by Christian people, and has no Sect dogma, no pet religion, that her members, the more tenaciously they hold this faith as a sacred trust which they dare not betray nor compromise, are tolerant and liberal in their esteem of all

who profess and call themselves Christians. The Catholic
Churchman is at once firm for the truth and loving and
large-hearted toward those who in the heat of the contest
between their own distinctive Shibboleths abuse and denounce him for maintaining only the very truths which
are at the foundation of their own religion. This peculiar
vice of sectarianism, disputatious intolerance, belongs as
well to the little narrow parties within the Church.

Such is the grand consentient testimony to the old Catholic truth presented by those large Christian bodies which
retain the ancient Divine organization of the Church. Even
the little fragments of the Church, the loose dissolving sects
which have cast off integral portions of Christianity, in a
wonderful manner are made unwittingly to bear the same
testimony; for although each has renounced some essential
part of the old Christianity, yet some have lost one and
some another part of the objective truth. *They do not agree
in their renunciations or in their newly-patented dogmas;* and
when you put the testimony of all together you find them
all concurring only in the old objective truth, of which each
carried away a part when it separated from the Body.

8. *Remote Antiquity of this Divine Provision.*

This wonder of the Providential government of God is
as old as the Church. God's ancient people apostatized
often and fearfully, so that once Elijah the Prophet believed himself to be the only living witness for God. Yet
through all these centuries of prevarication and adulterous
communion with idols the ancient Church, by its jealous
guardianship of the books of Moses, of the Aaronic Priesthood, of the Divine Ritual, constantly bore witness to the
old objective truth, and preserved it in its original integrity to be the occasion and the standard of every healthful

reformation; to be the rallying-ground to which the people could with assurance and confidence resort, when, repentant and ashamed, they would turn from their idolatries to seek the living God.

And now, if we who hold this old objective truth in its integrity, in its Divinely-appointed forms, were but one fortieth or one hundredth part of our actual numerical strength, our testimony to that truth would be just as plain, as certain, and as valuable, and as complete a vindication of the faithfulness of God, as if it were borne by all the myriads of professing Christians in the same unadulterate integrity. For the Divine provision for the security and perpetuation of the life-giving truth is that the Church, the whole Catholic Church, shall never cease to hold and teach this truth in its old Divinely-given forms, whatever may be the fantasies and follies commingled with that teaching in any given age or place. The promise that the gates of hell shall not prevail against the Church is fulfilled by this adorable miracle of Providence and grace. The assertion that "The Church is the Pillar and Ground of the Truth" is abundantly substantiated when this Catholic Church of all the ages witnesses to the One Truth once for all revealed, and proposes that truth to men in the old Divinely-chosen forms. It is this Catholic Church, holding and teaching the same unalterable truth in all places and at all times, which in the Creed we profess to believe.

When the mocking question was once asked, "Can any good thing come out of Nazareth?" the sufficient answer was "Come and see;" and all in every age can come and see that this is the old truth once for all delivered.

We hold this eternal truth in its integrity not only for ourselves, but for the world and for the generations that are to come after. The smallness of our numbers is no cause for faltering or for failure. Must Elijah apostatize because the whole nation was idolatrous? Should Athanasius conform to the imperial and courtly standard of Christianity and go with the time-serving Bishops because he seemed to be almost alone in the confession of the true faith?

9. *The Objective Truth thus witnessed not the Subject of Compromise.*

Some persons seem to consider Christian unity as a thing entirely of human consent, to be attained by mutual claims, concessions, and compromises. They have revived in their conception of the Church the exploded theory of The Social Compact, advanced in the eighteenth century, to account for the existence of human society. Their notion of Christian unity is that the various denominations should enter into a "reciprocity" treaty on the equitable principle of "give and take," and upon the foundation so adjusted re-establish the broken unity of the Church.

This theory appears to leave out of view altogether the fact that the Church is a Divine creation, and has received all its essential characteristics, all that constitutes its unity, from God. Man, therefore, has nothing to do with this foundation but to be built upon it. He can make no agreement or concession or concordat in relation to it. To recognize and accept this Divine basis of unity is the first and indispensable condition of unity. Then, if opinions and practices outside of this basis have produced divisions between those who possess the constituents of the unity which God has ordained, these opinions and practices on either side may properly be made the subject of agreement, compromise, and mutual concession. It is possible many of these opinions and practices might be retained by their respective partizans, as matters of opinion, not to obstruct or interfere with the Divinely established unity.

I confess that I have seen no signs of such a consummation. The abjuration by a few leading men in different denominations of the monstrous opinion that sectarian division is itself an absolute good, is a long way off from a practical return to unity by those denominations. The probabilities seem rather to be that each of these organized bodies will run its natural course to the end, dividing and subdividing, and getting further and further from its original point of departure. As one consequence of this process of disintegration, and gradual departure from the faith, individual members of them all will be induced to look more earnestly into the Divine constitution of the Church, and unite themselves to the Christian body which retains in perfect integrity that Divine constitution, adding nothing thereto, and imposing no terms of communion inconsistent with that provision of infinite wisdom and love.

It does not matter how small in point of numbers may be the Communion which clearly possesses these characteristics. God's truth does not depend upon majorities. The history of the world and of the Church proves that if it had been committed solely to such guardianship it would have been irrecoverably lost long ago. The All-wise Revealer of truth knew what was in man, and therefore provided a guardianship of that truth which would save it from the destructive power of the transient caprice, pride and passion of men. Even the objective truth thus carefully enshrined has not prevented deadly errors and base corruptions. But that objective truth has remained, its own sufficient witness, to suggest and to secure timely Reformations. Only by the influence of these Reformations has the true religion been saved from the corrupting power of majorities.

The Anglican communion in this country—the Protestant Episcopal Church—is indeed an inconsiderable body. There will be the less sacrifice of pride, therefore, for members of all the larger denominations to find in her the Providential possessor, in its original integrity, of that essential truth of which we all are in search.

The strongest motives appeal to earnest Christian men to come into the communion of this unsullied branch of the Catholic Church. They may not find in her, in any prominence, the special and favorite symbol of their own denomination. And neither will they find in any such prominence, if at all, the dogmas and peculiarities which they have been accustomed to oppose in rival denominations. But they will assuredly find all that they have held in most sacred and reverent estimation as the food of their spiritual life and the warrant for their hopes of heaven. In the basis of unity which she maintains is the only realization of that grand test of truth proposed by Vincent of Lerins, A. D. 434, and so universally approved. "That we hold that which has been believed *everywhere, always and by all—quod ubique, quod semper, quod ab omnibus*—for that is truly and properly Catholic, as the very meaning and derivation of the word show." (Commonitory, Sec. 2.)

To this primitive and permanent unity of Christ's mystical body it is, by the Providence of God, the high vocation of the Anglican and American Churches to call back their wandering brethren of every name. Upon this ground alone can the Sacramental host of God's anointed again be marshalled and conducted to victory over the enemies of man's salvation. These scattered members of Christ's fold can each impart as well as receive advantage by uniting together upon this common ground. Each Christian body has carried almost to perfection in its isolation some one distinguishing trait of discipline or policy. It will be the happiness of the members of each to impart this element of strength to their common mother when they return into her bosom. And the truth will need all the strength that can thus or any way be gathered for the coming conflict with error. Defiant infidelity and a grossly corrupt Christianity threaten with destruction the saving truth that God has revealed.

That politico-religious institution which now numbers a majority of those who are called Christians, and which has for its centre an earthly kingdom, by the aid of the Divine armory which it has sacrilegiously combined with that secular dominion, is gradually extending its power over the world. The almost unlimited control of men and money which superstition gives to this power enables it to operate with overwhelming influence in America. Cathedrals, churches, colleges, schools, rise as if by magic at its will, and the worshipers to fill them come obediently from the crowded countries of Europe. The looser sects can present very little resistance to the advances of this great power, except a mass of prejudices which can easily be removed, and from which the reaction is always proportioned to the amount of previous ignorance and to the violence of feeling which was founded on that ignorance. The astounding boldness of the pretensions of this sect will wither and overawe the minds of the weak and the credulous, of the young and the imaginative. Yet another class will be attracted by the congeniality of the superstitions of that elaborate system of deceit to the corrupt imaginations of the human heart. There is a religious instinct in every human being which requires to be satisfied. True religion can only satisfy that instinct at the expense of a conflict, severe and continued, with the master passion of the soul. Superstition appeases that instinct without provoking any contest with the strongest natural affections of man's perverted nature. Hence the avidity with which men embrace, and the tenacity with which they hold, superstitions which offer them the consolations of religion, and do not demand the renovation of their nature.

But the greatest accession to this same communion will be of that large class who cannot bear to be in a minority. Let the time come when elections shall be decided and offices bestowed by the votes of this religious party, and then will be repeated in this country, on a larger scale and with more decisive results, that mighty revolution, which in many nations of Europe characterized the close of the sixteenth and the beginning of the seventeenth century, and which has been so graphically described by Ranke. At that period whole nations which had abandoned the superstitions of Romanism, wearied with the dissensions of the imperfect systems that had been substituted for it, at the very first breath of persecution, at the first touch of arbitrary power, returned into the embrace of the sorceress from the pollution of whose enchantments they had so recently escaped. Vast numbers of similar sectaries in this country will become subjects of the Romish obedience under similar circumstances, and then the contest will be narrowed to a final struggle between Infidelity and Romanism leagued together on the one hand, and the ancient Christianity which by the holy Apostles was delivered, by the glorious army of martyrs confessed, and by the holy Church throughout all the world continually held. By meek endurance, by heroic constancy, by patient continuance in well-doing, must the Church of God again be tried, refined and purified, that she may be worthy to share the triumph and to enter into the glory of her Lord, at the close of this last fiery conflict. For of the result of this trial there can be no doubt. We know Him who hath said, "My strength shall be made perfect in weakness;" and "My grace is sufficient for thee;" and "He shall reign until He hath put all enemies under His feet." As this contest comes on and becomes more imminent and deadly, those of our separated brethren who would be valiant for the truth, who with holy emulation will rejoice to be counted worthy to suffer persecution for the name of Jesus, will learn that they must give up their miserable divisions, abandon their parti-colored standards and modern symbols, their human and ever-changing organizations, and rally around the one glorious standard of the Cross, and stand firmly together upon the old foundations of the Catholic Church, with her universal Creed, her holy Sacraments, her Divinely instituted ministry. Thus alone can they offer any effectual resistance to the anti-Christian powers which are trying to subvert the most sacred interests of religion and humanity. Now the fitful, passionate and ill-directed efforts of rival sects are more hurtful to themselves than to the enemies of the truth. All untruth feeds upon their divisions and grows thereby. And not less disastrous will be all attempts to wage a political war upon these adversaries. Such a contest is utterly foreign to Christianity, and nothing but confusion and defeat can come from it. To all who would be the honored champions of the truth to the Romish and the Protestant sectarian, to all who love the Church and the Savior of the Church, we offer the Unity which Christ established, as the tower of the Church's strength as the secret which Christ himself has said should teach the world that God had sent him: "That they all may be one; as thou, Father, art in me, and I in thee, that they also may be one in us; that the world may believe that thou hast sent me." (St. John, 17, 21.) Already a cheering voice comes from the noblest and devoutest members of the Roman Church, from Italy itself, accepting this basis of unity, and pledging all their energies to secure its general adoption.

In a letter to the Rev. F. Meyrick, in 1865, Ottavio Tasca, a distinguished layman, says—"Good Italians no longer recognize the Pope either as king or as despot over the whole of Catholicism. We want a Reformed Catholic Church, a national Italian Catholic Church, modelled after the primitive Church of Christ. God grant me courage and perseverance in this holy enterprise. *Si Deus pro nobis, quis contra nos?*" A like response has just reached us from distracted Mexico, torn and convulsed by the terrible struggle between awakening intelligence and depraving superstition.

Until the blessed consummation comes for which the Savior prayed, it is the duty of all to improve to the uses of charity even our unhappy divisions, by recognizing that imperfect unity which virtually subsists between those who stand together upon any part of the Divine foundation. Those who claim as their common inheritance the one Faith once for all delivered, and the same precious word of God, may joyfully own the sanctity and power of these bonds, however widely they may be separated by other differences.

O, Almighty God, who hast built Thy Church upon the foundation of the Apostles and Prophets, Jesus Christ Himself being the chief corner stone; Grant us so to be joined together in unity of spirit by their doctrine, that we may be made an holy temple, acceptable unto thee; through Jesus Christ our Lord.

THE INCARNATION.

CHAPTER I.

THE EFFECT OF THE INCARNATION UPON HUMAN NATURE.

In the preceding work I have assumed this great fact—
The Incarnation—as the essential basis of all Christian
truth. Especially is this profound mystery, the immediate
and necessary source of the truth which, because it is so
commonly denied or neglected, I have more largely maintained, the gift of The Holy Spirit, to be the guide and
helper of humanity in every condition of this earthly state
of probation. Assuming this fundamental fact, I omitted
to state with proper distinctness the essential meaning and
pervading nature of this fact, as it is presented to us in
the revelation of the WORD MADE FLESH. The present
state of religious thought makes such a statement more
necessary now than at any recent period.

Every now and then it becomes necessary in the history
of society and of the Church to go back to first truths—to
elemental principles. It is not so much that these first
truths come to be formally denied, but that, being universally acknowledged and taken for granted, their very
familiarity hides from us their depth of meaning. That
great Christian truth—The Incarnation—has been for
some ages an illustration of this tendency. While all
devoutly acknowledge it in the Creed, and with heart and
mind confess it to be at the foundation of Christian faith

(3)

and hope, yet the intense contemplation in later times of the sacrificial death of Christ, and of the external and judicial effects of that sacrifice as an offering for sin, has greatly obscured our conception of the full meaning and the pervading effect of The Incarnation in the economy of salvation.

§1. THE OLDER RELIGIONS RECOGNIZE THE INCARNATION. 1. The Incarnation of Deity—God becoming man—man exalted to communion and fellowship with God—is the meeting-point of all the higher religions of the world. Only when the degradation produced by multiplying sin, and by increasing ignorance, had reached an extreme limit, did men exchange this conception for Fetich worship, for the adoration of creatures lower than themselves as gods.

All the older religions, which are also the higher, are instinct with this conception. It was an ennobling principle, which served to elevate the peoples who entertained it, inspiring them with lofty thoughts and with cheering expectations. The gloom, the darkness, and the crushing bondage of heathenism only settled down upon the nations as this grand conception of the primeval religions was gradually obscured. No sufficient account of the universal prevalence of this idea, and of its organic connection with the ritual of all these religions, can be found except in the fact which the Divine word makes known, that a primeval promise given to the Parents of mankind, and incorporated into a primeval ritual, made it the common inheritance of all the nations.

History assures us that the nations which retained most faithfully in freshness and vividness this ennobling truth have been the brightest, the most elastic, and the most capable. This has been emphatically true of those peoples who, as composing the Church of God, have preserved this truth in its uncorrupt integrity. And since the actual coming of the Son of God in our nature the Christendom which exists as the realization of this truth witnesses to the whole earth its generous and elevating influence. By the inspiration and power of this grand fact in human history the earth itself has been subdued, and the strongest powers of nature brought under subjection to man's control. A higher task than this has been essayed and measurably accomplished. The corruption of man's own nature, indwelling sin, the usurped dominion of the Devil, have been successfully encountered, and in myriad instances in every age gloriously overcome.

§ 2. THE AU-
GUSTINIAN THE-
OLOGY OBSCURED
THE DOCTRINE OF
THE INCARNA-
TION.

2. For a long time the Incarnation was considered of little more import than as a necessary foundation for the merit and virtue of the expiatory sacrifice, and for the forensic distribution of the benefits of that expiation to those elect persons for whom only it was designed. The Augustinian theology presumptuously undertakes to answer the question which our Lord and Master refused to answer, "Are there few that be saved?" In the mediæval ages it answered this question dogmatically by the double affirmation that only a few elect could be saved and that all the elect would be baptized. Add to this the accordant dogma of the indefectibility of grace, and you have that tissue of contradictions, of arbitrary assumptions, and of narrow technicalities which have been the opprobria of Christianity, and a fruitful source of unbelief in all the history of the Church.

In the second generation after the Reformation the Sacraments grew into disrepute with an active and earnest section of the Protestants, and came to be regarded as little better than dead forms and beggarly elements. Discarding therefore the Sacraments from all effectual operation, these persons retained the theology of Augustine under

its modern name of Calvinism, and affirmed it to be the
only pure gospel. As a natural reaction from this phase
of error multitudes have renounced the Gospel itself as
thus represented.

Romanism, in settling down upon its own distinctive
basis as a sect, retained in vigorous exclusiveness the
sacramental part of the mediæval system; and while some
of its schools adhered firmly to the Augustinian theology,
other schools gradually softened the sterner and more re-
pulsive features of that theology, and have come very near
to the Pelagian heresy.

The Christian consciousness of that immense majority
of the English and American Church which revolted
from the narrowness of Puritanism has held with more
or less distinctness the true sense of the Incarnation, and
has consequently assigned to the Sacraments their actual
meaning and purpose in the economy of salvation.

The confused and imperfect conception of the meaning
and effect of the Incarnation is painfully exhibited by the
accepted representations of the beginning of spiritual life,
in both the Romish and the Puritan systems of theology.
Both assume a partial redemption. The Romish view of
this partial redemption is that the beginning of spiritual
life is in Baptism. The baptized therefore are the elect,
and they only can be saved. The Puritan version of the
same dogma is that spiritual life begins at the so-called
conversion of the adult subject, and that therefore Christ
has no connection with our nature until this epoch in the
personal history of the elect.

Few of our own people, imbued as they must be with
the genial and catholic spirit of the Liturgy, can hold
either of these systems in their naked severity, for both
are hopelessly at variance with that spirit and with fact,
experience, and consciousness. Every one is compelled to

modify one or the other systems more or less distinctly. But such has been the pervading influence of the Augustinian theology upon the thought and speech of Christendom that the language of one or the other of these systems is familiarly used by writers and preachers, and men array themselves into hostile parties, having for their shibboleths the terminology of the Romish or of the Puritan version of election. It is very easy for the partisans of each of these systems to point out the error of their antagonists; and, seeing that error so plainly, they cling with more intense devotion to their own cherished dogma as the only refuge from the falsehood mutually charged. Thus the vain contest between these related but warring errors continues from age to age.

§3. SPECULA-
TIVE VIEWS CON-
CERNING ORIGI-
NAL RIGHTEOUS-
NESS AND ORIGI-
NAL SIN.
3. In trying to determine this question of the beginning of spiritual life in man, both the opposing schools of theology have undertaken to declare the precise nature of that "original righteousness" which was the condition of man before the fall, and of that "original sin" which became his condition after the fall. To attempt to elucidate one obscure subject by the light of another far more obscure is not a very hopeful task. The endless mazes of this inquiry are fruitful themes for subtle disquisition, but can bring us no nearer to a solution of the actual problem of humanity. For in all the conflicting theories upon these subjects both parties seem to have forgotten that whatever may have been the meaning and effect of that death incurred by the first apostasy, neither Adam nor his posterity were permitted to remain in that state, for instantly upon the sentence and its execution came the redemption in Jesus Christ. In Him human nature was once more touched by the Divine nature, and revivified by the Life-giving Spirit, and placed in a new state of probation, under the new economy of

32

grace.   Hence to determine what man is or would be without grace is an absolutely insoluble and therefore idle problem, because there is not a single element of known fact for its solution beyond the revealed description of the fruits of nature and of the fruits of the Spirit; and this description is given in terms which apply to that complex state of redeemed humanity in which the fruits of both in some degree appear.

The Romish theologian, J. A. Moehler, gives an elaborate account of the speculations of the Schoolmen and of the Protestant and Romish Divines on the question of original justice and original sin.   While defending the dogma of his own party, he often makes very sound and just reflections, although inconsistent with the position he is obliged to defend.   In one place he says:

"Now it is an universal truth, holding good of all, even the highest orders and circles of intellectual creatures, . . . that no finite being can exist in a living moral communion with the Deity save by the communion of the Holy Spirit.   This relation of Adam to God, as it exalted him above human nature and made him participate in that of God, is hence termed a supernatural gift of Divine grace, superadded to the endowments of nature.   Moreover, this more minute explanation of the dogma concerning the original holiness and justice of Adam is not merely a private opinion of theologians, but an integral part of that dogma, and hence itself a dogma."

Again he says: "Divinity must stoop to humanity if humanity is to become divine.   Hence did the Son of God become man in order to reconcile humanity with the Godhead. . .   Divine grace must ever compassionately stoop to our lowliness, and impart to our sin-polluted faculties the first heavenly consecration, in order to prepare them for the Kingdom of Heaven and the receiving of Christ's image." (Symbolism, pp. 116, 178.)

This is a very accurate description of the effect of the Incarnation upon our humanity, and it is borne out by all the phenomena of human history. For it is manifest that good and evil, a reaching after God and a fearful depravity, have struggled together in that humanity in all ages and in all nations, as the same writer very beautifully proves when he describes the high attainments · of heathen morality and religion. But when he ascribes these results to unassisted nature he simply contradicts the above profound conclusions.

¶4. MODERN THEORIES A RE-PRODUCTION OF ANCIENT HERE-SIES CONCERNING THE INCARNA-TION. 4. The two theories which give rise to this confusion, and which refer the commencement of spiritual life in man one to baptism, the other to conversion, are a reproduction in a modified form of the ancient heresy which made the Incarnation to be the union of the Divine Nature with a human person, the Man Jesus, and so to have consecrated only that person, already a perfect human being. In opposition to this heresy the truth, elaborately established by the Church as the meaning of the Creed, is that HUMAN NATURE, the common nature of us all, was assumed by the Son of God, and consecrated by the adorable mystery— God with us: The Word made Flesh.

The exhaustive labors of the Fathers and Councils of the fourth and fifth centuries, accurately defining the truth of the Incarnation, in opposition to many successive heresies, have virtually determined the very question which is now bandied back and forth between the advocates of these two opposing systems in regard to the beginning of spiritual life in man. The doctrine of the Incarnation, so clearly settled by the Fathers, teaches us that the Son of God assumed to Himself in the person of Christ the

second Adam—not another human person, not this or that
man, but human nature—in indissoluble connection, *thereby
enduing that nature*, as it successively comes into being in
each person, with His life.   It is *this life* which makes the
subject of it, whether infant or adult, capable of admission into the Church—THE MYSTICAL BODY OF CHRIST—
by Baptism, there to be fed, nourished, and strengthened,
and perfected by all the means of grace and growth.   This
truth alone gives an adequate account of all the phenomena
of human life and character in the matter of salvation.

§5. HISTORY OF
THE DOCTRINE.   5. It will help to remove the confusion
and imperfection of the popular conception
of the Incarnation to look back at the successive distinctions and definitions by which this fundamental truth was
clearly and immovably established.   That truth is indeed
positively stated in the original Creed of the Church, both
in its Western and Eastern form.   But as misapprehensions of this truth—common enough with the masses of
Christian people—were magnified by obstinate and perverse teaching into heresies, the faithful pastors of the
Church were compelled to express the same truth more
clearly, not by changing the words of the Creed, but by
defining with all the accuracy and subtlety of which language is capable the very essential meaning of the Creed.
This exposition of the Creed by the General Councils is
given positively in the form of definitions and of ecu-
menical letters, and negatively by anathemas specifying
the particular errors to be avoided.

The whole brood of confusions and denials which center
around the mystery of the Incarnation are summarily
contained in the skeptical question of the Jews in the
very presence of our Lord, when he declared His flesh to
be "the life of the world."   "How can this man give us
His flesh to eat?"   (St. John vi, 51, 52.)   The mystery

at which they stumbled was that the Son of God, the Divine Nature, could be so united to human nature in the Person of the humble Man they saw as by that union to communicate life—the life of God—to all men. It was the mystery of the Second Adam, Christ, the new beginning of redeemed humanity; imparting His exalted nature just as effectually and universally as the first Adam had imparted his corrupt nature to the whole of his descendants.

The first error on this subject was that of the Gnostics or Docetæ, who taught that "our Lord's body was but a phantom, and that he came not in the flesh, but in appearance only." This teaching was in the life-time of the Apostles, and was so fully rebuked by them as never to have been revived. Afterward Arius maintained that the Son of God did not take human nature, but a human body only, and that the Divine Word was in the place of the soul. Apollinarius went a little further, and said that our Lord took a human body and a sensitive or animal soul, but that the place of the rational soul was supplied by God the Word. On neither of these suppositions was human nature taken into union with the Deity, and Christ, although truly the Son of God, was not at all the Son of man; and so the Son of God was not "made man," as the Creed affirms.

Long after these errors were disposed of, and "in Christ the verity of God and the complete substance of man were with full agreement established throughout the world" (Hooker, book v, sec. 52), Nestorius taught, either directly or by necessary implication, that "there were not only two natures but two persons in Christ; viz., the person of God the Son and the person of the man Jesus Christ." This statement really denied the doctrine of the Incarnation, because by its terms our human nature was only in contact with the Divine Nature in the Christ, and was not taken

up into the Divine Nature to make of the two natures
one indivisible person. This error was condemned by the
Council of Ephesus, A. D. 431.

Again, Eutyches, with the fancy, so common in our day,
that the best way to escape from an error is by getting as
far away from it as possible, in opposition to the Nestorian
doctrine of two persons in Christ, asserted that the divine
and human natures of Christ, although originally distinct,
yet "after their union became but one nature, the human
nature being transubstantiated into the divine." But this
statement equally denied the fact of the Incarnation—God
made man—because it left no human nature to subsist in
indissoluble union with the divine nature. And so the
Fourth General Council—that of Chalcedon—defined that
"in Christ two distinct natures are united in one person,
without any change, mixture, or confusion." (Har. Brown,
art. 2, sec. 1.)

The circle of definitions fencing in this part of the Creed
from human perversion was thus complete. The result of
the whole is the establishment of the position that it is an
inadequate and deceiving conception of the Incarnation to
suppose that the Son of God was united to a human person—one unit of the myriads composing the human race.
For then the indwelling of the Godhead would only have
redeemed and sanctified that one person, and *human nature*
must still have subsisted in unrelieved corruption and depravity.

And the vice is just the same, the deviation from the
essential meaning and determination of these definitions is
just as wide, if for one person we substitute any limited
number of persons, *leaving out human nature.* The denial
of the true nature and pervasive healing-power of the
incarnation is the same, whether we say that the *persons*
who alone receive the vivifying virtue of the Incarna-

tion are arbitrarily selected by a secret decree, or by
the visible designation of Baptism, or by "the will of
man," the conscious choice of the offer of salvation implied in conversion.   Each of these assertions is alike and
equally the denial of the fact and meaning of the Incarnation as defined by the early Church.

Hooker beautifully states this conclusion and its consequences: "It pleased not the Word, or Wisdom of God,
to take to itself some one person amongst men, for then
should that one have been advanced which was assumed,
and no more; but Wisdom, to the end she might save
many, built her house of that nature which is common
unto all; she made not this or that man her habitation,
but 'dwelt *in us*.'   The seeds of herbs and plants at the
first are not in act, but in possibility, that which they
afterward grow to be.   If the Son of God had taken to
Himself a man new-made and perfected, it would of necessity follow that there are in Christ two persons, the one
assuming and the other assumed; whereas the Son of God
did not assume a man's person to his own, but a man's nature to His own Person; and therefore took *semen*, the seed
of Abraham, the very first original element of our nature,
before it was come to have any personal human subsistence.   The flesh and the conjunction of the flesh with
God began at one instant; . . . so that in Christ there
is no personal subsistence but one, and that from everlasting." (Hooker, book v, sec. 52.)

§ 6. HUMAN NA-
TURE ACTED,
SUFFERED, AND
TRIUMPHED IN
CHRIST.

6. And it is our nature, the nature of
every child born into the world, that is
thus redeemed, purified, and exalted.   And
therefore of the myriads—more than half of
the human race who die in infancy—we know by faith in
the Son of God that they have been taken from the evil
to come, to be with Him of whose nature they partake.

For these have not by actual sin crucified the Son of God afresh, nor stamped out from their nature the lineaments of the Divinity, reimparted by the Incarnation, nor driven away the Holy Ghost, by whom the union of each one of the redeemed with Christ is mysteriously effected.

It is in the light of this transcendent truth that we must view all the deep and far-reaching facts recorded in the history of our incarnate Lord, beginning with the Baptism and immediately subsequent Temptation in the wilderness, and ending with His ascension and session at the right hand of God. Christ, true Man, and by the infinite love of God the Representative Man for us and on our behalf, and *as containing in Himself the whole race of man*, immediately after His public Ordination at His Baptism encounters and overcomes all the temptations to which that race is subject. The wiles of the Devil, the lust of the flesh, the pride of life, all the evil by which man can be brought into subjection, are condensed into those recorded temptations of our Lord as OUR REDEEMER. He resisted and overcame them, and all who are His can also resist and overcome them by His might and in his strength, and so achieve in union with Him the life eternal which He has won for that nature which He wears and has consecrated. With a right perception of this great truth, how miserably jejune, mean, and trifling is the bastard rationalism which would convert into myth or parable or illusion this profound and pregnant fact, this stupendous crisis in the long trial of humanity!

And so of all the other mysteries of our redemption. They are the sufferings, actings, and triumphs of *our nature* in His Person. We have seen how perspicuously the "judicious" Hooker states the true doctrine of the Incarnation, as expressed in the Creed and as defined by the early Councils.

In a subsequent passage he beautifully unfolds the necessary effect of this Incarnation upon the whole race of man. "Thus much no Christian man will deny, that when Christ sanctified his own flesh, giving as God and taking as man the Holy Ghost, He did not this for Himself only, but for our sakes, that the grace of sanctification and life which was first received in him might *pass from Him to His whole race, as malediction came from Adam to all mankind.* Howbeit, because the work of His Spirit to these effects is in us prevented by sin and death possessing us before; it is of necessity that as well our present signification unto newness of life as the future restoration of our bodies should presuppose a participation of the grace, efficacy, merit, or virtue of His body and blood; *without which foundation first laid there is no place for those other operations of the Spirit of Christ to ensue.* So that Christ imparteth plainly himself by degrees." (Ec. P., book v, sec. 56.)

In the same profound sense of this truth Jeremy Taylor says: "God sent into the world His only Son for a remedy to human miseries, to ennoble our nature by an union with Divinity," . . . that we might "with free dispensation receive the influences of a Saviour with whom we communicate in nature." (Life of Christ, part i, sec. 1.)

An ancient Collect composed by St. Leo, the great champion of the truth of the Incarnation against Nestorius, says: "O God, who art pleased to save by the nativity of Thy Christ the race of man which was mortally wounded in its chief, grant, we beseech Thee, that we may not adhere to the author of our perdition, but be transferred to the fellowship of our Redeemer."

The Rev. J. H. Blunt, who sometimes uses the language of the mediæval version of Augustinianism, in his account of the festival of Christmas, breaks loose from the narrowness of that theology, and expands to the full conception

33

of the adorable mystery in these words: "And even beyond the immediate influence of the Church it is found that the Christmas gladness of the Church is reflected in the world around; and a common instinct of *regenerated human nature* teaches that world to recognize in Christmas a season of unity and fellowship and good will, of happiness and peace." (An., p. 77.)

All these human representations fall short of the emphatic expression of the same truth by St. Paul when he elaborately describes the admission of the Gentiles into the visible Church, the mystical body of Christ, by the similitude of a graft. It is essential to a graft that it must be alive, and even possess a life somewhat of the same nature with the stock with which it is to be united To insert a dead branch into a stock would simply wound the latter, and could by no possibility transfer the life of the stock into the branch. And even a living branch of an altogether foreign nature can not be successfully grafted into any stock. To give sense and meaning therefore to this favorite illustration of the Apostle, the Gentiles must be regarded as possessed of spiritual life analogous to that of the Church, previous to their engrafting by Baptism into that Church. St. Paul thoroughly recognizes and affirms both conditions. For the Gentiles are described not only as *living* branches, but as branches of a "*wild* olive-tree" to be grafted into the "*good* olive-tree."

Now the life here referred to, which enables men to believe, repent, and turn unto God, and so be capable of Baptism—of engraftment into that "mystical body which is the blessed company of all faithful people," must either be natural, the "relics of the fall," as Pelagius maintained, or supernatural, *the effect of the Incarnation produced by the Spirit*, as the Church has held in opposition to Pelagius.

St. Augustine (cited by Wall, vol. i, pp. 380–1) states

the question between Pelagius and the Church thus simply: "Inasmuch as the question about reconciling man's free will and God's grace is so intricate that while one is asserted the other may seem to be denied; if he (Pelagius) would grant that God does not only give us a power of doing well, but does also assist us in the willing and doing of it, the controversy would be at an end. . . . What great matter were it for him to say this, especially where he undertakes to handle and explain that point? Why should he there defend *nature* only?"

"The precise offense here charged against Pelagius," says Harold Brown, "is that he refused to refer all effectual power in man to do or to will that which is good to supernatural grace, but persisted in attributing such power to nature, thereby consequentially denying that the Holy Ghost is the only Giver of spiritual life."

Alas! for the weakness of our nature! The very Fathers who, guided by the Holy Spirit, so clearly determined that it was our common nature which was assumed and sanctified in the adorable mystery of the Incarnation; that, as Hooker states it, "the grace of sanctification and life, which was first received in Him, might pass from Him to His whole race, as malediction came from Adam to all mankind;" the very Fathers who announced this grand and comprehensive truth, so flagrantly departed from it as to restrict the benefits of this Incarnation, the grace of God, and all participation of Christ to that very small number of mankind who might be admitted to the Sacrament of Baptism.

§7. FURTHER TESTIMONIES TO THE EFFECT OF THE INCARNATION ON HUMAN NATURE. 7. In a previous chapter I have shown that in the first virgin faith of the Church, in the earliest ages, a far wider, more generous, and Christ-like spirit prevailed. To the testimonies then collected out of the scanty remains

which have come down to us I add the following from
Irenæus and from St. Clement: "For it was not merely
for those who believed on Him in the time of Tiberius
Cæsar that Christ came, nor did the Father exercise His
providence for men only who are now alive, but for all
men altogether, who from the beginning, *according to their
capacity* in their generation, have loved and feared God,
and practiced justice and piety toward their neighbors,
and have *earnestly desired* to see Christ, and to hear His
voice." (*Irenæus* v. *Her.*, book iv, chap. 22, sec. 2.)

This passage becomes more beautiful and expressive
when compared with the language in which the coming
Messiah was announced by the Prophet Haggai, "And
THE DESIRE OF ALL NATIONS SHALL COME."

St. Clement, the first in the bright array of the Christian Fathers, and whose Epistle to the Corinthians stands
next to Holy Scripture, uses many incidental expressions
in that beautiful book, which show his sense of the glorious comprehensiveness of the work of Christ as performed
for the whole race of mankind. In chapter 4 he says:
"Let us look steadfastly to the blood of Christ, and see
how precious His blood is in the sight of God, which, being
shed for our salvation, has obtained the grace of repentance *for all the world*. Let us search into all the ages that
have gone before us, and let us learn that our Lord has in
every one of them still given place for repentance to all
such as would turn to him. Noah preached repentance,
and as many as hearkened to him were saved. Jonah
denounced destruction against the Ninevites, howbeit they,
repenting of their sins, appeased God by their prayers *and
were saved, though they were strangers to the covenant of God.*
Hence we find how all the ministers of the grace of God
have spoken by the Holy Spirit of repentance."

Here it is abundantly evident that St. Clement recognizes the grace of Christ and His mediation prevailing in all the ages and in all the world as the source of all the goodness of men. In chapter 14 he speaks of "that faith by which God Almighty has justified all men from the beginning." And in the same spirit, "All the ages of the world, from Adam even unto this day, are passed' away; but they who have been made perfect in love have by the grace of God obtained a place among the righteous, and shall be made manifest in the judgment of the kingdom of Christ." (Chapter 21.) And to show who, in his estimation, were these "righteous" in all the ages, he *classes together*, in the next chapter, the Gentiles and the Covenant people as "strengthened by the grace of God" to do many glorious things.

₂8. SYNODICAL ACTION OF THE CHURCH OF EN- GLAND ON THIS QUESTION. 8. This very point has been solemnly determined by the Convocation of the Church of England, as appears from chapter 36, canon 36, of Overall's Convocation Book: "It is generally agreed upon amongst all Christians that from the creation of mankind during the times aforesaid there hath always been one Universal or Catholic Church, which began in Adam, and afterward, as his posterity multiplied, both before and after the flood, was dispersed over the face of the whole earth, and whereof the Son of God likewise was always the head and sole, though invisible, monarch. The foundation of which Church was ever one and the same rock; to wit, Jesus Christ, the promised 'seed of the woman that should break the serpent's head;' and as many persons, families, societies, and companies as truly believed in that blessed Seed, without exception of any sort or distinction of people, were the true members and parts of the Catholic Church."

After tracing the progress of this Church down to the calling of Abraham, the chapter goes on:

"Besides, hitherto all the world being as one people, if there were then any visible Churches at all upon the earth, it can not be truly said that the calling of Abraham out of Chaldea, and the erecting of the true worship of God in his family, did make them to be in worse case than they were before. If Churches before, they so continued after, though superstitious and idolatrous Churches. Again, it is generally held that God did not therefore distinguish the Jews from other nations and people, and settle His public worship amongst them as purposing thereby that His Catholic Church in their times should consist only of them and their nations, and such other proselytes as would be circumcised and join themselves unto them; but much more because by that means the truth and certainty of all the promises and prophecies concerning the coming of the Messiah might be faithfully and diligently observed, and kept in one nation, and visible, known place and people. For it is plain in the Scriptures that after the said distinction many of the Gentiles served God and believed in Christ, and were thereby made the true members of the Catholic Church, though they were not circumcised nor had any meddling with or dependency upon the Jews."

"So that the Catholic Church, consisting from the beginning till Abraham's time of such only as were afterward for distinction's sake called Gentiles, although God was pleased to bestow His mercies more plentifully upon that one particular Church of the Jews deduced from Abraham than upon any other, or indeed upon all the rest, for the principal causes before specified; yet they were not utterly so rejected or cast out of God's favor but that many of them did continue as dutiful children in the lap and bosom of the Catholic Church."

The canon which follows this chapter, and formally

enacts the principles more largely declared in it, is very notable and of great interest.

"CANON 36.

"If any man therefore shall affirm either that during the continuance of the Old Testament the merits of Christ's death actually to come were not sufficient to save all true believers; or that there was then no Catholic Church; or that at any time there was any other rock but Jesus Christ, the blessed Seed, upon whom the Catholic Church was then built; or *that many of the Gentiles were not always, for aught that is known to the contrary, true members of the Catholic Church;* or that Christ Himself was not the sole head or monarch all that while of the whole Catholic Church; or that the said Catholic Church, after the members of it were dispersed into all the places of the world, was otherwise visible than *per partes;* or that Noah did appoint any man to be the visible head of the said Catholic Church; or that the High-priest among the Jews had any more authority over the Catholic Church of God than King David had over the universal kingdom of God; or that the said High-priest had not greatly sinned if he had taken upon him or usurped any such infinite authority, *he doth greatly err.* PLACET EIS." (Book i, chap. 36.)

"*He doth greatly err.*" And all who concur in thus defaming the grace of God by restricting that grace to narrow sections of mankind do "greatly err." The refusal of Christian teachers to maintain and publish this grand comprehensiveness of the Gospel, while holding fast all dogmatic truth in the same Divine connection, is the crying opprobrium of modern religion. The failure to hold these truths *in their just connection* throws off one section of the community into the wildest libertinism of speculative opinion, and contracts another section into a narrow exclusiveness of dogma irreconcilable with the exercise of a generous and salutary influence upon the higher classes of minds.

Thus it appears that the principle which I have so earnestly pressed, and which has been as earnestly opposed, was Synodically affirmed in stronger language and by a more expressive representation by the whole Church of England in the Convocation which assembled in the year 1603 and continued its session to 1610. It was a grand and beautiful presentation of this great truth, worthy of the Church of England in her palmiest days, to describe all the generations of believing men in all the earth as composing the one Catholic Church of God. However corrupt and idolatrous in its parts, that Church was still within the covenant, and all its members were reached by the life-bestowing power of the Incarnation, and recipients of the grace that offered salvation.

The faith by which these men believed and worshiped, however inadequate the object of that faith, and however imperfect that worship, was itself the precious gift of God to all men through Jesus Christ our Lord. We are called upon in these later days to vindicate the certain existence of faith as a ruling power of the human soul, in opposition to the Atheists, who deny that there is any such faculty in man as faith. The Atheists base their denial upon the transparent sophism that because there are so many differences and even oppositions in the objects of faith, therefore there is no such faculty as faith. They forget that the corrupt use of a faculty is just as certain proof of the existence of the faculty as the right use of it.

It will be easy to prove against these men that this universal gift of God has been in all nations and ages the foundation and essential condition of morality and of social order, of all real knowledge and of all human progress.

Surely Christian men will not come to the assistance of this atheistic party, and deny the existence of the faith that produced these results, because the blinded hearts of men gradually obscured and hid from them the true and proper object of faith, the One Eternal God. The English Convocation, in the action just referred to, and in the very spirit of St. Paul's account of the same gradual apostasy, significantly meets this objection. In the chapter above cited they say: "Likewise after the flood all Noah's offspring, being one Church under him, and grounded upon Christ, the true foundation of it, although afterward, when they were settled in their several countries allotted unto them, they swerved greatly from that purity in religion which Noah had taught them, yet they had still their priests, their sacrifices, and some outward worship of God among them."

So then, as the Convocation plainly affirms, these Gentiles still used this inestimable gift of God to some good effect, although they had lamentably lost sight of the One True Object of faith. The same comprehensive principle is often referred to in other parts of this work, as especially in book ii, chap. 11.

The universal grace of God through Christ vouchsafed to all men, and "saving," as Bishop Andrews says, to all who will rightly use it, must now be confessed a recognized doctrine of the Church of England, and surely will not again be spoken of as a novelty in that Church or in ours.

The Canons set forth in this book only failed to become law for want of the signature of King James I., who feared that some expressions in them peered too curiously into the foundation of his royal prerogative.

9. BISHOP AN-
DREWS.
9. In suggestive connection with this determination of the English Convocation there is a curious and learned treatise by Bishop Andrews, enti-

tled "A Discourse of Ceremonies Retained and Used in Christian Churches." Bishop Andrews, who was certainly a member of that Convocation, instances in this treatise a great number of particulars in which there is a striking agreement between the Heathen and the Christian polity, custom, and worship. And this, he argues, not in derogation of the Christian practice, but in proof that these Heathen customs and worship were parts of that primitive ritual which God had given to His Catholic Church, as the above-cited canon speaks, and which, being right and proper in themselves, and suitable to the nature and necessities of men, were continued in the Jewish Church and in the Christian Church. So that the difference between Heathen and Christian in this respect is not so much in outward observance or in the original principle of both, but in the utter and foul corruption of the first, together with the loss of the true knowledge of God. The Christian religion and worship are the old primitive religion and worship, cleansed from all base defilements; pure, and with the true knowledge of God restored and enlarged.

§10. RICHARD HOLT HUTTON.   10. To these ancient testimonies let me add a very instructive fact occurring in our own time. Richard Holt Hutton, a distinguished member of a distinguished English family of thinkers and scholars, early trained in Unitarian negations, and for many years tenaciously holding the tenets of that sect, found his way out of darkness into light through a clear perception of this great truth which he saw to be involved in the very nature of the Incarnation. From his admirable and suggestive essay, entitled "The Incarnation and Principles of Evidence," I take the following passages:

"The Incarnation, if believable, seems to me to throw a strong light on the seeming contradictions of human nature—contradictions which are only brought out into

sharper relief by a fuller knowledge of the Creator. . . .
The knowledge we have gained either humiliates and
crushes us, or produces an artificial elation. We either
crouch with the highest of purely Jewish minds, or become
urbanely self-content with the Pelágian-Unitarian thinkers.
We either cry, 'Woe is me! for I am undone, because I
am a man of unclean lips and dwell amongst a people of
unclean lips; for mine eyes have seen the King, the Lord
of hosts!' or we congratulate ourselves that we are, by
inherent right, children of God, 'born good,' as Lord Pal-
merston said, and have no profound need, therefore, of
purification at all. The humiliation alone, and the exaltation alone, are alike false to the facts within us and
destructive of the true springs of human hope.

"What we want is some *universal* fountain of Divine
Life within us which shall yet not blind us in any way to
the truth that we ourselves are not by our own right children of God, but only become so through One who is.
We need a reconciliation of the fact of the unhealthy
egoism of our own individualities with the equally certain
fact of a Divine Light struggling with that egoism and
claiming us as true children of God.

"The Incarnation alone helps us adequately to understand ourselves; it reconciles the language of servile
humiliation with the language of rightful children. Both
are true. The unclean slave and the free child of Heaven
are both within us. The Incarnation shows us the true
child of God—the filial will which never lost its majesty,
which never tasted the impurity of human sin—and so
still further abases us; but then it shows him as the incarnate revelation of that Eternal Son and Word whose filial
light and life can stream into and take possession of us
with power to make us like Himself. The Incarnation
alone seems to me adequately to reconcile the contradictory

facts of a double nature in man—the separate individuality which has no health of its own, and turns every principle to evil directly it begins to revolve on its own center, and the Divine nature which lends it a true place and true subordination in the kingdom of God. 'We are not,' said Athanasius, '*by nature* sons of God, but the Son in us makes us so; also God is not *by nature* our Father, but He is the Father of the Word dwelling in us; for in Him and through Him we cry, Abba, Father.' It is obvious that Athanasius uses the word 'nature' here in a much narrower sense than Bishop Butler. In the largest sense it *is* our true 'nature' to live in and through the Eternal Word. But what he meant—namely, that not by virtue of anything in our own strict *personality or individuality*, only by virtue of the divine life engrafted upon that personality or individuality, do we become sons of God—seems to me the very truth which St. John reveals: 'He came unto *his own* and *his own* received him not, but as many as received him to them gave he power to become sons of God.' This teaching, and this alone, seems to vindicate the divine nature *in* us without leading us into the delusion that it is *of* us."

Elsewhere this clear thinker says: "Surely all the expansive power of Christianity—all that adapts it to the purpose of the ages—has been directly due to the faith in a 'light that lighteth every man which cometh into the world,' and in the incarnation of that light in the human life of Jesus of Nazareth."

The generous and scriptural views of the fullness of the redemption that is in Christ Jesus which at first prevailed in the Church soon gave way before the natural intolerance of the human heart and the narrowness of the mere theological intellect, and presently we hear the very Fathers who, under the guidance of the Holy Ghost, in the General Councils vindicated so nobly the great truth, that in Christ human nature had been assumed, redeemed, and sanctified, restraining all this wealth of love to the baptized. This technical and Christ-defaming dogma they sternly carried out to its apparent consequence, and remorselessly consigned all unbaptized infants, as well as adults, to everlasting damnation. At the same time they held, as we have seen, that supernatural grace is necessary to produce that faith and repentance which are required as conditions of Baptism; or, as Hooker expresses it, "a participation" of Christ, "*presupposed as the foundation first laid of all the other operations of the Spirit of Christ, to issue.*"

Put these two propositions together, and the combination is a clear denial of the possibility of repentance and faith to any but the baptized. And as these graces are the condition precedent, the condition *sine qua non* of Baptism, the two statements deny the possibility of Baptism to those who are not already baptized. That is to say, if both statements are to be received as true, they logically destroy the Christian Religion by resolving it into contradictory and mutually destroying affirmations. Both, therefore, can not be true. That which is but a fuller expression of the Creed, and the very sense of the definitions of the early Councils, must be confessed as true; and the other, which contradicts it, is of necessity false.

The issue between these two contrasted views of human nature and its relations is distinct and plain. It will not do to play fast and loose with these systems, and use indifferently the language of both. When the Puritan Calvinist affirms that a man can have no participation of Christ and no spiritual life until he is converted, he plainly affirms with Pelagius that the natural man apart from Christ is capable of those Christian graces, faith and repentance, which are the necessary antecedents of conversion. When another person uses the language of mediæval theology, and says there can be no participation of Christ and no spiritual life without Baptism, he also affirms with Pelagius that the natural man can exercise those highest functions of spiritual life, faith and repentance, which are conditions *sine qua non* of Baptism. For these same parties to turn around then and denounce Pelagianism as false is to make Christianity a tangled web of contradictions and inconsistencies, the very result which has driven so many plain people away from Christianity.

§11. BAPTISM AND THE AGENCY OF THE CHURCH IN THE MATTER OF SALVATION.

11. A striking illustration of the circle in which the human mind moves occurred the other day in connection with this subject. When, in answer to his inquiries, I stated this doctrine of the Incarnation to a young divine, he inquired, "Of what value then is the Church, and what is the use of Baptism?" They were the very questions which the Jews put to St. Paul eighteen hundred years ago. When he argued the salvability of the Gentiles through Christ, the Saviour of the world, their puzzled inquiry was, "What advantage then hath the Jew? or what profit is there in circumcision?" It was easy to return to our querist the answer which St. Paul gave to the objectors of his day, "Much every way."

The greatest of all truths becomes a falsehood when severed from its divine connections. So universal redemption has been perverted to the dogma of universal salvation, irrespective of human freedom. The spiritual life thus imparted to humanity by the Incarnation, like all derived life, must be nourished by continual supply from the Fountain of Life, or it will die. Our Lord has ruled the whole case by a multitude of teachings. He is the Body, we are the members. He says emphatically, "I am the Vine, ye are the branches. If any man *abide* not in ME, he is cast forth as a branch, and is withered; and men gather them, and cast them into the fire, and they are burned."

Where the Gospel is preached, where the revealed will of God is made known, there faith, worship, and the sacraments are the constituted channels of spiritual nourishment to the redeemed. Cut off by unbelief or by wanton neglect from these channels of supply from Christ the Fountain, the pre-existing life of the soul shrinks, decays, perishes. Place a compress upon the arm sufficient to prevent the continuous flow of blood and nerve power to the parts below: how soon would the vigorous life of that strong and steady hand be fatally impaired, and after a while mortification would ensue, and amputation of the dead and gangrened member become necessary!

Human will perversely exercised acts as this compress, cutting off the rebellious man from the Fountain of Life. It is this will which refuses to use the means and channels of grace, choosing this world and its lusts as a sufficient portion, and the bondage of Satan in place of that service of God which is perfect freedom. The very process, in the analogous illustration, has been precisely described by the Lord of life: "I am the true Vine, and My Father is the husbandman. Every branch in me that beareth not fruit He taketh away." (St. John xv, 1.)

Human freedom, human will, mysteriously concur with the Divine will in all the relations between God and man. The Divine will makes the earth fruitful; but man must plow and sow and wait for the increase. The life of Christ has been imparted to all men by the Holy Ghost in the adorable mystery of the Incarnation; and the means by which that life may be so vigorously maintained, nourished, and developed in this world as to secure eternal

life in the world to come, have been freely placed within
the reach and subject to the use of all to whom the Gospel is proposed—to whom "the Kingdom of God has
come." Through these channels rightly employed spiritual food, power, growth, enlargement, continually come to
our nature to purify it, to assimilate it more and more
perfectly to the nature of the Word made Flesh. Because
He will have none but a free-will worship, God requires
His redeemed to accept or reject the use of these means of
grace, the channels of His life and power. By Baptism
we are reborn into that glorious kingdom which came
down from Heaven in the Person of the Incarnate Lord.
Then, as citizens of that kingdom, we have the freedom,
the unrestricted use, of all the precious means and mysteries of salvation.*

This is the meaning and the use of Baptism. This is
the value of that Church of the living God which is the
mystical Body of Christ. This is the answer which St.

---

* L'Estrange carries on the analogy between natural birth and spiritual
birth in Baptism further than I have done. Speaking of Baptism, he says:
"And to that custom of washing new-born babes Mr. Mede, another very
learned man, hath applied it. Indeed the analogy and conformity between
Christian Baptism and that custom is concise and proper, both in relation
to the laver and also to regeneration: in relation to the laver, because
as the laver or elemental water doth wash away and cleanse our bodies
from filth contracted, so doth the mystical washing of the Holy Ghost
purge our souls from all further pollution; in relation to regeneration, for as
it is at our generation, so it is in our regeneration. At our generation, or birth,
when we were born men, we were washed, so are we when we are born Christians, and washed from a pollution exactly agreeable also. When we were born
we were washed from the pollution we contracted from our parent's womb;
when we are new-born we are washed by Baptism from that original sin
which is derived to us from our first parents." (Alliance of Divine Offices,
page 353. Anglo. Cath. Lib.)

My friend, Dr. Everhart, in an able article in the Am. Quar. Church Review,
had presented the same feature of the analogy in a very forcible way some
years before I found the above confirmation of his view from so high an
authority.

It gives me pleasure to refer in this connection to a small but admirable
pamphlet, entitled "Birth and New Birth," by the Rev. Edward J. Stearns, A. M.

Paul furnished to the ancient Jew and to the modern inquirer. "Much every way; chiefly, because that unto them were committed the oracles of God," *all the constituted channels of knowledge and of grace.* "Therefore," he concludes, "being justified by faith, we have peace with God through our Lord Jesus Christ: by Whom also we have access by faith into this grace wherein we stand, and rejoice in hope of the glory of God." (Rom. iii, 2; v, 1, 2.)

Those who make Baptism to be the first conveyance of spiritual life to our nature, and those again who restrict that life to the conversion of the adult subject, do both, although in different degrees, detract from the essential value of the Church of God as the appointed agency of salvation. Instead of being, as some suppose, a human expediency, or at best a mere accident of Christianity, that Church is constantly spoken of by our blessed Lord as the synonym of Christianity, as the comprehensive formula for the whole body of truth. He Himself commenced his public ministry by preaching "the kingdom of of God is at hand;" and by "preaching the *Gospel of the kingdom.*" The Apostles were sent forth to "preach the kingdom of God;" and again the seventy are commanded to "say unto them, the kingdom of God is come nigh unto you."

That gross exaggeration of the necessity of Baptism which induced the ancients to allot damnation to all unbaptized infants, came from a failure to appreciate the transcendent mystery of the one Kingdom of God established on earth as the refuge and home of the redeemed, of those who, being first "made alive in Christ," are received into that kingdom for nurture, for protection, for the continued supply of His grace, His life, His strength. Thus undervaluing the ministry of the Kingdom on earth,

34

they understood our Lord in His conversation with Nicodemus to mean by "the Kingdom of God" exclusively
the state of eternal glory. Therefore they supposed our
Lord to say that no one without Baptism could see or enter
into eternal life. Many were the shifts, evasions, and
subterfuges to which the more compassionate theologians
were driven to escape from the cruel consequences of this
palpable misrepresentation. And out of them all has
come the Romish conceit of a "*Limbus Puerorum,*" a
sort of milder hell for the unbaptized children. But our
Lord's words on this occasion were the same as when he
certainly spoke of that Kingdom which he had established
in the world as the appointed ministry of salvation to His
redeemed. And this He himself distinctly affirmed when
He added, "If I have told you *earthly* things and ye believe
not, how shall ye believe if I tell you of heavenly things?"

It would be apart from the meaning and purpose of the
Gospel to tell us anything of the provision which God has
made for the preservation and development of the life of
quicked humanity in those to whom the Gospel has never
been proposed; but it is plain to see how the moral life
had decayed in all heathendom, ancient and modern, for
want of the Church with its life-sustaining Sacraments
and fructifying Word.

In the following passage St. Augustine lays down broad
and generous principles in regard both to Baptism and to
Conversion, which should have preserved his own and succeeding generations from much of the technical narrowness of his own theology. Speaking of infants who can
not believe, and of the penitent thief who was not baptized, he says: "By all which it appears that the sacrament of Baptism is one thing, and Conversion of the
heart another: but that the salvation of a person is completed by both of them. And if one of these be wanting,

we are not to think that it follows that the other is wanting; since one may be without the other in an infant, and the other was without that in the thief: God Almighty making up, both in one and other case, that which was not *willfully* wanting. But when either of these is willfully wanting, it involves the person in guilt. And Baptism indeed may be had where conversion of the heart is wanting; but conversion of the heart, *though it may be where Baptism is not had,* can not be where it is contemned: for that is by no means to be conversion of the heart to God where the sacrament of God is contemned." (Cited by Wall, vol. i, chap. 15.)

CHAPTER II.

OBJECTIONS TO THIS VIEW OF THE INCARNATION.

1. A DIFFICULTY in the way of the reception of this truth is found by some persons in the implication contained in the language of Article 13: "Works done before
§ 1. ARTICLE 13. the grace of Christ and the Inspiration of his Spirit are not pleasant to God, forasmuch as they spring not of faith in Jesus Christ; neither do they make men meet to receive grace, or (as the School authors say) deserve grace of congruity: yea rather, for that they are not done as God hath willed and commanded them to be done, we doubt not but they have the nature of sin."

Literally taken, the article strongly affirms the very truth I have been advocating, that the grace of God goes before and inspires all good works. But the article contemplates more than this. Evidently it has not in view at all the question now before us. Its sole purpose was to deny a Romish conceit derived from the mediæval Schoolmen. Its special determination is against the doctrine that men may by good works "deserve grace of congruity." Being thus limited in its scope, the *implication* in the first clause ought not to be *strained into the positive assertion* that men may do good works without the grace of Christ. All that the article asserts is that those who reject or despise that grace can not by good works merit or purchase the grace they have so contumeliously treated.

But why should we try to make a verbal technicality,

if ever so obstinate, override two of the most incontrovertible facts? One of these facts universal observation
attests, that the baptized and the unbaptized, with equal
advantages of Christian culture or equally neglected, do
not manifest any difference of religious knowledge and
feeling except that which is common to any other persons
in either class. The second fact is contained in and required by the same formulary in which the technical objection is found; viz., that the most characteristic graces
of the Spirit, the energetic movements and strivings of
spiritual life—Repentance and Faith—must be exhibited
by the unbaptized adult as the condition of baptism.

§2. A NEW
TRANSLATION OF
JOHN iii, 3-5.
2. Again it is suggested that the word
translated "born" in the conversation of our
Saviour with Nicodemus properly means
"begotten." The word by itself may be rendered either
way, and the proper meaning must be determined by the
context. The context here precludes the rendering " begotten." For the question of Nicodemus, "How can a
man be born when he is old? Can he enter the second
time into his mother's womb and be born?" is capable of
an answer corresponding to the physiological facts of the
analogy. To substitute "begotten" for the translation so
long used by the Church makes the intended analogy utterly incongruous. A living person, old or young—and in
the Christian mystery the old must become as "a little
child"—may be "born again" from the womb of nature
into the Kingdom of Grace. But for a living person,
conscious or unconscious, to be rebegotten is an entire
departure from the physical analogy. It is true that elsewhere, by a different figure, where the *implantation* of
faith and hope is represented, the word is properly rendered "begotten."

Again, to substitute "rebegotten" for "reborn" in this

place is to conform the passage exclusively to the Puritan theology, and to put out of view altogether the Church of God, and the agency of that Church in the whole work of salvation. If there is here in these declarations of our Lord nothing but a spiritual *conception*, the Church is left out of view, and has no proper or assigned agency in the development of the Divine life so imparted. That life, according to this rendering, so far as this passage teaches, will subsist and grow of its intrinsic energy, without any external means. But this supposition contradicts the concurrent voice of the Church in all ages interpreting this pregnant passage.

§3. THE WORDS OF ST. JOHN, i, 12.

3. In defense of those narrow and technical dogmas which deny that by the Incarnation Christ *quickened our nature* the words of St. John, i, 12—"As many as received Him to them gave He power to become the sons of God, even to them that believe on His name"—are cited by the two opposing classes as the warrant for their respective systems, and as the complete refutation of that more generous view of this stupendous mystery which makes it indeed the Evangel—glad news of great joy to all people.

To give such meaning to these words, to make them thus to circumscribe the glorious Gospel,• they are torn from their connection with the passage to which they belong, and put forward as an isolated and independent dictum. The words, "To as many as *received* Him," are declared to be emphatic and decisive of the whole question. But if we misinterpret these words into a denial of spiritual life, *of any participation* of Christ, to all who have not consciously *received* Him by hearing and believing, then all the infant portion of the race—even the baptized—are cut off from the benefits of the incarnation, and consigned therefore to the unrelieved darkness of eternal death!

Moreover, this interpretation makes this sentence a point-blank contradiction of the grand and more emphatic declarations that immediately precede it. "In Him was life, and the life was the light of men. . . . That was the true light which lighteth every man that cometh into the world." That cardinal principle of interpretation which requires us to give effect to all the parts of the same document, and so to combine them as to give to the whole a meaning which does not destroy or contradict any part, easily resolves the difficulty and removes the alleged objection. This principle of interpretation demands that we take this last declaration as cumulative; not narrowing or destroying what went before, but affirming the same truth in another and special application of it. In this sense the words, "as many as received Him," *are* emphatic. St. John passes from the contemplation of mankind — the race — visited and vivified by the Divine humanity, to the contemplation of the concurrent mystery—human will—freely and consciously accepting or rejecting this supernatural aid, this Divine election. The passage is a recognition of this freedom, this awful prerogative of redeemed humanity, and again affirms that to all to whom this life has come, and who consciously receive it, *power* shall be given to become the sons of God in the highest sense; power to resist and overcome the corruption of nature, the wiles of the Devil, and the temptations of the world, and to achieve the consummate meaning and glory of the Divine adoption.

The immediate context proves this meaning. After announcing the grand and universal truth above cited, the Evangelist calls to mind man's freedom and perverted will, and sadly recognizes the inbred sin which induced so many to reject Him, even His own covenant people. "He came unto His own, and His own received Him not." Turning again from this disheartening contemplation to consider the virtue of the new life which can cure this distemper of humanity, he joyfully exclaims: "But as many as received Him to them gave He power to become sons of God." The whole of this passage plainly refers to the limiting declaration, "His own received Him not;" and instead of limiting the universal proposition first announced, is simply a qualification of the bar which human will consciously exerted puts to the full and consummate operation of that universal truth. The whole declaration is equivalent to the words of our blessed Lord, reported by the same Evangelist, and a like recognition and assertion of human freedom in the whole economy of redemption, "And this is the condemnation, that light is come into the world, and men loved darkness rather than light because their deeds were evil." (St. John iii, 19.)

§4. A TRAN-
SCENDENTAL OB-
JECTION.

4. Nearly all the objectors to that view of the Divine Life set forth in this work as having its necessary initiative in the mystery of the incarnation dwell much upon an imagined consequence of the fall, as, using the language of the Bible and the Church, I have spoken of that portentous fact. It is declared that "in a being in such a condition there would be no place of entertainment for the Divine Spirit; that it would remove him as far from the possibility of salvation as if he were a beast, a stock, or a stone." I have never been able to comprehend the force or meaning of these representations. I am not sufficiently acquainted with the essence of the human soul, or with the limits of the vivifying power of the Divine Spirit, to affirm that human nature can be beyond the reach of influence from that Spirit. Certainly the Scriptures do not encourage us to set limits to the Spirit's power. A Prophet once inquired, "Can these dry bones live?" And Jesus said, "If these should hold their peace the very stones would cry out."

I have simply affirmed with the Church, that man in his own nature, untouched by the Divine humanity of his Redeemer, is "very far"—"*quam longissime,*" as far as possible according to his nature—"gone from original righteousness." What that ruined nature would have been without the incarnation, in its essence and possibilities; how much of the defaced image of God remained in man, we are not told, and therefore we can not know. Only it is certain from the testimony of the Scriptures and of the Church that to make this fallen creature capable of loving and of doing good, of loving and seeking after God, the Spirit of God must move upon his heart, quicken his nature, and impart at once the desire and the capacity for communion with God. And this transcendent spiritual operation is not by mechanical force upon brute nature, but by inclining and co-operating with the human faculties. The work of the spirit to this extent has been procured for human nature in its entirety by the adorable mystery of the incarnation of the Son of God. The objection to this Christian affirmation, founded upon any supposable or imagined state of human nature, is to me simply unintelligible.

§5. A WORLD-WIDE FIELD OF PHENOMENA OUTSIDE OF REVELATION TO BE ACCOUNTED FOR.

5. That the revelation makes the Church and its ministrations the way of salvation is but the synonym of the fact that the Church is an integral part of the revelation, and that all to whom the revelation comes must accept this appointed way. But there is a world-wide field of phenomena outside of the revelation which can not be overlooked. The revelation does not distinctly treat of these phenomena; neither does it state formally the being of God or the immortality of the soul. It assumes these and many other verities as the basis of its positive teaching. I have simply formulated some of these all-pervading phenomena, and exhibited their relation to the Gospel and to the king-

35

dom of God, on the principles abundantly supplied by the revelation itself. A broad and intelligible basis is thus presented for the positive teachings of the revelation.

To demand that the revelation shall be always nakedly presented to the minds of men as a mere arbitrary and technical system, apart from the universal truths which itself assumes and recognizes, is to deal unfairly with the Gospel, is to put it out of relation with the thoughts and hopes and affections of men and with the better spirit of the age in which we live. If the ministers of this Divine truth are determined thus to present it in severe isolation from all accordant truth, as a system outside of humanity, it will be rejected, as they see, by a large class of the better minds. Not so was the revelation given. It was given to men with mind and capacity to see and consider and entertain all the phenomena of life and character and condition contained in the world's history. It was given, not as an isolated fact, unconnected with any other truth, but as a component part of a beautiful harmony of the universe. And it contains the principles, large, liberal, and pervading, by which its own special truths may be rationally connected with these universal phenomena of human character and destiny submitted to our view. And so, as we have seen, the early Church received and understood the revelation.

§ 6. HUMANI-TARIANISM. 6. The reaction from the stern, narrow, and technical theology insisted upon by many theologians of a later period and in our own time has produced that widespread humanitarianism which is so painfully affecting the Christian faith. It has become a familiar observation that every heresy, every revolt from loyal submission to Christian truth, has come from the fact that the Church in a particular age has slurred over or left out of view some great truth. When, by the progress of knowledge or by other providences, this neglected truth is made especially prominent, and the current theology stiffly refuses to accept or acknowledge it, then the men of fiery zeal and of contracted vision on the other side give to their one dominant idea an unnatural development, and make it by disproportion an excrescence upon Christianity, or use it as a reason for rejecting Christianity. So, the progress of thought and the enlarged knowledge of mankind in our age have brought into unaccustomed prominence the contrast between the narrow and technical theology which restrains all the wealth of Divine love, all the glorious mediation of the God-Man, to the small number of the baptized or of the consciously converted, *and those grand and universal facts of human life and character presented in an appreciable degree by all men,* "which," St. Paul assures us, "show the work of the law written in their hearts." (Rom. ii, 15.) Nothing but the narrowness of view produced by the exclusive study of an artificial system could hide from men this better aspect of redeemed humanity, and prevent them from recognizing the gracious influences of the Spirit of life and light working out in all nations the generous problem of the same Apostle, "If the uncircumcision keep the righteousness of the law, shall not his uncircumcision be counted for circumcision?" (Rom. ii, 26.) Revolting from the partial theology which presents this strong contrast between its own artificial system and the plainest facts of observation and consciousness, men renounce the Christianity so presented, and undertake to build up another one-sided system out of these facts of observation and consciousness, disregarding revelation altogether. Humanitarianism, in all its varied phases—the popular conceit that unaided nature worked itself up from brutishness to fetichism, and then to Christianity, and now is passing beyond Christianity, and that last fearful impiety, that "humanity is God"—this system owes much of its currency, I believe, to a reaction from the denial of the pervading influence of the Incarnation upon the race; to a reaction from the stiff refusal of Christian teachers to behold and confess the Eternal Spirit prompting and bringing to good effect the good and the beautiful wherever they have appeared in human affection and conduct. I have endeavored to point out the Christian way of terminating this miserable conflict *by reconciling with Christian dogma* these universal facts upon which humanitarianism relies, and clearly exhibiting *the relation between these facts and the supernatural revelation*—"THE KINGDOM OF GOD."

I have connected these unquestionable phenomena with the revealed fact that a portion of the Christ-nature has been given to all men through the Incarnation; that the taint of sin derived to every man from the first Adam has been as fully met in every man by the virtue derived from the Second Adam; that through Christ the whole race has been visited and touched by a living power of righteousness commensurate with and equal to the corruption of nature. The proper place and work of the Church in this Divine economy of grace is another essential fact which partial systems distort or leave out of view. In that Church is provided the food for the new Christ-life, corresponding to the food which in the kingdom of nature is required for the preservation and growth of the physical life. Worship, prayers and praises, Sacraments, and all Divine offices; instruction by hearing and reading the Word of God, by sermons, exhortations, and catechisings, supply the necessary food for the new life of the soul.

By Baptism we are brought into this Church, reborn into the Kingdom of Grace, where is stored all this bounteous provision for the nurture and development of the

spiritual life—a provision so abundant that it even over-
flows to the nurture of multitudes beyond the pale of the
Church. In the catechism the same truth is otherwise
expressed by the language that in Baptism we "are made
members of Christ;" that is we are thereby incorporated
into His true and mystical Body, "which is the blessed
company of all faithful people." (Communion Service.)
We are thereby truly united to Him, "the Head," by
being made members of that glorious "Church which
is His Body, the fullness of Him that filleth all in all."
(Eph. i, 22, 23.) Under this similitude there flows from
Christ the Head, through constituted channels, living
power. The truth is the same however varied may be
the imagery by which it is expressed.

By this appointment of material channels of grace, requiring the concurrence of human will and agency in
their *use* with Divine power in their *operation*, that great
and awful fact of man's nature, FREEDOM, is recognized
and provided for as an integral part of the Divine economy of salvation. For those innocents indeed who are
not permitted in this world to arrive at an age to know
and to choose between good and evil, God Himself makes
the choice. By virtue of the Incarnation and of the sacrificial life and death of Christ, He purifies them by His
Spirit from the taint of sin, and saves them from the peril
of damnation. But all others must choose for themselves
according to their varied opportunities. Life and death are
set before them. Where the Gospel is preached that life
is manifested—distinctly showed forth—in Christ. Life
through union with Christ! Death out of Christ—death
separated from Christ! The sacraments provide the means
and the opportunity of making this choice, sensibly, pal-
pably, beyond the chance of doubt or misgiving. They
are outward acts which all the senses witness, which all

around us witness.   By the right use of these sacraments
we abide in Christ and are nourished by His Spirit.   More
and more of His life is imparted to us, and we live by
Him.   But if we neglect and despise these sacraments,
then we as truly despise and reject the union with Christ
which they symbolize, convey, and perfect.   And then,
according to the economy of grace, the life of Christ originally imparted to us as the means of our probation, is
gradually withdrawn, the moral pulse beats with feebler
stroke, the Spirit warns in fainter tones, the conscience
loses its sensitiveness and becomes at ease, and presently
the self-destroyed soul is as the limb severed from the
Body, as the branch broken from the Vine, fit only for the
burning.

CHAPTER III.

REGENERATION IN ITS MANIFOLD ASPECTS.

1. At a time of unusual agitation in our Church upon the subject of Regeneration, and the connection of Baptism with Regeneration, it seemed to me that if the light of the great truth, the Universality of the Grace of God in Christ Jesus our Lord, could be brought to bear upon these vexed questions, the differences between the disputants might be resolved into harmless logomachies. A logomachy, while unresolved, instead of being harmless, is the most mischievous and hopeless of all controversies. For each party is contending for a truth, and for want of a mutual understanding can never come to an intelligible issue.

§1. Summary.

Since that time—twenty-five years ago—the great truth which I advocated has forced itself, against the barrier of a narrow and technical theology, into more general acceptance; so that it is affirmed in our Mother Church that the recognition and full allowance of this truth must be laid at the foundation of all successful missionary work among the more cultivated heathen peoples.

Since that time, also, the progress of the controversy has brought the disputants to the ultimate terms of the question on either side, so that it can be more easily taken hold of, and its real quality discerned. I propose, therefore, to

offer here a few additional considerations bearing upon the
present advanced state of this unprofitable contention.

2. And, first, it gives me very great pleasure to present
from the pen of one of the clearest thinkers of our Church
and country, the late Dr. Samuel Seabury, a
strong vindication of the great truth I have
tried to restore to its proper prominence.
From the volume of his "Discourses," published in 1874, I take the following lucid statement:

§ 2. REGENER-
ATION AS THE
FIRST CONTACT
OF THE DIVINE
WITH THE HU-
MAN NATURE.

"By his act of disobedience Adam lost the life in which
he was created, and was thus changed from an obedient to
a disobedient, from a happy to a miserable being. Into
this state of apostasy, or separation from God, the descendants of Adam are born, and from this state the Son of God
interposed to redeem them. He was promised to Adam
immediately after the fall, and with the promise came
the thing promised; for the promises of God are never
fallacious, but always true. The fallen Adam and his
posterity were thus made capable of faith and repentance—acts which can not be acceptably exercised without the Holy Spirit. The Holy Spirit was given as
the principle of a new life, by whose powerful energy
man was made capable of being reclaimed from his
apostasy.

"In a restrained and qualified sense, therefore, the Son
of God assumed human nature instantly on the fall of
Adam. He assumed the human nature so far as to communicate to it by the energy of the Holy Spirit the capacity
or principle of a new and holy life. Unless all men have
this capacity the Gospel would be preached in vain, for
none could respond to its call. If man, in virtue of his
own will, reason, and conscience, or any of the natural
powers that belong to him as man, could recover himself

from his apostasy, then Christ died in vain; if man, in virtue of his natural strength, could do the least conceivable thing which would be effectual toward his recovery, then would he share with Christ the merit and glory of redemption.   Neither of these consequences can be admitted; and we therefore conclude that the Eternal Word, from the moment of the fall, assumed human nature for the accomplishment of His gracious purpose; so assumed it as to be in and with it, though not of it, as the principle of a new and heavenly life, bestowing on it the capacity of being re-united to God in the life of obedience and happiness which was lost by the fall." (Discourses, pp. 72–3.)

This great gift of God to man, providing for the fallen creature a new life and a new capacity for holiness, was not only a *fact* in the counsel and eternal purpose of God, and by consequence a *fact* in the actual condition of human nature, but it was *a fact revealed, as the object of Faith*, and as the pregnant sense of all the worship and of all the sacrificial rites of mankind.   The mysterious promise, the Seed of the woman shall bruise the Serpent's head, illustrated and enlarged by a continuous stream of prophecy, and by all the *services of primeval worship*, was the solace and comfort of all nations, inspired the hopes and directed the faith of the whole world.

The growing and various corruptions of this faith and worship gave occasion, first to the call of Abraham, and afterward to the establishment of the Mosaic Polity.   The chosen people thus were made the special guardians and keepers of the truth.   But the rest of mankind did not then and therefore cease to believe in God and in the promised redemption.   They did not then and therefore cease to offer the worship, however corrupted, which embodied and showed forth that faith.   On the contrary, this worship and this faith retained their hold upon the world, and were the salt and savor of humanity, down to the actual birth of Christ, and in some nations long after. It is true that by lapse of time and by the progress of corruption the traditional faith became more and more obscured. And St. Paul, in his address to the Athenians, expressed the actual condition of the religious mind in that time and country, "Whom, therefore, ye ignorantly worship, HIM declare I unto you." (Acts xvii, 23.)

And now a new element in this wondrous provision of eternal wisdom for the salvation of the world becomes prominent. The Desire of all nations has come. The object of the faith of the whole world through all generations—the Divine, Human Redeemer; "God, manifest in the flesh"—is revealed in time, the Babe of Bethlehem, the Fulfiller of the Law, the Teacher of the Nations, the One Sacrifice for the sins of the whole world. And yet on the eighth day after His human birth He is brought into the narrow pale of the Jewish Church by Circumcision. And at the close of His ministry He commanded that all nations as they were converted should be brought into His earthly kingdom by Baptism. This earthly kingdom of Christ is indeed far wider and more comprehensive than Judaism; but compared with mankind, for whom Christ came and lived and died, it has continued to be a very narrow circle. In contemplation of the corresponding problem in the old time, St. Paul had asked, "Is He the God of the Jews only?" The same question, with its satisfying answer, belongs equally to the same problem in its Christian form. Is He the God of the Christians only? Is He not the God of the Heathen also?

When we look back and see that but for the restricted Jewish Polity all true religion would have disappeared from the earth before the coming of Christ, we must admire the Divine wisdom which attached such blessings to Circumcision and such severe penalties to the neglect of it, because through this Circumcision the Jewish Polity was maintained and perpetuated, and so the truth was preserved.

Again, when we see that without the Christian Church to keep the Scriptures and to proclaim the Gospel, there would have been, since the Apostolic age, no Scriptures to keep and no Gospel to proclaim, we are compelled to acknowledge and adore the Divine wisdom which has connected with that Baptism, *by which alone the Church is preserved and perpetuated*, such rich blessings, such glorious promises.

It would seem reasonable to suppose that it was in contemplation of His design to appoint Baptism as the condition and instrument of maintaining the new form of the visible kingdom of God, that our blessed Saviour *adopted and incorporated forever into the language of Christian faith and worship* the Jewish formula of speech which made the Baptism of a Proselyte, the incorporation of a stranger into the Jewish Polity, to be a NEW BIRTH. In its original application this language and the idea it conveyed were familiar to all the covenant people. But the application of a figure of such pregnant meaning to themselves, the proud and highly-privileged citizens of the kingdom, was the hard saying which they could not understand. The declaration was to their minds revolutionary and destructive— a complete reversal of all their cherished preconceptions of Messiah's kingdom. To them that kingdom was to be the triumph and the world-wide dominion of Judaism. The representation which made it to be a new Polity, in relation to which Jews and Gentiles stood alike as strangers, and into which both alike were to be introduced on equal terms by a New Birth, was painfully offensive, and beyond their present capacity of comprehension.

For keeping together in their appropriate place and relation the two essential truths of the dispensation of grace—first, the gift through Christ and by the Holy Ghost of spiritual life to all men, to make them capable of faith and obedience; second, the obligation laid upon all to whom this grace is fully revealed to be in visible union with the external kingdom which God has established in the world—the figure of a new birth is singularly appropriate and expressive. For natural birth is neither creation nor conception. It is the entrance of a living creature into new and higher relations.

Is the human mind too small to contain both the parts of this great truth? Is the range of human vision necessarily so contracted that but one side of this glorious manifestation of the grace of God can be seen by any one person? Must the children of God forever stand on opposite sides of the shield of faith, each proclaiming the half truth which he sees, and contradicting and reviling his brother because he only sees and proclaims the other half?

The objection constantly made, and from opposite quarters, to one or the other of these two truths, and of course to their combination as before represented, is the assertion that New Birth and Regeneration, sometimes used as its equivalent, are words of too lofty and spiritual significance to be restrained to the narrow and frigid sense of a mere change of state and of relations. Therefore it is contended by one school that Baptism is indeed Regeneration, and that Baptism must, by the force of the word, mean the first and transcendent communication of spiritual life, the Christ-life to our dead nature, thereby denying the first of these truths. The answer which the confessed phenomena of universal humanity gives to this theory is so overwhelming that only those can hold it whose minds are capable of intrenching themselves out of sight and out of reach within the narrow circle of a system of technicalities and arbitrary definitions.

Another school with equal emphasis affirms that these lofty words—New Birth, Regeneration—are degraded by applying them to Baptism and to the formal admission of a child of God into the visible Church. These words, it declares, are wholly and intensely spiritual, and designate that transcendent operation by which the Eternal Spirit first visits and vivifies the dead soul of man, and by which that soul *consciously receives* the grace, and *turns* to God in a life of faith and holiness.

This theory, like the other, may be confronted with a vast array of phenomena of human life and history utterly irreconcilable with it. But I am more anxious to point out the element of truth which is in both these systems, and gives to them their vitality and force.

The words we are considering are the loftiest in human language, and contain the noblest conceptions of human capacity and destiny of which the human mind is capable. Arbitrarily and exclusively to restrain them to Baptism, or to any form of admission into the visible kingdom of Christ, is to circumscribe within narrow limits their boundless import. They reach to and express those transcendent relations between God and man by which it was provided in the everlasting covenant that the taint and curse of sin in human nature should be cured by the contact of the Eternal Spirit with that nature, thereby to restore the degenerate child of man to purity, to holiness, to God, to heaven. The Regeneration sweeps through the whole compass of the Divine decree and of the Divine acts, by which this glorious consummation is accomplished, and includes them all. It has a beginning, a progress, and an end—a consummation far above the reach of human imagining; for "Eye hath not seen, nor ear heard, neither hath entered into the heart of man, the things which God hath prepared for them that love Him." (1 Cor. ii, 9.)

The beginning of Regeneration, in this its true and legitimate meaning, is in that contact of Christ by the Spirit with human nature in its entirety, by which the essential evil of an apostate nature is met and resisted by the granted power to exercise a living faith in God and goodness, to repent of sin and to yearn after holiness. This beginning of the regeneration, of the new creation in Christ Jesus, belongs to mankind, the free gift of God to a fallen world. Then, also for mankind, there is a continuous process by which God in His Providence seeks to nurture this better life of humanity, to strengthen it for the conflict with evil, and to enable it to bring forth the fruits of righteousness.

§ 3. REGEN-
ERATION AS
THE CONSCIOUS
CHOICE OF GOOD
AND REJECTION
OF EVIL.
3. In this process is included that crisis in the personal history of most men, that turning point of character and destiny, when good and evil stand before us in tangible and contrasted shape and lineament, and the soul, the will, consciously chooses and gives its allegiance to one or the other. And when, under the light of Christian truth, this choice is made, in the only way in which it can so be made, by accepting Christ as Redeemer, Master, Lord, and God, then this fruitful crisis in the Regeneration is not only rightly called Conversion, but it deserves for its eminence to be termed, and our brethren are right in calling it, Regeneration.

Even this momentous crisis in the normal condition of each man has been verified more or less distinctly, in personal experience,-in all ages and among all nations. The perpetual struggle between the higher aspirations and the evil nature of men is a confessed phenomenon in the history of mankind always and every where. And whenever the opportunity has been presented of looking at the moral history of individual men, we find that this very choice of good and rejection of evil, this determination to follow the higher aspirations and to resist and mortify the evil tendencies of nature, has been distinctly made in a vast number of instances outside the pale of Judaism and of Christianity.

The admired and beautiful fable, the choice of Hercules, in which is set forth this universal conflict between right and wrong, between moral good and evil, and the conscious choice of the good in opposition to all the allurements of vice and to all the strongest propensities of nature, is reported to us by a heathen writer long before the birth of Christ, and through successive generations its persuasive teachings have helped to influence for good Christian children and Christian men. Of the oldest of the great dramatists of Greece—Æschylus—Bishop Meade, of Virginia, has written:

"He is pre-eminently the theological poet of Greece The great problems which lie at the foundation of faith and practice—the same problems which are discussed by Job and his three friends—are the main staples of nearly all his tragedies. . . . It must be confessed that his theology is surprisingly healthy, sound, and truthful in its essential elements. The great doctrines of hereditary depravity, retribution, and atonement are there in their elements, as p lpally as in the sacred Scriptures. Would that modern poets were equally true to the soul of man,

the law of God, and the Gospel of Christ." (Bible and
Classics, pp. 417, 422.)

The same distinguished prelate quotes from a younger
dramatist very much to the same effect. Sophocles, in
relation to the eternal rule of right, says:

> "These are no laws of yesterday; they live
> For evermore, and none can trace their birth.
>
> True piety alone defies the grave;
> Let mortals live or die, this blooms forever.
>
> Conscious of right,
> The soul may proudly soar."

The Bishop (p. 425) sums up a long and interesting dis-
sertation with this conclusion:

"We may thus see how God could save those heathen,
by means of the remaining light handed down by tradition,
which becomes a law written in the hearts of men by the
SPIRIT of God. . . . Through the mercy of God and
by the power of His Spirit they were made humble and
devout, by the instrumentality of that truth which they
held." (*Ibid.*, p. 499.)

These citations are taken from the instructive work
of Bishop Meade, because in the use which he has made
of them the position I am maintaining is strongly supported by his high and persuasive authority.

There must have been such a crisis as that described in
Xenophon in the life of those great and good men whose
history adorns the annals of all nations, and who, by un-
faltering adherence to right, by uncompromising resistance
to evil, by noble self-sacrifice for the good of others, filled
up the measure of a godly life, furnished us in the Scriptures, more perfectly, in many instances, than the average
attainment of Christian men. Surely of these illustrious
witnesses of the sanctifying power of the Spirit we may say

that their part in the Regeneration, in its second and higher meaning, has been unmistakably proved, according to the very letter of Holy Writ. "For if ye live after the flesh, ye shall die; but if ye through the Spirit do mortify the deeds of the body, ye shall live. For as many as are led by the Spirit of God, they are the sons of God." (Rom. viii, 13–14.)

§ 4. REGENERA-
TION AS THE AD-
MISSION OF THE
CHILD OF GOD
INTO THE KING-
DOM OF GOD BY
BAPTISM.

4. But, as we have already seen, there is another marked and decisive period in the Regeneration, under the Christian form of the Covenant, when the heir of salvation is solemnly admitted into that kingdom of heaven which God has established on the earth for the refuge and home of His redeemed. The absolute necessity for the continued existence of this kingdom, to preserve the truth, as well as to nurture the religious life, we have before considered. Not only to preserve the truth, but to manifest it to the world, and to prove it, and to show its continuous transmission from age to age, is this kingdom essential. Take away this testimony, and the Bible, even if it had in its integrity been preserved in the world through all the convulsions of society, would have been subject, like any mere waif of literature, to such a sneer as this from one of the bitterest enemies of Christianity. The writer to whom I refer, speaking of himself, says:

"His refusal of the *creative hypothesis is less an assertion of knowledge than a protest against the assumption of knowledge*, which must long, if not forever, lie beyond us, and the claim to which is the source of manifold confusion upon earth. With a mind open to conviction, he asks his opponents to show him an authority for the belief they so fiercely uphold. They can do no more than point to the Book of Genesis or some other portion of the Bible. Pro-

36

foundly interesting and indeed pathetic to me are those attempts of the opening mind of man to appease its hunger for a cause." (Tyndall, Belfast Address, p. 14, Preface.)

The writer of this sentence forgets that the Book thus mockingly described as mere human guess-work has been handed down through all the ages as the authentic record of a Divine Society, an established social organism, coeval with mankind, claiming and exercising authority over the moral and spiritual nature of men. This spiritual kingdom of God upon earth, older than all civil Polities, authenticates this Book as a revelation from God, given to this spiritual kingdom from time to time, and witnessed "by many infallible proofs," by miracles and prophecies, and by the accordant testimony which its truths find in the hearts and consciences of men. The certain existence and the known history of this kingdom, and the moral sphere in which it rules, are FACTS, outside, indeed, of physical phenomena, but none the less facts, to be considered and treated of as a substantive part of human knowledge and experience. These facts are not within the range of the *physical* sciences, but they are prominent and incontestable phenomena of *historical and moral* science. And it is the transparent fallacy of this school that it mistakes physical science for the sum of all knowledge. These facts of historical and moral science can no more be put away and destroyed by a sneer or a conjecture than any facts of natural history or of chemistry can be so disposed of.

The kingdom of God, thus appointed to rule and to bear witness in the sphere of morals and religion, has also been endowed by its King with spiritual graces, for the nurture and development of the spiritual and moral nature of man. Therefore the solemn admission into this kingdom, with the chartered grant of all its privileges, immunities, and graces, is fitly called regeneration, as being a *fruitful and eminent incident* in that transcendent operation of the Holy Ghost by which depraved and sinful men are made sharers with Christ of a Divine nature, and joint heirs with Christ of a heavenly inheritance.   The great Head of the Church emphatically termed this controlling and fruitful incident in the spiritual life of each one of his disciples a New Birth; and the Church has but echoed His words in her Baptismal Office, from the beginning.

§ 5. REGENER-
ATION AS THE
FINAL PURIFI-
CATION OF THE
REDEEMED.
5. But the Regeneration is not exhausted or completed by this act, efficacious though it be.   It is to go on, in a continuing progress, from grace to grace, from strength to strength, in the transformation of a degenerate and sinful nature into the Christ-likeness, into the completed pattern of the Perfect Man.   The Regeneration, in its highest and fullest sense, can only be at the great consummation, at the end of this economy, when the number of the elect is made up, when there shall be a new heavens and a new earth, and when the Son of Man shall sit down in the throne of His glory.   Then, in the perfected Regeneration, all who have followed Him on earth in self-denial and in doing good shall be admitted to share with Him in the glories and joys of His everlasting kingdom.

§ 6. DIFFI-
CULTIES.
6. The spirit of partisanship has especially raged around that incident of the Regeneration which the Church, using the language of her Lord, emphatically calls the New Birth—the admission of the child of God into the kingdom of God by Baptism.   This controversy is maintained in perpetual activity, by the exaggeration of the effect of Baptism on one side, provoking a corresponding depreciation of the effect of Baptism by the other side.   And both parties ap-

peal to the Catechism, as containing the indubitable proof
of their respective assertions. It would seem that this very
fact ought to make both parties a little less positive and a
little more modest in claiming for their antagonist positions
the unquestionable authority of this venerable formulary.
Instead of this reasonable hesitation and diffidence, the
two parties become more clamorous when it is proposed
to reconcile the passages to which they respectively appeal,
by pointing out a meaning which satisfies and embraces
both. Neither party seems willing to part with a long-
cherished, tenderly nursed, and constantly recurring source
of difference and contention. It is a pretty quarrel as it
stands, and they will tolerate no interference to appease it.

The favorite sentence of those who claim for Baptism
the first bestowal of spiritual life is the answer of the child,
"Baptism, wherein I was made a member of Christ, a child
of God, and an inheritor of the kingdom of heaven." That
these words can not be taken in the sweeping and exclusive
sense claimed for them by these persons might easily be
shown by the necessary principle of interpretation, that all
language must be understood in relation to the facts and
circumstances of which it treats. The known fact that
spiritual life — the Christ-life — has been possessed and
manifested by innumerable persons unbaptized precludes
this exclusive sense, and compels some qualification of the
terms employed. But there is an answer even closer
and, if possible, clearer than this. The Baptismal Service,
which is made by the reference a part of this very formulary, demands from the person to be baptized, as a condition
precedent, a profession of the most eminent graces of the
Spiritual or Christ-life — Faith, Repentance, Obedience.
The exclusive interpretation is, therefore, absolutely and
peremptorily negatived by the document itself. With what

qualification the terms in question are to be understood must be determined, perhaps only approximately, by the facts and circumstances of the case. This qualification has been suggested, and seems to me safe and sufficient. Baptism, as a Sacrament, the outward and visible sign of an inward spiritual grace, takes its subject out of the region of hypothesis and speculation in regard to his relations to God, and places him visibly and formally within the terms of the covenant of grace as a member of Christ, etc. This high transaction is made more solemn and determinate by the sanction of a mutual oath between the parties—God on the one side, man on the other. This qualification of the answer would be expressed by the addition of a single word, "wherein I was *visibly* made a member of Christ, a child of God, and an inheritor of the kingdom of heaven."

The more literal interpretation of the language in question, heretofore given, regards it as simply the affirmation that to be made a member of the Church by Baptism is to be made a member of Christ, because the Church is "the body of Christ."

Those on the other extreme, who deny that the Baptism of an infant is or can be the New Birth in any sense, cite as conclusive proof of their position the definition given in the Catechism of the "inward and spiritual grace" of Baptism, viz., "A death unto sin and a new birth unto righteousness." It is impossible and absurd, it is said, for this high spiritual attainment to be affirmed of an unconscious infant.

This objection brings us into the heart of the most solemn Christian verities. Can these words, in their full and unqualified sense, be properly affirmed in any case of the Baptism of an adult person? Is any man, the newly baptized or the mature Christian, actually *dead* unto sin? Is sin no longer present with him, to taint his soul or body, his thoughts, words, or actions? The consciousness of every Christian gives the answer of St. John to this question, "If we say that we have no sin, we deceive ourselves, and the truth is not in us." (1 St. John i, 8.)

The definition in the Catechism uses the words of St. Paul, and means what he meant when he described the state and condition of a Christian, "Know ye not that so many of us as were baptized into Jesus Christ were baptized into his death? That like as Christ was raised up from the dead by the glory of the Father, even so we also should walk in newness of life." "Reckon ye also yourselves to be dead indeed unto sin, but alive unto God through Jesus Christ our Lord." Then follows that fervid exhortation to make the *sacramental* death unto sin and life unto righteousness an ever-growing reality, by the continued mortification of sin, by continued and faithful obedience to the Spirit. "Therefore," he concludes, "we are debtors not to the flesh, to live after the flesh. For if ye live after the flesh, ye shall die; but if ye through the Spirit do mortify the deeds of the body, ye shall live." (Rom. vi, 3-4, 11; viii, 12-13.)

The whole passage is a description of the meaning and purpose of the Christian profession, and a vindication of the grace of God given to us to make that profession good.

The Baptismal Office faithfully embodies this elaborate and inspired description of the meaning of Baptism. It is, on our part, the solemn and sworn *renunciation* of sin, the solemn and sworn *vow* of allegiance to God, and of submission to be led by His Spirit. It is, on the part of Almighty God, the sworn promise that His grace shall be sufficient for us, to enable us, as long as we try to be

REGENERATION IN ITS MANIFOLD ASPECTS.   61

faithful, to make that renunciation and that vow of obedience effectual. And this view of the Sacrament is clearly
and precisely expressed in the concluding exhortation of the
office: "Remembering always that Baptism representeth
unto us our profession; which is to follow the example
of our Saviour, Christ, and to be made like unto HIM;
that as He died and rose again for us, so should we, who
are baptized, die from sin, and rise again unto righteousness; continually mortifying all our evil and corrupt
affections, and daily proceeding in all virtue and godliness of living."

The two vows of renunciation and obedience in the Office
explain unmistakably the "death unto sin and new birth
unto righteousness," in the contemplation of this Sacrament, to be the rejection of one allegiance and the choice
of another.

All is in the future, except the profession—the vow—
on the one side and the grace given on the other. These
constitute the *sacramental* death unto sin and life unto
righteousness. The *actual* death unto sin and life unto
righteousness are to be accomplished *in futuro* and continuously, as the consequence, the design, and the meaning
of the Sacrament.

And here let us gratefully observe that this plain meaning of the Baptismal Office, provided for our use by the
Holy Church, is the faithful echo and rehearsal of the
meaning which Holy Scripture has unalterably fixed to
the very same language. For in the passage of the Epistle
to the Romans, from which the Church has reverently selected her own phraseology, St. Paul is careful to explain
in less figurative speech the precise meaning of the language
now so painfully contested. In the very process of his argument, *as a reiteration of his previous statement* concerning

death and life, he says, "Know ye not, that to whom ye
yield yourselves servants to obey, his servants ye are to
whom ye obey; whether of sin unto death, or of obedience
unto righteousness?"   (Rom. vi, 10.)

Is not this Sacramental effect just as true and real in
the baptism of an infant as in the baptism of an adult?
The renunciation and the vow are the same; the grace
given is the same; the actual admission into the earthly.
kingdom of God, with its endowment of all the means
of grace, is the same.   Only the *modus operandi* of the
training is different.   The child is "under tutors and gov-
ernors," and the grace of God must give effect to their
discipline and instruction.   The adult is under the government of his own will and intelligence, and the grace of
God must co-operate continually and mightily with all the
instruments of his discipline, or the Sacrament will be
frustrate and of none effect.

§ 7. LANGUAGE INCAPABLE OF SUCH PRECISION AS TO PRECLUDE DIFFERENCES OF INTERPRETA-TION.   7. Even if all this should be allowed, yet.
it is earnestly insisted that the Baptismal.
Office should be so changed as to preclude
all doubt or possibility of difference in its
interpretation, to take away occasion for these elaborate
explanations of its meaning.

There are three sufficient answers to this demand.

1. The thing required is simply impossible.   Human
language is incapable of the precision which excludes
doubt, or a different understanding of it by different
minds.   Even if language were perfect, the demand would
require that all human minds should be alike in natural
capacity and in acquired culture, so that all should receive
from that language precisely the same impression.   Both
the terms of this hypothesis are notoriously untrue.   A.
high legal authority has said that it took two hundred.

years of judicial interpretation and many millions of pounds sterling to ascertain the meaning of the English Statute of Frauds. Compose a new Baptismal Office, and doubts about its construction will arise at once. And in another generation, with changing currents of thought and with changing circumstances, the doubts and difficulties will be indefinitely increased. Now we have an Office, to the meaning of which we are at least assisted by common usage, and by the concurrent or conflicting estimation of the best minds of three centuries.

Those two conflicting forms of thought, which have prevailed, not only in the Church, but in the world, from the beginning of society, will inevitably differ and dispute over any religious formula that can be expressed in words. They separate into parties, and dispute over every form of civil constitution and of government.

The possible constructions of the venerable Office which is now the heritage of the Church have been ascertained by three centuries of use and exposition. And every one can know with certainty that it bears one or the other of these interpretations, between which he can freely choose according to the bent of his own mind. But a *new Office*, or the *old one essentially changed*, launches us upon a sea of uncertainties.

2. Besides this sufficient reason for retaining the old, it must be remembered that, as we have seen, the present Office embodies the language and thought of inspiration. *And precisely the same questions circle around the Baptismal Office as around the words of Holy Scripture.* For the Church then to embody in this Catholic formula one of these interpretations, to the exclusion of the other, would be to affect a wisdom higher than the wisdom of GOD, and possibly to be guilty of a corruption of His word.

37

3. Again, I think it will be conceded by most Church-men that this Office was composed by men of deeper insight into spiritual things, and of a clearer perception of the analogy of faith, than the men of this generation.· The stirring events of the time, the intense concentration of intellectual and spiritual force upon abstract truth *then*, in contradistinction to the diffusion of that force *now* over a new world of physical research, produced very naturally that deeper insight and clearer perception. May we not hope that a generation may yet arise capable of entering fully into their spirit and into their labors? In the mean time, let not the Church throw away the precious heritage they bequeathed to us, and take in its place the fancies and superficialities of an age which recognizes John Stuart Mill and Huxley and Tyndall and Herbert Spencer as its prophets and guides.

CHAPTER IV.

THE INCARNATION AS EXPRESSED IN THE HOLY EUCHARIST.

1. IT is delightful to see how a great truth when fully conceived throws its cheering light not only through large spaces, but into corners and caverns where hard questions and painful difficulties have intrenched themselves in gloom and darkness. The Incarnation — the quickening of humanity through the human nature of Christ — is the one transcendent mystery of the Gospel, which but reappears in varied forms in all other mysteries in the Divine Word and in the Sacraments. Against this fundamental fact of Christianity the hearts of men have stumbled in all ages, wherever and however it is exhibited.

§ 1. TRUTH EMBODIED IN MATERIAL FORMS AND ACTIONS.

To help us to *apprehend* this profound mystery—not to enable us to *comprehend* it, for then it would cease to be a mystery, and would be less than the least of God's manifold works of wisdom and power, but to help us to apprehend and believe this mystery of our salvation — the Scriptures have exhausted the powers of human speech in presenting the same truth in varied forms and by the most striking similitudes.

To this effect is the sixth chapter of St. John; in which by the similitude of Himself as bread from heaven, upon which men feed, and it becomes the nourishment, the strength, and the very substance of their bodies; by the similitude of His flesh and blood to be eaten and drunk, our Saviour announces the intimacy and reality of the

union between Himself and His redeemed; and that the
spiritual life of humanity is derived solely from this union;
and that salvation and eternal life depend entirely upon
the continuation and consummation of this union. Precisely the same cardinal truths of the Christian religion
are presented to us in other forms. Christ says, "I am
the door; by Me, if any man enter in, he shall be saved."
"I am the Way, the Truth, and the Life." St. Paul
says, "We are members of His body, of His flesh, and
of His bones." (Eph. v, 30.)

The Sacrament of Regeneration, the New Birth of water
and of the Holy Ghost, represents and effectually seals the
same glorious mystery in one divinely-ordained form, in
which God and man meet together as co-actors in a solemn
covenant of adoption and grace on the one hand, and of
faith and fealty on the other.

The Sacrament of the Body and Blood of Christ is the
divinely-ordered expression and the effectual seal of the
same adorable mystery, in which God and man again meet
together; man as the faithful and penitent recipient, God
as the Almighty Giver of the life of His Son; thus continuing, strengthening, and perfecting that union between
Christ and the believer which is the only life of humanity—the only hope of salvation.

To conceive rightly of the Sacraments of Christ's religion is to conceive rightly of that religion. For all its
holiest truths are embodied in those Sacraments, made
concrete in material forms and actions. And one of the
purposes for which those sublime truths are so embodied
is that we may the more readily apprehend them. The
plainest and simplest way, therefore, of teaching Christian
truth is to employ and interpret these divinely-appointed
forms of that truth. And the favorite and most successful method by which the truth in every age has been

assailed and corrupted has been by a subtle and tortuous misinterpretation of these holy mysteries. We have seen how the Sacrament of Regeneration has been abused, and made the battle-ground for perpetual conflict between opposing errors. In like manner the Holy Sacrament of Love has been turned into the unhappy occasion of fratricidal strife by the perverse ingenuity of erring men.

§ 2. TRANSUB- 2. The blessed Sacrament of the Body
STANTIATION.   and Blood of Christ has been perverted by superstitious folly into a monstrous fable, insulting alike to God and man, by which Religion has been degraded almost to the level of Fetich worship, and Christianity placed in direct antagonism with those very faculties of men by which alone its own truth can be perceived and recognized. The varied and beautiful imagery of our Lord in His discourses, together with His own blessed Sacrament, expressing a sublime and glorious mystery, are thus changed into a revolting figment which overturns the nature of a Sacrament and frustrates the whole meaning, purpose, and teaching of the Divine instruction and of the Divine institution.

The gross and carnal fable of transubstantiation invents a miracle as useless as it is profane in place of the Divine miracle of grace intended by the Sacrament. For, observe, the natural effect of bread and wine is only to nourish our bodies; but consecrated by the Holy Ghost their *ordered Sacramental* effect is twofold; first, to be the *effectual seal* of our personal union with Christ; and secondly, to be the channel to convey to us Christ Himself, to be the spiritual nourishment of soul and body.

For this mighty miracle of grace superstition substitutes her poor pretended miracle, and affirms that the bread and wine have been changed into the natural Flesh and Blood of Christ. But the natural effect of flesh and blood is

68

only to nourish our bodies as bread and wine do; so that after all this sacrifice of sense, reason, Scripture, and the common meaning of language, this gratuitous miracle, has not advanced us one single step beyond the simple use as food of unconsecrated bread and wine. For the Divine institution, *under this representation of it,* consisting simply in the supposed conversion of bread and wine into flesh and blood, and our feeding upon them, there is no place in this pretended mystery for the Sacramental union with Christ, which the real mystery was intended to symbolize, continue, and strengthen. Even with the aid of the hypostatical union, with all its possible and, in this connection, revolting consequences, you get not beyond this, except by abandoning "the letter," which truly in this case "killeth" the most profound and glorious mystery of our Religion.

It is painful to have to write or to think of these consequences; but it is an unhappy necessity to answer men according to their folly. Allow to these men the pretended literal meaning of the words of institution, supplemented by all the effect claimed for the hypostatical union in this transaction, and the result is merely that the communicant has received, *as food for his body,* the dead or living Christ, the flesh, blood, soul, and Divinity of the crucified and risen Saviour. But where is the place in this process for "the strengthening and refreshing of our souls by the Body and Blood of Christ, as our bodies are by the Bread and Wine," as the true Sacrament provides? All the power and glory of the Divine institution are expended and lost, under this theory, in providing a little nourishment for the body, and in the *mere subjective excitement which the thought of such a repast may occasion.* The real spiritual benefit is thus reduced to the very lowest point of the Zuinglian fancy.

To attain the true purpose and meaning of the Sacrament, to make it the communication of Christ to us, to dwell in and consecrate our whole nature, the Romanist is compelled to rely upon a truer and higher meaning of the blessed words of institution than that poor pretended literal meaning out of which his monstrous fable has been constructed. He must add to this letter that killeth a belief in the power of the Holy Ghost consecrating the supposed flesh and blood to their instituted purpose and effect, to nourish both soul and body, to be the communication of very Christ to us. This supernatural and glorious effect, the real meaning of the institution, is altogether beyond and aside from the mere reception as food of the Flesh and Blood and the whole person of Christ. And in the real Sacrament ordained by our Lord, according to the plain and obvious meaning of the words of institution, Bread and Wine are consecrated to this very supernatural and glorious effect. So that this weary circle of folly and stultification leads to no end, accomplishes no purpose, except to degrade religion, and to be used as an instrument for the degradation of the human soul.

We have spoken of transubstantiation as founded upon the alleged literal meaning of the words of institution; but it really seems to be an abuse of language to call that a literal meaning of the words which does not express their plain and obvious meaning, according to the ordinary forms of speech.

The necessary construction of human language conveys spiritual and abstract truths by words derived from material and sensible images. The mystery of the Eucharist is in the real meaning of the words of institution. The so-called "literal" acceptation of those words does not properly involve a mystery, but is simply a violation of the elementary principles of language, an insult to the

Divine Speaker. For Christ used human language in its ordinary forms, addressing it to human intelligence. The words were used to convey a certain meaning in accordance with the most common form of human speech. Men say they will humbly take these words in what they call their literal meaning, whatever contradiction it may give to sense and reason. But in doing this they take the words senselessly and *leave out the meaning.*

The words correspond in character with many like expressions of the same Divine Teacher, and all of them are as plain as ordinary language can be. "I am the door;" "I am the vine;" "I am that bread that came down from heaven," referring to the manna in the wilderness. Must we "humbly," as these persons say, take these words in what they call their literal meaning? Must we make our Lord to be a piece of deal-board manufactured into a door? Must we think of Him and "adore" Him as a grape-vine planted in the earth? The pretended literal meaning of all these expressions is no mystery, but simply senseless and contradictory. The unfathomable mystery is in the plainly-intended meaning, according to the ordinary usage of human speech, not in the literal meaning of the words.

The mystery is the union of Christ with us—begun by the Incarnation, continued and perfected in each child of God by this and other means of grace and spiritual growth. The mystery is Christ giving Himself to us when He gives us bread and wine, consecrated to represent that body and blood which with our whole nature He assumed for our sakes. The mystery is Bread and Wine consecrated to be the *effectual seal*, the instrument, therefore, by which He conveys Himself to us. The symbolism in that Divine mystery is that Christ is as truly united then to our souls and bodies as the consecrated elements are to those bodies. It is amazing that sensible men will obscure this great truth by a perverse taking of our Lord's plain and simple words. The Jews, who were offended by the great mystery first disclosed to them by our Lord in the conversation related in the sixth chapter of St. John, took not his words in the gross and carnal sense now contended for by some. The communication of the life of Christ to men, thereby uniting them to God, was the profound and puzzling truth which they gathered from those words, and which inflamed their hearts with madness. This is the fundamental fact of Christianity, the one pervading mystery which is continually reproduced in various forms all through the institutions and mysteries of redemption.

§ 3. THEORY OF IDENTITY, OR UNION OF CHRIST WITH THE ELEMENTS.

3. Transubstantiation and Zuinglianism are by our formularies alike denied and forbidden to be held. It is to be feared that some radical extremists in one direction in our Church do hold this last-named form of error concerning the Holy Eucharist, making of it a bare remembrance. Lately there has arisen in the Church of England, as an extreme and passionate reaction from the deadening Erastianism of the last century, an active and zealous party which, with some admirable traits, is unhappily distinguished by its denunciation of the English Reformation, and by its painful effort to assimilate as near as possible to Rome without incurring the legal penalty of ejection from the English Church.

It is almost a matter of course that this party should have its admirers and imitators in America, although the external reasons for the existence of such a party do not exist here as in England. It was a fatal mistake of some of the younger clergy and divinity students of the last generation to have thrown themselves warmly into the current of the earlier "Oxford movement," with its turbid stream of mingled truth and error; unmindful of the fact that all the truth of that movement had long before become "familiar science" to American Churchmen. The changed constitution of the civil legislature and the dawning suspicion of possible disestablishment, which helped to start the movement in England, had long been accomplished facts in this country, and had forced our people to study and comprehend the Divine Constitution of the Church as the necessary warrant for their organization, doctrine, and worship. And so the teachings of Seabury and White and Hobart and Ravenscroft, of Bowden, Chapman, and Cooke, had settled for us, on immovable foundations of reason and evidence, the truths which these Oxford professors were painfully feeling after.

It was during this earlier movement that the doctrine of the Eucharist was depraved for a section of English and American Churchmen by a new theory put forth as a milder substitute for Transubstantiation. The writer who first formally stated and with laborious ingenuity expounded this theory was Robert Isaac Wilberforce, then "Arch-deacon of the East Riding." This task he accomplished by the publication of quite a large volume a year or two before his avowed secession to the Church of Rome. The book abounds with sophistries and misrepresentations; but it exercised a large and pernicious influence in both countries, because it was received as a genuine utterance of English Churchmanship.

The theory of Wilberforce is that although the Elements remain bread and wine, retaining their natural substance, yet after consecration, "by a law of identity without parallel," the flesh and the blood, and consequently the whole Person of Christ, are inseparably united to the Elements, and being in the Elements and upon the Altar, should be adored there. "Hence it comes to pass," he says, "that this Sacrament consists of two things, a Subject and a Predicate, which are united into one by a law of identity which is without parallel." (Page 133.) "When it is said then that the relation between the Subject and the Predicate in our Lord's words of institution is that of sacramental identity, it is meant that the outward and inward parts, the *sacramentum* and *res sacramenti*, are united by the act of consecration into a compound whole. Such was the efficacy of our Lord's original benediction; such continues to be the force of the same words when pronounced by Him through the mouth of His Ministers. For they are *creative* words, like those which called the world into existence." "The outward and the inward, retaining each their own character, are united into a heterogeneous whole." (Page 135-6.) "Christ's Body, therefore, may be said to have a form in this Sacrament, namely, the form of the Elements, and to occupy that place through which the elements extend." (Page 176.)

In more than one place he tells us that the supposed contradiction between the Church of England and the Church of Rome on this subject is "verbal rather than real, in language and not in thought." (Page 143.)

This mischievous theory, remitting us to the worst corruptions of mediævalism, and engrafting upon Christianity the very principle of all heathen idolatry by identifying the Deity with the Symbols of His Presence, has recently received a very extraordinary indorsement in the judicial opinion of Sir Robert Phillimore, Dean of the Court of Arches, in the case of Shepherd v. Bennett. And the "adjudicated words" of the defendant, Bennett, are now adopted as the shibboleth of the new party. They are as follows:

"I believe in the real, actual Presence of our Lord under the form of bread and wine upon the altars of our churches," and "I myself adore and teach my people to adore Christ present in the Elements under the form of bread and wine, believing that under this veil is the sacred Body and Blood of my Lord and Saviour Jesus Christ." It is true that the Supreme Court of Appeal indignantly denies the assertion of the Judge of the court below that these words express the doctrine of the Church of England or of her great divines; nevertheless it affirms that judgment, refusing to condemn the defendant for the use of these words.

The issue is now therefore fairly joined between the old Christian doctrine of the Eucharist and this "new-fangled conceit," as St. Bernard called one of the later articles of the Romish Creed—the immaculate conception of the Virgin Mary. And this issue must be tried in both countries upon the broad ground of reason and Scripture. I have no fears of the result. Because with the warning example of Rome before us in the same progress of superstition, and with the absorbent power of that communion to take up intractable impurities from any source, our Church will continue to give, in the future as in the past, a clear and certain testimony to all the great verities of Christian religion.

4. With a strange forgetfulness of the terms of their new dogma, its advocates take up the stereotyped claim of Rome in regard to Transubstantiation, and affirm that the "letter" of the words of institution is "the sure warrant" for their theory.

§ 4. ILLOGICAL APPEAL OF THIS PARTY TO THE LETTER OF INSTITUTION.

We have already seen as to the Romish figment, and the same is just as true of all its cognate theories of identity, impanation, consubstantiation, and sacramental union in the sense that Christ is in the Elements, that it is a violent departure from the literal or any other sensible meaning of the words, *according to the established and familiar usage of human speech.* But if you once allow such a force to be put upon language and common reason as to admit the absurdity of Transubstantiation, then there is a sort of logical adherence to the letter in that conceit. For if the Elements are no longer Bread and Wine, they may be, according to the letter, the Body and Blood of Christ, and consequently the whole Person of Christ. But this new device is, in any possible aspect of it, an entire departure from the alleged letter. Take any of the terms in which the new dogma is expressed, and they are all alike a departure from the letter. For if the elements remain bread and wine, then it is a departure from the literal meaning to say that they are *likewise* the Body and Blood. It is an unauthorized addition to say that they *contain* the Body and Blood, or that the Body and Blood are *united* with them. Certainly our Lord says nothing of this sort. As the martyr Ridley has pointed out, our Lord does not mention two substances, but one only. He does not say this Bread *and* My Body, but "This is My Body." This necessary departure of all the later theories from the mere letter throws us back either upon the mediæval fable of Transubstantiation, or upon the legitimate and recognized sense of the words—the proper literal meaning according to the *usus loquendi* of all human speech. This bread represents My Body; is now by My Divine word constituted the efficacious symbol of My Body; so that he that receiveth rightly this Bread receiveth Me.

Dr. Pusey and a part of his followers are quite emphatic in expressing their rejection of Transubstantiation. The distinct language of our formularies requires this rejection. But the special theory of Transubstantiation is only a surviving specimen of scholastic nonsense. The theological vice of this famous relic, as of its kindred errors, is that it confuses the Deity with the symbols of

His presence—with the instruments of His power—and
localizes HIM *in or under material forms;* and when the
Deity, *so localized,* is worshiped by outward acts of adoration, those bodily acts, by the necessity of our condition,
are directed to the material forms. In the instance of a few
gifted persons, the *mind* may pass beyond the visible symbol to the invisible God, but the prostrations and other
bodily acts are made to the symbol as representing the
Present Deity. And this is precisely the description of
that vast system of heathen idolatry which had overspread
the earth. The heathen worshiped the Deity in the symbol—the sun, the moon, the stars, or the graven image;
and the higher minds among them, as among the Roman
Catholics, made that purely intellectual distinction between
the worship of the Deity in the symbol and the worship
of the symbol, which Mr. Bennett did not make except
upon constraint. Alas! for the multitudes who are incapable of this distinction!

I am persuaded that many of the objectionable forms
of expression now applied to this Divine mystery are a
mere juggle of words, growing out of the confusion and
obscurity incident to a thousand years of verbal controversy. The mystification began by the departure, in an
age of ignorant conceit, from the proper and accustomed
meaning of words used according to the ordinary forms
of speech, and putting upon these words, *under the plea of
adhering to the letter,* an arbitrary, forced, and impossible
meaning. This departure once made, and the changes
upon these abused words continually rung by innumerable
disputants, produced a mistiness and indistinctness of conception which affords no basis for mutual understanding or
for settlement, but gives the unhappy occasion for inter-
minable disputation without the possibility of getting
nearer to the truth by an intelligible issue.

5. The words of institution and all the words of our blessed Lord in regard to this Holy Sacrament, accord with the most common facts of human intercourse and with the best established usage of human speech.

§ 5. The Real Presence as taught by the Church.

One of the most familiar forms of speech is to give to a constituted symbol of a thing the name of the thing, or as St. Augustine expressed it, "He calls the Sacrament of so great a thing by the name of the thing itself." One of the most common facts of social life in all ages is the transfer of property, of any kind or value, by the delivery of an agreed symbol of that property. Nine tenths of the business transactions of the world have always been effected by the operation of these two principles. A warehouse certificate will pass the possession and property of a rich cargo to an indefinite succession of purchasers. All transfers of lands and houses are made by the delivery of a piece of paper duly written, signed, and sealed. In either case the certificate and the deed must be executed *according to the precise terms of law*, or they are nullities. It is in accordance with this universal principle that both the Christian Sacraments have been made effectual by the Divine love and power to the accomplishment of their intended supernatural purpose.

This plain conclusion brings into view another source of ambiguity and indistinctness on this sacred subject.

There is all the difference between the Presence of Christ in the Sacrament and the Presence of Christ in the *material elements* of the Sacrament as between a blessed truth and a pernicious error. A competent knowledge of that *law which is universal reason*, and of which Hooker speaks so grandly, will teach us how utterly mistaken are those persons who speak of Christ as enthroned on the altar, or as the victim on the altar, or as being on the altar in any special sense, *in or under the species of bread and wine.* This language and the ideas conveyed by it are an entire departure from our Lord's institution, a plain misconception of the meaning of the Holy Sacrament. The consecration has indeed changed the *character* of these elements from common bread and wine into holy and effectual symbols of a transcendent and adorable mystery. This consecration makes possible a Real Presence of our Lord, to be distinguished as well from that general Presence by which the Deity is everywhere as from a so-called Virtual Presence by which faith and other Christian graces are increased. This Presence is so real that when the consecrated symbols are received, *according to the institution,* then Christ imparts Himself to the faithful communicant to be the life, the strength, the nourishment of the new nature in Christ Jesus. This Sacrament, like the other, is a continuing part of the one pervading mystery of the Incarnation, by which Christ becomes more and more one with us and makes us one with Him. And this most true and effectual Presence is involved in the nature of this Sacrament as one whole and entire thing.

To descend from this height and to represent the Presence as in the Elements, or on the Altar, or in the hands, is not only a departure from the sublime meaning and the very words of the institution, but is a direct contradiction of the definition of this Sacrament contained in our Catechism. According to that definition, the consecrated bread and wine become the "sign of an inward and spiritual grace," "the Body and Blood of Christ," "*given unto us.*" "The inward and spiritual grace" is neither "visible" nor "outward" in the Elements. These Elements, the "outward and visible sign," are simply and purely, says the definition, the "*means whereby we receive*" the inward and spiritual grace, "and a *pledge* to assure us thereof." To represent "the inward and spiritual grace," "the Body and Blood of Christ," to be in the elements, or under them, or to have any relation to them, other than the instituted one of mediate cause and effect—"a means and a pledge"—is a direct contradiction of this definition.

The mistake is flagrant and fatal which changes the place of this adorable mystery from the communication of Christ to us by the power of the Holy Ghost through this instituted "means" to the poor substitute of veiling Christ in or under the Elements, upon the altar, or in the hands. By the institution of Christ the Bread and Wine are changed indeed, not in "substance" nor in "accidents," but in character and meaning. There is no mystery at all in the appointment of these material symbols of power and efficacy. This appointment is in plain accordance with universal custom and common speech. The mystery is in the spiritual grace given to us—the constituted power and efficacy. This mystery is deep, transcendent, "the tremendous mystery," the "miracle of grace," in the contemplation of which we may all take up the heart-cry of the late excellent Hugh Davy Evans whenever he approached the altar, "Lord, I believe; help thou my unbelief."

That the mystery is *here*, in the communication of Christ to us, and not where it has been improperly placed, in an imagined alteration of the substance of the bread and wine, or in a supposed hiding of Christ within or under the material elements, is, by logical necessity, involved in the nature of this Sacrament. I suppose that every jurist will concur in the correctness of the following proposition.

A POSITIVE INSTITUTION, as contradistinguished from a natural thing, can only exist as an entirety. You can not change or divide it. It subsists as a whole, or not at all. This Sacrament is a POSITIVE INSTITUTION. As such it

38

must be observed according to its terms, or it is not ob-
served at all. The changed or mutilated thing is a nullity.
The Sacrament is not celebrated. Now, the reception of
the consecrated Bread and Wine by the faithful is an
integral, essential, and component part of the Sacrament.
Without this completion the positive institution of our
Lord has not been complied with, and has no existence.
All that went before fails of its effect, and is as if it had
not been done. Christ is truly and ineffably present in the
Sacrament, but only where the Sacrament is complete,
where the Sacrament is, when the Elements are received
according to the institution. Then Christ gives Himself
to the communicant. To speak of Christ as on the Altar,
either as King or Victim, is aside from and in derogation
of His institution. It is a presumptuous departure from
that institution, an unwarranted change of its terms. The
Elements are only consecrated to their instituted purpose,
viz., to represent the Body broken and the Blood shed,
and to be received and eaten, as the condition on which the
living Saviour will communicate Himself to His people.
The immediate purpose of the consecration of the elements
is that they may be received and eaten. Previous to this
commanded duty and purpose they may indeed be a
Eucharistic and Commemorative Sacrifice. But as yet
there is no Sacrament. The main particular of the divine
institution is not performed. Christ is not otherwise
Present up to this point than as He is Present in all
Divine offices, as the effectual Mediator and Priest. The
REAL PRESENCE of Christ, *in its highest sense as the blessing
of this Sacrament,* by the very necessity of the institution,
can only be IN THE PARTICIPATION OF CHRIST by the faithful recipient of the consecrated elements. For then only
is the Sacrament which Christ ordained complete. Then
only are the terms of this positive institution complied

with and its meaning accomplished. Then only is it the SACRAMENT OF THE BODY AND BLOOD OF CHRIST.

§ 6. PRETEND- ED AUTHORITIES FOR THE NEW THEORY.
6. Some of the bolder advocates of the new theory of the Eucharist do not hesitate to denounce the English Reformation and the whole body of Anglican divinity which has followed it as uncatholic, and only to be mentioned with contempt. Another section of the party, at the head of which we must now place the learned Dean of the Court of Arches, stoutly maintains that this fantastic notion has been held by the early Christian Fathers and by nearly all the great Divines of the English Church.

My treatment of this claim must be summary, but I trust it will be sufficient. Many volumes have been written for and against this claim, so far as the early Fathers are concerned, in regard to the related theory of Transubstantiation. The same testimonies from antiquity which refute the Romish figment are equally strong against the more recent position. To these testimonies, as gathered by our great Divines, I must in general refer. But all these testimonies must be considered in the light of two leading facts.

As I have said, the words of institution, in the strongest possible sense, according to the ordinary usage of human language, can only mean that this Bread is the effectual Representative of My Body given for you. This Cup represents My Blood shed for you. By these representatives of My Body and Blood I give myself to you, so that I may dwell in you, and you in Me. The Representatives thus constituted properly receive, in all human speech, *the name of the things they signify.* The Christian Fathers, freely and without reserve, adopted this language in this sense, and expanded it in varied forms, as the basis of their exhortations to reverence and sanctity, and to a just

conception of the amazing mystery which this language
involved, never dreaming of the gross departure from the
plain meaning of this common form of speech which
mediæval and modern conceit has made. Such words of
the Fathers are now quoted in favor of Transubstantiation
and of this later and kindred error. But when the Fathers
themselves incidentally speak of the same thing in other
language, and so interpret their own meaning, we see that
they intended no such abuse of human language as is now
ascribed to them. Any one of the many places in which
the Fathers thus incidentally explain their own sense would
be sufficient to vindicate their memory and their intelligence from the reproach of so taking the words of our Lord
as to leave out the meaning. Happily these places are
numerous. The two facts I referred to are conclusive upon
this point.

(1) St. Augustine employs the common and well-under-
stood *usus loquendi* in regard to the Lord's Supper as the
most familiar illustration by which to explain a difficulty
which had been proposed to him growing out of the form
of administration of Baptism. The question was, how can
the sponsors truly answer that an infant believes? St.
Augustine's solution of the difficulty is, that the answer
may properly be made in conformity with the established
usage that a *representation* or *Sacrament* of a thing receives
the name of the thing itself. "The Sacrament of faith is
faith," and so the infant receiving the Sacrament may
rightly be said to believe. Whatever we may think of
the justness of the conclusion, the material point in this
determination is the common and familiar examples which
Augustine adduces of that form of speech upon which he
relies. "When Good Friday is nigh we say, To-morrow or
next day is our Lord's passion; on the Lord's day we say,
This day our Lord arose. Why is there nobody so silly as

to say we lie when we speak so, but for this reason, because
we give names to those days from the representation they
make us of those on which the things were indeed done."
His second example of the same usage of speech is the
common way of speaking about the Eucharist. "Was
not Christ in His own person offered up once for all? and
yet in the Sacrament He is offered in the Church not only
every Easter, but every day; nor does he lie who being
asked says He is offered. For Sacraments would not be
Sacraments if they had not a resemblance of those things
whereof they are the Sacraments; and from this resemblance they *commonly have the names of the things themselves.*
As therefore the Sacrament of Christ's Body is after a
certain fashion Christ's Body, . . . so the Sacrament of
faith is faith." St. Augustine adds: "The Apostle on this
same subject of Baptism says *we are buried together with
Christ by Baptism unto death;* he does not say we *signify* a
burial, but uses the word itself; *we are buried.* So that he
calls the Sacrament of so great a thing by the name of the
thing itself." (Epist. 23 to Boniface.) If St. Augustine
deemed that there "is nobody so silly as to say we lie when
we speak so," what would he have thought of the possibility of perverting this form of speech into a literal
affirmation?

(2) Another conclusive testimony to the sense in which
the ancients used and understood this Sacramental language is furnished us by Ratramn in his celebrated treatise.
He quotes St. Augustine as teaching that *the people who
receive are* represented by the Eucharistic elements in the
same sense in which Christ is represented by them.
Ratramn adds: "But in this other, which is celebrated in
a mystery, there is a figure not only of the proper Body
of Christ, but also of the people that believe in Christ.
For it beareth the figure of either Body, that is, of the

Body of Christ, but also of the people that believe in Christ. For it beareth the figure of either Body, that is, of the Body of Christ, which suffered and rose again, and of the people who in Christ are born again and quickened from the dead." (Sec. 95–8.)

If there were but these two testimonies to the sense in which the Fathers used the figurative language of the Eucharist, these would be amply sufficient to save them from the reproach of believing either that the elements were "changed" into His Person, or that he was "identified" with the elements in a mystical conjunction.

This opinion, that the water mingled with wine in the Cup represented the people *in the same mystical sense in which the wine represented Christ,* was not the singular thought of Augustine, or of Ratramn quoting this Father, but was the commonly received exposition from very early times. For St. Cyprian, rebuking an ancient folly which has been revived in our time, viz., the offering of water in the Eucharistic cup instead of wine, says: "For whereas Christ says, *I am the true vine,* the Blood of Christ is not surely water, but wine. Nor can His Blood, whereby we have been redeemed and quickened, appear to be in the Cup when the Cup is without that wine, *whereby the Blood of Christ is set forth.* . . . . For because Christ loves us all in that He bore our sins also, we see that in the water the people are intended, but that in the wine is shown the Blood of Christ. But when in the Cup water is mingled with wine His people are united to Christ, and the multitude of believers are united and conjoined with Him in whom they believe." (Epistle 363 to Cœcilius.)

Plainly St. Cyprian and the men of his time have never conceived of any difference between the representation of Christ and the representation of the people who believe in Christ, in this Holy Mystery.

About the time in which St. Cyprian lived, A. D. 250, the work entitled "Constitutions of the Holy Apostles" is generally believed to have been published. In this work the Eucharist is often mentioned in terms which preclude the modern fancies, as for example: "Instead of a bloody sacrifice He hath appointed that reasonable and unbloody and mystical one of His body and blood, which is performed to *represent by symbols* the death of the Lord." (Book vi, chap. 23.) "Offer the acceptable Eucharist, the *representation* of the royal body of Christ." (Book vi, chap. 30.) "We also, our Father, thank Thee for the precious blood of Jesus Christ, which was shed for us, and for His precious body, *of which we celebrate these representations, as He Himself appointed us, to show forth His death.*" (Book vii, chap. 25.)

The words of our Lord in the sixth chapter of St. John, referring to this Sacrament and to our union with Him, have been so constantly misrepresented by the depravers of the mystery that it will be profitable always to keep in mind the sense in which they were understood by the early Church. Origen says: "There is also in the New Testament a letter which kills him who doth not spiritually understand those things which are said; for if we take according to the letter that which is said, EXCEPT YE EAT MY FLESH AND DRINK MY BLOOD, *this letter kills.*" (Homilies on Leviticus, cap. 10.)

St. Augustine gives more copiously the same testimony. In his treatise *De Doctrina Christiana* (lib. 3, tom. 3, p. 53), laying down several rules for the right understanding of Scripture, he gives this for one:

"If the speech be a precept forbidding some heinous wickedness or crime, or commanding us to do good, it is not figurative; but if it seem to command any heinous wickedness or crime, or to forbid that which is profitable or beneficial to others, it is figurative. For example: *Except ye eat the flesh of the Son of man and drink his blood, ye have no life in you.* This seems to command a heinous wickedness and crime; therefore it is a figure, commanding us to communicate of the passion of our Lord, and with delight and advantage, to lay up in our memory that His flesh was crucified and wounded for us."

I do not suppose that St. Augustine in the last words of this extract expresses the fullness of his own conception of the meaning conveyed by the figurative language of our Lord. But this comment by the two most illustrious teachers of the Church in different ages upon those pregnant words of our Lord, by which he signified the mystery of the Incarnation and the showing forth of that mystery in this Sacrament, should drive away forever that wretched travesty of these words and of His Holy Sacrament which makes the blessed Saviour teach that He puts Himself in the place of His appointed Symbols, or that He hides His sacred Person under the veil of these Symbols, to be first adored and then eaten by His people. The grossness of this fable was not too coarsely described by Averroes, an Arabian philosopher, as quoted by Archbishop Tillotson: "I have traveled over the world and have found divers sects, but so sottish a sect or law I never found as is the sect of Christians; because with their own teeth they devour their God whom they worship."

Tillotson quotes in the same place a saying of the great Roman orator expressing a common rule of language, which should confound his Christian countrymen and their copyists with shame: "When we call," says he, "the fruits of the earth Ceres and wine Bacchus, we use but the common language; but do you think any man so mad as to believe that which he eats to be God?" (Tillotson's Works, vol. ii, serm. 26.)

One of the most painful attempts at argument by this party is the comparison of the supposed union between Christ and the Elements to the hypostatic union between the Divine and the Human nature of Christ. Gelasius and Theodoret are cited as authorities for this notion. Gelasius shall answer for himself. The passage relied upon is: "Surely the Sacraments which we receive of the body and blood of our Lord are a divine thing, so that by *them* WE are made partakers of the Divine nature; and yet it ceaseth not to be the substance or nature of bread and wine; and certainly the *image* and *resemblance* of Christ's body and blood are celebrated in the *action* of the mysteries."

Gelasius does not *compare* anything which takes place in the Eucharist to the Hypostatic union, but he *illustrates* that union, as against the Eutychians, by the *completed* "*action*" of the Holy Mystery. For as the consecrated bread and wine, he argues, though endowed with the mysterious power to make us "partakers of the Divine nature," yet retain their own nature; so the human nature of Christ remains in its own integrity, notwithstanding its mysterious relation to the Divine nature. Neither the Fathers nor our English Divines had conceived of this modern substitute for Transubstantiation, and therefore their language was not guarded against it. But they all alike speak of the Eucharist only in its proper aspect, as *one entire thing—as the completed action.* They know nothing of a Divine mystery halved, and the nature and properties of either portion made the subject for curious speculation. They thought not of bread and wine becoming "partakers of the Divine nature," but of themselves, the redeemed, by the use of these elements made "partakers of the Divine nature." "*Divinæ efficimur consortes naturæ*" are the words of Gelasius, and immediately afterward he calls these con-

39

secrated elements the "image and representation of the
body and blood."

Archbishop Tillotson, who receives honorable mention in
the Oxford Catena, shall tell us about Theodoret: "The
second is of the same Theodoret, in his second dialogue
between a Catholick under the name of *Orthodoxus* and an
heretick under the name of *Eranistes*, who maintaining
that the humanity of Christ was changed into the substance of the Divinity, (which was the heresy of Eutyches,)
he illustrates the matter by this similitude: 'As (says
he) the symbols of the Lord's body and blood are one
thing before the invocation of the priest, but after the
invocation are changed and become another thing, so the
body of our Lord after his ascension is changed into the
Divine substance.' But what says the Catholick Orthodoxus to this? Why he talks just like one of Cardinal
Perron's hereticks. 'Thou art (says he) caught in thy
own net, because the mystical symbols after consecration
do not pass out of their own nature, for they remain in
their former substance, figure, and appearance, and may
be seen and handled even as before.'" (Works, vol. ii, pp.
110–11.) So it seems that the earliest approach to the
Wilberforce theory was made by the Eutychian heretics in
their vain struggles to find arguments to support their error.

On the same page the Archbishop furnishes the testimony of "Facundus, an African Bishop who lived in the
sixth century." I copy this passage because, like most of
the authorities I have cited, it incidentally and therefore
most assuredly tells us the *animus*, the mind and meaning
of the Fathers in all their speeches concerning both the
holy Sacraments. "Upon occasion," says Tillotson, "of
justifying an expression of one who had said that Christ
also received the adoption of sons, he reasons thus: 'Christ
vouchsafed to receive the *Sacrament* of adoption both when

he was circumcised and baptized, and the Sacrament of adoption *may be called adoption,* as the Sacrament of His body and blood which is in the consecrated bread and cup is by us *called His body and blood;* not that the bread is properly His body and the cup His blood, but because they contain in them the mysteries of His body and blood. Hence also our Lord Himself called the blessed bread and cup which He gave to His disciples His body and blood.'"

Nothing can show the severe strain which can be put upon the mind by the exigencies of an argument engaged in the support of error more clearly than the use which has been made of the grand words of St. Paul: "The cup of blessing which we bless, is it not the communion of the blood of Christ? The bread which we break, is it not the communion of the body of Christ?" (1 Cor. x, 16.)

Instead of taking these words, as the Church has always done, to be the comforting assurance that this Holy Sacrament both testifies the union of Christ with His believing people and strengthens and perpetuates that union, these mistaken brethren profanely distort them into the assertion that there is a sort of hypostatic union between Christ and the Elements; that the bread and wine are the communicants, the partakers of Christ!

§7. MISREP-
RESENTATION OF
THE ENGLISH
DIVINES.
7. But the claim that this strange freak of superstitious fancy is the doctrine of the English Church, and of the great divines of that Church, is one of the most remarkable illusions of our time. The Wilberforce already mentioned is the author of this fable, as he is, for the English people, of the theory it professes to sustain. The theory indeed is as old as the Pseudo-Seventh Council, which established this dogma along with the worship of images. But the theory was not fashioned into the special shape of Tran-

substantiation until Paschasius Radbertus accomplished that feat in the year 818.

Now, when we think of the shadowy distinction between the two forms of this untruth, and that every vice of the one religiously conceived inheres in the other, it is sufficiently extravagant to imagine that Ridley and his fellow-martyrs deliberately perished at the stake in defense of this worthless and impalpable distinction!

In reading the English divines we must recollect that they were compelled to vindicate this Sacrament not only against the Romish figment, but with equal emphasis against the Zuinglian and Socinian degradation of the Sacrament into a *bare memorial*. Against this last-named reduction of the holy mystery they were called upon to assert strongly the *reality and virtue of consecration* in changing the Elements from their mere natural character into true and efficacious representatives of the Body and Blood of Christ, the appointed *media* for uniting Christ to the faithful recipients of these sacred emblems,

If, as is now alleged, the Church of England and her greatest divines had taught the Sacramental theory which furnishes a new pretense for the revival of ancient idolatry —a new reason for worshiping God in the Symbols of His Presence and Power which is the very essence of heathen idolatry—surely the great Hooker would have heard of this teaching, and in his exhaustive account of the views which had been held concerning this Sacrament would not have omitted that one which as a loyal Churchman he was bound himself to hold.

Leaving out of view the opinion attributed to Zuinglius, "that men should account of this Sacrament but only as of a shadow, destitute, empty, and void of Christ," he declares of the "Real Presence" but three statements of doctrine then known to Christian people: Transubstantiation, Consubstantiation, and that of the Church of England which he so grandly sets forth.   Of the fantastic Presence, which is neither of these three, but which talks so boastfully of "substance" and "objective reality," he had never heard.   It is true that in describing the two former he uses, as he was compelled to do, the very language by which the advocates of the Bennett doctrine now describe their theory.   For the distinction which these advocates profess to make between their notion and the old recognized errors is impalpable and incapable either of verbal expression or of mental conception.   And Aquinas, and after him Bellarmine, explain Transubstantiation in the very words used by the modern party in setting forth their doctrine; viz., that the Body of Christ is not "present after the manner of a *Body*, that is, in its visible form," but "it is present *spiritually*, that is, invisibly and by the power of the Spirit."   (Aquinas cited in Oxford Catena, p. 66.)

Can it be reasonably pretended that a distinct doctrine of the Eucharist, *of which Hooker had never heard*, was really held and taught by the leading divines in England before and in his time?   As only these two perversions of the Sacrament were in the thoughts of men in that age, there was no need of guarding their language against the imputation of holding a falsehood so near of kin as is this new theory to that which they were exposing with abundant learning and with merciless logic.   Therefore it is not difficult for an acute disputant like Sir Robert Phillimore to cull out of their writings numerous passages which seem to have that meaning, and so to construct a *catena* of seeming authorities for this poor fiction..   Happily in every case of any theological value there is enough in context, or in the avowed purpose of the treatise, to disprove the inference, and to vindicate the memory of martyrs and theologians from the disgraceful imputation of converting a sublime mystery of our religion into a worse than heathen superstition.

At the head of the list of English divines whom they thus calumniate these gentlemen place the name of Ridley, martyred for his rejection of the very doctrine for which this new theory is proposed as the equivalent. They have about as much authority for the rest as for Ridley. It will sufficiently expose the character and value of this *catena* to see how Ridley sustains the advocates who call him as a witness.

Almost at the opening of his treatise on the Lord's Supper Ridley seems unconsciously to anticipate and refute this modern conceit. For he says, if "the matter of the Sacrament" is not bread, then we "must needs grant transubstantiation," seeing that all learned men in England, so far as I know, both new and old, grant *"there is but one substance."* This is making short work of Mr. Wilberforce's theory of the "union" or "identity" of Christ with the elements. The martyr proceeds to state the question in a way which throws some light upon his conception of both the Sacraments: "If it is found that the substance of bread is the natural substance of the Sacrament, although *for the change of the use, office,* and *dignity* of the bread, the bread indeed is sacramentally changed into the body of Christ, *as the water in Baptism is sacramentally changed* into the fountain of regeneration, and yet the natural substance remains the same as it was before."

It would be difficult to state more precisely the effect of consecration in giving new character and meaning to the material elements of both the Sacraments. The conclusion of the same passage is equally decided in its condemnation of the practice attendant upon the new theory, as it was and is attendant upon the old. "Then that Godly honor which is only due unto God the creator, and may not be done unto the creature without idolatry and sacrilege, *is not to be done unto the Holy Sacrament.*"

Ridley discusses briefly, but well, the question of "figurative language." "How vain then is it that some so earnestly say, as if it were an infallible rule, that in doctrine and in the institution of the Sacraments Christ used no figures." But some say, if we thus admit figures in doctrine, then all the articles of our faith by figures and allegories will shortly be transformed and unloosed. I say it is a like fault, and even the same, to deny the figure when the place so requires to be understood, as vainly to make that a figurative speech which is to be understood in its proper signification." He then illustrates the distinction by that famous determination of St. Augustine that so many of the words of our Lord in the sixth chapter of St. John must be understood figuratively.

"It seems to command a wicked or ungodly thing; wherefore it is a figurative speech commanding to have communion and fellowship with Christ's passion." "Then surely Christ commanding His disciples in His last Supper to eat His Body and drink His Blood seemeth to command in sound of words as great, and even the same inconvenience and ungodliness, as His words do in the sixth chapter of St. John; and therefore they must, even by the same reason, be likewise understood and expounded figuratively and spiritually, as St. Augustine did the other."

After citing Chrysostom he mentions an argument of the Papists that unless we allow that the *substance* of the bread is gone we must admit "the absurdity of impanation," and adds: "What manifest falsehood is this, to say or mean that if the bread should remain still, then must follow the inconveniency of impanation? As though the very bread could not be a Sacrament of Christ's Body, as water is of Baptism, except Christ should unite the nature of bread to His nature in unity of person, and make of the bread God." Here again Ridley seems to have anticipated the new theory, but only to speak of it as a thing too extravagant to be supposed. Further on he quotes Tertullian: "Jesus made the bread which He took and distributed to His disciples His Body, saying, "This is My Body;" that is to say, saith Tertullian, a "figure of My Body." Ridley adds: "In this place it is plain that according to Tertullian's exposition Christ meant not, by calling the bread His Body and the wine His Blood, that either the bread was His natural body or the wine His natural blood; but He called them His Body and Blood because he would institute them to be unto us Sacraments, that is, *holy tokens and signs of His Body and of His Blood;* so that by them remembering and firmly believing the benefits procured to us by His Body, which was torn and crucified for us upon the Cross, and so with thanks *receiving these Holy Sacraments* according to Christ's institution, we might by the same be spiritually nourished and fed to the increase of all godliness in us." How like is this to that sentence in the Communion Service where Christ is declared to be "our spiritual food and sustenance in that Holy Sacrament!" Ridley adds: "Origen, Hilary, St. Augustine, Ambrose, Basil, Gregory, Naziansen, and other old authors likewise call the Sacrament a figure of Christ's Body." Further on, quoting again Tertullian, who had said that "the bread was made a *representation* of His Body," Ridley says: "Now I pray you, what is it to say that Christ has made a representation by bread of His Body, but that Christ had instituted and ordained bread to be a Sacrament to represent unto us His Body?" It will be tedious and unnecessary to give more of the testimonies from the Fathers which the Reformer has collected.

I had occasion to cite these same passages not long ago

in vindication of the martyr, as well as like passages from Bishop Wilson and many others, and here is the best answer which a respectable advocate of the new theory could give:

"But to avail for your argument it is not enough for Ridley or the Fathers to say that they are figures, types, tokens, or Sacraments; but they must also say that they are figures, types, tokens, and sacraments of an *invisible part, which is not united to them,* but which comes to the soul after reception." That is to say, when a man tells you, pointing to a portrait, "that is a good likeness—representation—of my father," unless he is careful to add, "but my father is not actually in the portrait or united to it," we must understand him to mean that his father is in the portrait *in propria persona!*

I conclude this vindication of Ridley with a passage from Edward VI.'s Catechism, to which the martyr gave his dying testimony:

"The supper is a certain thankful remembrance of the death of Christ; forasmuch as the bread representeth His Body, betrayed to be crucified for us; the wine standeth instead and place of His Blood plenteously shed for us. And even as by bread and wine our natural bodies are sustained and nourished, so by the Body, that is, the flesh and blood of Christ, the soul is fed through faith and quickened to the heavenly and godly life. . . . . . Faith is the mouth of the soul, whereby we receive this heavenly meat, full both of salvation and immortality dealt among us by the means of the Holy Ghost."

With the same recklessness Bishop Andrews is cited, when in the very treatise from which his words are taken, the answer to Bellarmine, he was refuting this notion. In the following passage Andrews declares that "the holy symbols" are the Body and Blood of Christ in the same

sense in which the Passover was His Body and Blood.
The whole passage is in full and plain accord with Catholic and Scriptural teaching, and utterly irreconcilable
with the new theory.

"Nay it must be *hoc facite*. It is not mental thinking or
verbal speaking, there must be actually somewhat done to
celebrate this memory. *That done to the holy symbols that
was done to Him, to His body and His blood in the Passover;*
break the one, pour out the other, to represent how His
sacred Body was broken, how His precious Blood was
shed. And in *corpus fractum* and *sanguis fusus* there is
immolatus. This is it in the Eucharist that answereth to
the sacrifice in the Passover, the memorial to the figure.
To them it was *Hoc facite in Mei præfigurationem*, Do this
in prefiguration of Me. To them *prænuntiare*, to us *an-
nuntiare;* there is the difference. By the same rules that
theirs was, by the same may ours be termed a sacrifice.
In rigour of speech neither of them; for to speak after
the exact manner of Divinity, there is but one only sacrifice, *veri nominis*, properly so called, that is, Christ's death.*
And that sacrifice but once actually performed at His
death, but ever before represented in figure from the beginning; and ever since repeated in memory, to the world's
end. That only absolute, all else relative to it, representative of it, operative by it. The Lamb but once actually
slain in the fullness of time, but virtually was from the
beginning, is, and shall be to the end of the world. That
the center, in which their lines and ours, their types and
our antitypes, do meet. While yet this offering was not,
the hope of it was kept alive by the prefiguration of it in
theirs. And after it is past, the memory of it is still kept
fresh in mind by the commemoration of it in ours. So it

---

* The Bishop uses the word "Sacrifice" as equivalent to "Propitiatory and
Meritorious Sacrifice."

was the will of God that so there might be with them a continual foreshadowing, and with us a continual showing forth, the 'Lord's death till He come again.' Hence it is that what names theirs carried, ours do the like; and the Fathers make no scruple at it, no more need we. The Apostle in the tenth chapter compareth this of ours to the *immolata* of the heathen; and to the Hebrews *habemus aram*, matcheth it with the sacrifice of the Jews. And we know the rule of comparisons, they must be *ejusdem generis.* . . . .

"From the Sacrament is the applying the Sacrifice. The Sacrifice in general, *pro omnibus.* The Sacrament, in particular, *to each several receiver, pro singulis.* Wherein that is offered *to us* that was offered *for us;* that which is common to all, made proper to each one, while each taketh his part of it; and made proper by a communion and union, like that of meat and drink, which is most nearly and inwardly made ours, and is inseparable forever." (Sermon vii, on the Resurrection, quoted by Dr. Pusey in his letter to the Bishop of London, page 31.)

I have given the foregoing passage at length, not only because it is a complete vindication of Andrews from the stigma which has been cast upon him as an authority for the new dogma, but because it is a very gratifying confirmation of my previous teaching in the body of this work, in sections 2 and 5, of chapter xv.

Overall, Cosin, Thorndike, Taylor, Beveridge, Wilson, and others, receive the same free handling. In regard to some of their extracts from these authors, the writers citing them are either unable to see, or do not care to see, that the passages which they parade refer usually to the Presence of Christ to the faithful when the Sacrament is complete, by the devout reception of the holy symbols, and not to the alleged *actual* Presence in or under the Ele-

ments before reception. Sometimes indeed the reference
is to that Representative Presence produced by consecration. And of this Representative Presence many grand
and lofty expressions are freely and properly used. "Glorious things are spoken of thee, O city of God."

Again, these two kinds of Presence are often combined
in the thoughts and in the language of the writers of every
age. In the fervor of exhortation or of devotional composition, they do not stop to distinguish with cold, logical
precision the different shades of meaning which may be
attached to their glowing words. And even if they had
never explained themselves, it would be an outrage to
put upon their language the gross and unnatural meaning involved in the theory of Transubstantiation or of
Identity. For the most part they do amply explain and
vindicate their meaning from this misconstruction. The
passages which make this vindication in regard to the
early Fathers have been triumphantly produced over and
over again by the English divines. Now, strange to say,
we have to employ the same method for the vindication
of these very divines from a like imputation.

Bishop Cosin, one of the authorities most relied upon
for the new opinion, has happily explained his meaning.
The following extract is from page 345 of the fifth volume of Cosin's works, in the "Library of Anglo-Catholic
Theology:"

"True it is that the Body and Blood of Christ are sacramentally and really (not feignedly) present, when the
blessed bread and wine are taken by the faithful communicants; and *as true it is also, that they are not present but
only when the hallowed elements are so taken,* as in another
work (the History of Papal Transubstantiation) I have
more at large declared. Therefore whosoever so receiveth
them, *at that time when he receiveth them,* rightly doth he

adore and reverence his Saviour there together with the Sacramental Bread and Cup, exhibiting his own Body and Blood unto them.   Yet because that Body and Blood is neither sensibly present (nor otherwise at all present but only to them that are duly prepared to receive them, and in the very act of receiving them and the consecrated elements together to which they are sacramentally in that act united) the adoration is then and there given to Christ Himself, neither is nor ought to be directed to any external sensible object, such as are the blessed elements.   But our kneeling, and the outward gesture of humility and reverence in our bodies, is ordained only to testify and express the inward reverence and devotion of our souls toward our blessed Saviour, who vouchsafed to sacrifice Himself for us upon the Cross, and now presenteth Himself to be united sacramentally to us, that we may enjoy all the benefits of his mystical passion, and be nourished with the spiritual food of His blessed Body and Blood unto life eternal."

Every one must admire in this passage the clear, discriminating precision with which Cosin distinguishes the Catholic doctrine of the Presence from that poor conceit which a modern party dubs with the exclusive name of Catholic.

Very like to the above expression of doctrine is the following, taken from Cosin's "History of Papal Transubstantiation," chapter iv, section 5: "And we also deny that the Elements still retain the nature of Sacraments when not used according to Divine institution, *that is given by Christ's ministers and received by His people;* so that Christ in the consecrated Bread ought not, can not be preserved to be carried about, because *He* is present only to the communicants."

I will here present in connection the testimony of an old

and of a recent English divine — Dr. Pusey quoting and
adopting with full approval the views of Dr. Brevint.   The
decisive passage I am about to give from the letter to the
Bishop of London proves either that the writer was practicing the *"Reserve"* which is recommended by a portion
of the party, or that at the date of this letter (1851) he
had not *"advanced"* to the present position of that party.
The Doctor quotes first some of the higher class of Romish
writers, who maintain, in opposition to the new theory, that
Christ "is *not* contained, as circumscribed or locally under
the Sacrament;" and then, quoting St. Augustine, adds:
"I can not think that these words, any more than those of
St. Chrysostom, which are adduced controversially, *imply
any local adoration.*   I had no such thought in my mind.
But believing that he was then in an especial manner present, I could not but think that we knelt, not only as
receiving so great a Gift, but in reverence for His Presence."   In connection with this sentence he cites, as further
expressive of his own view, the following from Dr. Brevint:

"The second is an act of adoration and reverence, when
he looks upon that good hand that hath consecrated for
the use of the Church the *memorial* of these great things.
Since, by the special appointment of my God, these *representatives* are brought in hither for this Church, and among
the rest for me, I must mind what Israel did when the cloud
filled the tabernacle.   I will not fail to worship God as
soon as these Sacraments and Gospel-clouds appear in the
sanctuary.   Neither the ark, nor any clouds, were ever
adored in Israel; but sure it is, the ark was considered
quite otherwise than an ordinary chest, and the cloud
than a vapour, as soon as God had hallowed them to
be *the signs* of His Presence.   Therefore, as the former
people did never see the temple or the cloud, but that
presently at that sight they used to throw themselves on

their faces, so I will never behold these better and surer Sacraments of the glorious mercies of God, but as soon as I see them used in the Church *to that holy purpose* that Christ hath consecrated them to, I will not fail *to remember* my Saviour, *whom these Sacraments do represent.*" (Letter, pages 54-5.)

Jeremy Taylor, with his luxuriant imagination, his rapturous devotion, his unequaled richness of language, might be expected to speak of this holy mystery in very lofty. and unguarded terms. Accordingly the octavo volume issued at Oxford in 1855, composed of a *Catena* of authorities alleged in support of this theory, furnishes many extracts from this English Chrysostom, which would go as far to sustain the theory as any language which can be quoted from ancient or modern writers. Yet even Taylor sometimes descends from the sublimities of rhetoric to teach in plain and simple words. In his treatise on "The Real Presence and Spiritual," from which many of these glowing extracts are taken, he in one place defines precisely and briefly what he means by "The Real Presence." He says: "But we by the Real Spiritual Presence of Christ do understand Christ to be present, as the Spirit of God is present in the hearts of the faithful, *by blessing and grace; and this is all which we mean* BESIDES THE TROPICAL AND FIGURATIVE PRESENCE."

It well illustrates the Spirit in which the *Catena* above mentioned has been constructed, that this decisive definition, interpreting all the rest, has been carefully *omitted.* This passage, again, illustrates the utterly illusory nature of all the rhetorical and devotional language quoted from the Fathers and from our own divines, to prove the unchristian dogma imputed to them. And yet again the distinction here so precisely presented by Bishop Taylor between his conception of "the Real Presence" and "the

Tropical and Figurative Presence," *coupled with the exalted terms in which he speaks of either and of both in undistinguished connection*, beautifully illustrates the true sense of similar language employed by other writers. Generally it may be said that what Jeremy Taylor calls the "Tropical and Figurative Presence" preceding writers designate as the "Sacramental Presence," the "Mystical Presence," the "Presence in a Mystery," and such like. It is very interesting to see how cautiously Ridley adheres to these forms of expression in the conferences in which his accusers and judges were trying to entrap him.

Thorndike and Overall seem to be more relied upon than any others to support the assertion that the Bennett doctrine was held by the English divines. And certainly, if we did not know the purpose for which they wrote, and the error against which they were contending, many of their expressions would seem to justify this appeal. We must recollect that in their day, as it has continued to be, the danger of the Church of England was principally from the rationalistic and spiritualistic impugners of all the externals of religion. These two parties, very opposite in some particulars, united in eviscerating from the sacraments all power, mystery, and vitality. I have myself been present when, in an assembly of professed Christians at a so-called Communion, the Sacrament was explained by the officiating minister as similar to the custom of drinking wine to the memory of General Washington on his birthday! The spiritualistic party made religion to consist entirely of faith and feeling.

To vindicate the dignity and reality of this Sacrament, and the Divine efficacy of consecration, Thorndike especially is very strenuous in insisting upon the connection between the consecrated Elements and the Grace of the Sacrament. The Bread, he says, is the Body, and the

Wine the Blood, not only as "significative, but exhibitory."
As he properly argued, if the Elements are bare signs, to
which no grace is adjoined, and if Christ is received by
faith only, then He could be received by the same faith
without the signs; and so the Sacrament may be entirely
dispensed with.   And this we see to have been the practical result of the same vicious principle in our own day.
Against this notion Thorndike proves the reality and efficacy of consecration in making the Elements to be the
Body and Blood of Christ, representatively and effica-
ciously.   "And," as he adds, "what a gross thing it were
to say that our Saviour took such care to leave His Church,
by the act of His last will, a legacy which imports no more
than that which they might at all times bestow upon themselves."

Keeping in view this purpose of his argument ought
be sufficient to clear Thorndike from the charge made
against him.   But he has been more explicit in relieving
himself from the imputation.   He, as well as Cosin, is very
emphatic in his enunciation of a principle which I have
dwelt upon at some length, and which is utterly irreconcilable with the theory for which he is quoted as authority.
He strongly affirms the position that until the completion
of the sacrament by the reception of the Elements there is
really no sacrament.   From a much longer passage to the
same effect I take these words, "True it is indeed, inasmuch as the appointment of our Lord Christ is not com-
pletely executed by consecrating the Eucharist, but by
respectively delivering and receiving it, you may truly say
that by virtue of these words, 'Take, eat, this is my Body,
this is my Blood,' that which every man receives becomes
the Body and Blood *to him that receives it.*"

In another place Thorndike uses words which plainly
interpret all the strong expressions about the Sacramental.
40

Presence in the Elements by virtue of consecration. "So
that the Body and Blood in the SACRAMENT turns to the
nourishment of the body, whether the Body and Blood IN
THE TRUTH turn to the nourishment or damnation of the
soul."

In this sentence the writer uses "Sacrament" in contrast
with "Truth" in the same sense in which St. Ambrose
long before had used "Image" in contrast with "Truth,"
as in this passage which I take from Canon Trevor on The
Eucharist:

"Truly we offer, but so that we make a remembrance
of His death.   We offer Him always, or rather we offer a
remembrance of His Sacrifice.   The Shadow in the law,
the Image in the Gospels, the Truth in the heavenly places.
Of old a lamb was offered, a calf was offered; now Christ
is offered.   Here in *image*, there in *truth*, where He inter-
cedes for us with the Father as our Advocate." (P. 212.)

Every one must see that language like this interprets
and plainly declares the intended meaning of the same
authors when they employ language more rhetorical and
figurative.   In the same connection Canon Trevor says:
"The language of Ambrose with respect to the sacrifice
of Christ in the Sacrament is defined by His disciple St.
Augustine, who often affirms that Christ is immolated in
the Sacrament, but with this explanation subjoined:"

"That is, the immolation of Christ is represented and a
remembrance of His Passion is made." "The Flesh and
Blood of this Sacrifice before the Advent of Christ was
promised through victims of similitude.   In the Passion
of Christ it was exhibited in *the very truth*; after His Ascension it is celebrated through a Sacrament *of remembrance*."
(P. 213.)

No one can read Thorndike's elaborate commentary on
the Eucharistic Service, and not see how utterly foreign to

his thought was this conceit now attempted to be bolstered up by his authority.   He declares the effect of the consecration to be, "that the elements, by being deputed to become this Sacrament, begin to be what they were not, that is, visible signs, not only to figure the sacrifice of Christ's cross, but also to tender and exhibit the invisible grace which *they represent to them that receive.*"   And he condemns the Church of Rome for altering the canon of the Mass, "on purpose that this Sacrament might not be called a figure of the invisible grace of it."   And yet, he adds, "nothing can be more cross to this doctrine of the *now* Chu·ch of Rome than their own service;" citing in proof these words of the present canon: "*Ut nobis corpus fiat, dilectissimi Filii Tui Domini nostri-Jesu Christi.*"   With great earnestness he denounces the sacrificial doctrine of the Roman Church, now so much insisted on by the new school in our Church.   He maintains against this pernicious novelty that there is no pretense or expression of such a doctrine in the early Church.   (See the whole passage in his treatise on "The Service of God in Religious Assemblies," Works, vol. i, Anglo-Catholic Library, pp. 324–366.)

In like manner Bishop Nicholson has been misrepresented.   In his account of the Sacraments he uses the very illustration of a Deed which Wilberforce and his followers denounce as pure Calvinism.   He says: "They are pledges to assure us of this grace.   For the Sacrament is as it were a pawn left us by God in the hand of the minister to give us acquiescence and ground of confidence that the graces promised shall be surely performed.   Of which that we doubt the less it is called a seal.   For God, not content with the general offer of His promises, out of His mere mercy hath thought fit to seal them to every particular believer, having a regard thereby to their infirmity.

In an indenture we have the conditions agreed upon betwixt both parties set forth and represented, after sealed and delivered.   A covenant God hath made with man for salvation and for grace, without which salvation can not be had; and by the Sacrament it hath pleased Him, as in a fair deed to represent it, to convey and make it over, to seal and deliver it unto us."

In treating of The Supper he says: "That which is more material to know is the change of these (the Elements), which is wholly sacramental, not in substance, but in USE. For they remain bread and wine still, such as before in nature, but consecrate and set apart to *represent* our Saviour's passion, and *exhibit and seal to a worthy receiver the benefits of that passion.*"

Referring to the "great disputes there are *How* Christ is present in the Sacrament," he makes a conciliatory attempt to resolve the various terms of theologians into a question of relation: "My intention is to put the fairest interpretation upon different expressions and so reconcile exasperated brethren.   That the Sacrament is in the predicament of relation will be, I doubt not, easily granted me, and under that logical notion I would thus define the Eucharist: The Eucharist is a Sacrament instituted by Christ under the elements of bread and wine, to represent, exhibit, and seal the passion of Christ and the benefits thereof to a worthy communicant.   In which definition we meet with all those things that are necessary to set forth the nature of a relation." (Exposition of the Catechism, Lib. Ang. Cath. Theol., pp. 156, 178.)

If our New-Light brethren would consent to have their pet words resolved into the terms of this definition, there would be an end of controversy with them on this subject.

It is really refreshing to turn from the mistaken comments of these modern discoverers, who copy from each other garbled texts, and read the grand old authors to whom they so confidently refer us. Hammond, in his Practical Catechism, furnishes a good specimen of this refreshment. First, he illustrates the words of our Lord in the institution of the Eucharist by the circumstances of the Paschal feast. "The Lamb that was drest in the Paschal Supper and set upon the table was wont to be called The Body of the Passover, or The Body of the Paschal Lamb, and Christ seems to allude to this phrase when he saith, *This is my Body;* as if He should say, The Paschal Lamb, and the Body of it, the memorial of deliverance out of Egypt, and type of my delivering myself to die for you, I will now have abrogated, and by this Bread which I now deliver to you I give or exhibit to you this other Passover, my own self, who am to be sacrificed (my Body which shall presently be delivered to death) for you, that you may hereafter (instead of that other) retain and continue to posterity a memorial and symbol of me. This for the words (*my Body*), but then for the whole phrase or form of speech (*This is my Body*), it seems to be answerable to and substituted instead of the Paschal form (*This is the* bread of affliction which our fathers ate in Egypt); not that it is that identical bread which they then ate, but that it is the celebration of that anniversary feast which was then instituted, as when in ordinary speech we say on Good Friday and Easter-day, This day Christ died, and This day Christ rose, when we know it was so many hundred years since He died or rose; which example is adapted to this point in hand by St. Augustine in his Epistles."

He afterward shows that "*the whole action or administration, i. e.,* do you all that I have done in your presence, take Bread, break, bless it, give it to others, and so commemorate me: the breaking and distributing, taking and eating this Bread, is the Body of Christ."

Hammond then learnedly discusses the relation of the heathen and Jewish sacrifices to this Sacrament, as indicated by St. Paul, and concludes: "Thus, *the Cup of blessing which we bless,* or (as the Syriack), *the Cup of Praise, i. e.,* the chalice of Wine, which is in the name of the people offered up by the Bishop or Presbyter to God with Lauds and Thanksgivings, *i. e.,* that whole Eucharistical action (and that exprest to be the action of the people as well as the Presbyter by their drinking of it) is the communication of the Blood of Christ, a service of theirs to Christ, a sacrifice of thanksgiving, commemorative of that great mercy and bounty of Christ in pouring out His Blood for them, and a making them (or a means ordained by Christ to make them) partakers of the Blood of Christ, not of the guilt of shedding it, but, if they come worthily thither, of the benefits that are purchased by it, *viz., the washing away of sin in his Blood:* so in like manner the *breaking and eating of the Bread* is a communication of the Body of Christ, a sacrifice commemorative of Christ's offering up his Body for us, and a making us partakers, or communicating to us the benefits of that Bread of Life, strengthening and giving us grace. And both these parts of each part of this Sacrament put together are (parallel to what was said of the Israelites and Gentiles) a mutual confederation betwixt us and the crucified Saviour; on our parts an acknowledging Him for our God and worshiping Him, and on His part the making over to us all the benefits of his Body and Blood (*i. e.,* his death), grace and pardon, to sanctifie and to justifie us."

A little further on he says: "This *breaking, taking, eating of the Bread,* this whole action is the real communication of the Body of Christ to me, and is therefore by some ancient writers called by a word which signifies the *participa- tion* (communication and participation being the same, only one referred to the giver, the other to the receiver), the very giving Christ's Body to me; that as verily as I eat the bread in my mouth, so verily God in heaven bestows on me, communicates to me, the Body of the crucified Saviour." (Pages 401 to 412.) The whole treatment of the subject is profound and exhaustive. I quote from the original edition published in 1662. The copy I have once belonged to Thomas Lewis, of Augusta County, Virginia, and was probably brought to Virginia by some worthy Churchman nearly two hundred years ago. If our people could be nourished with such solid food, they would be in little danger of being "carried about with every wind of doctrine, by the sleight of men, and cunning craftiness, whereby they lie in wait to deceive." (Eph. iv, 14.)

An *ad captandum* argument, strongly urged by Wilberforce and his followers, is to represent the Catholic doctrine of the Eucharist as pure Calvinism, adopted by the English clergy, *in simple ignorance*, from the Genevan reformer. Now as these gentlemen have triumphantly cited Cosin as a witness and an *authority*, let us hear his testimony on this point. In the work before quoted (volume iv, page 167, Anglo-Catholic Theology) he says:

"Now because great is the fame of Calvin (who subscribed the Augustan Confession and that of the Switzers) let us hear what he writ and believed concerning this sacred mystery. His words, in his Institutions and elsewhere, are such, *so conformable to the style and mind of the ancient Fathers, that no Catholic reformer would desire to use any other*." He then quotes from Calvin abundantly to prove this assertion.

What reliance can be placed upon the pretended authorities of a party which ostentatiously puts forward

Beveridge as a witness for its fable, and as an advocate
for "Eucharistic adoration," when just a casual turning
to his dogmatic works, as it happened to me, presents us
with testimony after testimony to the exact contrary?

In his "*Oratio Canonica ante Synodum*" Beveridge mentions "Eucharistic adoration" as one of the worst corruptions of Popery! In the syllabus of a formal discourse on
Idolatry he divides that sin into two classes; 1. Heathenish; 2. Romish saints, EUCHARIST, images! (Thesaurus
Theologicus, volume iv, page 394.) In several other ex-
positions of the blessed Sacrament itself he says, in one
place: "1. What it is in itself—Bread (1 Cor. x, 16);
2. What it *represents* unto us—the Body of Christ. *Hæc
oblatio est figura corporis et sanguinis Domini nostri Jesu
Christi. St. Ambrose.*" And a little further on: "Observe,
2. *Eat*, not take and *lay up*; not take and *carry about*;
break, not take and *worship*; but take and eat." (*Ibid.*,
volume iii, page 114.) Again, in another place: "What
are we to understand by these words, *This is my Body?*
I. Negatively, not that it is really the Body of Christ, or
transubstantiated. This, 1. Is not grounded on Scripture;
2. Contrary to the Scriptures; 3. It takes away the nature
of the Sacrament, there being no sign. II. Positively.
This is my Body; that is, the Sign and Sacrament of my
Body. (See Gen. xvii, 10, 11; Exod. xii, 11.) *Hoc est
corpus meum, id est, figura corporis mei* (Tertullian). *Non
enim Dominus dubitavit dicere, hoc est corpus meum, cum signum daret corporis sui* (St. Augustine)." Again, "It is
Bread we eat and Wine we drink in the Sacrament, not
the real Body and Blood of Christ." And yet again: "It
is a Sacrament wherein, under the outward Signs of Bread
and Wine, Christ is *signified* to us. The end: to remember Christ's death. To represent it. To offer it. To
convey it too. To seal it, not *signum* only, but *sigillum*."

And in an explication of 1 Cor. xi, 29: "1. What by eating and drinking? Not the Body and Blood of Christ, but Sacramental Bread and Wine. . . . 2. What by not discerning the Lord's Body? *Non discernens a cibo communi.* S. Hieron. . . . . Ignorant Receivers. . . . . . 3. That know not the nature of the Sacrament, even that it is an ordinance instituted by God, wherein, under the outward Signs of Bread and Wine, Christ, with all the benefits of His death and passion, is represented, sealed, and conveyed to the worthy receiver." (*Ib.*, pages 116, 121, 125, 128.)

The whole teaching of Beveridge is to the effect of these brief extracts. In like manner some devotional expressions of Bishop Wilson have been misconstrued into the very opposite of his *formal teaching* in his sermons. And in every instance that which is said by the cited authority of the communication of Christ to the faithful receiver, when the Sacrament is complete, is, with strange confusion of thought, referred by these advocates to their fancied communication of Christ to the Elements, while yet the Sacrament is inchoate — the Divine command not yet obeyed.

§ 8. THE TWO THEORIES *de modo* A SAD TRIFLING WITH A HOLY MYSTERY.

8. These two aspects of a common theory, Transubstantiation and Identity or Sacramental Union, seem to me to be a very sad trifling with a holy mystery. For what is the Divine command which is thus travestied and played upon? Look at the words of Institution: *Take, eat. Drink ye all of this. This do in remembrance of Me.* Do what? Is any promise or blessing annexed to the mere breaking of the bread while saying these or any other words? Is not the communication of Christ to us, the partaking of Christ by us, the substance and meaning of the whole transaction? Is not the eating of the Bread, the drinking of the Wine,

41

the precise LETTER of the Command? Is not the partaking of Christ the essential SPIRIT of that command?

In an age of growing superstition and ignorance men
were not content to rest in the Divine power to give the
promised blessing whenever the Divine command is
obeyed, but must supplement the sublime simplicity of the
Mystery by a little humanly-conceived machinery. And
so, to assist the Divine Omnipotence in fulfilling His word,
to make it easier for Christ to impart Himself to His faithful people, the MANNER, *the intermediate process* by which
this miracle of grace is accomplished, must be reasoned out
by human wit, and reasoned out in such a way as to afford
a resting-place for the superstitious weakness of the times.
So the familiar form of speech used by our Lord in desig-
nating the Symbols of His Body and Blood was perverted
into the degrading conceit of an actual union of Himself
with these simple Elements; and this corruption was
presently, with more exact logic, developed into Transubstantiation.

Happily, PROVIDENTIALLY, the gross fiction was met
and refuted in the very age in which it was proposed.
Ratramn on the Continent, the old Saxon Homily for
Easter, about a century later in England, with effective
logic and abundant learning, rebuked the novelty and vindicated the Holy Mystery. But, as Alexander Knox has
well said, the corruption was in accordance with the spirit
of the age and the refutation against that spirit, and so the
miserable falsehood prevailed, accumulating around itself
other and kindred corruptions. All the modern questions
and confusions on this subject come out of this original
departure from the Divine institution.

All our great Divines mourn over this fatal departure.
Jeremy Taylor, in the beginning of his treatise on "The
Real Presence and Spiritual," says: "We may say in this

mystery to them that curiously ask what or how it is, *'Mysterium est;'* 'It is a Sacrament and a mystery.' By sensible instruments it consigns spiritual graces; by the creatures it brings us to God; by the body it ministers to the spirit. It was happy with Christendom when she" was content "to believe the thing heartily and not to inquire curiously."

Archbishop Bramhall, in his answer to de la Militiere, is very emphatic in his condemnation of this unhappy questioning *de modo:* "No sooner was this bell rung out, but as if Pandora's box had been newly set wide open, whole swarms of noysom Questions and Debates did fill the schools." After giving a long and mortifying list of these subtle questions, and stating the simple *fact* of the Presence—*neque Con., neque Sub., neque Trans.*—he concludes: "This was the belief of the Primitive Church, this was the faith of the ancient Fathers, who were never acquainted with these modern questions *de modo*, which edifie not, but expose Christian religion to contempt."

A singular illustration of the continued fecundity of this unhappy disputation *de modo* has just appeared in a pamphlet, which undertakes to demonstrate the *manner* of Christ's Presence, as in the elements, by a bran-new interpretation of the Catechism. This new version is founded upon a new mathematical axiom, that a part is equal to the whole. Wilberforce and his followers multiply the two parts of this Sacrament, as defined in the Catechism, into three. This writer reduces them into one, and essays the astounding logical feat of proving that one of two *parts* of a thing is the whole, and that the other *part* is something else! Doubtless there will continue to be new items to be added to Bramhall's catalogue of "noysom questions" growing out of this unhappy tendency to explain the manner of Christ's Presence in the Eucharist.

In defining and refining, trying to construct a dogma which will suit them, and yet differ sufficiently from that of Rome to save their consciences, the advocates of the theory of "Identity" are careful to tell us that the Body of Christ which is in the Elements is not that natural Body which was born of the Virgin, nor that spiritual Body which is now in heaven, yet it is a true, real, and substantial Body. A Body which is neither in heaven, nor on earth, nor under the earth, is indeed a wonderful creation of human ingenuity. I sometimes wonder whether these enthusiastic brethren do really believe this shadowy fiction, or whether they have not persuaded themselves that it is necessary for the due and effective influence of religion on the common run of men to have something for superstition to feed on; and that to enable the now pure Church to which they belong to compete successfully in the race for popular power with Romanism and other isms she must furnish to the vulgar fancy at least one idol *for easy worship.* It is the same natural and rationalistic conception which induced Aaron to yield to the clamorous solicitations of the people, and make the golden calves *for the better satisfaction of their devotional feelings.* If this is the thought and the purpose of our brethren, they have strangely forgotten the divine and holy mission of the Church of God to be the Witness and the Keeper of THE TRUTH. Departures from that truth there will ever be in every possible direction, and especially in those directions in which the mere affections of nature do most strongly lead. The forms of religion that have been most skillfully molded in conformity with these corrupt leadings will always command the popular suffrage and be able to wield the controlling power of numbers. For in reality the bodies which have adopted these corruptions are but a part of the world itself, in one of its moods, taking on the guise and aspect of religion. But it is the sublime calling and charge of God's Holy Church, whether composed of few or many, to keep the truth in uncorrupt integrity, to bear witness to the truth among all peoples and in every generation to the end of the world, for the real healing of the nations.

9. Let us briefly sum up the testimony to the truth ₰ 9. RECAPITU- which the Church is commissioned to bear LATION. upon this important subject — The Sacrament of the Body and Blood of Christ.

We learned before that "by the word Sacrament" the Church means an "outward and visible sign of an inward and spiritual grace *given unto us*." The "inward and spiritual grace" is not said to be given to the Elements, or united to them "by a law of identity," or sent down upon the altar to be recognized by the eye of faith. The sole expressed relation of the "inward and spiritual grace" is that it is to be "given to us," the believing partakers of the consecrated elements, according to our Lord's words, "Take, eat; this is my Body." The definition goes on to tell us that the Sacrament is both "a means whereby we receive" "the inward and spiritual grace given unto us" and "a pledge to assure us thereof." Here the Church happily distinguishes, emphatically declaring the grace of consecration whereby these inert substances are made the instruments of producing supernatural effects. And she further declares that they are "the *means*" whereby *we receive* the spiritual grace which they were constituted *to represent*, and which comes directly *to us* from the Fountain of all grace. They are, moreover, "*a pledge to assure us thereof;*" that is, to make us certain, if we believe God's word, that as surely as we have received the visible sign, so surely we have received the spiritual grace. The same logical formulary goes on to tell us that "the outward part or sign of the Lord's Supper" is "Bread and Wine, which the Lord hath commanded *to be received.*" "The inward part or thing signified" is the Body and Blood of Christ, which "are *spiritually taken and received* by the faithful in the Lord's Supper." So the act of the believer receiving is ever made a part of "the outward and visible sign" and the essential condition of "the inward and spiritual grace."

This figment of "IDENTITY" destroys the nature of a Sacrament, as Transubstantiation does. A Sacrament is the consecration of an outward and visible thing to be the symbol of an inward and spiritual grace given unto us. By this pretended "*law of identity*" the symbol and the gift are combined into one. The symbol does not *represent* the gift and *convey* it, but *contains* it. The spiritual grace is first given to the symbol. As I have shown, this theory of the *manner* of Christ's Presence is not only unwarranted, but is a flagrant departure from the institution it professes to illustrate. According to that institution and to the precise definition of it given by the Church, the *especial Presence* of Christ which *belongs to this Sacrament* can only be in the actual partaking of the consecrated emblems according to His command. They have been consecrated to be the instruments of conveying Christ to the believer when they are received. Only in the reception, when the command is obeyed, can this promised effect be produced. Then only is the Sacrament which Christ ordained complete when *our duty and His promise are brought together in one.* Then Christ fulfills His promise and becomes "our spiritual food and sustenance in that Holy Sacrament." Then we may adore Him as truly, mystically, and spiritually Present, uniting Himself to us. We must not adore Him in the Elements, for He is not in them; they are but the material instruments used by His grace to give Himself to us, humbly obeying His command; they are the "means" to convey to us this great gift, and the sensible "pledge" to assure us thereof.

It is needful for the due apprehension of this blessed mystery to keep clearly in mind the distinction, to which I have before adverted, between the REPRESENTATIVE character of the symbols—the Consecrated Elements—and the *actual communication of Christ to the faithful communicant.* And if this protracted examination can result in bringing this distinction more clearly to the mind of believers it will not have been altogether in vain.

By CONSECRATION the Elements are *changed* from common bread and wine into true REPRESENTATIVES of the Body and Blood of Christ.   The Fathers, our standard divines, and the clergy and laity of this day, properly call these *representatives by the names of the things they signify,* in accordance with the common use of language.   It is therefore altogether proper to say that Christ is Present on the Altar by these His Representatives, the appointed symbols of His Body and Blood.

When the Sacrament is *complete,* by the doing of that which the institution commands and requires—the feeding upon these consecrated symbols—then there is another and higher kind of Presence, a Presence real, spiritual, and substantial—Christ giving Himself to the faithful Communicant, as a consequence and the perpetuation of the Incarnation.

This twofold Presence—*representative* by the consecration of the Elements, and *actual* by the communication of Himself to the faithful receiver—satisfies and explains all the expressions quoted by Romanists from the Fathers, and by Sir Robert Phillimore and others from them and from the great divines of the English Church, and RECONCILES THESE EXPRESSIONS WITH OTHERS OF THE SAME WRITERS WHICH SEEM TO HAVE A CONTRARY MEANING.

It is a vain and profitless exercise to quote from the Fathers, or from our standard English divines, isolated passages which seem to have a Romish sense, or that modification of the same sense proposed by Mr. Bennett and his coadjutors, and rebutting these by other passages from the same authors expressing an entirely different meaning, without taking pains to find out the general scope and character of the writing thus abused. It is amusing as well as instructive oftentimes to trace up to the authors from which they were originally taken these stock quotations quoted and requoted by a long succession of controversial writers relying upon each other, and find that the passages in their proper connection are altogether innocent of the meaning they have been put forward to sustain. It is an acknowledged canon of interpretation that figurative language, however copious, must be construed in the sense of plain and unfigurative language used by the same writers. No writer can be fairly judged of except by the general purport of his work. The Scripture has been wrested to intolerable meanings by this use of isolated passages, by the neglect to read every part in the light of the "proportion of faith." So it must be with every written composition.

How worse than idle it is, for instance, to try to make St. Augustine speak in the sense of one or the other of these parties, by the quotation of any number of passages which seem to have either of those meanings, when he has so explicitly informed us that this language is figurative and has no such meaning, and that in his time and before no person was "so silly" as to give to it any such meaning!

The fair and candid application of the principle of interpretation just referred to, that a writer is to be judged of by the general tenor of his work and not by isolated expressions, and the clear recognition of that *double* Presence

above mentioned—REPRESENTATIVE in the Symbols, REAL
and SUBSTANTIAL in the Communion of the faithful—will,
I am sure, explain and reconcile the seeming contradictions in all the standard Divines of the Church, earlier
and later, on the subject of the Eucharist, and effectually
vindicate their intelligence and their memory from the
aspersions of the depravers of this Holy Sacrament in
every direction.

NOTE

CANON LIDDON ON THE LOCAL PRESENCE.

Under stress of reason and argument, the leading champions in this country of the Phillimore dictum have very emphatically denied that the Eucharistic Presence in which they believe is a LOCAL Presence. Under like stress in England, Canon Liddon seems to have denied any *Local* Presence in the Eucharistic Elements. In one of the letters drawn out by Mons. Capel, the Canon says, "So in the next quotation, the prepositions 'beneath' and 'in' must be abandoned if they are supposed seriously to define a local relation between the consecrated elements and the Eucharistic gift."

This denial that the assumed Presence is *local* appears to me to scale the heights of an irreverent play upon sacred words. A Real Presence, IN THE ELEMENTS, which IS NOT LOCAL, is simply a contradiction in terms. It is an affirmation and a denial of the same thing. By thus stripping the words of all sense and meaning they become blank words, and the formula they compose is a blank formula, and expresses nothing. The only use to which such a blank formula can be put is to make it serve as a rallying cry for party, and the starting-point of any depravement of the Holy Sacrament which it insults.

As long as this empty formula is retained and insisted on, it is not the less but the more dangerous for this emptiness. For the human mind can not thus be mocked. If men receive this formula, even as a harmless thing, by the necessity of the mind's action, they must put a meaning into it. And any possible meaning of such a formula is mischievous, untrue, and a fatal corruption of the Sacrament. These same disclaimers and abjurations of offensive and carnal meanings, in the Romish doctrine of the Eucharist, have been made over and over again by the more creditable Divines of that Communion. But the dogma remains, to be the seed-bed of noxious errors, and to be the warrant for forms of worship hardly differing from heathen

(121)

idolatry, and subversive of the first principles of Christian religion.

In striking contrast with this confusion and contradiction, the Church doctrine of the Eucharist dwells upon the Local Presence. The efficacious SYMBOLS of the Body and Blood of Christ, memorials of his sacrificial death and redeeming love, *are upon the Altar.* The Elements have been changed, by the act of consecration, into those *efficacious Symbols,* and the faithful are exhorted to "DRAW NEAR with faith," not to adore Christ in the Elements, but to "take this Holy Sacrament to your comfort;" to receive these appointed Symbols, and in worthily receiving them to receive Christ Himself.

That Canon Liddon is in substantial accord with this doctrine of the Church is evidenced by another more grateful utterance. Commenting upon these words of one of his critics, "When God's Minister is giving the bread God is giving the Lord's Body," he inquires, "Is the gift of the bread the actual means whereby the Lord's Body is given, or is the Lord's Body given quite independently? If the former, he and I are not likely to differ much."

As far as I know, all Churchmen, except the maintainers of the Phillimore dictum, hold, in the very words of Mr. Liddon, that "the gift of the bread *is* the actual means whereby the Lord's Body is given." The reception of the consecrated Bread and Wine—the Representative Body and Blood of Christ—is coincident with the spiritual reception of Christ himself, and is "*the means whereby*" we receive Him. The Phillimore dictum, on the contrary, makes the gift of the Bread and Wine to be, not "*the means whereby*" we receive Christ, but the very gift of Christ himself, inexplicably confused and mingled with these Elements, in some unimaginable, and to my mind, profane and revolting union.

If instead of holding on to this mischievous formula, now by their own admissions reduced to emptiness, these earnest brethren in both countries would ingenuously confess that in the reaction from a cold and rationalistic theology, and in the fervor of an enthusiastic temperament, they had made a mistake, which the healthy process of searching examination has removed, they would give peace and assurance to the Church, and secure for themselves the grateful commendation of the members of Christ's kingdom.